Culture, Politics, Race and Diaspora:

The Thought of Stuart Hall

Caribbean Reasonings

Caribbean Reasonings

Culture, Politics, Race and Diaspora:
The Thought of Stuart Hall

edited by
Brian Meeks

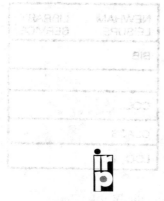

Ian Randle Publishers
Kingston • Miami

Lawrence & Wishart
United Kingdom

First published in Jamaica, 2007 by
Ian Randle Publishers
11 Cunningham Avenue
Box 686, Kingston 6
www.ianrandlepublishers.com

National Library of Jamaica Cataloguing in Publication Data

Culture, politics, race and diaspora: the thought of Stuart Hall / edited by
Brian Meeks

p. ;   cm. – (Caribbean reasonings).

Bibliography : p.   . – Includes index.
ISBN 976-637-272-1 (pbk)

1. Hall, Stuart, 1932–   2. Culture.   3. Political sociology.
I. Meeks, Brian   II. Series

306   dc 21

First published in the UK, 2007 by
Lawrence & Wishart
99a Wallis Road, London E9 5LN
www.lwbooks.co.uk

ISBN 978-190-500-761-5

British Library Cataloguing in Publication Data
A catalogue record for this book is available from the British Library

Cover and book design by Ian Randle Publishers
Printed in the United States of America

Caribbean Reasonings
Series Editors
Anthony Bogues
Rupert Lewis
Brian Meeks

Table of Contents

Acknowledgements

The conference that generated the articles in this volume could not have been successfully staged without the invaluable care and attention of the staff of the Centre for Caribbean Thought — Adlyn Smith, Allan Bernard and Sonjah Stanley Niaah. Adlyn, Allan and Dahlia Cole also gave invaluable support in the final editing and indexing of the volume. The members of the Marcus Garvey Movement — a student group at Mona — provided voluntary liaison and manpower assistance which helped to make things run smoothly. Special thanks are due to the staff of the Mona Library, in particular Charmaine Salmon and Gracelyn Cassell for a detailed and textured exhibition on the life of Stuart Hall. Christine Randle at Ian Randle Publishers (IRP) gave her full and generous support while always keeping a stern eye on the production schedule. The generational change at IRP is obviously in very good hands. Judith Wedderburn of Friederich Ebert Stiftung, Jamaica, provided generous help for this and other conferences of the Centre. Many thanks to then University of the West Indies (UWI) Vice Chancellor Rex Nettleford and Mona Principal, Kenneth Hall, for their invaluable and multi-faceted support for the Conference and, more generally, to the Centre for Caribbean Thought. A special word of thanks is due to my associate directors of the Centre and series editors of *Caribbean Reasonings*, Rupert Lewis and Anthony 'Tony' Bogues, who continue to be tremendous sources of inspiration and balance. Brown University — Tony's institution — must be acknowledged for their vision in co-hosting a series of conferences far away from their Rhode Island home. Finally, the conference would not have been the same without the presence of Stuart Hall who came with his wonderful wife and intellectual partner Catherine and actively participated, despite great personal difficulty, throughout the entire proceedings. To both of them, I extend the ultimate Jamaican greeting: 'Nuff respect'!

Introduction: Return of a Native Son

Brian Meeks

When Stuart Hall sat at the podium to deliver his closing speech to the Third Caribbean Reasonings Conference at Mona in June 2004, there was a hushed air of expectancy in the packed lecture theatre. For many in the audience, Stuart Hall was either entirely unknown, or a vague mythical figure encountered sporadically on reading lists, or in copies of well-thumbed articles in the library reading room. Hall spoke with few lines of notes and glanced at them even less frequently. Then, for some 90 minutes, without hesitation or falter, he engaged in a rolling and building narrative of his personal history, of diaspora and its meaning, of Marxism and globalization, of the role of the intellectual and of his own place in all of it. At the conclusion, there was a thunderous, standing ovation, which seemed to roll on far beyond the boundaries of politeness. Stuart Hall, after more than half a century, had at last, come home.

Hall was born in Kingston, Jamaica in 1932. The son of 'brown', middle-class parents, he attended Jamaica College, from which he gained the Rhodes scholarship to study at Merton College, Oxford in 1951. While at Oxford, he grew close to people on the Left, including Marxist scholar of culture Raymond Williams. Radicalized by the 1956 Soviet suppression of the Hungarian workers' uprising, he became a leading member of the university-based new left movement. In 1957, he left Oxford and founded the *Universities and Left Review* (*ULR*) in London. Hall edited the *ULR* for three years after which it merged with the *Northern England Reasoner* to become the *New Left Review* (*NLR*), which he steered and edited for its first year. The *NLR*, still published regularly, remains today among the leading international journals of culture, social criticism and politics. In 1964, Hall was appointed a Fellow at the newly formed Birmingham Centre for Contemporary Cultural Studies. It was at Birmingham, where he later became director, that he cemented his reputation as a leading global scholar of the second half of the twentieth century. Not only was he at the helm of the forging and definition of the discipline of cultural studies, but he also managed to nurture an entire cadre of young intellectuals who continue to make remarkable contributions in the fields of cultural studies and social criticism. Outstanding scholars including Paul Gilroy, Hazel Carby, Larry Grossberg, Dick Hebdige, Bill Schwarz, Angela McRobbie and many others, stand as living testimony to Hall's success as a teacher and nurturer.

Beyond these accomplishments, of course, are Stuart Hall's own significant contributions to contemporary social and political discourse. It would be redundant to rehearse here the details of his work, as this is the subject of much of the remainder of this volume, yet it might be relevant to focus for a moment on the core question of his methodology. More consistently than anything else, Hall has been praised for his scholarly prescience. In studies like *Policing the Crisis,*[1] he predicted and sketched the social bases for the rise and political consolidation of Thatcherism in the UK and the implications therein for the worldwide triumph of neoliberalism. There is, however, an equally common criticism of his work that hangs on the notion that it is too eclectic, that earlier positions are in conflict with later ones and there is too much inconsistency for it to constitute a new, powerful and coherent theoretical perspective.[2]

The possible answer to this seeming disjuncture between analytical strength and apparent methodological flabbiness lies in an urgent need to rethink the meaning of Hall's eclecticism. The suggestion here is that his insightful success in grasping the meaning and significance of conjunctural 'moments' cannot be de-linked from his methodological approach. Hall's methodology might be described as an approach that never abandons a materialist reading of history, yet always seeks to explain material forces as operating through social and cultural categories, which possess their own dynamic and establish their own inner mechanics of operation. From such an angle, apparently clear-cut phenomena are not always quite what they appear to be. Racism as a system of oppression may retain certain essential features, but its ideological tools of maintenance as well as institutional structures, are constantly in motion. Thus, as he suggests in his concluding remarks at the end of this collection, historically there has not been one racism, but many racisms. Equally, the forms of resistance to racism are constantly changing, in response to changes in the oppressive structures themselves as well as for quite independent, extraneous reasons. Thus, a methodology that vegetates in the realm of fixed certitudes, not unlike a camera with a slow shutter speed, will picture the conjunctural moment as a blur, not a sharply defined image. In Hall's apparent eclectic madness, therefore, is a purposeful method grounded in the recognition that while it is essential to have a deep empirical understanding of a social moment, it is equally important to appreciate the permanency of movement and, alongside it, the role of human agency in the shaping of events. Both requirements demand a certain theoretical fleetness of foot to capture the (albeit) fleeting image.

The essays that constitute the remainder of this collection, all derive from presentations made at the 2004 Caribbean Reasonings Conference. They all, in different ways, contend with Hall's methodology, his philosophy, as well as many other dimensions of his rich and textured intellectual career. More importantly, however, they serve to reconnect his work to the social context of his island of birth, Jamaica and the wider Caribbean. While Hall has written intermittent, though penetrating essays on Caribbean culture and politics and has produced one of the better documentary television series[3] on the region, it would be difficult to argue that the Caribbean, outside of metropolitan diasporic concerns, has been at the centre of his intellectual focus. Yet, Hall's significant contribution to cultural studies has influenced a relatively small but influential and growing cadre of Caribbean scholars, located both at home and abroad. Some of the issues they contend with help form a central aspect of this collection.

The volume itself is divided into three sections, with an introductory prologue and ending with Hall's own closing remarks to the conference. In the Prologue, Rex Nettleford, himself an icon of Caribbean culture in both theory and practice, presents Hall to a Caribbean audience and suggests his relevance to an understanding of the current moment of neoliberal globalization. In Part I, Metropolitan Engagements, focus is given to Hall's work in Britain in relation to contemporary politics, the black Diaspora, feminism and popular culture. In Part II, Theory and Critique, Hall's earliest study, *The Popular Arts* is discussed alongside counterpoised positions held by Lawrence Grossberg and Charles Mills on the character of his writing on race. In Part III, Caribbean Contingencies, the emphasis shifts from the exposition and critique of Hall's work, to an exploration of aspects of the Caribbean condition through approaches inspired in smaller or greater measure by Hall. Essays related to slavery, power and violence in Jamaica, contemporary Jamaican politics, dancehall culture and the Caribbean Diaspora in California, all suggest the influence of Hall's work in the critical study of Caribbean culture, society and politics. In the epilogue, Stuart Hall reflects on his work and his long journey from Kingston to London, to Birmingham and now, finally, back to Kingston again. Presented here in miniature is the sweep of his intellect, the breadth of his interests and the seriousness of his political commitment to both imagine and contribute to the making of a better world. As Michael Rustin argues in his insightful summary of the character of Stuart Hall's political approach:

> Hall does not see himself as a political optimist — pessimism of the intellect, facing up to the real, have been his watchwords. But there has been something deeply hopeful about his commitment to finding people who will listen and respond, if one shares one's attempts at understanding with them. Many have done so.[4]

Hopefully, many more from the Caribbean and its far-flung diasporas will share in these critical debates centred on Stuart Hall's rich life and work and arising out of this remarkable gathering at the University of the West Indies in Kingston, Jamaica.

Notes

1. Stuart Hall, C. Critcher, T. Jefferson, J. Clarke and B. Roberts, *Policing the Crisis: Mugging the State and Law and Order* (London and Basingstoke: Macmillan, 1978).
2. See, for instance, Chris Rojek, *Stuart Hall* (Cambridge: Polity Press, 2003); and in this volume, Charles Mills, 'Stuart Hall's Changing Representations of Race'.
3. See Stuart Hall, *Redemption Song* (London: BBC/Ambrose Video, 1991).
4. See in this volume, Michael Rustin, 'Working from the Symptom: Stuart Hall's Political Writings'.

Prologue:
The Caribbean and Cultural Studies: More than Grimace and Colour

Rex Nettleford

This volume is for me a most welcome initiative on the part of the Centre for Caribbean Thought. It honours the work of a Caribbean intellectual polymath who, whatever may be the pedigree of his intellectual preparation, is now known for the new ground(s) he has broken in intellectual discourse. He has done so not in the crass manipulation of the received wisdom which a man of his generation could not have escaped but by the creative use of such wisdom to advance the discourse on human thought and development and, in the process, to add frontiers to the landscape of knowledge which, as is now well known, is by no means the exclusive province of those who not only came and saw but conquered.

He is quite rightly regarded as a seminal contributor to the still developing field of Cultural Studies, but dynamic enough to be an undoubted and reliable source of intellectual energy for the generation of ideas, of philosophy (both political and moral), and of maxims of prudence (the gift of orature). It is an inspiration, as well, for both the tradition of resistance to human oppression and the quest for freedom and autonomy which have been core aspirations for the half-a-millennium history of millions of souls on both sides of the Atlantic, and without doubt in his Caribbean.

Stuart Hall is a creative thinker, synthesizer, cultural activist, university teacher and the sort of guru who as public scholar has worked extra-murally, giving to the ivory tower welcome openings to reality and moats of access to the goodwill of would-be detractors once they became the beneficiaries of the engagement by the academy with the wider community.

Through his exercise of intellect and imagination he has therefore been able to bring much light to the quest for self and society, as well as the heat of passionate engagement directed against the reactionary postures and iron-clad certainties of those Western leaders who in their zeal to rid the world of evil empires and troublesome trade unions

1

too easily confused the baby with the bathwater. Yet he is too well-honed an intellect to get stuck in cozy hypotheses which, however useful in one set of circumstances, would wish to defy being subjected to disproof, modification or reformatting. He brought to debate and to his measured activism much grace and civility; even charm which some might well have mistaken for weakness but which hit home nonetheless, despite the sheen on the sword or the foam-rubber around his knuckle duster.

I, for one, found a kindred spirit in this deceptively gentle warrior in his embrace of what has come to be called 'Cultural Studies'. For the Cultural Studies enterprise has had on its agenda of concerns such items, which have challenged ones like myself, as multiculturalism, race, ethnicity, politics, identity, diasporas, diversity and their play on modern, postmodern and postcolonial dispensations. Stuart Hall has addressed or engaged them all.

The problematique of diversity and multiplicity is indeed evident in 'multicultural societies' — from the one that he left back here to the one which has long adopted him as a homeboy. In plain Jamaican, wherever him tun, macka jook him (whatever path he takes he gets pricked by thorns). So he remains the quintessential Caribbean man — part-African, part-European, part-Asian (his older sister seeing him in his crib chose the East Indian part of Asia), part-Native American but totally Caribbean. Such heterogeneous confusion clearly poses a problem for those who perceive themselves as tenants of a homogenous world — usually the parts thereof with the luxury of persistent hegemonic power, whether military, economic and, by extension, cultural. But this is at the same time a welcome, if awesome, challenge for some multicultural aggregations which are bent on progress from the separate-but-equal mode of relating to the more organic intertextuality of their postcolonial existence producing for their tenants the texture of tapestry and that dynamic process of continuing negotiation for place and purpose on the part of individuals and groups, whether ethnic-, class-, or occupation-specific, but functioning in clearly delineated geographical spaces.

Such cultural heterogeneity indeed differentiates aggregations so perceived from 'liberal constitutions', and modern, western nation states which are predicated on the (usually unspoken) assumption of cultural homogeneity organized around 'universal liberal individualist secular values', a view Professor Hall admits is shared by at least one other scholar, Goldberg, who has looked seriously at cultural diversity.[1]

Reading the professor further, I knew I could depend on him to produce a typology to help clear up the conundrum that the notion of 'multiculturalism' presents to all who must find place for the ideas that emerge from efforts to invest existence with meaning, or to endow nonsense with sense and bring harmony to the dissonance that the cacophony of multiplicity and plurality implies. So guru and teacher that he is Professor Hall offers his reader a fascinating scheme of classification of the single term with distinctive variations on the theme, starting with conservative multiculturalism which he tells us insists 'on the assimilation of difference into the traditions and customs of the majority'. I immediately asked myself how we position the Caribbean where a politically useful numerical majority has long been called upon to function as a cultural minority, a situation that lands us in unending contestation resulting in creative chaos and admittedly challenging possibilities. Even here one is tempted to further ask, 'possibilities' for what?

But he also identifies liberal multiculturalism which he says 'seeks to integrate the different cultural groups as fast as possible into the mainstream provided by a universal individual citizenship, tolerating only in private certain particularistic cultural practices'. I ask, could this apply, to that Trinidadian or Jamaican Eurocentric nationalist urge promoting Westminster nation-building despite the presence of ones like Rastafarians, Muslimeen or inflammable university 'eggheads' on campuses of the University of the West Indies (UWI) and beyond who look to India, Ethiopia, Mecca or Moscow for psychic sustenance? But there is also pluralist multiculturalism which 'formally enfranchises the differences between groups along cultural lines and accords different group-rights to different communities within a more communal or communitarian political order'. West Indian cultural pluralists with M.G. Smith as patron saint could here be accused of this brand of multiculturalism with a record of spirited dialogue in the well-known stratification versus pluralism debate.

Professor Hall further identifies what he calls commercial multiculturalism which he says depends on private consumption to solve or 'dissolve' the problems of cultural difference which would otherwise breed disunity. Could this be something of a kindred spirit to pluralist multiculturalism, making chutney highly saleable and digitized calypso or reggae/dancehall chase quite handsome profits alongside less marketable Brahms, Bach and Beethoven sonatas and symphonies which are counterpoised in a less than muted controversy that persists in Jamaica? To this Professor Hall adds yet another category — that of corporate multiculturalism (public or private) which 'seeks to "manage" minority differences in the interest of the centre' as is supposedly evident in uptown electronic media ads utilizing downtown elements: 'As you quint, money in yuh hand' roars a dancehall artist for Jamaica National International Money Transfer in a full page *Gleaner* ad. Or is public corporate multiculturalism to be found in the manipulation of the folk material by middle-strata governments who may be insensitive to the intrinsic value of many a traditional or contemporary popular artistic form but always ready to use it liberally when needed to entertain visiting potentates or tourists and then to send the entertainers back into their barrios, ghetto yards or rustic clearings where ironically the real creativity finds form and energy?

Then there is critical or revolutionary multiculturalism which challenges as a matter of course, if not of duty, power and privilege, and 'foregrounds'. Professor Hall echoing the view of McLaren[2] states that the hierarchy of oppressions and movements of resistance seeks to be 'insurgent, polyvocal, heteroglossial and anti-foundational'.[3] Our recent history covering the decades of the 1960s and 1970s was all this and more. Jamaica to be sure has been rich in all such indulgences (some would say 'afflictions') from Rastafari to Black Power with variations ranging from Designer Dread through ragamuffin 'stylee' to the more recent bold and daring defense of slackness.

The typology by Professor Hall is engaging and as I read it I found myself trying to find a slot into which I could snugly fit the Caribbean. No such luck! I was virtually forced to have our region embrace together and separately all the types of the multiplicitous phenomenon as is our wont, through interconnecting the variables even in oxymoronic tension to produce something distinctive and different from the original source of each ingredient. Biologically, the region is after all well endowed with douglas a-plenty, brownings in abundance, coolie royals, chinee-royals ('chigros' as Ian Fleming once described them) and unspecified 'others' many of whom have a way of claiming Scottish ancestry as if to dissolve the melanin and lactate the coffee.[4]

It is such cultural diversity that is fast becoming a defining element of Third Millennium Planet Earth as it has been of this Caribbean region from as early as the late seventeenth century. It is this phenomenon which will increasingly engage or challenge the much bruited globalization that spells homogeneity for the centres of power inebriated with their hegemonic powers. Though Orlando Patterson in a recent essay draws attention to the fact that 'the argument that homogenisation is resulting in the homogenisation of the world ignores the increased vitality of local cultures and ethnicities in recent times and the complexity of global cultural diffusion, in particular the extent to which so-called peripheral regions are increasingly contributing to American popular culture and to the world music scene'.[5] Even the 'peripheral' Caribbean cannot be seen as a single monolithic cultural space. It is in fact the cultural diversity that has long challenged the region to find ideal, form and purpose, thus guaranteeing to our people at home and abroad creative coping skills in globalization in the face of such dominant agenda items that turn on economic development, borderless financial transfers, trade and saleable services underpinned by the market neoliberalism of a postcolonial, neocolonial, postmodernist dispensation; and all of this, lest we forget, driven/ inspired by the knowledge-economy in the age of the all pervasive information technology revolution.

It is no surprise that our honouree is a creative thinker, teacher and university man. I am, therefore, driven to share some recent thoughts I have been addressing on whether universities are losing their reputation as a home of culture and if so should it matter.

Are universities losing their reputation as the home of culture? To a certain extent they may well be. The communications technology revolution has introduced rival agents of cultural formation. The internet, CD-rom, radio, television, and visual images from the galactic spheres transform the entire planet into a 'global village' as the saying goes. In our Caribbean as elsewhere the 'CNNization' of consciousness is all but complete. The entire world now knows what Iraq looks like and gets nightly news of terrorism in action and recently a virtual surfeit of the funeral rites of a dear departed former US President. Lifestyles not only of the rich and the famous but of the poor and the destitute unfold minutely on the box. And people rush from campus classrooms to dorms or private homes to catch 'The Bold and Beautiful', 'The

Young and the Restless' or any other going soap opera that keeps us in serialized animation.

The university no longer has a monopolistic or near monopolistic hold on our cultural formation if ever it had! The World Trade Organization (WTO) is going after higher education in its commodification enthusiasm and is about to liberalize higher education as a service. The borderless education that distance learning already offers is about to be enhanced by the free access to the minds of different people in the name of globalization. Many see this as a threat to the deepening and heightening of particularistic cultural investigation, analysis and explanation which have long enriched the business of learning and the advancement of knowledge, into equations of mixed variables giving to universal life and living the textured diversity which the very globalization which threatens homogenization will need, to have the planet's inhabitants learn to live together rather than just side by side.

Universities have traditionally provided such a laboratory space in the preparation of skills and expertise which have gone beyond the walls and groves of academia to make a difference in a variety of fields ranging from the arts and humanities through the social sciences to the natural and medical sciences. So, does the loss of such cultural guardianship matter? Yes, it does. And it matters even more to those of our more recent universities faced with the task of positioning themselves in a fluid globalized environment which must surely mean firm rooting in the soil even while the branches spread into the open, but must so do with the strength to withstand the whirlwind of dynamic change.

Universities are universally endangered, and are likely to be of little use in the foreseeable future if they ignore the implications of tying education too narrowly to a specific job or skill area. For that is the 'text' while university education is concerned no less with the 'context'. Universities dare not yield to the temptation of churning out Management Studies graduates bereft of knowledge of the deeper forces of the societies they are set up to serve. For such forces take on ideal, form and purpose precisely at the point where people spend most of their waking lives, namely, the workplace — itself a battleground for rights and justice. The training of the engineer must produce more than a technical wonder. He or she ends up, after all, 'engineering' situations involving human beings whose emotional quotient may figure more than the IQ expected in any given set of circumstances. This is as true for the civil engineer called upon to construct a bridge on terrain where the soil structure is unsuitable but which must be erected at a certain spot because of the political interests of a particular member of parliament who must deliver to his or her constituents or lose the next elections. The trained lawyer without inkling of jurisprudence or of the sociological/political/cultural realities of his arena of practice (the wider society) is likely to become the jackass many say the law already is. The education of such key skills for development requires more than over-specialized and exclusive technical training. Medical education cannot escape the cultural contexts which determine professional efficacy and human understanding. The culturally diverse Caribbean is more than well placed and equipped to contribute to the global discourse on the role of university education in human development in preparation for the twenty-first century. Yet in their self-doubt and lack of confidence too many Caribbean people (and no doubt many ex-colonial developing countries) still tend to follow what the North Atlantic has done, is doing or is likely to do, ending up usually a generation behind erstwhile masters in their own explorations and experimentations in the field. The generation of ideas, concepts, conceptual frameworks and hypotheses rooted in keen in-depth observation, analysis and reflection on one's own history and existential reality, local and global, is an imperative not just for gaining self-knowledge but for economic development which depends on much of that very knowledge of self in terms of the grasp of one's creative potential and capacity for action.

One area of serious concern for all of us is the delivery of the sort of education to our people so that they grab a hold of their destiny, take decisions in their own interest consonant with the demands of a country that may be poor in material wealth but rich in human resources; so that they can command mastery over the legacy of that spirit of independence, of self-reliance, individual initiative and the capacity for coordinated social action towards mutual growth, many of which values were bequeathed us by our forebears who ploughed the land and made the society safe for human habitation.

There are, in any case, a certain number of human values that need to be activated and kept alive in human-scale communities like ours —

values such as the dignity and responsibility of the individual, the freely chosen participation of individuals in communities, equality of opportunity and the search for a common good and cultural certitude, all of which can be realized through the field of education.

In the Commonwealth Caribbean, the neglect of culture as integral to education persists among many in the public bureaucracy and the teaching profession. This is so despite some of the clearest evidence that many of the people who have had anything of value to say about this region are those who have exercised their creative imagination to make sense of the region and of human historical experience, providing a realm of thought with more than grist for the mill of discourse, debate and programmes of action which depend on a sense of self-worth.

That sense of self-worth, that self-esteem which bolsters the confidence in self, leading to giving of self to the growth and development of society through mutual trust in coordinated action, is necessary. It is possible only when we are able to discover and to keep re-discovering who we really are, how our lives have been forged from that textured history of the past half-a-millennium and how our place is determined in the world — a complex, groping world, itself in search of certitude and ways of coming to terms with something like the physical environment which admittedly we have all despoiled and degraded. The anxiety is the result clearly of an acute sense of crisis about the future of self and society. The anxiety is universal — meaning it is everywhere on Planet Earth, making ones like Stuart Hall who have plumbed the depths of the conundrum that is cultural diversity, a necessary point of reference in the quest for meaning.

Many of us in the Caribbean have had to pursue this quest from the margin. I have never regretted that quite frankly. In any case with so many centuries of apprenticeship in sabotage, many find it congenial to be subversive and it also gives one a bird's eye view of things. One is even better able to locate oneself a little easier than if one were submerged in the Establishment. Many of us in the University of the West Indies certainly found our way and were able, through outreach, to extend our activities into the wider community all over the Caribbean and even beyond as contributors to human development. Much of this has of course taken place through the work of the artists and public scholars/intellectuals like Stuart Hall whose work in the Open

University has been able to engage the wider community and the kindred souls to be found there.

The economists and planners notwithstanding, it is the creative artist and cultural activist who have plumbed the depths of our anguish and our possibilities, producing words and music, movement and myths, syntax and satire. With these have come hard cash which is precious foreign exchange to the monetarists and bottom-line advocates, many of whom are yet to view such artistic output as productive variables in the development equation rather than as self-indulgent exercises that cannot contribute to the per capita income, the gross national product (GNP) and the gross domestic product (GDP). The buzz phrase 'cultural industries' has been uttered frequently more recently. So there is hope. But where there is a change in perception, such change should find drive and energy in universities through their scholars critiquing, analysing and disseminating. Some of the most insightful, gems of thought by Stuart Hall have come in essays critiquing visual arts presentations as in his piece entitled 'Maps of Emergency: Faultlines and Techtonic Plates'.[6]

Planet Earth needs the lessons which cultural activists (individual and collective) have taught for the journey into this new millennium. For nothing short of an expansiveness of thought embracing a new vision of a groping rainbow world, a new sense of self and new ways of knowing to underpin new ways of living, can guarantee us safe conduct throughout this kaleidoscopic millennium.

Derek Walcott states that: 'the sigh of history rules over ruins, not landscapes.... Antillean Art is the restructuring of our shattered histories'.[7] He sees history as a self-redeeming, self-accepting story of people, culture and their significance in the order of things. He defines history, 'not as records of monuments and empires in habitual celebration of domination and the humiliation of large hordes of humanity, but rather as a self-redeeming, self-accepting story of one's person, culture and of one's ultimate significance in the order of things'. His sojourn at the University of the West Indies certainly helped in the honing of this vision. What an excellent mission statement for political planners and the deliverers of higher education to the generation that will inherit the twenty-first century. What has mattered in the Caribbean is that presence of the creative artist and of kindred souls to be found among genuine intellectuals who exercise creatively their imagination and intellect to enable what was once Africa's, Asia's and Europe's encounters on Amerindian soil to further forge in the crucible of the Caribbean heritage, a viable plural or complexly multicultural society of great intertextuality where people are content to at least attempt to live together. It is largely through the exercise of the creative imagination that we have come to understand the dynamics of these past 500 years of becoming, producing in all of the Americas (including our own Caribbean) genuinely new peoples, and a new sense and sensibility of sufficient substance and uniqueness to make a difference in the development of humankind. I speak not of that 'New World' of which Columbus spoke despite the fact that he found people here, but of the New World which is the result of those early encounters and the ones that followed slavery, indentureship and colonialism.

The best among many Commonwealth artists, by definition, have no problem with being the creatures of all their ancestors — the textured, complex, concentrated, offspring of the willful accidents of modern history. This is true of Commonwealth Caribbean artists like Walcott, Kamau Brathwaite and George Lamming as it is of Ngugi Wa Thiongo of Kenya, Nadine Gordimer of South Africa, Chinua Achebe of Nigeria, Arundhati Roy of India — all of whom will have read Shakespeare, Marlowe and Dickens and, as I assured the Italians recently, Dante and Machiavelli too. That this reality endows the Commonwealth Caribbean person with a unique knowledge of the crafting of a new sensibility, not out of some void as in the Book of Genesis but out of the lived reality of differing cultures, is cause for celebration rather than for self-negation, self-contempt or self doubt. It is from that reality, I like to think, Stuart Hall has emerged intellectually secure along with the other encounters he has had in metropolitan Europe and colonized Africa — the continent as well as the Diaspora.

Some of these encountering cultures, one may recall, are afterall rooted in not only the old Graeco-Roman Judaic Christian origins, but also in African so-called animist belief systems, while still others are rooted in Hindu and Muslim cosmologies with the rich methodologies of Native aboriginal America in place ensuring that mythic connection between aboriginals and later arrivants to the Americas. The authenticity of the Native American made Alexander Bustamante claim Arawak ancestry in one of his more intuitive if mischievous moods and still has so many citizens of the Dominican Republic with a wee drop of the stain of Africa in their blood, designating themselves 'Indios'.

Despite the myriad influences via the colonial conditioning of yesteryear and cultural penetration in these globalized electronic times, the human being is able to retain a capacity for self-reflection and self-realization. That sense of self must be manifested in our capacity to distinguish through our actions what in us is autonomous from what is determined. Contrary to still commonly held beliefs, the writing of poetry, the composition of a piece of music, the creation of a play, the painting of pictures and so on are all forms of action and not modes of escape from reality. They are valid routes to cognition which the educational system ignores at its peril. There is every good reason to examine, analyse and finally diffuse findings with respect to their impact on and active determining of human life and living.

For every true artist understands the tension that exists between becoming self and having that self function as part of a wider whole. All art is, after all, mediated by social reality and the self has to reach out as well as in, if it is to make sense of the world we tenant.

It is now becoming universally recognized that the importance of culture to development has to do with the enhancement of the social capital, the sustaining of an ambience of civility (and civilization) based on the intellectual and cultural bedrock of any social aggregation whether it be tribe, nation or region.

Walcott was exposed, as were all of his generation who received an education, to antiquity and that meeting point of cultures in the Mediterranean which gave to humanity not only Greece and Rome (to be hijacked by those who were to feel they had a monopoly on culture, character and civilization) but also Egypt and the great monotheistic religions, as well as the thought systems and value-configurations of the Orient. Omeros,[8] a Walcottian masterpiece, may well be speaking to the inheritance from that crossroads civilization tenanted by kindred spirits of old. For are we not the creatures of that special creolizing process of becoming? An understanding of such civilizations is not possible without knowing the cultural context in which they flourished. Universities have long been an effective agency of transmission of this meaning of human life and living. The Cultural Studies enterprise can do much to facilitate this.

The alleviation of poverty, the current buzz phrase of the development school, could well begin with the alleviation of the poverty of spirit that breeds a coarsened sensibility and threaten to saddle entire populations with a paralysis of any will to innovate and creatively think through problems. Our artists understand why ones like themselves, have been able to achieve, because of their capacity and the good fortune afforded them to create. 'There is a form of exultation,' declares Walcott, 'a celebration of luck, when a writer finds himself a witness to the early morning of a culture that is defining itself.'[9] It is such exultation that one finds in much of the work and thought of someone like Stuart Hall in that 'ritual of the sunrise'[10] which follows.

Despite all that I have said, the neglect of the idea of culture being integral to education persists among many in the public bureaucracy and even in the teaching profession, including university academics, though there is no shortage of desire to have one's appetite temporarily titillated. But in fairness, I sense, the idea of Cultural Studies straying from the halls of Literary Studies and Critical Theory to other disciplines in the traditional university what with the increasing advocacy for interdisciplinarity as a driving force in pedagogy. The implied pluses for character formation in creative cultural engagement are also legion. The discipline that underpins the mastery of a craft through which all art finds expression, whether it comes from Renaissance classicists or Caribbean intuitives, from Mahler or from Marley from Shostakovich or from Sparrow, from Bryon or from Brathwaite, the demands made on continuous re-invention and re-creation of effort and application, the challenges encountered on the journey to excellence, habits of realistic self-evaluation, the capacity for dealing with diversity and the dilemma of difference, whether in the performing arts or in the key branches of sports (themselves for me part of the performing arts), constitute excellent preparation for learning to be (which is the stuff of ontology), learning to know (the substance of epistemology), and learning to live together (the essence of the creative diversity which characterizes human existence, a fact which is about to overtake the entire world). It is of seminal importance that university education must not only teach people to make a living, it must also teach them how to live.

The educational system, of which the university remains a vital hub, with the help of those who are charged with directing it (including governments), should take full responsibility for the promotion of dynamic interaction and coordination between artistic creativity and the general cultural enterprises on the one hand and on the other, policy domains such as education itself, working life, urban planning, and industrial and economic development strategies for the benefit of all. Annual National Economic Reports should stop listing culture in the 'non-productive' category.

One here speaks culturally to a totality of human experience as well as to a totality of meaningful articulations of environmental integrity, arguably the cause, occasion and result of one's culture. The teaching of science, for example, would do well to start with the natural environment where there is such an environment rather than with the computer whose place in the knowledge-economy is impatient of debate, let me hasten to say. But, it is that bifurcation of knowledge into science and the rest that has served to misguide many among the educated. I speak, then, of cultural intertextuality, not of play-safe multiculturalism.

One has had cause to invite the young generation of scholars in the University of the West Indies — a still growing groping institution — to become engaged in what is one of the most vital and critical of discourses with the resolve to be original, tough-minded, creative contributors to the exercise. The Centre for Caribbean Thought is one such response. For the intellectual and psychic liberation now necessary among us can be no one else's responsibility to achieve but ours. It is now conceded in large measure that both capitalism and apocalyptic socialism, in their would-be purest of forms have been basically acultural in their approach to development. Neither has really had a place for the specificities of experience culturally determined over time and among particular sets of people. Development, it was felt, had to be scientifically determined and pursued universally according to immutable laws, whether of the market or on the basis of unrelieved class conflict.

Any invocation of cultural particularities and differences has been considered reactionary or revisionist. And although popular cultural expressions have been tolerated, they have been obliged to appear, in both dispensations, as an ornamental folkloric element only despite the efforts of visionaries like Adorno and others to prove otherwise. Many who have abandoned this position have drifted indiscriminately towards another panacea — the culture of technology. But one task of education has to be to ensure that the source of technology — science — finds a central place in the educational process without prejudice to the humanities.

Perhaps it is culture with all its indices of language, religion, ethnicity, kinship patterns, artistic manifestations and their interconnectedness in the environment of power (political and economic) that really counts at this time in the important pursuit of education adapting to the changed and changing circumstances of the contemporary globalized world.

As someone once said of the American statesman, George Kennan, it takes the likes of Stuart Hall to be, 'counsellor, scold, our conscience, our lyric philosopher of loss and nostalgia [as well as of possibilities], our Ancient Mariner, our traveller in time and space, between the worlds of power and of feeling', [11] in an effort to avoid the abyss. It was the very George Kennan who once wrote what someone like Stuart Hall himself could well have written: that there is nothing in man's plight that his vision if he cared to cultivate it, could not alleviate. The challenge is to see what can be done, and then having the heart and the resolution to do it.

I believe Cultural Studies — the enterprise — beckons us to use the heart and show the resolution. It beckons us, as well, to emancipate ourselves from the status of the 'insignificant other' who is likely to be treated as a surrogate prostitute especially in the now hallowed tourist industry on which the entire region from The Bahamas to Tobago has come to depend, or as minstrels, as both our festival arts like carnival and our popular arts like calypsos and reggae are frequently mistaken to be by so many visitors to our sun-drenched, sea-washed, sand-fringed shores causing Pedroso, the Cuban poet, once to wail:

Are we no more than merriment?
Are we no more than rumbas, black lust, carnivals?
Are we no more than grimace and colour ?
Grimace and colour...[12]

I know there is at least one person who is sure that we are more than colour and more than that 'rictus of a smile'[13] as Walcott once described that grimace. That person carries the name of Stuart Hall whom, along with governments, teachers, fellow-academicians and the institutions of learning in whose name we all labour, I see to be major contributors to, and principal facilitators of, the cultivation of that kingdom of the mind so badly needed to produce a self-reliant, self-respecting, creative, tolerant, enterprising, culturally confident and productive community of souls not only for our Caribbean but for all of Planet Earth.

Notes

1. David Goldberg, *Multiculturalism: A Critical Reader* (London: Blackwell, 1994).
2. 'Peter McLaren: A Call for a Multicultural Revolution'. Gustavo Fischman Interviews Peter McLaren. *Multicultural Education* 6, no. 4 (Summer 1999): 32–34. P. McLaren, *Schooling as a Ritual Performance*, 3rd edition (Lanham, MD: Rowman and Littlefield, 1999).
3. David Goldberg, *Multiculturalism*.
4. These terms are colloquialisms used throughout the Caribbean for persons of mixed race. 'Dougla' is a term used particularly in Trinidad and Tobago to describe a person who is a mix of African and Indian. In Jamaica, the term 'coolie-royal' is used for such a person. 'Chinee-royals' are people of African and Chinese mixture. A 'browning' is a term used to describe a person (usually a female) with a lighter skin tone — usually a mix of African and Caucasian.
5. Orlando Patterson, 'Global Popular Culture and the American Cosmos'. The Andy Warhol Foundation for the Visual Arts. Paper Series on Arts, Culture and Society, Paper No.2. (1994):1.
6. Stuart Hall, 'Maps of Emergency: Fault-lines and Teutonic Plates', in *Fault-lines and Contemporary African Art and Shifting Landscapes*, eds. Gilane Tawadros and Sarah Campbell (Institute of International Visual Arts (inIVA), forum for African Arts, Prince Klaus Fund, London, 2003).
7. Derek Walcott, 'The Antilles: Fragments of Epic Memory (The Nobel Speech 1992)', in *What the Twilight Says*, by Derek Walcott (New York: Farrar Strauss and Giroux, 1998).
8. *Omeros* is the longest of Derek Walcott's three book-length poems, for which Walcott won the Nobel prize for literature in 1992. Taking its title from the Greek form of the name Homer, it draws analogies between characters in the *Iliad* and *Odyssey* and ordinary people in Walcott's native island of Saint Lucia. See *Omeros* (New York: Farrar Strauss and Giroux, 1990).
9. Derek Walcott, 'The Antilles: Fragments of Epic Memory (The Nobel Speech 1992)', 7.
10. Ibid., 79.
11. Robert Steel, 'George Kennan at 100', *New York Review of Books* 51, no.7 (April 29, 2004).
12. The Afro-Cuban poet, Regino Pedroso is quoted in an article by Roberto Marquez, 'Zombie to Synthesis — notes on the Negro in Spanish-American Literature', *Jamaica Journal* 11, nos.1 & 2 (1977).
13. Derek Walcott, 'The Antilles: Fragments of Epic Memory (The Nobel Speech 1992)', 81.

PART I

Metropolitan Engagements

1 | *'Working from the Symptom':*
Stuart Hall's Political Writing

Michael Rustin

Much of the writing we see about politics falls into two categories — each as unsatisfactory in its own way as the other. The first and by far the most common of these, which fills up acres of space in the newspapers every day, is commentary on the surface flow of events. Which politician has said and done what. What steps have governments announced, what policies have they promulgated. What response has been made to these by their political opponents. Who is gaining ground and who is losing it, by such indicators of public support as votes, press commentary, opinion polls, or more vaguely, 'mood', as in 'someone close to the Government said to me in the lobby earlier today'.

Organizations and institutions get a say in this accounting, as when their spokespersons announce their dissatisfaction or approval. Even social movements get a look in, if they can raise enough noise by demonstration or direct action to raise them above the threshold of invisibility. One can, and does, devour volumes of this kind of stuff on a daily basis whilst feeling in the end that one has learned little. What is being described here is of course the daily discourse of political practitioners, including the journalists whose practice is reporting and commentating.

At the opposite pole, lie more abstract and more scientific forms of discourse, developed by political scientists and sociologists. These trade in models of systemic equilibrium and disequilibrium, statistical trends, profiles of public attitudes, models of class composition and political affiliation, and the like. These methods can be illuminating, and one can even draw comfort from them. An example of a recent interesting piece of work in this genre is Judis and Texeira's (2002) book, the *Emerging Democratic Majority*, which predicted, on the basis of the changing demographics of the United States of America and the rise of a highly educated, post-industrial workforce to a leading position in the economy and society, an era of 'progressive centrism' — 'the emerging democratic majority' of the book's title. Cheered up by this volume, which I had acquired on a visit to the West Coast, I enthusiastically passed it over to Stuart Hall on my return home. 'It's somewhat optimistic,' said he sombrely, never one to be deluded by false dawns. (Two years later, he was unfortunately proved right when George W. Bush won his second term.)

Texeira and Judis are politically engaged writers — practitioners of academic forms of political science generally hold themselves aloof from political practice, distinguishing their 'value-neutral' stance from committed political commentary or polemic. A gap is thus established between everyday political practice, and the academic study of politics, one which is reinforced by the rewards attached to specialized academic production in contrast to writing for general publics.

Stuart Hall's political writing belongs to neither of these genres, and this has been one of the main sources of its originality and brilliance. What have always interested him are neither particular events, nor abstract models alone, but rather the connections between them. The questions for Stuart Hall have always been, one, how can we make sense of this or that particular phenomenon, in terms of a broader orienting theoretical conception. Secondly, how can we put the theoretical ideas on which all thinking about society depends to actual use, in explaining the situations and conjunctions which we encounter in an engaged political life. What has continually amazed me about Stuart Hall's political writing and speaking is the capacity he has to locate meaning in the everyday epiphenomena of politics, to see and identify the deep currents beneath the flotsam drifting on the surface.

Mapping Social Change

The starting point has always been Stuart Hall's recognition of how hazy and opaque political realities actually are. We think we know — everyone seems to speak with such confidence, all the time — but we do not. It is as if we are being carried along in a political mist, trying to discern new land-forms emerging and disappearing before our eyes. There are maps, which some people have great confidence in, and some of which have even been drawn by our own comrades, but unfortunately these are usually at least partly wrong. In the early days of his political writing, the landforms which Stuart Hall was most interested to understand were those of Britain's changing class society, which he began to map anew in three remarkable papers, 'A Sense of Classlessness' (1958), 'Absolute Beginnings' (1959) and 'The Supply of Demand' (1960), two of these published in *Universities* and *Left Review*[1] and one in *Out of Apathy*. What he noticed in these articles, and began to give a shape and explanation to, are the changes of social identity which were then taking place in Britain's class society. The papers describe both a new sense of individual freedom and opportunity brought about by relative prosperity and the emergence of a consumer-led economy, and the continuing inequalities and constraints which prevailed.

'Absolute Beginnings' is particularly striking in its interest in both of these dimensions. Its first part described the rejections and blockages inherent in the Secondary Modern School (this was a review of books by two teachers, Edward Braithwaite and Margareta Berger-Hammerschlag, but drew on Stuart Hall's own experience as a teacher in a south London school). The second part, elaborating a new cultural sociology of the young from the point of departure of Colin MacInnes's novel, *Absolute Beginners*, described the emancipations of identity and style which were then being accomplished by young people in the cities, and especially in London. These young people were conspicuous in Soho where *New Left Review* had its office, in the life of the streets, clubs, pubs and coffee bars, and in the style-oriented workplaces of the West End. It was a remarkable feature of those days that it took an intellectual community consisting of many exiles — from Jamaica, Australia, Canada, the USA, and individuals from rather marginal or sequestered native communities — to really appreciate what was going on in England at that time. The difference between the *New Reasoner* and the *Universities* and *Left Review* strands of the early New Left are encapsulated in the fact that the headquarters of the former lay in northern industrial Halifax, in Yorkshire, and that the latter had in effect just moved down from Oxford to what would soon be called Swinging London.[2]

In 'The Supply of Demand', Stuart identified at a very early stage the great problem which the emergence of consumer capitalism was going to pose for socialists. Many goods can and will be supplied by the market, and it would be stupid, arrogant, and patronizing, he noted, not to recognize that many of these bring genuine benefit to large numbers of citizens. It helped in coming to this conclusion that Hall shared and enjoyed the ways the people he saw around him dressed, danced, listened to music, and went to the cinema — socialist puritanism has never been part of his outlook. But the other side of the argument of the 'Supply of Demand' are all those goods that can not be provided through shopping, or as items of individual consumption — the health care, education, housing, and public space on which society as a bonded and moral entity depends.[3] The problem is how to refashion the supply of these public goods in ways which can compete with the seductions of the market, and of what 25 years later we came to call 'individualization', though much of its essence had already been identified in these early essays.

Hall argued that it was essential to attend to both aspects of the emerging market society which involved the satisfaction of people's needs, and indeed the creation of new demands whose fulfilment gave enjoyment, and to its considerable and inherent lacks. Unless one took full note of the creative and inventive capacities of the system one was basically opposed to, one had no chance of generating an effective oppositional response to it. This has been an almost universal principle in his political writings.

On the one hand, changes are taking place, which are pushing to the fore individualism, competition, and markets of all kinds. These forms of life have popular appeal, and would not be succeeding in winning assent and political support if they did not. There is no point in denial, in preferring an ideologically-driven view of reality to the world which is taking shape before our eyes. But on the other hand, we need to resist the remaking of the world by capitalism; instead we should be inventing alternatives to class society which are egalitarian, democratic, and solidarist, which celebrate difference whilst at the same time recognizing the equal worth and entitlements of all human beings. It is a tall order to hold together both sides of this argument, and it has always involved Stuart in an argument on two fronts. Socialist orthodoxy has been his antagonist on the first, since he has consistently held that conventional socialist beliefs about class structures, identities and their contradictions are untenable, and amount to a state of wilful denial of unwelcome realities. On the other side his antagonist has been on the right, since his commitment has been to promote an alternative socialist future, not to collude with the triumph of capitalism.

This has usually been an uncomfortable position to occupy, since those on the Left were often infuriated by challenges to their traditional view of the world, while those on the Right recognized an enemy when they saw one. A duality of this kind has been central to almost all of Hall's political thought.

The Crisis of the Social Order

In the second major phase of Hall's political writing, he took on a more complex task. This was nothing less than to chart the changing shape of class relations in Britain, as these were mediated in political and ideological terms over a crucial period of 20 years or so. The intellectual ambitiousness of this project has been to some degree obscured by the fact that its principal address, in true Gramscian spirit, has been not to the academy, but to participants in the political process itself. Even though much of the work was produced in universities, both in Birmingham at the Centre for Contemporary Cultural Studies, and at the Open University, even the mode of production within the university was unusual. *Policing the Crisis*, a work of political sociology of the highest standard, was published under the co-authorship of Stuart Hall and four other writers who were actually graduate students at the Centre during the writing of the book. Many of the remarkable papers which developed the arguments of *Policing the Crisis* were first published in *Marxism Today*, a monthly magazine which successfully sought a large public readership, and which made few concessions to the norms of academic writing.

A more intrinsic feature of this work which somewhat obscures its scope is the way in which it moves back and forth between particular instances and theoretical conceptions, refraining from developing a theoretical model which can be clearly abstracted from its particular there-and-then uses. It is easy to misremember this project in its narrower terms, as an attempt to clarify the phenomenon of Thatcherism, and later, in the debate about 'New Times', to find some viable political perspectives for the post-Thatcher period. It had this purpose, and was taken up as such by its directly political audience. But it was considerably more far-reaching in theoretical terms than this. In fact one cannot understand Hall and his colleagues' argument about Thatcherism unless one also understands the larger theoretical argument about order and conflict in British society in which they situated it.

The argument of *Policing the Crisis* and the subsequent papers is that Thatcherism was the solution — for British capital and its associated ruling class interests — to a problem. One had to recognize and understand the problem before one could understand the full scope and importance of the New Right's chosen solution to it. The analysis, in *Policing the Crisis*, of the long pre-Thatcherite phase of social crisis and deadlock, is as original as that of Thatcherism itself. Indeed, without the former, Thatcherism is indeed unintelligible and the Thatcher regime becomes instead merely an instance of inspired political opportunism by Mrs Thatcher and her associates.

Some on the Left criticized Hall's thesis about Thatcherism on the grounds that it misrepresented Thatcher as some kind of new departure, when she was surely a highly recognizable and familiar kind of Conservative. 'Weren't the Tories always in favour of the free market, and of law and order, so why is this anything special?' they said. What was naive about this reaction was its neglect of the larger framework of the analysis, of a social order which had been in a state of deep crisis for two decades. Thatcherism was not the first 'exceptional' response to have taken place in this situation. One thing that is remarkable about *Policing the Crisis* and its accompanying writings is that it charts all of this development, and the different tactical adaptations which different political formations made to its exigencies. Only on the assumption that nothing ever much changes in political life, and that the same battles are continually re-fought on the same ground, could one ignore all this, thus sparing oneself the necessity for much thinking.

What is the crisis which *Policing the Crisis* describes and explains? It was nothing less than a general crisis of social order in Britain, part of which was crystallized in the events and symbolism of 1968, and of the 1960s more generally. *Policing the Crisis* was successful in bringing together the many different dimensions of this crisis, and to connect them within a model of contested hegemony, developed from Gramsci's writings. The authors recognized the links between industrial insurgency (in miners' strikes which had defeated two governments, and in very high rates of strike action generally); a generally hyper-inflationary climate, which condensed an excess of demands for public and private goods of all kinds; and a sharply-contested moral climate, in which new claims to freedom of speech and behaviour, not least in the sexual domain, provoked an extreme conservative reaction, represented by such interventions as the Festival of Light, Mrs Mary Whitehouse's National Viewers and Listeners' Association, and the Black Papers which attacked 'progressive' orthodoxies in education. At the same time, the degeneration of the conflict in Northern Ireland into armed struggle, and broader fears of terrorism brought about across the world by groups such as the Red Brigades in Italy, the Weathermen in the USA, the Baader-Meinhof Gang in Germany, and the Angry Brigade in Britain, engendered an atmosphere of anxiety and paranoia.

Policing the Crisis describes the Selsdon Man phase of the Heath Government of 1970–74, and the cumulative repressive moves on which it embarked, before it was pushed by the miners into a return to the negotiated corporatism which had emerged in the 1960s as the dominant mode of managing class contradictions not only in Britain but across the western world. But then Heath chose to take on the miners in 1974, and lost his 'who governs Britain?' election, returning Harold Wilson to power for the second time to try once more to make this precarious settlement work. It was only when this collapsed, under Callaghan, in the 'Winter of Discontent' of 1978–79 that the way finally lay open to the more radical social recomposition accomplished by Thatcher.

In other words, Thatcherism emerged as a 'solution' to a crisis which had been developing for about 20 years. For much of this time, governments seemed to be at the mercy of forces they could not control, and regularly took over each other's ground (for example, in Heath's corporatist interventionism, and in Labour's repressiveness towards its own working-class constituencies), under the extreme pressure of events. One reason why the Thatcher government maintained its support despite the widespread economic damage it inflicted through de-industrialization, unemployment and so on, was because it seemed to have regained control of an 'ungovernable' situation. Indeed the Conservatives only lost office much later when they had visibly lost control of events, through 'Black Wednesday' and the exit from the Exchange Rate Mechanism, the mass resistance to the Poll Tax, and in their own internal splits over Europe.

The Origins of Thatcherism

If one part of the originality of Hall and the work of his colleagues was in describing the 'problem' of the crisis of order which led to Thatcherism, its other aspect was a brilliant grasp of the nature of the 'solution', the 'hegemonic project' of Thatcherism itself. Here, once again, the procedure was to connect the various particulars which made up the Thatcher moment, and see how they had been made to cohere through the exercise of political leadership and by their assemblage into a coherent ideological narrative. Central to all this was the issue of 'law and order' itself. This was not merely a matter of local instances of disorder (urban crimes or riots) but reflected anxieties about a much broader social condition. *Policing the Crisis* identified the issue of 'mugging', exploited by the Right in the same way as similar racialized anxieties had been exploited by Richard Nixon in the USA, as a particular focus of conservative mobilization, against the 'threats' posed by immigration and the growing ethnic minority presence in Britain. This issue brought race to the centre of Hall's published work, where it has remained ever since. It identified, at an early stage, a fundamental element in the disorganization of the left in the politics of the United States of America and Europe, namely the successful mobilization of working class anxieties to perceived competitors from ethnic minority groups. These anxieties had their economic root in the effects of de-industrialization and globalization on working class living standards and self-respect. The subsequent rise of the new right across Europe has shown how prescient this analysis was.

'Mugging' was important in the argument of *Policing the Crisis*, and in the analysis of Thatcherism as a major ideological and political formation. It had been an issue which the media, and Conservative politicians were able to seize on, as a signifier for much broader social anxieties and antagonisms. The idea of 'mugging' served to condense many different fears into one concrete object, indeed as we might now say it became a focus of unconscious fantasy. The various fears were of crime, of young adults perceived to be more sexual and dangerous than they were remembered to have been in the regulated past, and of course of black people, and immigrants more generally. *Policing the Crisis* was at pains to demonstrate how the opportunistic focus on this topic had been made possible by the elaboration of anxieties about immigration and race over a longer period, notably by Enoch Powell. Hall's contention was that although Powell might have been dismissed from the Heath government for exceeding the limits of acceptable rhetoric, he had in fact succeeded in his bid to change the entire political agenda. The potency of this signifier lay in the fact that the implicit reference of 'mugging' was unmistakably racial, while because this reference was implicit its racial connotations could be disavowed. If a certain kind of crime were on the increase, how could anyone reasonably object to its being reported, even if its perpetrators happened to be disproportionately black? It was not easy to argue that the reason why mugging had been selected for this exceptional level of media attention was because of its racial associations.

This argument in *Policing the Crisis* brought together, in the brilliant synthetic mode which characterized so much of the work of the Centre for Contemporary Cultural Studies and Hall in particular, several explanatory discourses. The 'new criminologists' in the National Deviancy Symposium, had noted that crime and deviance were not merely objective facts, but were culturally constructed entities (two of Hall's co-authors in *Policing the Crisis*, Tony Jefferson and Brian Roberts, were criminologists). The symbolic representation of crime and transgression by the media and by others with powers of public definition were important phenomena in themselves, perhaps as important as criminal behaviour itself. The idea of 'moral panics and folk devils' had already been placed by Stan Cohen (1972/2002) on the agenda of social science, and indeed of public debate more generally. Mugging had many of the attributes of the moral panic, and muggers were 'folk devils' par excellence.

But a more complex theoretical discourse was needed to demonstrate how an apparently rather minor issue like this could have a significant role in the transformation of political discourse, and in the conquest of a key field of ideological conflict. Fundamental to this was the idea that ideological formations were 'constructed' by discursive and political action, and were not, as Marxists had tended to believe, merely reflections of social realities. Politics was a practice with its own effects. This practice proceeded through the construction of discourses which gave a shape and meaning to the experience of subjects, and became the symbolic basis of collective identifications. It was vital to understand this as the New Right began its ideological advance. This thinking drew on Gramscian conceptions of the cultural dimensions of class struggles, and of the ways in which they could solidify in long-lasting regimes of class power, the famed idea of 'hegemony'. Laclau's charting of the autonomous role of ideological practice in the construction of Latin American populism was another important element of this analysis.[4]

Althusser's idea that the antagonistic relations of classes had an inescapably contingent or 'conjunctural' dimension provided a further resource for trying to map this ongoing crisis and the fateful outcome to it that was foreseen by Hall and his colleagues. While underlying configurations of power were relatively stable over long periods, in periods of instability and crisis the outcomes of struggles could not be predicted from economic determinism, or evolutionist presuppositions. Among the most important elements of uncertainty was political action itself, and the processes of persuasive definition and interpretation on which this always depended. Political identifications were always to a degree created and chosen, not given. The 'cultural turn' in the social sciences of which the Birmingham Centre was one of the most important embodiments in Britain in the 1970s enabled interpretation and definition — the work of the symbolic sphere — to be recognized to be a crucial element in the political process with a causal weight of its own.

The argument was not that the manufactured issue of 'mugging' had made Thatcherism possible, or even been a necessary condition of its success. It is rather that all political struggle proceeds through a process of antagonistic and competitive signification. The construction of an advancing bloc entails as one of its dimensions the attachment to one another of chains of signifiers through which different collective subjects are able to recognize themselves and make common cause with one another. Bringing off these semantic linkages and equivalences is one of the principal tasks of political leaders when they put together a following. It is through this process of signification, in part, that a social bloc is constructed.

Policing the Crisis and the essays which followed provided an anatomy of a shifting discursive field, in which many crucial and disputed terms figured. In a liberal democratic system in which power is won by parties through elections, it is inevitable that struggle by signification will happen serially and by accumulation. The news media and the insatiable appetite of the consumer public for novelty further determines that representations continually change their form — even though one can discern persisting objects of reference beneath the shifting patterns. To be sure, the cyclical electoral system does generate its own natural climaxes, and these lead parties to attempt condensations of very complex representations into summary versions of themselves, and their opponents. The analysis of Thatcherism described the process of construction, maintenance and evolution of a whole programme of representation of this kind, including its adaptations to opportunities — such as that provided by the Falklands War in 1981 — when these arose.

It is consistent with this account of Thatcherism that so important a part was played in the development of its signifying structure by specialists in mass communication and mass persuasion from the advertising industry, such as the Saatchi Brothers and Sir Tim Rice. One can describe the construction of discourses and chains of signification in the language of cultural studies or sociology, but its actual practice in developed societies takes place through a highly specialized technical expertise. One might say that this apparently rather theoretical analysis of the discursive construction of Thatcherism influenced New Labour to give such great emphasis to the media, in the later construction of its own counter-project.

Much work was put into giving coherence to the method of analysis which led to the understanding of Thatcherism as a response to the organic crisis of British capital and social relations in the 1970s, and some elements of this theoretical synthesis are referred to above. Hall's approach, enumerated in countless apparently improvised speeches as well as in many articles over these years, had another, more intuitive component. This was evident in Hall's feeling for the significant detail, the turn of phrase, and the event given special attention, as starting points for his many explanatory forays.

From Symptoms to Crises

Hall began university as a student of English Literature, and on the completion of his undergraduate studies he began to undertake a doctoral thesis on Henry James. James was of course an exemplary practitioner and fastidious advocate of the literary method of beginning from particulars. Only from such particulars as can be registered in their full immediacy did he believe one could proceed as a writer to larger narratives or descriptions of fictional worlds. James approvingly quotes Ibsen, in this respect a kindred spirit, saying that he can begin a character from imagining the button on a man's coat, and he refers to the acorn principle, whereby very large literary undertakings start from tiny seeds. James's details of course give rise to novels with the most complex and fully-realized connectedness imaginable. Some of the satisfaction in reading them comes from the density and intricacy of meaning that is revealed as one proceeds, in particular as the world of the novel is made largely through the perception and understanding, or its absence, of each of its characters. James's worlds are intricately full of particulars, the author himself and his opinions, whatever they may be, deliberately remaining in the shadows, behind his characters.

One of the implicit aims of Hall's accounts of moments or periods in the life of a society seems to me to be that in principle they should be inexhaustibly full in their points of reference to the particulars of social experience. It seems that it ought to be possible, in this approach to political analysis, to start almost anywhere, since any thread one chooses to start from, once one pulls on it, will lead eventually to the centre or the totality. (Except of course that there is no stable centre or totality in this view, but always an evolving process.) One of the reasons why Hall has been such a gripping speaker and writer over the years is that his habit of starting where he happens to be, with the observed detail of the moment, creates a recognition in his audience of a common starting-point in experience, and they are then invited to participate in an exploration of its meaning. I have also seen people asking themselves 'where on earth are we going' as some of his eloquent narratives unfolded, finding the apparent lack of an obvious map or grid references rather disconcerting. But generally the outcome is that one follows a process of disclosure of connectedness and meaning from initially apparently inchoate or banal materials. 'A figure in the carpet' emerges, which brings a sense of discovery since it was not evident at the start of the journey.

The idea that sociological analysis can proceed from details to structures, from surface to depth, has affinities with psychoanalytic methods of investigation, when it is the 'material' being examined. Dreams which emerge in analytic sessions are a good example. These lead the analyst to explore with the patient the underlying unconscious configuration which is shaping his or her state of mind. Lacanian psychoanalytic ideas had some influence on Althusser's theory of conjunctures, helping to explain how an 'excess' of meaning and force could become concentrated in apparently contingent events. This Althusserian model of 'ensembles' of social relations and the 'conjunctures' which punctuate their development has a contemporary formulation in 'complexity theory' and 'chaos theory', with their 'butterfly effects' — the idea that a system can be tipped from one 'phase-state' to another in certain conditions by apparently minor or trivial events. The crisis which is examined in *Policing the Crisis* is of this kind. The issue of 'mugging' condensed energies which helped its political definers and operators — the Thatcherites — to move the system from one state to another, bringing about the tipping-over from its decaying 'corporatist' mode to its new form of 'authoritarian populism'. In this sense the particulars on which Stuart's analysis often focuses, or from which it starts, can be read as 'symptoms', as nodes of signification (and thus of solidarity and power) which can have transformative power. This may be analogous to patterns of psychic crisis in individuals and organizations (we have all known these) when some specific event or object becomes the projective focus of intense anxiety. The symptom, for Freud, was the psychic system's means of containing unbearable tensions. The alternative to the hysterical, phobic or obsessional symptom might be breakdown as the psychic system becomes overwhelmed with desire or anxiety. We may see the condensation of social conflicts in heavily charged signifiers of this kind — he unburied dead of the 'Winter of Discontent', the 'sleaze' of the late Major government, 'mugging' in the 1970s, the 'Weapons of Mass Destruction' of the last year or so — as symptoms of this kind. In each case they focused collective sentiments which led to or threatened a social convulsion or transformation. The psychoanalyst W.R. Bion called such moments in psychic life experiences which threatened 'catastrophic change', not a bad psycho-social description of the onset of Thatcherism.

We are here in fields in which structures have their effects, and become evident, only through particular elements of experience, including subjective states of mind. It is the latter which gives society and social processes their ability, their capacity to defy and transform law-like patterns. It is this principle of uncertainty and the unknown, to a point, which Hall has insisted we must attend to, if we are to learn anything about the actual world.

It is interesting to reflect on Hall's political writing over the years. With this reflection, is there anything we should now be doing with this exemplary method to understand our current political realities?

Where is the Social Crisis Today?

Hall himself has written some important essays on the successor epoch to Thatcherism and its weakened succession under John Major, namely that of New Labour. His recent paper, 'New Labour's Double Shuffle', looks characteristically beneath the surface of an excessively-discussed topic, that of media 'spins', and tries to make some structural sense of it. 'Spin', he demonstrates, has been a functional necessity for New Labour since the role it has chosen to occupy is to continue the Thatcherite programme of modernization and full 'marketization' of British capitalism, while having to maintain support for this project from its working-class constituency whose interests and values are contrary to such a programme. 'Spin' signifies the continuing necessity to find and impose descriptions which will achieve this impossible act of translation.

In previous Labour governments the compromises with capital, unavoidable to social democracy, were to some degree openly negotiated and contested within the Labour Party and the trade unions, and with a wider public opinion. In the new situation, the institutions where these arguments would previously have taken place have been pushed aside, and the very idea that ideological differences are there to be clarified and debated is rejected. New Labour is, in its own self-conception, unitary. It is the project of a vanguard, now incorporated in or close to government, which formulates its mission as 'modernization'. But since intractable political realities remain, conflicts and contradictions still have to be managed and in a different way than through the conventions of debate which accompanied the earlier settlement, which was essentially, as Ralf Dahrendorf (1959) put it, an institutionalized class compromise. Hall suggested that 'spin' was the new institutional device for mediating New Labour's project of modernization, in many respects a continuation of the Thatcherite programme to constituencies which retained other beliefs and interests.

The controversies over the Iraq War have subjected this device to exceptional strain. The contradictions of the situation were most intensely felt within the BBC, whose conception of itself as an institution through which differences and oppositions should be negotiated by accepted rules and rituals came into collision with the government's own media apparatus. The two chief officers of the BBC were forced to resign as a result, though wider public reactions and the government's continuing difficulties to win its argument over the war, has held off for the moment more lasting damage to the BBC's mission, as a key institution of mediation. Of course all this recalls Hall's earlier work, also undertaken in a period of intense conflict, on the conventions governing news broadcasting, as an instrument of managed consensus and compromise.[5]

As valuable as this 'Double Shuffle' intervention has been, there remains a notable difference between what we have available to us in the analysis of the present post-Thatcher conjuncture, compared with the complexity of analysis that was developed previously. The earlier analysis was based on a theory of a larger social crisis, to which Thatcherism was able to represent itself as a solution. There could have been no analysis of Thatcherism without the prior analysis of the organic crisis of disintegrating corporatism, of the eventual failed class deadlock of the post-war era. Thus, in order to understand where we are now, we need to understand why, in the final event, the Thatcherite regime disintegrated and was driven ignominiously from power. That moment was also the expression of a social crisis, objectively speaking. How could it have been, we should have asked, that the project of completing the 'Americanization' and full-marketization of British capitalism should have foundered so spectacularly on a popular demand for better public services and for some reasonable standards of altruism in public life? Thatcherism's victory must have been far from complete to have led to this outcome. It seemed we had been too overcome by defeat to have noticed that democratic social aspirations remained alive and even well, after all that battering. Perhaps there had even been an element of emancipation and invigoration brought about by Thatcherite populism and assertiveness, its own unintended contribution to the democratic cause.

New Labour believed that its only feasible mission was to continue a version of the Thatcherite programme, moderated in some respects, reinvigorated in others. It insisted on the most minimalist view of what the electorate would tolerate. It brought a renewed disciplinary force to the project of public sector reforms initiated by the more capable Conservative modernizers. As everyone knows, New Labour in power maintained Conservative-defined limits on public expenditure for a full three years after regaining office with one of the largest Parliamentary majorities ever. Those connected with *Marxism Today* were disillusioned with New Labour in office — the one-off revival issue of *Marxism Today* in 1998 put their critique forcefully[6] — but at that point they also found it hard to articulate an alternative political course. They had been among the foremost critics of the Old Left, insisting that progressive politics now had to be reinvented for these 'New Times'. *Marxism Today* had in this respect given intellectual substance to New Labour's project of modernization. But because the old 'container' for democratic aspirations was now so weak, and because the right had been in power for so long, there was nearly everywhere a tacit pessimism or minimalism about what was then possible.

But then, around the time of its second election campaign in 2001, New Labour underwent a partial self-radicalization. It then committed substantial resources to selected public services, notably health and education, and reaffirmed that its commitment to full employment, 'social inclusion', and its own 'war on poverty' was genuine. Why did this self-radicalization even take place, and what does this tell us about the ongoing social crisis in modern Britain? Is it possible that the weakness of the political expression of 'progressive' social demands led us to underestimate them, even to fail to notice their continuing existence? Is the New Labour's adoption of its second-term public services agenda its own recognition that it had no choice but to do this, if it wished to survive in power? The constituencies on which New Labour was seeking to impose its agenda of capitalist modernization, via the machineries of spin, had after all in some obscure way bitten back and imposed reciprocal demands of their own. The actual location of this social compromise — where the deals were done — remained a mystery. It seemed to have something to do with what went on in the Granita restaurant in 1997, and in the recurrent rumours of rows between the occupants of Numbers 10 and 11 Downing Street. But typically enough, these differences were read merely as conflicts of personality and ambition, and not as the expression of much deeper societal tensions.

Caesarism and Tony Blair

How should we think about the political role of Tony Blair, and the Third Way formation around him, in the light of all this? In his article, 'The Little Caesars of Social Democracy', Hall provided a brilliant Gramscian characterization of the project of the Social Democratic Party (SDP) in the early 1980s, in terms drawn from Gramsci's model of Caesarism as a condensation in the person of an individual leader (sometimes a collective leader) of social contradictions which it had not been possible to resolve by more constitutional means. The original exemplar of this model of analysis was Marx's *The Eighteenth Brumaire of Louis Bonaparte*, the classical text to which Hall's historical political analysis has also been closest. Should we not perhaps see Tony Blair as just such a 'Caesar', chosen by the Labour Party as a leader who was specifically not identified with Labour's own political culture, in order to win much broader cross-class support? Blair and his coterie's rejection of Labourism have often been represented in terms of political pragmatism rather than conviction. This is also how it has preferred to represent itself, as a necessary pragmatic solution to Labour's electoral problem, given the withering away of its traditional support base. The fact that Blair has also always claimed to be a conviction politician, with a principled agenda, has been somehow ignored as if the convictions themselves, whatever they were, did not matter. In so far as there plainly were such convictions, this at least had the advantage of showing that Blair was, in his own way, honest.

But suppose we do take Blair and New Labour's definite convictions seriously, and recognize that they have a fundamentally new project, that they envisage a different kind of social settlement altogether than 'social democracy'. By social democracy I mean the institutionalized, pluralist class truce of the earlier social democratic settlement, with its shifting balance of public and private sectors, and its significant 'neutral' constitutional space of mediation between 'countervailing powers' (made up of a civil service, of independent professions, of strong trade unions, of the judiciary, of public service broadcasting, even of autonomous universities). The alternative new project is for a system substantially dominated by capital, with a state whose role is to secure its conditions for existence not arbitrate between it and contending, even if subordinate social interests. The welfare state becomes conceived not as a bastion of alternative communitarian values, but as a means for the reproduction of the capitalist work ethic, and as a sphere in which new opportunities can be found for private capital accumulation. After all, in a post-industrial economy, if capital accumulation is barred from the spheres of health, education, social care and transport, its scope of operation is going to be severely constrained. The state has to be restructured in managerial terms, to ensure that market mentalities — what the Thatcherites used to call the 'Enterprise Culture'— are inculcated in every sphere of society, overcoming the earlier dualism of an individualist private and a broadly collectivist public sector. The managerial state becomes distinct from the arbitrating, conflict-managing state. Mostly the new model state has been successful in imposing its disciplines on other social institutions — its burgeoning systems of audit and inspection have been one mechanism for this — but it does from time to time meet resistance, from the judiciary, from the public service broadcasters, even from the doctors and the military.

It has been easy to see this as a juggernaut rolling all before it. But then why did this partial self-radicalization take place, why did the government commit itself to a substantial enhancement of collective provision, in the first instance in health and education, but perhaps shortly in an expanded programme of early years' child care also. The explanation may be that the sources of division which brought the social order to the point of collapse in the 1970s and 1980s have not in reality gone away, and remain latently if rather inchoately present. The petrol price protest movement of two years ago showed how great the latent potential for social disorder is, and how quickly a crisis can emerge apparently from nowhere. New Labour's insistence on its success in maintaining economic growth throughout its period of office has as its unspoken shadow its anxiety about what would happen if this were to falter. The splintering of the electorate in the June 2004 round of elections shows how volatile the political system has become, and how weak the hold of the major parties is on the social constituencies which they need to sustain them.

From this perspective, the change of course of New Labour in its second term, and the different public spending priorities it has adopted, were a prudent judgement of what had to be offered to the majority of the electorate if New Labour were to remain in office. The New Labour government remains, that is to say, a coalition in which the radical pro-capitalist modernizers whose leader is Blair, share power with a subordinate but still powerful group whose leader is Brown, who retain their social democratic commitments despite their endorsement of the Blairite modernizing project. This coalition continually threatens to unravel. If it moves too far to the New Labour Right, it risks the desertion of its working-class voters, and overt opposition from the trade unions, still important sources of party funding and support. If it moves too far to the Left, it risks antagonizing its tacit 'social partners' in business, and their press baron advocates, and losing votes in 'Middle Britain'. But there is a deeper, more long-term risk, or potential, that in so far as New Labour succeeds in office it *ipso facto* strengthens the democratic aspirations which were so beaten down by the years of Thatcherism. How is it to prevent the re-emergence of structures, institutions and agencies which will engender new social demands, and will want to renegotiate the terms of settlement between different 'social partners' and their value systems? In other words, success in demonstrating that Labour can win and keep power is likely to wake up its various constituencies to the idea that perhaps they can 'ask for more'. Adjustment to this changing balance of forces has already happened, as Labour's second-term programme showed. The ongoing stresses on the partnership between Number 10 and Number 11 Downing Street, between Blair and Brown, reflect these contradictions of power base and political purpose. Ken Livingstone's unique success for Labour in the recent round of elections is another indication of the emergence of more autonomous democratic institutions as a consequence of even modest achievements.

If 'Blairism' was a 'Caesarist' moment, what happens when it passes, as it inevitably must? Will the system again be pitched into crisis, with the reawakening of collective action, and a counter-response from the Right? Some unstable resolution of such a crisis from the Right is one possible outcome of that situation. Or can some routinization of this charismatic, Caesarist moment be achieved, stabilizing a lasting settlement between the contending conceptions of social order now contained within the New Labour system, and making such a social compromise into the 'common sense of the age'. Is it possible to set limits of possibility for the Right as the post-war welfare settlement successfully achieved 50 years ago? The argument here is that we would have a better chance to influence these outcomes if we were to return to the problematic of social crisis which Hall originally set out for us, and attempted to analyse this new conjuncture with the subtlety and complexity which he brought to its earlier moments. If we do this, we might even manage to catch up with the history of our own time.

A Postcolonial Intellectual

I want to conclude with some reflections on how Stuart Hall's Jamaican origin has been fundamental to his work. He went to England as a Rhodes Scholar when he was 18, and has lived there ever since.

A number of important analyses of contemporary British intellectual history have drawn attention to the vital contribution that has been made to it by émigrés and immigrants of various kinds. The central argument of Perry Anderson's essay, 'Components of the National Culture'[7] was that English intellectual life had been wholly revitalized by the arrival of successive generations of refugees from Europe, who had helped to overcome the insularity and anti-theoretical cast of English thought. Anderson and Nairn cite the influence of Wittgenstein, Malinowski, Namier, Popper, Berlin, Hayek, Namier, Gombrich, and Klein, among others. This was mostly a 'white' influx — more progressive figures, such as members of the Frankfurt School like Adorno, Horkheimer, and Fromm who went to America instead. The project of the later *New Left Review*, under Anderson's editorship, was to bring about a comparable exposure of British intellectual life to 'red' influences from abroad, in particular through the translation and assimilation of writing in the Western Marxist tradition — Lukacs, Gramsci, Althusser, Poulantzas, Benjamin and countless more. These became familiar figures in British academic life in the 1970s and 1980s, but were scarcely read in 1960.

Terry Eagleton, in his *Exiles and Emigres* (1970) developed this argument in the context of literature, drawing attention to the role of émigrés from the USA, Poland, Ireland, and also following Raymond Williams, the English working class in bringing new energies into a rather closed and complacent English literary culture. It is not difficult to update this argument by reference to the influence of later Irish, American, and postcolonial writers and interpreters, such as Heaney, Plath and Alvarez.

Stuart Hall's contribution, both in his individual work, and his contribution to the work of others around him, needs to be seen in this context, though the fact that he has found such a central place in one 'quarter' of English intellectual life (an initiator of the New Left, a founder of the major new discipline of cultural studies, holder of a major chair at the Open University, key figure in the critical analysis of the move to the Right in British politics since 1978, latterly the most influential theorist of issues of ethnic identity in Britain) may have somewhat obscured this aspect. What is significant, however, is how much of this influence and contribution has depended on Hall's origin, on his initial distance from the metropolitan society, and has not been merely incidental to it.

In fact, a great deal of the freshness and perceptiveness which the grouping of the New Left brought to British society and culture came from the fact that so many of them came from outside it. Charles Taylor (French Canada), Norman Birnbaum, Clancy Sigal, Norm Fruchter (USA), Peter Worsley (Australia), John Rex (Rhodesia, as it then was), Stuart Hall (Jamaica) are examples, well represented in the pages of *Universities* and *Left Review* and *New Left Review*. The other *New Reasoner* strand of this tradition, came from a different kind of 'outside', that of the 'small world of British Communism', represented in the Oxford–London New Left by Raphael Samuel, and by the larger group of New Reasoners. It was from these 'outsider' locations that it was possible to 'pick up' so quickly and sensitively what was changing in British social relations, and what was so limited about the standard political repertoires, whether Fabian or Communist.

Sensitivity to issues of empire and race were there from the beginning in this project. Suez — a late but it now turns out by no means the last paroxysm of the Empire — was one of the founding moments for the formation of the new left. The idea of 'positive neutralism' developed in association with the Campaign for Nuclear Disarmament (CND), drew heavily on the anti-imperialist identifications of ex-colonials such as Worsley, Rex Nettleford, and Stuart Hall, as well as on the commitment to find some space independent of both capitalism and state communism. This 'positive neutralism' looked to the non-aligned, post-imperial nations — India, Ghana, Indonesia, Egypt, and the Bandung Conference — for a new leadership. Gandhi's idea of non-violent resistance was also one of the inspirations of CND. Recognition of the role that race was going to play in the politics of the British Right also came very early, in the involvement of the New Left by Stuart Hall in particular, in the community politics of Notting Hill, one of the first areas where antagonism towards Caribbean immigrants became mobilized by the Right. Recognition of new kinds of freedom and expressiveness among young people in the cities, reported in the 'Absolute Beginnings' essay mentioned above, included noting that black youngsters, and cultural models for white young people which were being taken from black culture, were part of this. Colin MacInnes, who was one of the inspirations for Hall's essay, was another incomer, from Australia.

When youth culture came to be one of the foremost topics of investigation by the young researchers at the Centre for Contemporary Cultural Studies in Birmingham, the interfusion of different ethnic voices and styles, in music in particular, was a central and liberating discovery. It seemed that here for once ethnic differences were a resource which young people were celebrating and making creative use of, something which has continued to fertilize British popular culture to this day.

The analysis of Thatcherism developed in *Policing the Crisis* and in the subsequent *Marxism Today* essays began as a response to police and media activities which were focused on race in Birmingham, which is the context for much of the media analysis of the book. The issue of 'mugging' led the way to the recognition of the role of racial antagonism in the construction of the New Left, through Enoch Powell's success in racializing the political agenda (even though he was himself removed from office by Edward Heath), and through Thatcher's confident mobilization of racial anxieties (the danger of the 'swamping' — a term chosen with intuitive cleverness — of indigenous communities by immigrants). The analysis of Thatcherism in 'The Great Moving Right Show' and elsewhere note the reassertion of British national and imperial identity, against 'others' of several kinds, as one of its central ideological components.

Whereas in much of Hall's earlier work ethnicity has been a crucial dimension in a more inclusive political and cultural analysis, in recent years he has come to address its importance more directly. As questions of ethnic self-definition became important in the black community, and as the question of national and ethnic identities became important in multiracial and multicultural Britain, Hall made his intervention through his idea of ethnic hybridity, his insistence that ethnicities were made through processes of social and cultural definition, and did not exist as natural essences. This analysis drew on ideas of cultural construction developed within cultural studies, to explore issues of gender and sexuality as well as class and race. This argument drew attention both to the emergence of new identities — 'new ethnicities' — made possible by experiences of migration, of its second and third generation communities, and the many interactions with other communities that were taking place. It was also a critique of, and a cautionary warning against, ethnic essentialism and separatism among black radicals, in which he did not see much promise. His BBC television series on the Caribbean gave a memorable exploration to these ideas of ethnic hybridity and difference, exploring as it did the significant ethnic and cultural mixes — between African, Indian, British, French, Spanish, and North American inputs — that make the Caribbean islands so distinct from one another. As he has himself said, he did not know himself to be a 'West Indian' until he arrived in England, and found himself part of a small community made up of people — including a group of novelists — from Caribbean islands he scarcely knew, and had never visited. Another more recent television series made on the 50th anniversary of the docking of the *Empire Windrush* in 1948, which began the major post-war Caribbean migration into Britain, recorded the psychic disappointments and deep injuries inflicted on the new arrivals, who imagined Britain from its own idealized imperial representation of itself, and encountered something quite different, and mostly far from welcoming. However, one could draw more positive implications from the Windrush television series taken as a whole, since so much could be seen to have changed for the better since those early days.

Hall became active in the defence of the rights of black people in Britain, for example as a member of the Runnymede Commission following the Stephen Lawrence murder. In this context he has taken up positions which are militant in demanding just and equal treatment for black citizens, even though he has remained committed at the same time to the encouragement of cultural diversity.

The courses he helped to develop at the Open University, whose publications have much wider dissemination than any other degree programme in the UK, gave particular emphasis to issues of modernity, globalization, and identity, to which the history and consequences of empire, and the dimensions of ethnicity, are fundamental.

For the last few years, post-retirement and away from a formal institutional role in a university, Hall has undertaken more of his work within the context of ethnic minority cultural communities, notably in engaging with photography and the visual arts as expressions and explorations of ethnic identities in Britain. This work has given rise to significant writings, which are at this point probably rather less well known than his earlier work in cultural studies, politics and sociology. He is a very active chairman of the International Institute for the Visual Arts (inIVA) which is in the process of funding a major new cultural institute in London devoted to ethnic perspectives on the visual arts. If this project succeeds, as it will probably do, it will constitute a major addition to London's cultural landscape, giving a new centrality to multi-ethnic culture in London, and to the contribution of the various overseas Diasporas to which it is connected.

It should be clear then that Stuart Hall's postcolonial formation (Jamaica was not yet even independent when he left for university in Britain in 1951) has been fundamental to nearly all of his work. He has interpreted British society and culture from the perspective of someone who was both deeply formed by it, as a colonial citizen, but was also an outsider to it. His work has from the beginning made the British notice the significance of racial differences in their midst, and take some explicit note of their imperial identity as something to question and ponder. For most of Hall's career, he has always sought to connect one thing to another, to make ethnicity and colonization visible as part of a larger totality of culture or politics, and not to insist on their separateness. One can see in this an implicit 'strategy of alliances' on the Left, which aims to link anti-colonial and anti-racist politics — fundamental to Hall's position — to a broader ensemble of issues and antagonisms in relation to domestic political alignments in Britain, to the recomposition of cultural studies, sociology, and politics as fields of study, and earlier on to the issues of the Cold War. It seems probable that the strong tradition of anti-colonialism in British liberalism and on the Left, and the relatively peaceful transition to independence in some of Britain's former colonies, made this option more feasible than it would otherwise have been. There was always some receptive ground for anti-racist and anti-imperialist politics in Britain, reflected also for example in the vigorous anti-apartheid campaign. This approach has enabled Hall, as a postcolonial intellectual from Jamaica, to be accepted as a formative and deeply-admired figure on the left of British politics and cultural life. He has contributed substantially, in this way, to the acceptance and valuing of contributions to the national culture by those of diasporic origins, and to the cultural diversification of British life. The establishment of inIVA, will among other things, show how many others have been able to follow in these footsteps, even in a society which retains many racist and exclusionary habits of mind. It has been possible for Hall to do all this without making compromises or disavowals of his own commitments or integrity. One consequence of this is that he has remained a dissenting and non-incorporated figure in British public life, slightly awkward for even the Left-centre establishment to deal with. He has thus had less influence with mainstream Labour, and with its government, and has had a less visible media presence, than one might have hoped. It should be noted as a fact that despite Hall's considerable success in interpreting the Caribbean Diaspora in Britain to itself, and to the British, not much interest seems to have been taken until lately in these explorations in the Caribbean itself. But perhaps this is now changing.

There have no doubt been different ways of taking up the role of a postcolonial intellectual in the past 50 years. Stuart Hall's way of doing this has been to make himself fully at home in his country of migration, but spend a good part of a lifetime there trying to change its ways of thinking to take account of experiences of millions of people like him. British academic, cultural and political life is much better for his efforts than it would have been without them. Space has been made for others to continue this work. Hall does not see himself as a political optimist — pessimism of the intellect, facing up to the real, have been his watchwords. But there has been something deeply hopeful about his commitment to finding people who will listen and respond if one shares one's attempts at understanding with them. Many have done so.

Notes

1. *Universities* and *Left Review* was published between 1957 and 1959, and edited by Stuart Hall, Gabriel Pearson, Raphael Samuel, and Charles Taylor, and gave rise to the ULR Club in London, the Partisan Coffee House, and various other initiatives. Close links were formed with the northern-based *New Reasoner*, also founded in 1957 and edited by John Saville and Edward Thompson following their and others' resignation from the Communist Party after the Soviet invasion of Hungary. The two journals merged to launch *New Left Review* early in 1960, which Stuart Hall edited for two years until the end of 1961.

2. Rolf Lindner, 'Absolute Beginnings: In Search of a Lost Time', in *Without Guarantees: In Honour of Stuart Hall*, eds. P. Gilroy, L. Grossberg and A. McRobbie (London and New York: Verso, 2000) is a perceptive discussion of this article and its importance.

3. This argument was influenced by John Kenneth Galbraith's *The Affluent Society* (1958) which with its theme of 'private affluence and public squalor' provided the most effective critique of consumer capitalism in this period.

4. E. Laclau, *Politics and Ideology in Marxist Theory* (London: Verso, 1977).

5. Stuart Hall, *The Hard Road to Renewal* (London: Verso, 1980).

6. Though Stuart appears never to have had any illusions about New Labour.

7. P. Anderson, 'Components of the National Culture', *New Left Review* 50 (July– August 1969). Reprinted in P. Anderson, *English Questions* (London: Verso, 1992).

2 | Disorderly Politics: Reading with the Grain

Bill Schwarz

This paper derives from a larger exploration of the interrelations between Caribbean migration, from the West Indies to Britain, and the historical transformations we have come to know as decolonization.[1] Though my emphasis falls on Britain rather than on the Caribbean, I argue that the West Indian migrant played a privileged role in elaborating a critical conception of the colonial civilization of the British. I am sure, moreover, that this is a critique which we in Britain can still make work for us, today.[2] There exists, in other words, a peculiarly Anglophone precursor to postcolonial thinking which deserves to be better known in Britain than it is. This attempt to reveal the role of the diasporic West Indian in imagining the British world decolonized is not original. It is there on every page in George Lamming's *The Pleasures of Exile*, first published in 1960 and, though rather more difficult to extract, it is there too in C.L.R. James's celebrated (but very strange) book, *Beyond a Boundary*, which first appeared in print in 1963. Indeed, James himself always imagined that it was only the black migrant presence that allowed the formerly imperial nation finally to see itself — to recognize itself for what, historically, it was — and thereby, in his terms, to realize its own fulfilment. This is a classic Hegelian formulation elegantly turned inside out: the slave finally settles accounts with the master, forced by a profane history to do his job for him and to create a better future for humanity at large.[3] It is, equally, a formulation which suggests that within the mentalities of the white native population of Britain there occurred some blockage or inhibition which made their vision of empire disabling and partial.

C.L.R. James, George Lamming, Sam Selvon, Claudia Jones: all found themselves in the 1950s confronting the metropolis not only in its idealized codes, but in its actually existing lived forms. The disparities between the two, between the ideal and the lived, were largely what their writings in the 1950s were about. This, after all, was the touchstone of the Caribbean migrant experience.

What, though, of Stuart Hall? His career as a writer effectively took off in the 1960s rather than in the 1950s; it did so principally, though by no means exclusively, within the institutions of the academic world; and by the time this happened, he had settled to live not in the Caribbean, but in Britain. This makes him a rather different sort of figure from James, Lamming, Selvon and Jones. But not, I think, that different. The intellectual labour of decolonization in the Caribbean produced a rich conceptual legacy, of significance not only for the Caribbean but more generally. It appeared in many different registers and forms. As I have argued elsewhere, to differing degrees formally accredited intellectuals schooled in the institutions of British colonialism increasingly perceived the need to divest themselves of something of the cultural inheritance of empire.[4] In so doing, they necessarily found themselves confronting more directly their own, and their respective nation's, creolization. Indeed, we can witness the protracted and uneven recomposition of Caribbean thought as it strove to incorporate within itself the vernacular forms of the West Indian nations in the process of their seeking sovereignty. At every point, the formal legacies of colonialism vied with the vernacular, blacker, more fluid cultures which constituted the traces of slavery, of other diasporas, and of a long history of racial mixing. If popular life in the Caribbean represented the stratum of a cultural order in which the norms of the colonizers were least internalized, we can appreciate why at this moment — on the threshold of independence and after — popular forms assumed a new valency. In such circumstances, thought could lose its purity, become more profane, and new things happen. These intellectual transformations were active not only in the Caribbean, but in the diaspora too. This, essentially, is my point. In Stuart Hall's writings of the 1960s and 1970s one can hear — in Britain — the echoes of these distant events. More profoundly, if more difficult to demonstrate, his thinking in its very conceptual foundations can properly be understood as diasporic, as we understand the term in its specifically Caribbean inflections.

On this occasion, however, I want to go back in time and look at Stuart Hall's earliest published writings, in the 1950s, to see what they reveal about his diasporic locations. I do this in the spirit of an archaeological reading. So far as I know, the earliest published essay, on Lamming and Selvon, appeared in *Bim* in 1955.[5] In addition there are the later contributions to the political and cultural journal which he co-edited, *Universities* and *Left Review* (*ULR*). These comprise five essays and double that number of brief reviews, notices or editorial introductions, the essays addressing Conservatism, the recomposition of class, the figure of the adolescent, and schooling.[6] These themes were all moving to the centre of radical inquiry in Britain in the late 1950s, in part perhaps, because of the influence of the *ULR* itself. They are not well known now, and so far as they are recalled they are interpreted as precursors of what is sometimes designated as British cultural studies, or of that version of cultural studies which came into being institutionally at Birmingham University in the 1960s, with Stuart Hall as its principal intellectual inspiration.[7] The *ULR* writings, we should remember, were produced when Stuart himself was a very young man. They were written for the political moment, addressing conjunctural issues of the day which are now long forgotten. The pieces are, as well, often quite short. Whether in consequence, they compose an identifiable, given corpus, about which one can readily generalize must remain an open matter. As will be seen, my own concern here is with a few tiny fragments of what is in any case only a relatively small collection of writings. But in the spirit of Carlo Ginzburg, I think that these seemingly incomplete clues tell us a story of great interest.

A decisive issue, which gives form to this story and which is formative for Stuart Hall's thinking in these years, is decolonization: the collective historical process of becoming postcolonial. We know that in this period colonial issues were uppermost in his mind.[8] He arrived in a country, in 1951, in which colonial mentalities were pronounced, and in which statements lauding the necessary virtues of white supremacy — a supremacy conducted with due courtesies, of course — passed by unnoticed in public life, for there was nothing exceptional about them. A short while before Hall's boat from Kingston had docked at Avonmouth, Winston Churchill had been re-elected as prime minister, still determined that so long as he held office he would resist any move to liquidate the British empire. Yet imperial Britain unravelled with astonishing speed, the dreams of the ruling caste notwithstanding, and with a finality that no one had predicted.

Perhaps as startling as the speed of the decolonization of the empire was, insofar as its white subjects in the metropolis were concerned, its invisibility. Pretty much, overseas really did mean out of sight. So far as the naked eye could see, this vast critical dimension of British history was disconnected from the everyday life of domestic Britons. There were very few occasions when political events brought about by decolonization directly impacted upon the domestic nation. The most dramatic instance was during the war with Egypt (known in politer parlance as 'Suez') when an angry, monster demonstration filled Trafalgar Square in London on Sunday November 4, 1956 — attended too, we know, by Stuart. But this was one of the only occasions, or perhaps the only occasion, when the formal politics of decolonization, in the metropolis, broke free from the institutions of Westminster, and spilled out into the street. Even then, the wider domestic crisis, although deep, was relatively short-lived. The *Times*, at pains to point out that the mass of the British people were more immediately exercised by the antics of young blonde starlets than by the events unfolding in the eastern Mediterranean, was equally sure that the people 'still want[ed] Britain great.'[9] Both these propositions were probably right. We need remember that popular, domestic perceptions of decolonization were highly mediated, particularly dependent on the condensed cinema newsreel stories, projected either in monochrome or in early, dreamy technicolor, with their bizarre musical scores and even odder mock heroic commentaries.

This invisibility of decolonization, for the natives of the metropole, was one factor in accounting for the longevity of the last of the great dominating myths of the English: the conviction that the transition from empire to post-empire occurred as a well ordered, finished evolution, from one to the other, with no discernible hiatus or disturbance. This myth dominated public life, across the full spectrum of Westminster opinion, during the entire period of decolonization itself.[10] The very visible catastrophes of the French in Vietnam and Algeria (and later of the Portuguese in their African colonies) did much to give it credence. Until very recently the formal historiography served to abet this interpretation of a uniquely providential British, or English, experience — a historiography that embodies the final redoubt of an implacably Whiggish temperament, whose life is only now slowly passing away.

Yet decolonization, both in general and in its British forms, was anything but ordered. It represented, on the contrary, disorder. The clearest conceptual expression of this properly dissenting view came from another West Indian writing at this same moment — Frantz Fanon. On the opening page of *The Wretched of the Earth*, when he was attempting to grasp the significance of decolonization as a historical process, he argued that:

> Decolonisation, which sets out to change the order of the world, is, obviously, a programme of complete disorder.... It transforms spectators crushed with their inessentiality into privileged actors, with the grandiose glare of history's floodlights upon them.... "The last shall be first and the first last." Decolonisation is the putting into practice of this sentence.[11]

'The last', in Fanon's imagination, were the racially exploited. For them to become 'the first' would indeed signify 'complete disorder.' If classical colonial societies worked through race, as Barnor Hesse argued in his paper, then the act of decolonization generated, specifically, a racial disorder.[12]

Fanon was concerned with the Algerian situation, and with the relationship to metropolitan France. The French and British circumstances differed in many critical respects. It is clear also that his principal assumption was that the disorder he was theorizing would occur in the colony rather than the metropole. But what if we use Fanon's notion of disorderly decolonization to investigate the politics of the British metropolitan experience?

In the British case, as I see it, it is the disorder consequent upon decolonization which could not be spoken. It could not be spoken because it had no name. Decolonization, in the imaginary world of the British, necessarily meant order, not disorder. End of empire, within this logic, simply could not be a contentious or problematic or divisive issue. The empire had gently transmuted into the Commonwealth. All had gone rather well: tea on the lawn had been completed and stumps drawn. Decolonization could not be the cause of anything ill — save, perhaps, the envy of the French which naturally the English rather relished. To have followed Fanon and to have linked decolonization and disorder — to have named the problem — would have been to have opened the mind to untold horrors, for it would have required confronting the violence of the present and the violent legacies of the imperial past.

There were, of course, plenty of signs of disorder in the domestic British nations in the 1950s, despite all the relative stability. But the incomprehensibility which underwrote the public soul-searching of the time was due in part to the inexplicability of the malaise which seemed to prevail. Never had the population been more prosperous. For most people war seemed a long way off. The institutions of the British state were generally perceived to be operating smoothly. Smart Ivy League political scientists travelled to Britain to marvel at the workings of its society. For one of the most renowned of these figures, Harvard's Samuel Beer, Britain seemed to exemplify the truth of a classic sociological functionalism, in which every piece of the machinery of state and society meshed with the next. What was evidently, observably dysfunctional was troubling only to the extent that it lay outside this overwhelming domain where harmony ruled, and where political institutions worked. With time, and with a bit more pragmatic social engineering, they too could be fixed, and all would be well.[13]

Yet one of these dysfunctional groups for whom things looked significantly different were the migrants from the Caribbean. Though clearly a factor this was not due primarily to their social marginality, banished as they were to the borderlands of civic life. It had more to do with the unrealisable aspirations which they had carried with them, with their suitcases and their Sunday best. The story has been well rehearsed. West Indian migrants arrived in Britain with a powerful, if displaced, inside understanding of the codes of British civilization, which derived from the full force of a deeply colonized society. On arriving in Britain they encountered a discrepant reality, which in its lived forms barely conformed to the high ideals of British civilization which had been internalized back home. As Kamau Brathwaite has expressed, reflecting on his own journey, he had arrived as a young man at Southampton expecting William Shakespeare himself to be there, ready to greet the newcomer and future poet.[14] But unfortunately, as we know, Shakespeare was not there that day. There were many others he missed as well. Nor was there much evidence of a wider generous civic culture ready to welcome these black colonial Britons from overseas. This compacted West Indian experience, as I have suggested, inspired the early diasporic realism which we can find in the London novels of Sam Selvon and George Lamming.

A curious quality of this genre, though, needs to be emphasized. It might seem as if the act of crossing the seas, from the Caribbean to the mother country, would have created a literature which turned on the discrepancy between the dreams of the migrant and the realities of actually-existing England. But invariably this was not so. The fiction works to other imperatives. It describes a world in which the dreams of the migrant constitute the given reality, and the strange habits of the real, flesh and blood English, the unreal dream. This is the paradox which lies at the heart of the West Indian tradition of diasporic realism. England features in the novels, so radically removed from the collective migrant expectation, as an unreal phantasm.[15]

In the fiction we can get close to the phenomenology of the migrant experience. But this is where theory and politics started, especially in these years, in the imagining of black subjectivity as we can see in Fanon.[16] This same perception was also given a more overtly political turn, and this is what Stuart Hall's writings of the 1950s represent. The evidence is fragmentary. But even so he writes to the same effect, as if he had entered a somnambulant world in which everything was inverted: where the dysfunctional appeared functional, the unreal real, torpor vital, and where a deep but unspoken disorder masqueraded as order.[17] This I take to be the tenor of his *ULR* article entitled 'The deep sleep of England', where he sought to expose the great 'cleavage between the tone of our society, its manners and forms, and the gross realities.' His purpose was to argue for a more expansive conception of what politics was, in order to overcome 'the deep, immobilising contradictions of our culture', its 'frozen matrix.' With a nod to Matthew Arnold (rather than, as later, to Gramsci) he developed the theme that he and his generation were poised 'between two worlds, one dead, the other powerless to be born', and he derided the insularity of the English, 'sleeping the deep, deep sleep of England.'[18] These readings of the official civilization of the mother country were dominated by metaphors of death and decay — and, concomitantly, of an intellectual life commanded by 'dead souls.'[19]

An earlier *ULR* article provided a political analysis of the Conservative Party after the destruction, or self-destruction, of Anthony Eden in the aftermath of the war with Egypt in the autumn of 1956. I find the opening sentence by Stuart Hall, wonderful: 'The disorderly thrust of political events,' he says, 'disturbs the symmetry of political analysis.' This is indicative of a political intellect that refused all varieties of functionalism, and which operated in an entirely different mental world from that of Westminster and its academic derivatives. In the immediate aftermath of Britain's greatest crisis of decolonization, disorder and disturbance moved to the centre of his understanding of what British civilization had become. It made redundant, for him, the choreographed readings of political science. If disorder reigned, then political analysis too — 'theory' — needed to be recast, such that it could grasp the unruly contingencies brought about by events, and by the expansion of the domain of politics itself. For those who recall Hall's analysis of British Conservatism in a later age — in the age of Thatcherism — there is much in this early piece that they will recognize. (They would encounter, too, both in the 1950s and in the 1980s, Hall sparring with that ineffably true-blue ideologue of Toryism, Peregrine Worsthorne. Believing the entire ideology of British Conservatism 'obsolete and dangerous' in the 1950s, in thrall to 'the most rootless archetypal images', it is little wonder that Stuart was so fiercely provoked when it rose again from the dead, in the figure of Mrs Thatcher, in the 1970s and 1980s). He condemned, in 1957, 'the moral failure of the Left' and insisted on the need to understand how political ideas become rooted in popular life. He perceived in Conservatism after Suez 'an unstable blend' of the new and the old, 'conflicting tendencies ... held together in a state of comparative disequilibrium.' He used the language of individual pathology to search beneath the surface of the political event in order to ascertain unseen, subterranean movements in the structures of political life. The Conservative Party of Harold Macmillan had, he believed, become 'the pawn of irrational forces.' 'The old neuroses govern.' Suez itself he identified as an event of 'traumatic' effect that worked 'to strip away the masks of rhetoric, and to expose the repressed sources of Britain's policy and its consequences.' 'Conservatism,' he noted in closing, 'has disappeared into the wilderness of unreason, and it should be left there to sing among the nightingales.'[20]

In the writings of the late 1950s, Hall was explicit about the connections between the formal sphere of politics and subjectivity. 'The public and the personal life are deeply interrelated,' he insisted, 'and we must learn to comprehend them as a totality.'[21] The determination to hold together the political and the personal has been a constant feature of his thinking in the intervening years, even while the conceptual terminology has become more complex. But something else is being hinted at here as well. The degree to which he employed the language of the damaged individual psyche — irrationalism and unreason, neurosis, trauma and repression — in order to understand what was happening in the domain of politics is not innocent, or simply of stylistic significance. It signals a conceptual shift of great importance, indicating that unless these psychic dimensions of politics and public life could be uncovered political critique itself would be impoverished and incomplete — a theme which Hall and others pursued with renewed urgency during the crises of the Thatcher years.[22] It highlighted, too, the need to devise a method to reach, analytically, the disorder and disturbance at the heart of Britain's body politic.

We can see in these early writings of Stuart Hall, the apprehension that British civilization itself was generating a disorder and that this was systematic rather than contingent. It needed to be acknowledged, named and theorized. 'Everyone,' he wrote, 'can feel and smell the concentrations and arbitrary exercise of power in our society. But who can name them?'[23] Invariably, in the studies of Stuart Hall which are now emerging, his theorizations of the early New Left period, which the *ULR* articles represent, are placed squarely in the domestic frame.[24] I think, though, Fanon's insistence on the centring of decolonization is persuasive: it is exactly the disorder which pertains when the empire, in its final violent reckoning, comes home. Every aspect of the domestic civilization, visibly or invisibly, consciously or unconsciously, is touched by this. When this process remains unnamed or unspeakable, it is within the culture — to use Hall's own term — repressed. It is that repression, in particular, that needed to be confronted and, arguably, still needs to be confronted.

A few years ago there was a pattern for the protagonists of poststructuralist and postcolonial literary theory to make much of the fact that they were reading against the grain of the text. This involved reading a text for its silences and impossibilities or, more particularly within the postcolonial idiom, for its buried, subtextual colonial and racial imaginings. Much collective energy was invested in these interpretations, and many literary texts became famous all over again because they exemplified so clearly the versatility of the new critical approach. Every text demanded that it be read against the grain. But going back to Hall's writings of the *ULR* period I think the difficulty is less reading against the writing than learning to read what is there, and to read with the text. In part he has already done the work for us. His are fledgling postcolonial texts in their own right. Their formulations may not reach the level of analytical sophistication to which we have become accustomed. But they are alive, I believe, to the essential issues.

I know that the category of disorder requires greater specification. In the British instance all I would say here is that one effect of decolonization was the drawing away of the nation from the state, with serious long-term, profound consequences.[25] While the political managers reorganized the British state, relocating its overseas interests from the colonies to Europe, they did so in the teeth of opposition from a variety of nationalist or anglophile tribunes: from the upholders of British rule in the white settler colonies, from advocates of British traditions in the Dominions, and — at home — from those who believed that the state was conniving to destroy the heritage of the English people, especially in regard to encouraging black immigration. Populist ethnic imaginings drove the disquiet about the end of empire, in Britain and in its former possessions. The reactions may seem, in retrospect, out of all proportion to the transformations which the end of the empire in fact brought about, or even threatened. If the last were to become the first, as Fanon had supposed, decolonization marked merely the first chapter of the first instalment.

One visible moment of disorder in the metropolis occurred in the autumn of 1958 when, in Notting Hill and Nottingham, serious white riots erupted, directed toward local black migrants in the respective neighbourhoods. There was a small but serious fascist, and even Klan, presence; cries for blacks to be lynched were heard on London streets. Although the politicians, with the admirable exception of Norman Manley, were doggedly silent about the outrages which had taken place within a couple of miles of Westminster, the overwhelming explanation from the remainder of official opinion turned on the role of local white hooligans and teddy boys. (At least this was so in the first days of the crisis: thereafter — one can see this happening in the pages of the press — condemnation shifted from the native hooligan to the black newcomer.) The under-socialization of dispossessed young white adults was taken to be the root cause and, as such, mainstream, respectable

England could in no way be implicated. Not one of the press reports I have read even came close to suggesting that there could be a connection between the racial lessons Britons had learned in the colonies and the violence on the urban streets of the mother country.

A singular exception can be found in the pages of the *ULR*. The journal published a series of interviews with young white schoolgirls who were sympathetic to the riots, and a predictably terrible audit emerged. In an unsigned commentary, which bears Hall's stamp, the editors insisted that the problem was not one of an active racialist minority, but of the civilization as a whole:

> Behind each irrational phrase [of the girls canvassed] stand an impressive list of names — Kenya, Cyprus, Malaya, British Guiana, Southern Rhodesia: but in one sense at least, these youngsters know, with a terrifying and distorted precision, what the names stand for. Here is the primitive barbarism, the "black man", abused in a score of governors' houses, beaten in a hundred district officers' huts, but who has lived on to haunt the nightmare world of a fifteen year old girl. The terrible tragedy of colonialism — not the past only but the present as well — has at last come "home".[26]

These were, in the 1950s in England, unusual sentiments. Amongst the migrant West Indians, and I daresay amongst other colonial groups, they had a certain currency: they provide, for example, a dominating theme in Lamming's *The Pleasure of Exile*. But the connections between mentalities formed in the colonies and violence, particularly racial violence, at home were unable to cross the threshold of the cognitive world of the vast majority of native Britons. The predominant discourses of decolonization cannot even be said to have been immune to such arguments, for they barely registered as possibilities. The connection between colony and metropolis, in this instance, was not one which was observable to the naked eye, nor one which could be demonstrated empirically. To imagine this connection, and to name it, required dismantling the way of thinking which made it unspeakable in the first place.

Although this cognitive divide between native Briton and Caribbean migrant was real enough, it was not absolute. On October 3, 1958, while public opinion in Britain was still confronting the shock of the Notting Hill riots, in the Cypriot town of Famagusta it appeared that

EOKA (National Organisation of Cypriot Fighters) guerrillas were responsible for shooting dead the wife of a British soldier, a certain Mrs Cutliffe, and for the wounding of her daughter, Catherine, whose wedding dress the pair were hoping to buy. The local British garrison went wild, and embarked — with or without official sanction — on a frenzy of violent retribution against the local population, in which four civilians were murdered, several hundred injured and during which there occurred only two arrests. Donald Wise of the *Daily Express* claimed 'I have never seen troops so fierce.' *The News of the World* reported that 'something snapped in the soldiers' minds' and that 'gun law' prevailed. The *Times* believed that the troops were 'in the grip of sheer cold rage.' The *Observer* alone pointed out that the British army was in danger of finding itself in the same position as its French counterpart in Algeria. Unnerving in this reporting was the sophistry employed in order to engineer an apology for the actions of the military.[27]

This event inspired a young British author, John Arden, to conceive of a play which attempted to work through the repercussions of this episode, and to draw out into the open the links between the ferocity overseas and apologetics at home. Arden later claimed that he wrote his play, *Serjeant Musgrave's Dance*, 'on fire' with the hope that it would articulate what remained unspeakable about the interrelation between colony and metropolis. He sub-titled it 'An unhistorical parable', while at the same time admitting that he had drawn freely from his historical imagination in order to provide historical depth.[28] The play was first performed at the Royal Court in October 1959. It proved, however, a commercial flop. The distinguished drama critic of the *Sunday Times*, Harold Hobson, offered a characteristic view: 'Another frightful ordeal. It is time someone reminded our advanced dramatists that the principal function of the theatre is to give pleasure.... It is the duty of theatre, not to make men better, but to render them harmlessly happy.' Many were simply baffled by what they saw. Even on a later run, six years later, Hilary Spurling in the *Spectator* believed that 'Muddle runs through the whole play and by the end has reached truly startling proportions.'[29]

In the first issue of *New Left Review*, which had been put together in the closing weeks of 1959 and appeared in January the following year, Hall wrote a short notice. In the *ULR* he had, amongst his other writings, commented on the London theatre, and had filed admiring pieces on the young playwrights Shelagh Delaney and Arnold Wesker.[30] In *New Left Review* he noted that *Serjeant Musgrave* had been met with 'total incomprehension' and that it had been 'killed stone dead by the London critics.' Yet he believed it to be the first new play on war 'which makes any sense at all.'[31]

Serjeant Musgrave is, in the first instance, about disorder. It is set some time in an allegorical colonial past, in a situation of crisis and violence. A young soldier is murdered, and the army wreaks its vengeance, in a moment of unchecked disorder, during which women and children, as well as local men, were killed and abused. Musgrave, an Ahab figure who we would now recognize as a prototype of a Christian fundamentalist, and who craves order where he perceives disorder, deserts with three companions. His purpose is literally to bring home to the domestic British the horror of colonial violence. He can only do so, however, by begetting ever greater violence. The more he attempts to impose order — the term and its cognates are a constant refrain throughout the play — the more violence and disorder prevail.[32] 'Wild-wood mad we are; and so we've fetched it home.' And: 'Join along with my madness, friend. I brought it back to England, but I've brought the cure too — to turn it on them that sent it out of this country.' Or again, in the words of one of Musgrave's comrades: 'We've earned our living beating and killing folk like yourselves in the streets of their own city. Well, it's drove us mad — and so we come back here to tell you how and to show you what it is like.'[33]

What is of great interest, though, is that the play is not merely about disorder, but it also enacts it. In terms of plot and 'rounded character', the psychological motives of the protagonists are indeed 'muddled', as Arden himself subsequently conceded.[34] But the play is, as its sub-title confirms, a parable rather than an exercise in naturalism. It dramatizes disorder. More especially, it dramatizes the repercussions of colonial disorder in the metropole. The great skill of the play lies in the fact that the audience is not apprised of the colonial terror and counter-terror — the episode which produces the narrative which we see on the stage — until halfway through the third act. Knowledge of this primal event first arrives in the broken articulations of Musgrave's nightmare, when he screams in his sleep, defending his own role in the counter-insurgency his troop carried out. Only by listening to this repressed voice, speaking what otherwise is unspeakable, can the audience arrive at an understanding of the play, and grasp its inner, historical coherence. Otherwise it is indeed a muddle. If Musgrave's repressed and unconscious torment is disregarded, as merely the delusion of a nightmare, the play cannot have meaning. That so many audiences did find it incomprehensible is symptomatic of the larger social, cognitive misrecognition of what decolonization represented. For others, for whom the realities of colonialism held no secrets, Arden's narrative proved a revelation: the only play on this theme 'which makes any sense at all.'

I have had to make my argument by stitching together fragments of evidence. In themselves, these fragments cannot bear the weight of an abstraction like 'disorder.' For it to convince, I would have to draw a more comprehensive picture. But I think it important to register the tone of Hall's thinking at this time for, as I see it, it anticipated an understanding of 'the empire at home' which only effectively entered public debate some 20 years later — during the time of early Thatcherism, the war with Argentina in 1982, and the intense racial conflicts of the period. I have attempted here only to deploy a minutely-focused historical argument, which both pays tribute to Hall's perspicacity and which also reminds us again of the weight of the thought (those dead souls) against which he and others at the time were pitted.

One conceptual matter remains unresolved. I have been keen to think through the links between decolonization and disorder. Following Fanon, I suggested that decolonization brings with it disorder. At a different level of abstraction, however, in Stuart Hall's writings we can see that he typically presents politics as essentially disorderly, disturbing and asymmetrical.[35] He was always careful to separate himself from any hint of Marxist functionalism — affiliating instead with what we might call a Marxist dysfunctionalism, or maybe a dysfunctional Marxism. His response to the political crisis generated in the aftermath of the British invasion of Egypt in 1956, and of Eden's subsequent resignation, was indeed on the dysfunctional dimensions of the political event. But isn't that what politics is more generally? The unpredictable and the contingent are, for Stuart, always around the corner, 'disequilibrium' the name of the game. This is the Stuart Hall touched most deeply by Gramsci. For what Gramsci designated as the domain of the political is also a 'live', dysfunctional, disorderly domain, composed by myths and passions as much as by rational doctrines. From this Gramscian perspective, the genius of Machiavelli lay in his capacity to craft a formal philosophy which could grasp these dimensions of political reality. Machiavelli's was a political philosophy, according to Gramsci, which 'stimulates the artistic imagination' and which 'gives political passions a more concrete form.' It was neither formally systematized, nor made up of 'pedantic classification.' In this conception, politics is not only about rational calculation, but about the making of what Gramsci called a 'concrete phantasy.'[36] To think in these terms adds a further layer of meaning to the idea of 'the concrete', for it alerts us to the subjective identifications in which political objectives take shape, become embodied, and generate human passion. And these are terms which are not easily amenable to orderly regulation.

I would have to concede, then, that there are difficulties in following Fanon and in proceeding to theorize the operations of racial disorder in the metropolis in the moment of decolonization. But however this is resolved; the disorder provoked — not only in the colonies but in the respective metropoles — still seems to me a fruitful question to pursue. In France and Portugal disorder was proximate and visible. In Britain, at least for most of the native populations, it seemed to be neither. And yet it was not only migrants like Stuart who felt that disorder had moved to the centre of things in the late 1950s and 1960s.

Later, this apprehension increasingly came to possess the New Right, and directly or indirectly, through many displacements, the loss of empire registered as part of the story. Many years ago I interviewed Enoch Powell, the great tribune and philosopher of what later came to be called Thatcherism. He was candid about many matters. I pressed him, particularly, on a speech he had made in his old home neighbourhood of Northfield in Birmingham in June 1970. This was the occasion when he dwelt on the dangers of the enemy within. He explained to me that around the moment of 1968 he had opened a file so that he could catalogue all the seemingly inconsequential episodes in civil society where order and cultural authority had been flouted, and where what he termed insolence abounded. (This term comes from deep within the colonial lexicon.) He was anxious not only about the fact that this was happening, and that few of his colleagues seemed to understand their political import, but also because he was unable to name the disorders he recorded. In desperation, he simply called his file 'The Thing.'

I think naming this metropolitan disorder, on both the left and the right, has proved to be a problem. We do not have the terms on hand. Fanon offers a clue in believing that empire was at the heart of the matter. We need also remember that in Britain the New Right mounted its project in the name of law and order, in reaction to its composite, fantasized conception of disorder. (In the closing scene of *Serjeant Musgrave* the verdict is given that 'law and order [has] been established'.)[37] If, as Fanon had imagined, decolonization marked a challenge to the racial hierarchies bequeathed by the colonial order, then the reaction to this racialized disorder was indeed a politics which sought to reimpose the old colonial habits and mentalities of racial authority.

I have suggested that in the 1950s, Stuart Hall, in the company of other West Indians of his generation, possessed a peculiarly sharp appreciation of the consequences of decolonization on the civilization of the metropolis. At the time, they got as close as anyone to understanding what disorder beheld. We should also recall his prescience in grasping the historic significance, 20 years on, of the new politics of order, manifest in what used to be called the New Right, evident in his influential study, *Policing the Crisis* and in his early grasp of the nature of Thatcherism.[38] We are now in a historical position to grasp more clearly the profound interconnections between the two.

Notes

1. I am most grateful to the British Academy, who by paying my airfare made it possible for me to attend the Centre for Caribbean Thought conference for Stuart Hall at the Mona campus of the University of the West Indies.

2. I have argued this in 'Crossing the Seas' in *West Indian Intellectuals in Britain*, ed. Bill Schwarz (Manchester: Manchester University Press, 2003); and in 'Claudia Jones and the *West Indian Gazette*. Reflections on postcolonial Britain', *Twentieth Century British History* 14, no. 3 (2003).

3. See C.L.R. James, *80th Birthday Lectures* (London: Race Today, 1981), 48; and his correspondence with V.S. Naipaul during the moment of publication of *Beyond A Boundary*; C.L.R. James, *Cricket* (London: Allison and Busby, 1989), 116–18 and 130–33. I am drawing here from my 'Becoming Postcolonial' in *Without Guarantees. In Honour of Stuart Hall*, eds. Paul Gilroy, Lawrence Grossberg and Angela McRobbie (London: Verso, 2000).

4. Bill Schwarz, 'Stuart Hall', *Cultural Studies* 19, no. 2 (2005), from which I have borrowed certain formulations here.

5.   Stuart Hall, 'Lamming, Selvon and some trends in the W.I. novel', *Bim* 23 (1955). Also published in this issue were two of Stuart's poems. There is a typescript of a radio talk (April 21, 1958) on 'British Caribbean writers' in Hall's file at the BBC written archives at Caversham.

6.   Stuart Hall, 'The new Conservatism and the old', *Universities* and *Left Review* 1 (1957); 'A sense of classlessness', *Universities* and *Left Review* 5 (1958); 'The politics of adolescence', *Universities* and *Left Review* 6 (1959); 'Absolute beginnings' and 'The big swipe', *Universities* and *Left Review* 7 (1959).

7.   The only consideration of these writings I know, focusing on 'A sense of classlessness', occurs in an essay by Colin Sparks. This endeavours to show that the positions adumbrated by Stuart in the 1950s anticipate the kind of post-Marxist affiliations which he was proposing in the 1990s. I suppose that the purpose of this was to demonstrate that Stuart Hall had never been a (proper) Marxist, even at the height of his engagement with Marxism. Even so, Sparks's attention to the writings of the 1950s is cursory, and his argument is not mine. 'Stuart Hall, Cultural Studies and Marxism' in *Stuart Hall: Critical Dialogues in Cultural Studies*, eds. David Morley and Kuan-Hsing Chen (London: Routledge, 1996).

8.   Stuart Hall, 'The Formation of a Diasporic Intellectual' in *Stuart Hall: Critical Dialogues*, 492; and Stuart Hall with Bill Schwarz, *Conversations with Stuart Hall* (Cambridge: Polity Press, forthcoming).

9.   The *Times*, August 27, 1956.

10.   George Lamming, we might note, is still shocked at the fact that British fiction during the years of decolonization paid no attention at all to the various 'emergencies' which dominated the end of colonial life. The contrast to French intellectual life, as Lamming comments, is stark. Interview with George Lamming, London, October 31, 2003.

11.   Frantz Fanon, *The Wretched of the Earth* (Harmondsworth: Penguin, 1971), 27.

12.   Barnor Hesse, 'Stuart Hall and the De/colonial question', Paper presented at the Stuart Hall conference at the Centre for Caribbean Thought (University of the West Indies, Mona).

13.   I draw loosely here from the once much admired analysis of Samuel Beer, *Modern British Politics: A Study of Parties and Pressure Groups* (London: Faber and Faber, 1965). Beer had been observing British political life long before this was published, and it represented the culmination of this phase of his thinking. Somewhat later, he was forced to tell a different story: *Britain Against Itself: The Political Contradictions of Collectivism* (London: Faber and Faber, 1982). For a historical survey of these deep shifts in British political society, see Stuart Hall and Bill Schwarz, 'State and Society, 1880–1930' in *Crises in the British State, 1880–1930*, eds. Mary Langan and Bill Schwarz (London: Hutchinson, 1985); republished in Stuart Hall, *The Hard Road to Renewal: Thatcherism and the Crisis of the British Left* (London: Verso, 1988).

14.   In a talk at the Africa Centre, London, July 24, 2002.

15.   Not only in Lamming and Selvon, but in Naipaul too. The theme of disorder lies at the centre of his early novel, *The Mimic Men* (Harmondsworth: Penguin,1969), which he wrote between August 1964 and July 1966. It carries Naipaul's usual theme of disorder in the colonies, but the force of the novel lies in its recognition of the operations of disorder in the metropole, which at times is explicitly linked to the moment of decolonization. Here 'London and the home counties' represent 'the greater disorder', 8. This is a disorder which derives from the failure of the civilizing project, as well as — for the narrator and author — the experience of migration. In a

bizarre and wretched conclusion, after many attempts to 'impose order on my history' and to abolish 'disturbance' (243), order of a sort is found, in all places, in the rituals of a provincial English hotel.

16. I discuss this historical moment further in 'C.L.R. James, George Lamming and the measure of historical time', *Small Axe* 14 (2003).

17. This is a theme which runs through Marx's *Eighteenth Brumaire*, a text to which Stuart Hall was clearly attracted at this time: see 'A sense of classlessness'.

18. 'The deep sleep of England', *Universities and Left Review* 3 (1958): 86 and 87. The notion of an unconscious England he took from the closing pages of Orwell's *Homage to Catalonia*.

19. Stuart Hall, 'Mr Raymond and the dead souls', *Universities and Left Review* 4 (1958). Here his attack was aimed at the cultural pages of the *New Statesman*. In the same issue his anger was directed at the Royal Academy: 'Big sir and the oranges and lemons', at the same time placing in the line of fire Winston Churchill and Lord Hailsham.

20. 'The new Conservatism and the old', 21, 23 and 24.

21. 'The deep sleep of England', 87.

22. This came to be a distinctive feature of his later interpretations of Thatcherism. And see too, in the same vein, Jacqueline Rose, 'Mrs Thatcher and Ruth Ellis' in her *Why War? Psychoanalysis, Politics and the Return to Melanie Klein* (Oxford: Blackwell, 1993), and Heather Nunn, *Thatcher, Politics and Fantasy: The Political Culture of Gender and Nation* (London: Lawrence and Wishart, 2002).

23. 'The politics of adolescence', 2.

24. Chris Rojek, *Stuart Hall* (Cambridge: Polity Press, 2003); Helen Davis, *Understanding Stuart Hall* (London: Sage, 2004); James Procter, *Stuart Hall* (London: Routledge, 2004).

25. I discuss this further in *Memories of Empire, Vol. III. Disorder* (Oxford: Oxford University Press, forthcoming 2008).

26. 'The habit of violence', *Universities and Left Review* 5 (1958): 4. For later formulations along these lines, Stuart Hall, 'Racism and Reaction' in *Five Views of Multi-Racial Britain* (London: Commission on Racial Equality, 1978).

27. The quotes from the press come from Francis Williams's discussion, 'Fleet Street: Verdict on Terror', *New Statesman* (October 11, 1958). In its editorial, the *New Statesman* insisted that this was not an isolated incident. The best account can be found in Robert Holland, *Britain and the Revolt in Cyprus, 1954–1959* (Oxford: Clarendon Press, 1998), 285–88. It is clear that the Governor of Cyprus, Sir Hugh Foot, anticipated violence from the military as soon as he had heard what had happened, and that he conceded that many of those detained had 'been given a good deal of rough treatment.' What has not been conclusively established, however, is whether the initial attack was carried out by EOKA.

28. Cited in Malcolm Page, *Arden on File* (London: Methuen, 1966), 19.

29. Both cited in *Arden on File*, 23–24.

30. 'Taste of the real thing' and '*Roots*', *Universities and Left Review* 6 and 7 (1959).

31. Stuart Hall, '*Serjeant Musgrave*', *New Left Review* 1 (1960): 50–51.

32. When revising this paper I came across the following story: US exchange students from the University of Notre Dame were abused by local police in their dormitories in the Australian city of Freemantle. The abuse parodied the violence inflicted upon Iraqi citizens captured by US forces in Iraq, its purpose it seems to enact a symbolic retribution on the United States *Australian*, July 22, 2004.

33.   John Arden, *Serjeant Musgrave's Dance* (London: Methuen, 1966), 90, 92, 94.
34.   Cited in *Arden on File*, 21–22.
35.   I discuss this in 'Stuart Hall', from which I borrow here.
36.   Antonio Gramsci, *Selections From the Prison Notebooks* (London: Lawrence and Wishart, 1971), 126.
37.   *Serjeant Musgrave's Dance*, 98.
38.   Stuart Hall, Chas Critcher, Tony Jefferson, John Clarke and Brian Roberts, *Policing the Crisis: 'Mugging', the State and Law and Order* (London: Macmillan, 1978).

3 | *The Revolution Stripped Bare*

Gilane Tawadros

Introduction

A few years ago, the art critic of *Time* magazine approached Stuart Hall at an event of the International Institute for the Visual Arts (inIVA) and asked him who he was. 'I'm an academic,' replied Stuart, 'but I've given up the day job.' In 1994, Stuart Hall was approached to chair a new, nascent organization called inIVA that was the first in Britain to be dedicated to diverse contemporary visual arts and ideas from every part of the globe. He reluctantly agreed to take up the role on a purely temporary basis. As a contemporary visual arts agency, inIVA supports and promotes the work of artists, curators and scholars from diverse cultural backgrounds, seeking to make their artistic practices and ideas accessible to new and diverse audiences. inIVA creates exhibitions, publications, multimedia, education and research projects. Over the past decade, the organization has chosen to work without a dedicated exhibition space but across a variety of spaces that sometimes includes galleries and museums but also encompasses the street, the internet, universities, publications, nightclubs, historic houses, schools and many other sites. inIVA experiments with new ways to present contemporary art and engage new audiences. It takes risks on young, unknown artists and those not yet established in the mainstream art world and it works collaboratively with a truly global network of artists, critics and curators. In a relatively short period of time, it has built up a distinctive portfolio of projects including exhibitions, publishing and research, education and multimedia projects and reached audiences in excess of five million. Ten years later Stuart Hall continues to play a key role at the helm of the organization. He has steered us through difficult waters, preventing the ship from being grounded on the rocks of bureaucratic indifference, and sometimes, downright hostility to issues of race and representation; the tidal wave of expectations from artists and mainstream art institutions in Britain who want to define the organization in its own image; and, perhaps, most importantly, navigating inIVA through the straits of contending political, social and economic discourses that threaten to close down the space for critical artistic practice and rigorous intellectual debate. Some may view Hall's engagement with contemporary visual art as his hobby — the equivalent of intellectual gardening, after decades of hard graft at the coal face of sociology departments, Marxist debates and cultural studies conferences — I want to argue that some of his most significant work and cutting-edge ideas have been honed on the factory floor of contemporary visual art practice. This has been achieved through the process of cultural production, of transforming those artworks and ideas into exhibitions, publications, education and research projects, which are then contextualized, presented and disseminated through the public domain.

Too many intellectuals retreat into the hermetic space of the academy where, too frequently, ideas move between academics, getting caught in the bottleneck of academia and prevented from circulating to a wider public. Long before the current vogue for celebrity television academics (some of whom, like the historian Niall Ferguson are trying to persuade us of the merits of empire and colonialism in a new public discourse of revisionist history), Stuart Hall recognized the potential of the mass media to reach a wider audience beyond the academic space. Rather than seeing the academy as the privileged site for intellectual ideas, or indeed, for political struggle, he embraced the Open University, television, radio, newspapers and magazines as legitimate spaces for engaging a cross section of people in a dialogue about political and cultural ideas. Far from being a top-down, paternalistic appeal to the masses from the elevated heights of intellectual life, Hall has always viewed the public domain as a two-way street where ideas can be opened up, contested, negotiated and fought for.

Hall's engagement with the public domain provided both inspiration and an innovative starting point for inIVA's modus operandi that embraced the model of an agency or television production company, working simultaneously across a number of sites and spaces at the same time. inIVA developed a two-pronged approach: on the one hand, it works collaboratively with mainstream institutions (galleries, museums, publishers, universities) in an effort to diversify the mainstream; on the other, it develops autonomous projects that are realized on the street, in nightclubs and in the underground. Although presented and distributed to a mass audience, the artworks themselves are uncompromising in terms of the ideas and questions that they raise within the public realm: from Yinka Shonibare's interrogation of definitions of Britishness to Simon Tegala's engagement with issues of technology, identity and representation through to Keith Piper's rigorous critique of the exclusion of questions of race and representation from the digital domain.

Within the museum space, the central question, the issue which returns and returns with unfailing frequency, is the question of modernity. More precisely, this is the question of who can legitimately lay claim to modernism and to modernity. It is probably the most contentious issue, the one which provokes museum curators into a rage and which has, at times, set inIVA at odds with museums and galleries in Britain who, while articulating their desire to embrace difference and, most often, 'celebrate' difference, recoil from that embrace when it becomes apparent that it could turn into a serious, long-lasting relationship rather than a one-show fling.

According to Stuart Hall,

> the world is littered by modernities.... It is littered by artists, practising artists who do not regard modernism as the secure possession of the West, never regarded it as such but always regarded it as a language which was both open to them but which they would have to transform.... The history now has to be re-written as a set of cultural translations rather than as a movement which can be located securely within a culture, within a history, within a space, within a set of political and cultural relations.[1]

Hall has consistently challenged the epistemological security of a worldview grounded within a Western Eurocentric perspective that, almost pathologically, denies the interrelatedness, the interconnectedness, the inextricable intermeshing of different histories and narratives. He draws the crucial distinction between modernism as it is understood, as a particular historical movement located within a specific geographical space, and modernity as a collection of experiences and translations. In a discussion with Annie Paul and Steve Ouditt at inIVA in September

2000, entitled 'The Caribbean: Quintessentially Modern Zone', he addressed the question of modernity in relation to the Caribbean:

> I just wanted to start by reminding you that this session is called "The Caribbean: A Modern Space", and just to note that that is inevitably a provocative observation, because whatever you know about the Caribbean, what you do know is that it is not a modern space in the most obvious, banal sense of the term. That's to say, it's not marked by technological wizardry, excessive lifestyles and high metropolitan living, etc. It's not modern in that simple and obvious sense.... One of the senses in which we mean that [the Caribbean is a modern space] is, obviously, that it is a space of what I would call "cultural translation". Most of the people in the Caribbean were not originally from that area. The original people in the majority of the islands, certainly, and even in most parts of the mainland, of the English-speaking Caribbean, were decimated within 100 years. Everybody who has come to the Caribbean since then, comes from elsewhere; and there's something peculiarly modern about that inability to find a long-standing continuity with the place from which you've come ... if we think of traditional societies, at least, even though we know that traditional societies are always themselves rapidly changing and subject to migration and so on, those traditional societies are relatively slow-moving, where people tend to stay where they were born for long periods of time, and where the connections between people and communities are very long-standing. This cannot be said of the Caribbean. I mean, if it's a place of any distinctiveness, it is a place of distinctiveness where nobody is, in the obvious sense, "at home", where everybody is to some extent dislocated, and that sense of dislocation is a very modern experience. The sense of being "not at home", or what is sometimes called "unhomeliness", is a very kind of modern experience ... the sense of dislocation, of having many origins, of coming together from very different roots and of nothing remaining, as it were, fixed and stable over a very long period of time, and therefore what comes out of it, in terms of cultural practices, in terms of language, in terms of the arts, in terms indeed of political organisation, and in terms of the economics and so on, all of it is translated. Translation is at the heart of what Caribbean culture is about.[2]

Stuart Hall's understanding of modernity and its cultural translations is absolutely critical to understanding his work and his unique contribution to the cultural and political realm as well as the profound impact that he has had on artists, the formation of cultural institutions as well as critical writing on contemporary art and culture. As he writes:

> I regard translation as an unending process, a process without a beginning. Except in myth, there is no moment when cultures and identities emerge from nowhere, whole within themselves, perfectly self-sufficient, unrelated to anything outside of themselves and with boundaries which secure their space from outside intrusion. I do not think that either historically or conceptually we should think of cultures or identities or indeed texts in that way. Every text has a "before-text", every identity has its pre-identities. I am not interested in the notion of translation in terms of rendering what has already been authentically and authoritatively fixed; what I want to do instead is to think of cultural practices as always involved in the process of translating. Cultural processes do not have a pure beginning; they always begin with some irritant, some dirty or "worldly" starting point, if I can call it that. When I say "dirty", I mean that there is no pure moment of beginning; they are always already in flow and translation, therefore, is always from one idiom, language or idiolect into another. All languages have their own internal character, their own kind of ethos, their own space, and so it is therefore impossible to think of a perfect translation; no such thing exists. One has always to think of cultural production of any kind as a reworking, as inadequate to its foundations, as always lacking something. There is always something which is left out. There is always mistranslation because a translation can never be a perfect rendering from one space or one language to another.... One has to think of meaning as constituted by an infinite, incomplete series of translations. I think cultures are like that too, and so are identities.[3]

In rejecting wholeheartedly the notion of the 'original', the 'before-text', Stuart reveals the false dichotomy between the diaspora and the homeland or the nation state, whether in the context of debates about Britishness, immigrants and asylum seekers or in the context of debates about the postcolony, nationalism and national self-determination. There are two important aspects that need to be drawn out here: the first arises from the de-stabilizing/the shaking up/the explosion of the idea of modernity from its fixed, secure, authoritative base into a scattering of modernities, this idea of a whole spectrum of modernities 'littering the world.' This is a fundamental challenge to a unitary worldview or a settled, fixed translation of the world. It rather opens up the difficult and challenging notion that we simply cannot depend on any fixed or settled position but rather must engage with transition, movement and change with the proviso that our perspective therefore will always be partial, lacking and somehow incomplete. This is not a trendy postcolonial or poststructural theoretical position but an ethical political and cultural challenge to all authoritative and fixed positions wherever they are to be found geographically — North and South, Europe and the Caribbean, America and Africa — which seek to close down debate, to narrow or exclude, to erase or censor.

The second crucial aspect is this process of translation and movement between what is solid, concrete and material, and that which is not solid, immediately visible or able to be grasped and held. This is the space of difference but also the space of the artwork. It is the space that needs to be negotiated but is never entirely translatable. It is a space in which the subtle shifts and changes of a culture and society may be registered but not always visibly or perceptibly.

As Stuart Hall writes:

> Despite the sophistication of our scholarly and critical apparatus in art criticism, history and theory, we are still not that far advanced in finding ways of thinking about the relationship between the work and the world. We either make the connection too brutal and abrupt, destroying that necessary displacement in which the work of making art takes place. Or we protect the work from what Edward Said calls its necessary "worldliness", projecting it into either a pure political space where conviction — political will — is all, or into an inviolate aesthetic space, where only critics, curators, dealers, and connoisseurs are permitted to play. The problem is rather like that of thinking the relationship between the dream and its materials in waking life. We know there is a connection there. But we also know that the two continents cannot be lined up and their correspondences read off directly against one another. Between the work and the world, as between the psychic and the social, the

bar of the historical unconscious has fallen. The effect of the unseen "work" which takes place out of consciousness in relationship to deep currents of change whose long-term effects on what can be produced are, literally, tidal, is thereafter always a delicate matter of re-presentation and translation, with all the lapses, elisions, incompleteness of meaning and incommensurability of political goals that these terms imply. What Freud called "the dream-work" — in his lexicon, the tropes of displacement, substitution and condensation — is what enables the materials of the one to be reworked or translated into the forms of the other, and is what enables the latter to "say more" or "go beyond" the willed consciousness of the individual artist. For those who work in the displaced zone of the cultural, the world has somehow to become a text, an image, before it can be "read".[4]

Stuart Hall has a profound understanding of the significance of this space that has no parallel in the political and academic worlds. Perhaps, this is why those who know him as a political thinker, writer and activist and those who know him as an academic and a theorist do not immediately recognize the importance of this space for both his intellectual and political work: 'The problem is rather like that of thinking the relationship between the dream and its materials in waking life. We know there is a connection there. But we also know that the two continents cannot be lined up and their correspondences read off directly against one another.' This strikes me as a superb articulation of the difficulty of resolving the relationship between the artwork and the world but also the profound difficulty of resolving in any easy or instrumental way the relationship between Hall's engagement with the world of contemporary art and culture and with the world of politics and academia.

Negotiating this space between the world and the work is never easy. At times, it can be very difficult to square the contingencies of economics, politics and the social with the field of contemporary cultural practice. Art is not urgent in a visceral, material sense in the way that food, education, health are urgent. Art can be elliptical, uncomfortable, and infuriatingly difficult to pin down, to hoist to a particular political banner. After visiting South Africa, nine years ago, on the occasion of the Second Johannesburg Biennial, I was struck by how a major international 'art roadshow' made little sense in this racially-segregated and economically-divided country. It seemed to underline the futility of contemporary art in a context where there were so many other pressing social, political and economic issues. This impression was reinforced when I returned to London and the inquiry began into the brutal racially-motivated murder of Stephen Lawrence in South-East London. The question of the place of contemporary art in relation to wider socioeconomic and cultural issues was the subject of a number of lengthy conversations with Stuart Hall. In the course of these conversations, Stuart Hall re-articulated a position which, for me, has been one of the most important aspects of his work: namely, the understanding that acts of racism and racial violence are not isolated incidents or individual acts, removed from the cultural fabric of our lives. He has consistently argued that notions of cultural value, belonging and worth are defined and fixed by the decisions we make about what is or is not our culture. Those conversations had a profound effect on me and on the curatorial work that I subsequently undertook, in particular, *Fault Lines* — an exhibition and publication developed as part of the 2003 Venice Biennale — which was homage to Stuart Hall. The project, which included the work of artists from Africa and the African Diaspora, took as its starting point the idea of fault lines — of shifting tectonic plates, below the surface. Triggered by the effects of colonialism and postcolonialism, migration and globalization, these fault lines have had and continue to have a profound impact on contemporary art and culture. Among other things, the project dealt with the incommensurability of the dream of the postcolony, of the liberated nation state and its present reality and how the reality had failed so spectacularly to deliver to subsequent generations, as well as the continuing dependencies and effects of colonialism. It also tried to elide the misleading and erosive distinction between the diasporan 'other' and the authentic 'other' by creating connections between artists and ideas across different geographical spaces. Most importantly, perhaps, the project pointed to the space of the artwork as a space of possibility — a space of critique, of poetry, of reflection, of debate — a space to consider both the past and the future and a space which needs to be continuously fought for and defended as Stuart Hall has done so unceasingly. In the publication that accompanied the show, we published some writings of the Algerian writer and playwright Kateb Yacine:

All doctrines whether religious or philosophical, always lead to the castration of poets, who then become leaders of the chorus. Even in a progressive climate, true poets should manifest their divergent views. If they do not fully express these views, they will suffocate. That is their function. They create their own revolution within the political revolution; at the heart of trouble, they are perpetual troublemakers. Their tragedy comes when they are made to serve a revolutionary struggle; they neither can nor should base their work on passing appearances. A poet is the revolution stripped bare, the very movement of life in an unending explosion.'[5]

There is no doubt in my mind that Stuart Hall, apart from being an intellectual, political activist, academic, writer and all those other things, is also an artist who recognizes that the artist has a critical role to play; a role which is radical and revolutionary but which nonetheless should never be in the service of politicians or regimes of power. Stuart Hall, like Kateb Yacine's poet is indeed 'the revolution stripped bare, the very movement of life in an unending explosion.'

Notes

1. Stuart Hall, 'Museums of Modern Art and the End of History', Keynote address, 'Museums of Modern Art and the End of History' conference, Tate Gallery, London, May 1999. Republished in *Annotations 6: Modernity and Difference*, Stuart Hall and Sarat Maharaj (London: inIVA, 2001).

2. Stuart Hall's introduction to an inIVA Chat Room event with art historian Annie Paul and artist Steve Ouditt, entitled, 'The Caribbean: A Quintessentially Modern Zone', September 19, 2000. Republished in *Changing States: Contemporary Art and Ideas in an Era of Globalisation*, ed. Gilane Tawadros (London: inIVA, 2004).

3. Stuart Hall, 'Modernity and Difference: A Conversation between Stuart Hall and Sarat Maharaj', in *Annotations 6*, 36–37.

4. Stuart Hall, 'Assembling the 1980s: The Deluge – and After', in *Shades of Black: Assembling Black Arts in 1980s Britain*, eds. David A. Bailey, Ian Baucom, Sonia Boyce (London: Duke University Press in collaboration with inIVA and Aavaa, 2005).

5. Kateb Yacine, 'The Poet as Boxer', in *Fault Lines: Contemporary African Art and Shifting Landscapes*, eds. Gilane Tawadros and Sarah Campbell (London: inIVA in collaboration with Forum for African Arts and Prince Claus Fund, 2003), 127.

4 | Feminism, 'Race' and Stuart Hall's Diasporic Imagination

Avtar Brah

As students embarking on our PhDs at Bristol University in the late 1970s, a group of us decided that we would visit Stuart Hall in Birmingham. Totally in awe of him, we were not sure when, or indeed whether, we would succeed in getting an appointment to see him. We need not have worried because, despite his immensely busy schedule, Hall made time for an early appointment with us. Our visit to the Centre for Cultural Studies at the University of Birmingham where he was director, was memorable, not only due to the intellectual excitement generated during our meeting with Hall, but also because of the warmth with which he greeted us and the immense encouragement he gave to our fledgling ideas. Few intellectuals of his stature are that generous of spirit. Hall genuinely respects and values each person for his or her uniqueness, and I admire him for this as much as for his towering intellect.

I mention this encounter because politics of the personal are, in my view, central to any agenda for bringing about change for a better world. This is a lesson that feminism learnt quite early in its genealogy which was privileged through the well-known feminist slogan 'Personal is Political', that has been the subject of major political contestation both within and outside the academy. The controversy surrounding the politics of the personal posed novel questions about subjectivity, identity and politics. As is well known, feminist attempts at theorizing, teasing out and working through entanglements of the personal with the political, resulted in challenging the very basis of the modernist binary between the public and private spheres of life. Feminism laid bare the constructed nature of this seemingly natural binary and, at the same time, foregrounded the diverse ways in which various axes of power — class, gender, sexuality and so on — are implicated in the constitution and maintenance of a social formation. Feminists have been at the forefront of these debates on what has since come to be known as 'intersectionality', arguing that cross-cutting formations of gender, class, race, ethnicity, sexuality and so on, cannot be understood without reference to one another and to histories of slavery, colonialism, and imperialism. In the context of these histories, the notion that woman or man could be construed as a homogeneous category was vigorously challenged.

But how does one theorize the simultaneous effects of a variety of factors? There are different answers to this question but the question itself inscribes a common ground on which feminist work and the writings of scholars such as Hall cross paths. One answer to this question was attempted through recourse to the Marxist concept of 'class fraction'. However, for many Marxists, this concept remained class-centred even as it was designed to address sociocultural transformations that would be effected when different axes intersected. That is to say that, class was still the master signifier albeit differentiated by gender, ethnicity, or sexuality. And, feminist theory, especially anti-racist feminist theory, challenged this type of narrative of the primacy of class. For example, when women labour migrants to Britain from the former colonies were theorized as constituting a simultaneously racialized and gendered class fraction, the processes of racialization and gender were given similar prominence as class. A second important issue that marks a common concern in Hall's writing and feminist work relates to the problematic of agency. Both sets of writing interrogated a tendency in the literature of the late 1970s and 1980s to reify process and regard agency as if it were voluntarist and goals could be achieved by the exercise of sheer, conscious will power. Feminist debate and critique challenged this conception and argued instead that political movements such as feminism or anti-racism were best construed as representing historically contingent relationships across fields of discourses and practices, and that agency cannot be properly theorized without taking the workings of the unconscious into account. Such prising open of categories that were hitherto imagined as monolithic and the theorization of meaning as contingent began to connect with poststructuralist perspectives.

Feminist debates on 'intersectionality' were closely allied to those on 'difference'. Feminists debated 'differences' in terms of what it meant to experience life as a situated, context-specific subject, for example, as a black working-class woman or as a lesbian. Concurrent studies of social class differences, on the other hand, rarely understood class difference as an issue of 'difference', mainly because the concept of 'difference' in class-centred discourses tended to be reserved for talking about 'cultural difference' as it was made visible by the presence of minoritized ethnic groups. Some of us turned to Hall's work because this body of work interrogated those tendencies which pathologized minority ethnic and working-class cultures. Instead, Hall addressed these cultural practices in their own specificity and their own terms. In fact, working-class cultures represented a major focus of the work of the Centre for Cultural Studies in which they were treated with immense sympathy. In his attention to 'difference' Hall has deployed a combination of structuralist and poststructuralist perspectives ranging from Marx, Weber, Gramsci and Althusser to Foucault, Derrida and Butler. This particular brand of creolized theory has constituted a major advance.

Hall's encounter with Marxist approaches during the 1970s and 1980s was singularly productive. His readings of Althusser and Gramsci have been a major milestone within the conceptual repertoire of neo-Marxisms. From my point of view, what is important is that unlike many other neo-Marxists at the time, Hall treated issues of 'race' as an endogamous feature of advanced capitalist social formations in the West. Moreover, he did not treat 'race' as an add-on feature but explored it in its contingent relationship with other key features of the social formation. His 1980 essay titled 'Race, Articulation, and Societies Structured in Dominance', the 1986 essay called 'Gramsci's Relevance for the Study of Race and Ethnicity', and his televised lecture of 1978 — later published jointly by the BBC and the Commission for Racial Equality — left no doubt in any discerning mind that this was a whole new perspective on thinking about 'race', and about British society. In these essays he explores the processes whereby power is spatially and temporally dispersed within a social formation; and, how social antagonisms, including those crystallizing around 'race', are relationally diversified across the cultural field. In his approach to the study of 'race', culture and structure are thoroughly intertwined rather than conceived as poles of a hierarchy as implied by the base and superstructure model of classical Marxism. Questions of emotionality and psychic dynamics are paid due attention. As he says:

> I learned about culture, first, as something which is deeply subjective and personal, and at the same moment, as a structure you live....

From then on, I could never understand why people thought these structural questions were not connected with the psychic — with emotions and identification and feelings because, for me, those structures are things you live. I don't just mean they are personal, they are, but they are also institutional, they have real structural properties, they break you, destroy you.[1]

Hall's readings of Althusser and Gramsci make it almost impossible to sustain reductionist or totalizing perspectives. I said almost because, without Hall's interventions Althusser and Gramsci — with their primary, if not exclusive, emphasis on social class — tend to retain residual totalizing and reductionist tendencies 'in the last instance'. Hall's writings on race open new theoretical vistas, with their emphasis on historical specificity, the role of hegemony, the importance of intersectionality, and the way in which social differentiations such as class or race are lived:

[Any investigation into racism] would have to begin from a rigorous application of what I have called the premise of historical specificity. Racism is not dealt with as a general feature of human societies, but with historically-specific racisms. Beginning with an assumption of difference, of specificity rather than of a unitary, transhistorical or universal "structure"… one cannot explain racism in abstraction from other social relations…. One must start, then, from the concrete historical "work" which racism accomplishes under specific historical conditions — as a set of economic, political and ideological practice, of a distinctive kind, concretely articulated with other practices in a social formation. These practices ascribe the positioning of different social groups in relation to one another with respect to the elementary structure…. In short they are practices that secure the hegemony of a dominant group over subordinate ones, in such a way as to dominate the whole social formation in a form favourable to the long-term development of the economic productive base. Though the economic aspects are critical, as a way of beginning, this form of hegemony cannot be understood as operating purely through economic coercion. The constitution of this (racialised) fraction as a class, and the class relations, which ascribe it, function as race relations. Race is thus, also, the modality in which class is 'lived', the medium through which class relations are experienced…. Racism is also one of the dominant means of ideological representation through which the white fraction of the class come to live their relation to other fractions, and through them to capital itself.... Capital reproduces the class, including its internal contradictions, as a whole — structured by race.[2]

This highly complex and innovative theorization of race challenges the modernist metanarrative of universalism and points to new ways for analysing different historically-specific racisms. Understanding the role of differential racializations remains crucial today as we witness the mobilization of racism — especially the form of racism directed against Muslims — as one of the means with which new global imperialisms of the twenty-first century are being secured. The discourses of 'terrorist', 'civilization' and 'failed states' articulate in the representation of large regions of the world as being unfit to govern themselves. Gender plays a critical role in these representational regimes, as when the figure of the Muslim woman comes to be orientalized as passive and at the mercy of authoritarian men. These representations of people appear in all manner of global media where certain images (for example, images of women clad in hijab) and not others (for example, women doctors, engineers, educationalists and so on, performing their jobs with or without hijab) are selected, with the effect of mobilizing long-standing Western discourses of superiority. The recent legislation in France which makes the wearing of hijab in educational institutions illegal is the epitome of this tendency. The rhetoric of this discourse is so pernicious that even some feminists fall under its sway and view the women through the prism of orientalism. Overall these discourses re-articulate the fantasy of non-Muslims, especially the men, of unveiling the woman.

To conceptualize racisms in the plural, as Hall does, enables us to see how differentially racialized groups can themselves, in turn, become positioned in a discourse that racializes another group. For example, where there is anti-Muslim racism, all non-Muslims can potentially become implicated in anti-Muslim racism. In other words, attention to both similarity and difference between different racisms permits better understanding of contingent power effects in a given context.

Although Hall does not always directly engage with feminism, his work, as I have noted earlier, shares certain common problematics with feminism. There would seem to be a subtle underlying symbiotic relationship between feminism and Hall's work and there has been a substantial two-way traffic of ideas. During the 1970s and 1980s, feminist theories as well as Hall's work, as we can see above, were informed by conceptual repertoires drawn largely from 'modernist' theoretical and philosophical traditions of European Enlightenment. At this juncture, the shared project of socialism animated both Hall's work and the version of feminism we used to call socialist feminism. Hall's encounter with poststructuralist thought has generated a whole new outlook — one which subjects poststructuralist insights to scrutiny through a postcolonial lens. His work reminds us that postmodernist critique of modernist perspectives, including the latter's claims to universal applicability, had precursors within anti-colonial, anti-racist, and feminist critical politics and practice. He demonstrates how postmodern experience is diasporic experience par excellence:

> Postcoloniality, in a curious way prepared one to live in a "postmodern" or diasporic relationship to identity. Paradigmatically, it's a diasporic experience. Since migration has turned to be the world-historical event of late modernity, the classic postmodern experience turns out to be the diasporic experience.[3]

Postmodern/poststructuralist theoretical approaches found sporadic expression in Anglophone feminist works from the late 1970s. But, during the 1990s the poststructuralist variant within feminism became a force to reckon with. These theoretical and political dialogues produced some compelling insights including: (a) that, political subjects such as white or black, cannot be treated as if they are mutually exclusive entities, each carrying some unchanging transhistorical 'essence'. Political subjects and subjectivities are relationally produced historical forms; (b) that, the concept of 'agency' when reconfigured through poststructuralist appropriations of psychoanalysis, goes beyond conscious agency to include our psychic and emotional life. Hence conscious agency is viewed as deeply marked by unconscious processes; (c) that, the notion of a transparent experiential authenticity, often valorized in the practice of 'identity politics' is found as being problematic. Rather, experience, it is suggested, is best understood as the mediated process of making sense of the world symbolically and narratively; (d) that, poststructuralist insistence that meaning is relational; that identity and subjectivity are not 'products' but on going processes; that power can be both coercive and productive; that subordination can occur through modes of inclusion no less than exclusion means that poststructural paradigms have much in common with theoretical interventions made by feminists over the years. These poststructuralist insights find strong resonance in Hall's later work, especially in his writings on identity.

A key feature of Hall's later work and the work of some feminists during the 1990s and early twenty-first century is their concern to draw upon the strengths of both modern and postmodern theorization. In the process they interrogate the simplistic binary that creates a divide between modern and postmodern theory as if these are mutually exclusive formations. Hall's work is a testament to the productive potential of combining modern and postmodern insights. A wider interest in interdisciplinary theory may be seen to stem from a variety of reasons such as:

(i) an interest in analysing the effects of racism without recourse to the discourse of race. We do not belong to 'different races'; rather, we are differentially racialized through racism in differential hierarchies;

(ii) the need for theorizing ethnicity and cultural difference outside the imperatives of racism. Here, Hall's concept of new ethnicities has proved singularly productive;

(iii) the importance of understanding political identities as contingent forms of resistance;

(iv) the necessity of distinguishing between political identity as conscious agency and identity conceptualized in terms of subjectivity;

(v) the importance of analysing locality and globality as relational categories; and

(vi) the engagement with postcolonial contemporary migrations and to understand the role which diasporas play in global politics and identities.

One of the topics which Hall has analysed to great theoretical effect is that of identity. His 1996 essay 'Who needs identity?' is a powerful discourse on the subject. With so much ink already spilled on this issue, why, he asks, do we still need to address the question of identity? His answer to this is twofold: firstly, the deconstructive critique, especially that which is exemplified by the work of Derrida, points to a way of thinking about critiqued concepts in forms that do not necessarily demand that they be supplanted. Rather, they can be engaged with 'under erasure'. That is to say that, they can be used in their deconstructed form, dislodged from their previous regime. Secondly, the concept of identity remains critical because of its centrality to the concept of agency and politics. Rejecting an unmediated notion of agency and following Foucault, Hall argues that what is necessary is not so much a theory of the 'knowing subject' as that of 'discursive practices' and how the subject is constituted within discursive practices, so that far from abandoning the subject — a criticism often levelled at poststructuralist thought — the subject is reconceptualized. In underlining the issue of politics, Hall is fully cognizant of the feminist debate on 'identity politics' and the 'politics of location', the latter a critically innovative way in which feminism ironically theorized 'location' as the site of 'dispersal' across different axes of differentiation such as gender or class, so that there is a permanent deferral of a final enclosure. In line with his emphasis that identity is always a process of becoming rather than being, Hall focuses on processes of identification as the core thematic of the discussion. The concept of identification, according to him, is understood as drawing its meaning simultaneously from discursive and psychoanalytic conceptual frameworks. Discursively a construct, a process — identification is never completed once and for all. It is, he says, an articulation and a signifying practice which, 'like all signifying practices, it is subject to the play of differance'.[4]

From its psychoanalytic usage, the concept of identity signals emotional investment of a specific kind:

> It is, in the first instance, a "moulding after the other" which compensates for the loss of the libidinal pleasures of primal narcissism. It is grounded in fantasy, in projection and idealisation. Its object is as likely to be the one that is hated as the one that is adored; and as often taken back into the unconscious self, as "taking one out of oneself".... Moreover, they (identities) emerge within the play of specific modalities of power, and thus are more the product of the marking of the difference and exclusion, than they are the sign of an identical naturally constituted unity — an "identity" in its traditional meaning.... I use "identity" to refer to the meeting point, the point of suture, between on the one hand the discourses and practices which attempt to interpellate, speak

to us or hail us into place as the subjects of particular discourses, and on the other hand the processes which produce subjectivities, which construct us as subjects which can be spoken. Identities are thus points of temporary attachment to the subject positions which discursive practices construct for us.[5]

Here, then, is a singularly insightful pointer to take forward the debate on 'identity', using simultaneously discursive and psychoanalytic repertoires. The discourse of 'identity politics' where agency was seen as personified in individual bodies is here transformed into a 'politics of identity'. Hence, to assume a gendered identity is to develop identification with particular subject positions — for example, a feminist or anti-feminist subject position — the latter having been constituted within a variety of discursive practices and representational regimes. This subject of feminism is discursively interpellated and psychically invested. Since identities are constituted in and through difference, they assume meaning through its relation to the 'other', to what it lacks, or what is often called 'its constitutive outside'. But it is worth bearing in mind that the *other* is not a complete opposite of the *self*, neither is it totally outside the *self*, and, nor indeed is it entirely a lack. There is profound instability and ambiguity in the production of identity even as it may at times feel like a solid core. Politically, specific identity positions are constructed and played out through ongoing reiterative political processes.

Hall has a thoroughly diasporic imagination. By this I do not mean that this diasporic imagination is the direct result of his migration from Jamaica to study and later settle down in Britain. This journey is important, of course, because, like all immigrants, he has had to put roots elsewhere and his attachments to the place where he now lives are mediated through the specificities of his personal biography — of which he has cogently spoken in various places, and by broader factors such as his colour, his class background whilst growing up in Jamaica and later working as an academic in Britain, and his current status as one of the foremost thinkers of Britain. Rather, his is a diasporic imagination first and foremost because it is nurtured by an open mind that continually decentres any desire for fixity. This imagination makes novel connections as it travels between and across concepts, experiences and subject positions. It is an imagination that knows what it means when the boundaries of the familiar are left behind and new journeys are charted. It is an imagination that is tuned to and is deeply concerned about the voices of the subaltern; that listens to the pain and pleasures of 'migrancy' — what is gained and what is lost; and, it is an imagination that is animated by ethics of care and justice:

> But I am not and never shall be "English". I know both places (England and Jamaica) intimately but I am not wholly of either place. And that is exactly the diasporic experience, far away enough to experience the sense of exile and loss, close enough to understand the enigma of an always-postponed "arrival".[6]

Notes

1. Stuart Hall, 'Dialogues with Stuart Hall', in *Stuart Hall: Critical Dialogues in Cultural Studies*, eds. David Morley and Kuan-Hsing Chen (London: Routledge, 1996), 488.
2. Stuart Hall, 'Race, Articulation and Societies Structured in Dominance', in *Sociological Theories: Race and Colonialism*, ed. UNESCO (Paris: UNESCO, 1980), 338.
3. Stuart Hall, 'Dialogues', 490.
4. Stuart Hall, 'Who Needs Identity?', in *Questions of Cultural Identity*, eds. S. Hall and P. du Gay (London: Sage, 1996), 3.
5. Ibid., 4–5.
6. Stuart Hall, 'Race, Articulation and Societies', 490.

PART II
Theory and Critique

5 | 'The First Shall Be Last': Locating The Popular Arts *in the Stuart Hall Ouevre*

Grant Farred

Writers on the Left have been markedly more attentive than their liberal and conservative counterparts, recognising in Leavis's argument a cultural argument of great weight and influence.

— Francis Mulhern, *The Moment of 'Scrutiny'*

The Popular Arts is the forgotten Stuart Hall text, the work that has long since fallen into disuse, if not disrepute. It is a book not even remembered for being the 'first' work by Hall in two critical senses. It is 'first' not only in so much as it was the first book he published, surely noteworthy in itself in such a distinguished intellectual trajectory, but also first in that it set the trend for the collaborative Hall modality. Working with other scholars, writing together with those with whom he shares intellectual visions, political commitments, and theoretical tendencies, has always been a salient characteristic of Hall's career and it is a mode inaugurated by his first book. Later works such as *Resistance Through Rituals*, certainly the groundbreaking *Policing the Crisis*, and even *The Hard Road to Renewal* (Hall's only 'single-authored' book although even this work has some jointly-written essays), are all marked by the collaboration that is co-editing, cultural and political projects sustained by serious conversations among intellectuals seeking to constantly invigorate, rethink and challenge the Left.

However, while most of Hall's other works remain in print, or, at least, referenced, turned to again and again by scholars of cultural studies, politics and critical theory, a sad fate has long since befallen his first work. No one ever talks about *The Popular Arts*, ambitiously subtitled, 'A Critical Guide to the Mass Media', that Hall co-wrote with fellow secondary school teacher Paddy Whannel. There are, ostensibly, reasons enough why it is so neglected by cultural studies and Hall scholars alike. Originally published in 1964 (first made available in the USA only in 1967), it has been out of print for what seems like decades now.

An early work, *The Popular Arts* was produced in a 'nondescript' moment — not in the sense that it was unimportant, but that it was not marked by an 'epochal' characteristic. The book was published after Hall had resigned as the inaugural editor of the *New Left Review* and before the cultural studies project at the University of Birmingham, the Centre for Contemporary Cultural Studies (CCCS), was in any sense established. *The Popular Arts* was written before cultural studies was a recognizable project and when Hall was a different kind of intellectual, the New Left thinker who was also a secondary school teacher, a public figure without a tertiary academic appointment. It is also a text aimed at an audience distinct from the one for which Hall would later write. *The Popular Arts* seems designed to address classroom difficulties confronted by his then colleagues, secondary school teachers, rather than what we now presume to be Hall's primary audience: an international collection of university-based scholars, Leftist thinkers of all ideological stripes, and political activists.

Most importantly, however, *The Popular Arts* has been forgotten. Among the reasons why it is no longer read is surely because it is not presumed to be representative of Hall's work and, implicitly, not critically useful in the ways his other writings have proven to be. It is not only the a priori but the aberrant text, the book that, ostensibly, has little in common with his later work, deeply marked as *The Popular Arts* is by a critical admixture unusual in Hall's oeuvre. On the one hand, clearly evident is the influence of the early cultural studies writing of Raymond Williams, E.P. Thompson, and Richard Hoggart, and, on the other hand, there are regular glimpses of a text shaped by the thinking of Matthew Arnold and F.R. Leavis, cultural critics too easily conceived of by both cultural studies and literary scholars — for their obviously different reasons — as arch proponents of a canonical literature. Cultural studies' debt to the Arnoldian and the *Scrutiny* tradition (*Scrutiny* is the 'literary' journal that Leavis memorably founded and edited for a couple of decades), is often acknowledged by its historians. However, the canonical influence exercised by the 'Tradition' is seldom encountered as directly as in *The Popular Arts* where Hall's training in colonial education and his undergraduate and graduate work (in English and American Literature) at Merton College, Oxford, gave him direct access to the formalist tendencies so emphatically rejected by later cultural studies practitioners.

Where else in the Hall corpus would one find him saying, 'minority interests are not necessarily highbrow'. Or, in a perfect blend of Hoggart and Leavis, Yorkshire and fringe Cambridge (that off-campus place in the town of Cambridge from which *Scrutiny* was sustained by the massive efforts of F.R. and Q.D. Leavis), 'Mass culture destroys folk art, dehydrates popular art and threatens fine art. It has little sense of tradition, of values being modified by change. Instead there is an obsession with fashion and novelty; to be the latest thing is thought in itself a sufficient recommendation'. There is little complication here of categories such as 'highbrow', 'mass art' and 'folk art', categories unsustainable in later cultural studies work. In fact, within the span of two short intellectual generations Paul Willis and Dick Hebdige authored books on subculture, biker culture and music respectively, that attests to how rapidly *The Popular Arts'* critical categories were surpassed — another potential reason why Hall's first book fell into disuse and has been ignored for so long. Willis and Hebdige belong, of course, to the first generations of cultural studies scholars trained by Hall, among others, at the CCCS. Nor is Hall's later critical vocabulary, in which 'fashion' and 'novelty' are read as instances of a different, often oppositional, politics, available yet. In a later work such as *The Hard Road to Renewal,* Hall argues, broadly conceived, that both 'fashion' and 'novelty', the general innovativeness of the popular, are crucial to an oppositional politics in an authoritarian state such as Thatcher's Britain.

The Popular Arts is also neglected by critics because it represents an interstitial moment in cultural studies. Hall's book is a product of that moment between the first and the second generation of the new Left, the moment between the constitutive, founding events of '1956' and the 'institutionalization' of the practice at Birmingham's CCCS in 1964. Richard Hoggart served as the first director of the Centre, and five years later Hall succeeded him. *The Popular Arts* was a work conceived in a critically ambivalent cultural studies milieu. Equal parts Leavis and Hoggart, Arnold and Williams, *The Popular Arts* is representative of the kind of thinking that predominated the first two generations of cultural studies work, that moment when the field was beginning to define itself, produce its critical methodologies, shape its politics, and articulate its theories. Founding texts within the field, and for that reason routinely referenced, invoked, and recognized, Raymond

Williams's *Culture and Society* and Richard Hoggart's *The Uses of Literacy* bears as much of an Arnoldian imprint as *The Popular Arts* without suffering any critical neglect.

The 'Second New Left', the generation of Hall, Whannel and Perry Anderson (Hall's successor as editor at the *New Left Review*) is still, *The Popular Arts* reveals, moderately in the grip of Arnold, T.S. Eliot, and Leavis. *The Popular Arts* speaks of a generation still struggling to find its own, distinctive critical voice; as that 'Second New Left' matured, of course, it produced a series of articulations that would find fulfilment in the theoretical Marxism of Perry Anderson from the mid- to late-1960s on (an approach to New Left politics that so famously, and bitterly, pitted Anderson against E.P. Thompson), in the pages of the *New Left Review*, and, most notably, in the CCCS. In Birmingham, under Hall's guidance as director (from 1969 to 1979), the thinking of structuralists such as Claude Levi-Strauss and Roland Barthes and Marxists such as Antonio Gramsci and Louis Althusser was distilled and put to cultural studies use, radically transforming the field.

Much like Eliot uses 'tradition' and Leavis establishes the poetry and the novels of the past as a cultural bulwark, the Arnoldian gold standard (the 'best that's been said, thought, and written') against which all subsequent literature must be judged, so *Culture and Society* (1958), *The Making of the English Working Class* (1963) and *The Uses of Literacy* (1957) all look back, to earlier cultural, political, and literary moments. Williams traces the radicalism of the Romantic poets, Thompson finds inspiration and example in the Dissenters (metonymic for him of the 'working class that was present at its own birth'), and Hoggart — more historically immediate than the other two — invokes his own experience of inter-War Yorkshire life. These are all texts in which the past predominates. It is in this regard that *The Popular Arts* is such a crucial text. It is the first work in a nascent cultural studies tradition that, while critically indebted to the past (both the historical and the immediate past), breaks with that tradition. Williams, Thompson and Hoggart's texts, despite their aesthetic, political and ideological similarities and differences, their radical interpretation of the past, subscribe to the same temporal modality, producing an unlikely intellectual trajectory — one that leads from Arnold through Leavis to Williams.

The proclivity for the past is an orientation that *The Popular Arts* disrupts by installing a new temporal orientation. Hall and Whannel's text casts its glance away from the past toward the work cultural studies can, and will be called upon, to do. Within the cultural studies trajectory, *The Popular Arts* is the text that produces the caesura: it announces, however ambivalently, partially, and unevenly, the break between the 'old' mode of cultural studies and the form that has, with its varied manifestations, dominated after Hall assumed the directorship at Birmingham. Unlike its predecessors, crucial as they were, *The Popular Arts* looks, not forward, but, more importantly, to its own historical conjuncture: the culture of the present. *The Popular Arts* trains its critical eye, for the first time in cultural studies' then brief history, on the cultural production of the now, its artefacts, its effects on the current moment, and its affective relationship to — and representation of — the present.

Unlike *The Uses of Literacy* (with which Hall and Whannel's work has the most in common), *The Popular Arts* is the first cultural studies text not to look backward, toward a past, for either political or aesthetic answers and authors (such as Williams did with William Blake and Thompson did with William Morris) now long since dead. In *Culture and Society* and *Romantic to Revolutionary*, Blake and Morris are called upon to serve as examples of what cultural studies might do — and how it might undertake the project of providing a cultural model for doing contemporary politics. Instead, *The Popular Arts* showed itself to be cognizant of but not overwhelmed by the theoretical tools and the political purchase of the past; Hall and Whannel made those tools attentive to the cultural demands of the present. *The Popular Arts* is a work that was willing to craft a cultural theory about working-class and popular cultural practices that had only just begun, and that only in rare circles such as the Universities of Birmingham and Warwick (where Thompson's history project was based), to receive attention.

The Popular Arts is a text that stands, simultaneously despite and because of all the problematic critical traces it bears, as the inaugural Hall text. It is the work that sought to make cultural studies a practice of the present, it is a text that understood the value of but was not, unlike *The Uses of Literacy*, a prisoner to nostalgia. It is appropriate that Hall should have gone on to produce other texts with which most scholars of cultural studies are familiar. It is, however, also clear that

The Popular Arts is of a piece, on a critical continuum, with *Resistance Through Rituals* and *Policing the Crisis*. It is, arguably, a more groundbreaking text because it had less of a tradition to work with; it was compelled to make history not so much under cultural conditions not of its own choosing as under conditions with no real disciplinary history of which to speak. Given how crucial this first book was to Hall's trajectory, the problem is not that *The Popular Arts* has been too long forgotten, but that we have taken so long to remember it, to afford it its proper place in his critical oeuvre.

There is, historically, a strange, even a haunting connection between this rereading of *The Popular Arts* and Hall's relationship to the Caribbean, the site where Hall is now being honoured. From where we are now located in relation to Stuart Hall, 40 years after the publication of *The Popular Arts*, ours is a strange and poignant conjuncture: his status as the New Left(s) intellectual for decades already firmly established, celebrated and recognized internationally, it is only in the last decade — since 1996 — that his reintegration into the politics and theoretical debates of his native Caribbean has been achieved, and this with a difficulty still barely acknowledged. Almost half a century after he left Jamaica as Rhodes Scholar for Oxford's Merton College, Hall now stands 'first', in an elevated intellectual position, after decades of critical neglect in his native land during which his work was unread and his Caribbeanness disregarded. The occasion of honouring him in Jamaica makes appropriate — necessary, even — a re-turn to his first book as the Jamaican-born thinker takes, albeit belatedly, his rightful place as Caribbean thinker, his place among cosmopolitan West Indians such as C.L.R. James, George Lamming, Shani Mootoo, Sam Selvon and Walter Rodney.

A Text *Sui Generis*

The Popular Arts demonstrates the difficulty of articulating a critical cultural studies without precedent, of working to establish a tradition without a model. In attempting to distinguish in *The Popular Arts* between 'popular' and 'mass', where the overtones of Hoggart's veneration for 'folk' art is resonant, Hall and Whannel write: 'This process — the practical exclusion of groups and classes in society from the selective tradition of the best that has and is being produced in the culture — is especially damaging in a democratic society, and applies both to the traditional and new forms of high art.'

This is a critique of Arnold — the best that's been said and written is the critical truism that defines *Culture and Anarchy* and retains a distinctly Arnoldian flavour — especially in so far as Hall and Whannel operate within the strictures of 'traditional' and 'high art', albeit of the 'new' variety. However, what is even more evident in *The Popular Arts* is Hall and Whannel's opposition to the anti-democratic tendencies in Arnold's work, particularly sensitive as they are to the highly stratified, class-based nature of British society and the historic exclusion of the labouring classes from 'culture'.

It is for this (anti-Arnoldian) reason that there is, as is always the case with Hall, acute attention paid to the context of intellectual production and political and cultural critique. *The Popular Arts* was written in the high moment of the Welfare State, a historical conjuncture where — with the realities of Third World independence, the reconstitution of the British populace in the wake of the post *Empire Windrush* black migration (soon followed, of course, by Asian immigration from the subcontinent and the continuing stream of African migrants to the metropolis), and the new access of the lower middle and working classes to higher education — 'democracy' had very different implications for the British state and cultural critics of all stripes. Hall and his colleagues knew that British society was being rapidly transformed and that they, if their work was to retain any relevance, had to adjust to the conditions under which this new history was being made. Hence the declaration that, as if to qualify the Leavisite influence and enunciate its cultural studies predilections, a 'true training in discrimination is concerned with pleasure. It places its emphasis on what can be gained from the best that is available. It is careful not to define the best in narrow terms.'

Since it is a text *sui generis, The Popular Arts* betrays a conceptual ambivalence. It is a work that draws on Leavis and Arnold even as it simultaneously strains against those traditions, aware that it needs to break, and to break with, that mould of thinking, that another way of reading popular culture is not only necessary but possible, that it can be achieved only by working through — as well as beyond — the existing strategies for reading. By virtue of that ambivalence, a product of context, training, and intellectual tradition, what the 'best' cultural articulation might be — a la Arnold — is rendered theoretically and conceptually contestable. Most importantly, *The Popular Arts* ensures that what *Culture and Anarchy* considered 'best' can no longer be defined in 'narrow terms'.

It is for this reason that film constitutes such a crucial component of this study of the 'popular arts'. The 'origins' of *The Popular Arts* are the result of the several 'years (Hall and Whannel) have been lecturing on and arguing about the cinema and the mass media with a variety of audiences'. With its conception in high modernist technology, its capacity to reach record numbers of the populace, its vigorous, democratic youth, film is not only the quintessentially twentieth-century art form, it is also the form of entertainment where what is good, to say nothing of the 'best', is very much up for negotiation at the precise moment that Hall and Whannel are writing their book — a trend in film criticism and theory that, arguably, continues to today. It is an art form where the standards of critical judgment have not yet become ossified and where aesthetic 'taste' is still a matter of intense debate — this is not to say that film is not a medium where narrow definitions of what is good or bad do not apply, where discrimination has not already taken root; rather, it is to suggest that an incipient film studies is receptive to the kind of intervention offered by *The Popular Arts*.

If film is the art form most amenable to producing a new cultural criticism, then *The Popular Arts* derives its main conceptual support from the same place so intimately associated with making those movies that Britons flocked to see — the USA — and a musical genre synonymous with articulating the struggle of the black underclass, in both its antebellum and post-Reconstruction formation: jazz. The jazz and the blues produced by African-Americans, a major cultural repository of African-American struggle, a musical form that transformed understandings of race, culture, and even political morality in the 'Roaring 1920s' America (what with the many associations made among the black jazz artists, the overwhelmingly white patrons at the Cotton Club in Harlem, and speakeasy ambience that pervaded that historical moment). Through this critical gesture Hall and Whannel internationalized, racialized (in a way they could not when discussing popular culture in a Britain which did not yet have the 'black public' face that was then still a decade or so away), and complicated the distinction between folk and mass art. While jazz belonged to a particular folk — African-Americans — during the 1920s it officially became 'America's' music — art, as it were, for the masses, both white and black, the history of slavery and the re-articulation of the African-American experience captured in a new century, by new generations of musicians, by a music that would encapsulate in its chords, harmonies, and arrangements for the propensity for black creativity. Jazz, like the 'blues', 'grew out of a common experience, an experience central to the life of a whole people, which they transposed into art', an art that gave voice to the epistemological lineage of African-Americans. It was this art that would produce the modernity of bebop flourishing in the geniuses of Thelonious Monk, Charlie Parker, Sonny Rollins, and, of course, Miles Davis, that was everywhere during the moment that Hall and Whannel were preparing *The Popular Arts*.

When critiquing jazz, Hall knew that he could not say, as he and Whannel do in the opening chapter (in a tone and language that is sharply redolent of Hoggart in *The Uses of Literacy*), that 'much that is produced under the name of "entertainment" is shoddy and third rate, and some of it is profoundly debased'. There is no possibility in Hall's contemplations on this music for any alignment with Theodore Adorno's largely pejorative conception of the popular, no chance of him dismissing jazz in the fashion of the Adorno and his Frankfurt School colleagues. Even at this early moment in his cultural studies career, Hall's regard for the popular and his radical politics distanced him and Whannel from the elitism that marks Adorno and Horkheimer's work; if anything, there is something Benjaminian about *The Popular Arts*. In any case, jazz had too much history, it encoded too much transatlantic black suffering, survival and triumph over racist adversity, to be 'third-rate'; under no circumstances could it be denounced as 'debased'. In the terms of *The Popular Arts*, the 'return of the younger jazz musicians after Parker to the blues and to "soul" is directly connected with the new urgency with which Negro minorities in America are seeking their identity and their freedom within the American community'. Spoken like a historically conscious cultural critic, like a jazz aficionado, and like the jazz drummer Hall had been during his student years at Oxford, when the young Jamaican scholarship boy played in a jazz band that included other students and a West Indian bus driver who lived in the town.

'Revaluation'

The Popular Arts, viewed from a historical vantage point that has rendered it obscure, presents itself as the text that has to be — in Leavis's terms — 'revaluated' because it set the paradigmatic terms for the way in which Hall's work would unfold. (Revaluation is Leavis's critical re-examination of a series of 'Great' figures in English literature, from Pope to Shelley, his attempt to situate them within the context of a reconceived tradition of literary scholarship.) Embryonic in *The Popular Arts* is the pre-eminent Hall modality after the late-1960s: an interrogation of race and the popular, in its many manifestations. Already present in *The Popular Arts* is the way in which Hall's writing would draw upon a range of cultures and resonate with a number of constituencies throughout the globe; this 1964 text contains within it a critique of the 'urgency' that characterized African-American life during the Civil Rights and the Black Power Movements of the 1950s, 1960s and 1970s. *The Popular Arts* would find its echoes, its ideological fulfilment, in *Resistance Through Rituals, Policing The Crisis* and *The Hard Road to Renewal*, all works that seek to intervene in the various crises that marked the lives of black immigrants, youth, and the British left over the course of almost two decades — the mid-1970s through the early 1990s.

The theoretical, political, and conceptual germ of these later Hall texts have their prototype in *The Popular Arts* because, as Hall and Whannel say, 'Popular art ... is essentially a conventional art form, values and attitudes already known; which reassures and reaffirms, but brings to this something of the surprise of art as well as the recognition.' There is, through *The Popular Arts*, a case to be made for the value of close reading by cultural studies and its proponents. This text is not an argument for the commonly (and too uncritically) held belief, a belief held both by cultural studies scholars and their detractors, that the popular always tells critics what they expect to find, that its 'conventionality' — its hermeneutic 'predictability', if you will — would be not so much uncovered as 'reassured' and 'reaffirmed'. *The Popular Arts* implicitly advocates a different approach: through a serious engagement, that mode of criticism works without any certainty of outcome, through the ambivalent melding of Leavis and Hoggart, of the *New Left Review* and *Scrutiny* into a critical apparatus, popular arts are revealed to be ambivalent, uneven, as much a site of resistance as a source of unreflective pleasure, as much determined by historical context as the capacity of artists to offer a soulful hermeneutics of the moment — that rare moment when, in the terms of *The Popular Arts*, the popular jazz vocalist Ella Fitzgerald and the classical opera singer Maria Callas can be deemed comparable, artistic equals even. Close reading, as Leavis often argued, was not about excluding context; it was simply about making it count in the weightiest historical and cultural moments. In Hall's case, the capacity to read culture closely was about the possibility of finding out what he and Whannel did not know. *The Popular Arts* demonstrates that the text, as much as the context, can yield an understanding of popular culture the authors did not expect. However, as all cultural and literary critics know, neither every text nor every reading will produce something previously unknown. What Hall and Whannel demonstrate is that their particular brand of cultural reading — and the nature of the insights it yields — is closely tied to the kinds of (incipiently Left) political, cultural, and textual distinctions they make in *The Popular Arts*. It is the ideological force, if you will, that girds Hall's analysis in *The Popular Arts* that leads to the production of such a rich critical ambivalence. Close reading on its own, of the New Critical (such as that practised by Cleanth Brooks) variety, would not have enabled such a politically textured reading of film or jazz.

It is for these deeply historical and political reasons that the ambivalence in *The Popular Arts* opened up the popular to a new kind of scrutiny. The encounters with the popular are an instance of how not to render cultural studies a formulaic practice. Instead, to read closely is to always live with the textured and textual reality of never knowing the full complexity of the popular. It is the lesson in *The Popular Arts* that would make Hall's Gramscian analysis of Thatcher so critical to the Left in *The Hard Road to Renewal*. Cultural arguments of 'great weight and influence' are only sustainable if they are produced through surprise, and conceived in critical and theoretical ambivalence. No cultural studies scholar has read culture, politics, ideology and, in rare moments, the literary, more carefully, in more surprisingly innovative ways, than Stuart Hall. We need only look to *The Popular Arts*, at a critical conjuncture when it was most difficult to recognize the value of reading culture in its own moment and against the formalist tendencies of the historical conjuncture, to understand how integral reading closely with one's eye attending to the immediate historical moment itself has always been to Hall's work.

If Hall's work is rightly understood as definitive for cultural studies, then *The Popular Arts* simultaneously affirms and complicates his centrality. This text offers an unexpected glimpse into how cultural studies was formed and an unusual mapping of its critical genealogy. This first book by Hall also reintroduces, in complicated and sometimes un-nuanced ways, the vexed and difficult issue of the aesthetic into cultural studies. What, if any, is the role of the aesthetic in cultural studies? Have cultural studies scholars, with their eye trained on the political, the popular, and the politics of resistance, among others, ceded the aesthetic entirely to the 'literary'? Does such a dismissal of the popular matter? What is the danger of this, particularly because there is a distinct politics to the ways in which aesthetic valuations circulate, perpetually sparking a debate to which cultural studies scholars, in their engagement with the popular, are implicitly responding to?

More importantly, however, tracing the Hallian genesis provides a surprising — only because of the neglect *The Popular Arts* has endured — insight into how early cultural studies, out of a combination of innovation and historical necessity, formed the thinking of Stuart Hall. *The Popular Arts* makes clear why, on the occasion of honouring Hall, we need to read him not only closely, but completely. Every new text, as T.S. Eliot so assuredly remarked in his famous essay 'Tradition and the Individual Talent', changes the relationship among existing texts. Eliot's critical sentiment might also be extended to every neglected text within a particular author's body of work: the reintroduction or, the first critical introduction of a disregarded work alters the relationship of every other text within a thinker's oeuvre. It changes the scholar's view of the 'new' work and it recalibrates the relationship amongst the 'existing' works. At the very least, it provides critics with a different, if not strictly new, place to begin the work of — as Leavis might have had it — Hallian 'valuation'.

References

Hall, S. 1980. *The Hard to Renewal.* London: Verso.

Hall, S., C. Critcher, T. Jefferson, J. Clarke and B. Roberts. 1978. *Policing the Crisis: 'Mugging', the State and Law and Order.* London: Macmillan.

Hall, S., and T. Jefferson, eds. 1990. *Resistance through Rituals: Youth Subcultures in Post-War Britain.* London: Routledge.

Leavis, F.R. 1936. *Revaluation: Tradition and Development in English Poetry.* London: Chatto and Windus; Toronto: Macmillan.

Mulhern, Francis. 1980. *The Moment of 'Scrutiny'.* London: Verso.

6 | *Stuart Hall on Race and Racism: Cultural Studies and the Practice of Contextualism*

Lawrence Grossberg

This paper starts with a simple and I hope obvious argument: that Stuart Hall's work on race cannot be separated from his work in cultural studies, and in particular, from his commitment to a radical contextualism.[1] The fact that it often is, especially in the USA at least, is partly due to the very different histories of cultural studies and of the variety of black and Afro-American studies programmes and their relations to cultural studies.

But I want to place that argument in the larger context of the relation of cultural studies (and Hall's work in particular) to theory. In one sense, it is clear that cultural studies is not a theory, which is not to say that it is not theoretical. This is because the project of cultural studies is to construct a political history of the present,[2] and it does so in a particular way, a radically contextualist way. Thus, it seeks to avoid reproducing the very sorts of universalisms (and essentialisms) that have, all too often, as the dominant practice of knowledge production, contributed to making the very relations of domination, inequality and suffering that cultural studies tries to oppose — politically, analytically and strategically. In other words, cultural studies as a project seeks practices capable of embracing complexity and contingency, and of avoiding any sort of reductionism.

I want to interpret Stuart Hall's work on race and racism in the context of his own long-standing commitment to a radically contextualist practice, rooted in part in his continuous struggle with Marxism in general, and in particular, with the notion of historical specificity, made so eloquently visible in his key, extraordinary essay, 'Marx's Notes on Method: A "Reading" of the 1857 Introduction', first published in *Working Paper in Cultural Studies* 6 (1974) after circulating as a mimeographed paper for some time.[3] This piece offers an original reconsideration of the materialist method as radically contextualist and anti-reductionist.

Without making theory a simple reflection or expression of its context, Hall quotes Marx: 'even the most abstract categories . . . are nevertheless . . . themselves likewise a product of historical relations and possess their full validity only for and within these relations'.[4] Or as he puts it a bit later, a contextual materialism seeks 'the mutual articulation of historical movement and theoretical reflection, not as a simple identity, but as differentiation within a unity'.[5] Hall offers a method of theorized empiricism: 'The method thus retains the concrete empirical reference as a privileged and undissolved "moment" within a theoretical analysis without thereby making it "empiricist": the concrete analysis of a concrete situation'.[6] Hall embraces the inseparability of the theoretical (discursive) and the empirical, the epistemological and the historical. Hall acknowledges that '[t]his may be theoretical work of a seemingly loose kind, porous but not without rigor. It is always connected to the specifics of a concrete moment'.[7] This is the significance of Hall's often eloquent refusals to claim the mantle of theorist, where the key to his practice is more often described as an attempt to go on theorizing, or to know when to stop theorizing:

> I have a strategic relation to theory. I don't regard myself as a theorist in the sense that that is my work. I am interested always in going on theorising about the world, about the concrete, but I am not interested in the production of theory as an object in its own right. And therefore I use theory in strategic ways . . . it's because I think my object is to think the concreteness of the object in its many different relations.[8]

And again: 'cultural studies . . . can only really work by moving from historical conjuncture to historical conjuncture using an evolving theoretical framework which is not conceptually purified'.[9] Hall's theoretical positions are often the result of 'poaching' and re-articulating concepts offered elsewhere.

For Hall, the appropriate level of analysis — and theorizing — is always at the level of specific contexts, or what he sometimes calls conjunctures. It is the level at which any social reality is overdetermined, existing as a configuration of relationships that are constantly open to re-articulation. At this level of the concrete, relations are themselves articulated, not into a simple unity but into a condensation of differences, an articulated unity. Analysis at this level involves mapping the 'redisposition of elements within a configuration'.[10]

The notion of contextualism in cultural studies is the idea of 'relationality', an idea that postulates a relation that precedes — is more fundamental ontologically — than the terms of the relationship. A practice is not anything by itself. It is what it is — for example, an economic practice, and an economic practice of a particular sort — only within a set of relations. Hence, if you will, all events are contexts, all the way up to the social formation itself. Any event or context is an articulated unity. In that sense, all events, all practices are condensations, articulated unities, overdetermined realities. Contextualism, in cultural studies at least, argues that just because something is a historical construction, the effect of an articulation, does not mean it is not real, that it does not have real effects, that it does not matter to people. Such discursive realities do not deny the reality of the non-discursive, but the existence of non-discursive realities does not mean that the historically produced discursive realities can be simply wished away or merely 'deconstructed'.

The work of Stuart Hall is one of the most resonant and original theoretical, even philosophical discourses available to us. Hall is not about the evasion of philosophy but its re-articulation into a radically contextual practice, culminating as it were in his attempts to locate race and racism, first in a particular conjunctural and hegemonic struggle and second, in an even broader context of global transformation and struggle. This is, of course, only one way of cutting into his work — and into cultural studies but I believe it is a useful one. Starting with other notions — contingency or complexity, for example, would result I presume in similar but also different arguments. Or one could begin with Hall's consistent and principled opposition to closure, fixity, essentialism, universalism and so on, where what is important is the specific form and practice of his opposition. Again, I believe you would end up in a similar but different place.

In the preface to Julien and Nash, Mark Nash notes 'the degree to which the USA misunderstands and misrepresents (Hall's and Isaac Julien's) work'.[11] And in a rare moment, in an interview with David Scott, Hall admits, 'people sometimes misunderstand what I'm saying. They don't think they disagree with me as much as they do'.[12] Too often, Hall's work on racism and identity is taken to be another instance —

more generous, more eloquent, maybe even more interesting — of a theory of difference, of anti-essentialism, of hybridity — as if that were or could be the end of the story, as if one could separate this work from his position in cultural studies.

I think it is too often forgotten and too easy or convenient to forget that Hall's work on racism and, moving out from there, on identity in its various forms is undertaken in the context of and in response to questions about the changing social formation — and the place occupied and work done by race and racism in the reorganization of the social formation. My argument again is that in developing his own materialist critical practice, one that takes seriously 'the determinateness of thought within the present organization of social formations', [13] Hall's theory of race/racism — as well as that of Paul Gilroy, Isaac Julien, Kobena Mercer, Hazel Carby and others — stands as one of the most consistently radical practices of a philosophy of contextualism available to us. Thus, Hall always locates, contextualizes, his work on race, as when he declares: 'I have never worked on race and ethnicity as a kind of subcategory. I have always worked on the whole social formation which is racialized.'[14]

The 'misunderstanding' that Nash and Hall note may result in part from a certain misreading of the stories Hall has told about the development of cultural studies in Britain (and especially at the Centre for Contemporary Cultural Studies (CCCS)). Too often people conflate these narratives of a discursive institutional project with the story of Hall's own political and intellectual biography, [15] forgetting that every individual has her or his own path through cultural studies. Thus, in 'Cultural Studies and its Theoretical Legacies', [16] Hall narrates the history of the political problematics at the CCCS — class, feminism, and race. Up until the 1970s, race was, he suggests, a significant absence at the Centre, until certain institutional struggles and social events — located in a particular conjuncture in which race was central — forced it onto the agenda.[17] But Hall's story is not the same as that of the Centre. It may not have been until the 1970s that he found the point of intersection for his concerns with race and racism, and his work at the Centre, but his career has been consistently involved with questions of race and racism. This should be unremarkable given the role of various Afro-Caribbean students (including Hall) in the formation of the New Left. Questions of race and imperialism were, after all, a vital part of the New Left's critique of Marxism. What Hall[18] has recently called his own 'Bahian' moment in the 1950s was continued into some of his earliest publications, such as 'Black Britons'.[19] This suggests that any discussion of the place of issues of race and ethnicity in both Hall's career and in Cultural Studies cannot be separated from the particular social formation in which the discussion is located and where it is directed.

Hall is rigorously consistent about this: 'I don't claim for my particular version of a non-essentialist notion of race correctness for all time. I can claim for it only a certain conjunctural [for the moment, read 'contextual'] truth.'[20] That truth can only be 'discovered' through demanding and rigorous work. There is nothing relativistic about the claim of the validity of this non-essentialist notion of race in the context of a particular social formation. There is nothing paradoxical — in the form of Mannheim's dilemma about relativism itself — about Hall's contextualism, since it can claim — and it need only claim — truth within its context.

One of the most interesting consequences is the way Hall treats poststructuralism, its practice of deconstruction and the various binaries that it deconstructs.[21] For Hall, the logic of deconstruction, of dissemination, of differance, 'must always be read in the context of colonisation, slavery and racialisation; they must not be read as an alternative to, but as part of their internal logic'.[22] Notions that are too often assumed to challenge the stable binarism of dominant structures of power — including notions of hybridity, syncretism, third space — are not escapes from or solutions to the binary organizations of asymmetrical power but are in fact products of '"the disjunctive logic" that colonisation, slavery and [m]odernity introduced'.[23] Note the import of this claim: not only is Hall denying (with a nod to Bhabha) that one 'can identify a point of enunciation that is neither one nor the other, that breaks the binary and speaks in-between', for that 'in-between' is itself part of the binary — condensation and dissemination — always implicating power already.[24] The real question for Hall[25] is not how to escape or deny the binarism, for that would entail ignoring the context. Rather, 'you have to keep asking why the binaries reappear'.[26]

As Hall explained it to me in another context: 'deconstruction is a vital move — showing that the binaries are really examples of differance'.[27] Deconstruction moves essential binaries to the level of historical differences. Hall yet refuses to think that a theoretical critique of binarisms is sufficient. For him, since concretely, any binarism is really an overdetermined difference, power always continues to maintain the binaries in historical realities.

> This is possible because language and power are not the same but power intervenes in language (representation) to secure certain effects.... This doesn't make deconstruction useless . . . only necessary but not sufficient. We need ceaselessly to deconstruct the binaries. But only politics can make this critique historically "real in its effects".[28]

Hall's work on racism begins from a 'rigorous application of ... the premise of historical specificity'[29] in which the object is the organization — by power — of the social formation as a configuration of unequal positions and relations. This particular contextualism sees racism as a way — or a historically changing set of ways — of dividing and distributing the population:

> There have been many different racisms — each historically specific and articulated in a different way within the societies in which they appear. Racism is always historically specific in this way, whatever common features it may appear to share with other similar social phenomenon. Though it may draw on the cultural and ideological traces which are deposited in society by previous historical phases, it always assumes specific forms which arise out of present — not the past — conditions and organisation of society.[30]

Hall continues:

> This is a warning against extrapolating a common and universal structure of racism, which remains essentially the same, outside of its specific historical location. It is only as the different racisms are historically specified — in their difference — that they can be properly understood as a product of historical relations and possess ... full validity only for and within those relations.[31]

Racism exists only in relation to other social relations:

> One must start, then, from the concrete historical 'work' which racism accomplishes under specific historical conditions — as a set of economic, political and ideological practices, of a distinctive kind, concretely articulated with other practices in a social formation . . . . The question is not whether men-in-general make perceptual distinctions between groups with different racial or ethnic characteristics, but rather, what are the specific conditions which make this form of distinction socially pertinent, historically active.[32]

Thus we cannot assume that attitudes of racial superiority produced plantation slavery, but rather must begin by understanding that slavery (as a response to historical conditions and needs) produced particular forms of racism.

The context is the beginning and the end of our research. The trajectory from the beginning to the end provides the measure of our success at mapping, at arriving at a better description/understanding of the context. Thus, Hall begins his now classic essay, 'What is this "black" in black popular culture' this way: 'I begin with a question: what sort of moment is this in which to pose the question about black popular culture'.[33] The answer of course always pulls one into the work of contextual analysis and self-reflection.

Since the context determines the specific question, always at least partly political, it also determines 'the strategies of cultural politics with which we attempt to intervene . . . and the form and style of cultural theory and criticising'.[34] Hall's contextualism is complete and consistent, from the refusal of *Policing the Crisis* to define mugging apart from its 'shaping context' to Bailey and Hall's reiteration of the argument Hall first proposed in 'Deconstructing the Popular':[35]

> It is perfectly possible that what is politically progressive and opens up new discursive opportunities in the 1970s and 1980s can become a form of closure — and have a repressive value — by the time it is installed as the dominant genre.... It will run out of steam; it will become a style; people will use it not because it opens up anything but because they are being spoken by it, and at that point, you need another shift.[36]

Or as Isaac Julien put it, 'Territories and ideas have to be explored politically through construction and reconstruction, then thrown away, if we are to change the master narratives and conventions'.[37] Nevertheless, one might suspect, reading Hall, that, at least sometimes, he does seem to speak in terms that begin to approach the general if not the universal, usually framed in terms of logics — the logics of modernity, capitalism, identity and so on. Yet, at least as early as 'Marx's Notes on Method', Hall clearly qualified the place of — and utility of appeals to — highly abstract and quasi-universal practices, forces or structures that transcend any and every particular relations or contexts, or that can be seen as the subject of an 'evolutionary historical development'. For example, he reminds us that Marx rejects the notion of 'production in general', instead recognizing that the claim of a general or abstract production is both a product and a claim of a particular conjunctural capitalism. But Hall also rejects taking this argument too far into a radical particularism:

> No doubt there are certain general features to racism. But even more significant are the ways in which these general features are modified and transformed by the historical specificity of the contexts and environments in which they become active.[38]

Of course the notion of 'general features' is an opening through which almost anything can enter, raising the problem of the concrete universal in a contextual form. Hall's answer seems to make 'general features' into a historical-empirical category rather than a logical one (of abstraction) or even a trans-contextual one, more akin to what he calls 'tendential combinations . . . which while not prescribed in the fully determinist sense, are the "preferred" combinations, sedimented and solidified by real historical developments over time'.[39] Interestingly, one example he uses is the connection between capitalism and free labour, suggesting a quite radical de-essentialization of capitalism itself. The 'general' then seems to slide into 'the reworking of the tradition under the force of the present conjuncture . . . A reworking that precisely delivers the much more complex idea . . . of the "changing same"'.[40] That is, every appeal, even to the apparently general or abstract, has to be understood contextually.

To put it differently, Hall does not deny the importance of abstract categories, such as commodification. For Hall, this is not the level of analysis at which critical work has to be done. While an abstraction like commodification may tell us something about what distinguishes capitalism from feudalism, it does not necessarily help us distinguish capitalism from other forms of market economy, and it does even less to help us understand historical and geographical differences amongst specific configurations of capitalism, precisely what we need to understand if we hope to imagine new futures, and new strategies for realizing them.

To take my argument any further, I must now return to Hall's theory of context, some of its own specificity. The first thing that needs to be acknowledged is the potentially paradoxical nature of any such theory, for a philosophy of context must surely also be a contextual philosophy. Hall, like the best cultural studies, I think, approaches his contextualism, more 'practically'.[41] At the same time, using the notion of context must not be allowed to flatten all realities, to singularise every territory, as if talking about contexts necessarily makes every system of relationality equivalent, or puts every territory on the same plane or scale.

The second thing that needs to be clarified is the specific way in which cultural studies — and Hall — approach the relationality of contexts. I have thus far allowed context and conjuncture to be conflated but I must now prise them apart. It is not enough to understand that Hall is a contextual theorist (and perhaps, although he would shy away from the claim, a theorist of the context). It is not coincidental that Hall's work on race arises simultaneously with, and is inseparable from, his analysis of the rise of Thatcherism. Hall's particular practice of contextualism involves his location within and his efforts at the diagnosis of a conjuncture.[42]

A key to this move can be seen in the place of race in the typically told narratives of cultural studies, especially as recounted by Hall in his powerful 'Theoretical Legacies' article.[43] Alongside a narrative of political problematics (class, gender and race), there is a theoretical narrative. As Hall puts it, 'movements provoke theoretical moments. Historical conjunctures insist on theories'.[44] Now, in the narrative of the essay, there are two explicitly acknowledged theoretical moments: Marxism, and what Hall calls 'the linguistic turn'. From the latter Hall claims to have derived some of his most central theoretical assumptions or demands: living with difference; the productivity of reproduction; and the importance of subject positionalities.

But there is no third theoretical turn. I want to suggest that the third theoretical moment, corresponding — loosely speaking — to the introduction of the problematic of race — that is to say, what enabled Hall to think race in a new way — was defined by the notion of the conjuncture, and depended on what I have elsewhere called a second reading of Gramsci at the CCCS — not the humanistic Gramsci of Raymond Williams and *Resistance through Rituals*, and not the structuralist (Althusserian) Gramsci that dominates so much contemporary cultural theory, but a reading located — as it were — between these two. This is a radically conjuncturalist Gramsci, one focused on the social formation as a complex articulated unity or totality. This was the moment at which Hall and some other people at the CCCS began to contextually theorize the notion of context itself.

Writing about *Policing the Crisis*, Hall says:

> If you'd just taken race as a black issue, you'd have seen the impact of law and order policies on the local communities, but you'd have never seen the degree to which the race and crime issue was a prism for a much larger social crisis. You wouldn't have looked at the larger picture. You'd have written a black text, but you wouldn't have written a cultural studies text because you wouldn't have seen this articulation up to the politicians, into the institutional judiciary, down to the popular mood of the people, into the politics, as well as into the community, into black poverty and into discrimination.[45]

The centrality of the notion of a 'conjuncture' to cultural studies, and in fact, the emergence of a different model of cultural studies around an understanding of context as conjuncture, depends on a radically conjuncturalist Gramsci, one focused on the social formation as a complexly articulated unity or totality (that is nevertheless not an organic totality). A conjuncture is a description of a social formation as fractured and conflictual, along multiple axes, planes and scales, constantly in search of temporary balances or structural stabilities through a variety of practices and processes of struggle and negotiation.

Hall is, in a recent set of interviews, quite explicit about this 'intellectual perspective' of cultural studies: 'It has an intellectual vocation to produce a critical understanding of a conjuncture, a cultural-historical conjuncture'.[46] And again, speaking of the collective project of the Centre: 'The commitment to understanding a conjuncture is what from the beginning we thought cultural studies was about'.[47]

Actually, conjuncturalism requires but is not equivalent to contextualism; not all contexts are conjunctures. If contextualism understands any event relationally, as a condensation of multiple determinations and effects,[48] a conjunctural analysis defines a specific set of critical and analytical practices. According to Hall, a conjuncture describes 'the complex historically specific terrain of a crisis which affects — but in uneven ways — a specific national-social formation as a whole'.[49] It is not a slice of time or a period but a moment defined by an accumulation/condensation of contradictions, a fusion of different currents or circumstances.

If a context is always a complex, overdetermined and contingent unity, a conjuncture is always a social formation understood as more than a mere context — but as an articulation, accumulation, or condensation of contradictions. If contextualism embodies the commitment to the openness and contingency of social reality where change is the given or norm, conjuncturalism looks to the changing configuration of forces that occasionally seeks and sometimes arrives at a balance or temporary settlement. It emphasizes the constant over-determined reconfiguration of a field producing only temporary stabilities. Some conjunctures may be characterized by a profound — organic — crisis while others are characterized by smaller uncertainties, imbalances and struggles and still others may appear to be settled or at least characterized by more 'passive revolutions'. Similarly, conjunctures have differing temporal scales: some are protracted and some are relatively short in duration.[50]

Moreover, Hall makes it clear that such conjunctural analyses cannot be understood as totalizing projects (in which everything is connected to everything else). And perhaps even more importantly, Hall makes it clear that he is 'not driven to a general philosophical proposition that conjunctures are all that we can study . . . . There are many other different forms of working. Not all histories . . . need be conjunctural histories'.[51] But it is at the level of the conjuncture that Hall believes that knowledge can be most usefully and concretely articulated to political struggles and possibilities, and it is at the level of conjunctures that cultural studies works.

Conjunctural analysis (as a theoretical practice) poses at least two key interrelated problems: The first is a task of 'judging when and how we are/are not moving from one conjuncture to another.' That is why the primary question for cultural studies is always 'what is the conjuncture we should address'.[52] The second, closely related, demands that every analysis must try to get the balance right — between the old and the new (or in Raymond Williams' terms, the emergent, the dominant and the residual), between what is similar and what is different, between the organic and the conjunctural (and the accidental).[53] Thus, the appeal to certain logics or processes is not necessarily a retreat from radical contextualism but partly a demand for further analysis of the complexity of the conjuncture in terms of both spatial scale and temporal duration, expanding the possibility that the analysis of a conjuncture opens onto a multiplicity of overlapping contexts, of contexts operating at different scales, and of what we might call embedded contexts. At the very least, this enables us to recognize that while conjunctures are largely constituted as national formations, they are increasingly and deeply articulated into and by international, transnational and global practices, relations, processes and institutions.[54]

The conjunctural model of cultural studies that I am alluding to here is commonly associated with the work done in Britain, around the twin poles of race and Thatcherism, by Hall, Gilroy, Clarke and others, in such important and exemplary works as *Policing the Crisis* and *The Empire Strikes Back*.[55] Of course, there is much more to the Gramsci invented by this reading than just a conjunctural model of cultural studies' contextualism; notions of hegemony, common sense, organic intellectuals, also played an important role in transforming cultural studies, and its approach to contemporary political struggles. It is a short but significant distance from the contextualism of Hall's essay on Marx's method to the collaboratively elaborated conjuncturalism — sometimes described as a theory of articulation — that enabled a collective body of work on Thatcherism (*Policing the Crisis* predicted the rise of Thatcherism), race (Gilroy as well as the striking 'Race, Articulation and Societies Structured in Dominance'),[56] and on the almost seamless articulation of the two problematics. A theory of articulation understands history as the ongoing effort (or process) to make, unmake and remake relations, structures and unity (on top of differences).[57] If reality is relational and articulated, such relations are both contingent (that is, not necessary) and real, and thus, never finished or closed for all times.

In the case of the Centre's work on the articulations of race in and to Thatcherism, the specificity of the conjuncture was defined by the existence of what the Centre, following Gramsci, called an organic crisis. Let me quote Gramsci here:

> A crisis occurs, sometimes lasting for decades. This exceptional duration means that incurable structural contradictions have revealed themselves (reached maturity) and that, despite this, the political forces which are struggling to conserve and defend the existing structure itself are making every effort to cure them, within certain limits, and to overcome them.[58]

Roger Simon takes up the argument:

> If the crisis is deep — an organic one — these efforts cannot be purely defensive. They will consist in the struggle to create a new balance of political forces, requiring a reshaping of state institutions as well as the formation of new ideologies; and if the forces of opposition are not strong enough to shift the balance of forces decisively in their direction, the conservative forces will succeed in building a new system of alliances which will re-establish their hegemony. Beneath the surface of the day-to-day events, an organic and relatively permanent structural change will have taken place.[59]

There are, no doubt, problems with using a vocabulary of crisis, which seems to imply a normative moment of stability and implicitly, an organic unity. Still there are moments when the instabilities and contradictions appear at almost every point of the social formation, and when the struggles become visible and self-conscious. *Policing the Crisis* argued that Great Britain was in the midst of such an organic crisis; the analysis of 'mugging' that is the empirical starting point led the analysis to that crisis. Yet it was only in the context of that crisis that one could even identity mugging as a problem. The authors saw the organic crisis as part of a longer history of the post-war social formation, and argued that 'no adequate conjunctural analysis of the post war crisis yet exists on which we could hang our more immediate concerns'.[60]

It is in this context of conjunctural philosophy that we can understand Hall's notion of identity as a relentlessly historical question, as not only complex and contradictory ('the play of difference across identity', a politics of multiple identities), as always in process, always constituted in and by representations (narratives of self), as involving identifications rather than stable identities, as the suturing (or temporary attachment) of subjectivity and discursive positions. Moreover, in the present conjuncture, Hall distinguishes two regimes of racism: race and ethnicity (where the latter refers to the culturally constructed places of enunciation). But for Hall, not all identities are cultural, and there is no guaranteed relation between political, economic, and cultural identities. This is of course by no means an adequate summary of Hall's contributions to the theory of identity. One would have to point out that Hall (and others to be sure, especially Paul Gilroy) have gone beyond the Lacanian/Althusserian theory of interpellation by raising questions of belonging and identification: how one takes up, attaches oneself to or invests in particular subject positions? Identities have to be seen as the 'point[s] of sutures between discourses that attempt to interpellate us and processes that construct us as subjects that can be spoken'. They are 'point[s] of temporary attachment to the subject positions which discursive practices construct for us'.[61] At the same time, 'Identities actually come from outside. They are the ways in which we are recognised and then come to step into the place of the recognition which others give us. Without the others, there is no self, there is no self-recognition'.[62]

Hall has been struggling with the duality apparently suggested here for some time. This duality might be described as the tension between belongingness and otherness. In part, he is wrestling here, as he often does, with another theorist, in this case Foucault's theory of discursive practices, which attempts to radically historicize and multiply the category of the subject. Foucault was interested in looking at the 'different modes by which ... human beings are made subjects ... subject to someone else's control and dependence and tied to his own identity by a conscience and self-knowledge'.[63] At the same time, for Foucault, the problem of subjectivity explores the 'practices by which individuals are led to focus attention on themselves'.[64] That is, for Foucault, interiority or psychic reality is a relation within and between exteriorities, which I might describe as the result of the discursive production and structuring of affect. Finally, according to Foucault, psychoanalysis as a theory of lack or negativity (the other is always a constitutive and disruptive outside) is a historical discursive description/production of one mode of subjectivity — perhaps the dominant one of many in contemporary societies. Therefore, while its effects are real, it cannot be taken up as a tool for critical conjunctural analysis.

Yet Hall acknowledges that interiority is 'at the heart of the modern conception of individuality' and thus presents itself as the way to reconcile belonging and difference, particularity and liberty. Hall does, especially in his more recent work, increasingly appeal to a kind of interiority, however metaphorically: 'The right for example to live one's life from within — not as it is imposed or dictated simply from outside — but from within, to give it a kind of authenticity from within'.[65] In this way, belongingess as particularity, as a concrete universal, precisely becomes the condition of possibility of 'personal liberty'. But this means that Hall ends up having to take a partly defensive posture — acknowledging that he is running the risk of letting liberal universalism back in.

Here again, we have to read Hall's apparent appeal to the general if not the universal, usually framed in terms of logics, as themselves contextual, so that we might consider his deployment of a vocabulary of belonging and an appeal to interiority (and 'futurity' I might add) as an attempt to respond to the conjunctural challenge of multiculturalism, a challenge posed by the organic crisis.

But as the above discussion suggests, organic crises are not easily settled once and for all, nor is there a single settlement that continues to re-establish itself. Rather, any number of temporary and unstable settlements may be offered or tried, until finally, the crisis is resolved, often through radical reconfigurations of the social formation itself. But even if the result is a period of relative structural stability, it is still always both unstable and temporary. While Thatcherism ('neoliberalism') provided a sort of resolution to the organic crisis of the conjuncture, nevertheless many of the features and elements of that conjuncture have continued to characterize the ensuring conjunctures, which must nevertheless be understood to define a radically different conjuncture. Thatcherism's solution, that is, itself rearticulated the crisis producing different contradictions and new crises, to which Blair offers a different settlement. While we can assume that elements of that older crisis continue to exist, albeit in different conjunctural articulations, the conjuncture itself has changed and demands new possibilities. That is to say, a lot has changed since the 1970s. Thus Hall observes that the conjuncture — and the place of race in the various struggles, possible settlements and manifestations of instability — has continued to change in Britain since the 1970s. He contrasts the black politics of the 1970s and 1990s, and concludes that things have moved 'into a new kind of ethnicised politics of difference' in which 'Blackness is no longer necessarily a counter or resistance identity, as it was in the 1970s. The political resonance of black identity has shifted significantly over the last 10 or 15 years.... The period when black politics was the politics of community struggle seems to be profoundly in recession.'[66] Black politics has taken 'on a decidedly more individualist cast'[67] partly in the context — the conjuncture I would say — of the new entrepreneurial culture and economy.

In fact, Hall suggests that over three or four decades, 'we have been passing through at least three, maybe more, differentiated ethnic identity moments,'[68] defined by new axes along which structures of radical difference move. This is partly the result, Hall continues, of a new round of Americanization but, as a result, we can now anticipate the possibilities for a genuinely multicultural Britain. But of course, multiculturalism does not guarantee the end of racism. On the contrary, it poses the new challenge of facing the tension between difference and equality as part of a larger transformation: 'The issue of cultural identity as a political question now constitutes one of the most serious global problems as we go into the 21st century'.[69] It is in this spirit that Hall claims that this is 'a highly transitional moment, a very Gramscian conjuncture that we are in — between the old state that we can neither fully occupy or fully leave, and some new state toward which we may be going, but of which we are ignorant . . . [we are] living in the moment of the post'.[70] This lovely somewhat Hegelian imagery suggests that we are in the midst of a rather prolonged organic crisis, what I have described as a war of positions among competing conceptions and configurations of modernity, with all the complexity it embraces.

Standing as we are in the midst of the present conjuncture — without an adequate analysis, I might add, we cannot escape the fact, according to Hall, that 'we are in the deconstructive moment', a moment of political and theoretical unsettling and destabilizing. In such a moment — caught between any possible settlements as it were — criticism can only proceed by 'putting terms under erasure', choosing to use a term — race, identity, interiority, psychic, economy, autonomy — knowing that it is inadequate to the challenge. The problems of identity and difference (of individuality and collectivity, of particularity and universality) cannot be addressed apart from the analysis of the complex conjunctural struggles organized around the very categories and structures that the old conjuncture has thrown up to us, and that the new conjuncture has not yet replaced — in all their complexity. This problem cannot be answered outside the analysis of the contemporary struggles over the very category of individuality, which has itself become a crucial site of contestation, again from any number of directions including communitarianism, corporatism, and various religious and scientific formations. In the end, the analyses of the particular political sites depend on an analysis of the conjunctural crises of which the very instability of any possible answer is constitutive.

But Hall also suggests another possibility for the conjuncturalism of cultural studies at the present moment:

> Cultural studies has got a lot of analytic work to do ... in terms of trying to interpret how a society is changing in ways that are not amenable to the immediate political language.... Cultural studies requires a huge bootstrap operation to lift itself out of its earlier agenda . . . so that it can come face to face with these much larger, much wider, much broader, more extensive social relations. I am struck by how much potential work there is, and I feel that cultural studies is not aware of its new vocation. It could be called on to act at the leading edge of measuring new ways of both understanding and implementing social and historical change.[71]

I believe this at least suggests another possibility and poses a question to and within a materialist, radically contextualist, practice. It proposes a more experimental and positive practice which need not end up with the same categories with which it begins, that might help to call new concepts into being, experimenting with another language, pointing toward what can only be called the coming conjuncture, that is, the future, following something like a line of flight out of the contradictions of the contemporary conjuncture.[72] If a radical contextualism is a significant philosophical practice and that, in some sense, is the basis of Hall's cultural studies (not as a specific and systematic set of propositions, but as a practical and contingent tool), then Hall has to be recognized as one of its most consistent and rigorous exponents. For Hall, the solution to the most perplexing theoretical questions that challenge us as we try to unravel the contemporary conjuncture in search of other possibilities cannot be solved in the abstract but only as part of an ongoing conjunctural analysis. Conjuncturalism is a philosophy born out of and in response to the conditions of contradiction, crisis and rupture. Without the modesty that conjuncturalism teaches us, any theoretical position is in danger of reproducing the very sorts of universalisms that Stuart Hall has spent his career fighting against. But in the end, I also believe that Hall's conjuncturalism demands a kind of philosophy of hope by which one looks toward a future that is not yet visible.

Notes

1. This paper was given at the conference: 'Culture, Politics, Race and Diaspora: The Thought of Stuart Hall' at the University of the West Indies, Jamaica, June 2004. It has been substantially revised and parts of it are derived from my paper, 'Cultural Studies: The life of a project, the space times of its formations (or What's the matter with New York?)', *Cultural Studies* 20, no.1 (2006). I thank Stuart Hall for his generous time and helpful comments on earlier drafts.

2. I use this phrase to both signal a connection with and a distance from the project of Foucault. Although I do think Foucault is a radical contextualist, his theory of the context—and the level of abstraction on which he operates—is significantly different from that which I will present here as the practice of cultural studies. To put it simply, Foucault does not operate at the level of the conjuncture but rather at the level of what we might call, with a nod to Heidegger, the epoch. Moreover, Foucault's philosophy is organized around the paired concepts of problematic/event, while Hall's are more typically organized around notions of conjuncture and articulation, but that may be in part because Hall, perhaps more consistently than Foucault, eschews the ontological. I am grateful to Eduardo Restrepo for our discussions on these issues.

3. Stuart Hall, 'Marx's Notes on Method: A "Reading" of the 1857 Introduction to the Grundrisse', *Cultural Studies* 17, no. 2 (2003): 113–49.

4. Ibid., 134–35.

5. Ibid., 137.

6. Ibid., 128.
7. Stuart Hall with Bill Schwarz, *Conversations with Stuart Hall* (Cambridge: Polity Press, forthcoming).
8. Stuart Hall, (interviewed by David Scott) 'Politics, Contingency, Strategy', *Small Axe* 1 (1997): 141–59.
9. Ibid.
10. Stuart Hall, personal conversation, April 10, 2005.
11. Isaac Julien and Mark Nash, 'Dialogues with Stuart Hall', in *Stuart Hall: Critical Dialogues in Cultural Studies,* eds. D. Morley and Kuan-Hsing Chen (London: Routledge, 1996), 476.
12. Stuart Hall, 'Subjects in History: Making Diasporic Identities', in *The House that Race Built* (New York: Pantheon, 1997), 289–99.
13. Stuart Hall, 'Marx's Notes on Method: A "Reading" of the 1857 Introduction to the Grundrisse', 136.
14. Stuart Hall, (interviewed by Les Terry) 'Not a postmodern nomad', *Arena Journal* no. 5 (1995): 53–54.
15. I do not mean to ignore those many people who do embrace Hall's work in all its complexity and even extend it as they engage with it.
16. Stuart Hall, 'Cultural Studies and its Theoretical Legacies', in *Stuart Hall: Critical Dialogues in Cultural Studies,* eds. Morley and Chen (London: Routledge, 1996).
17. Another common mistake in reading histories of cultural studies is to assume that the narratives of dominant concerns and trends encompass the entirety of work in cultural studies. Thus, as early as the late 1960s, both individually (for example, Trevor Millum's work) and collectively (the first collective research was a study of story from a women's magazine called 'Cure for Marriage'), issues of gender were present at the CCCS, despite their almost total absence in the historical narratives.
18. Stuart Hall, 'Thinking the Diaspora: Home–Thoughts from Abroad', *Small Axe* 6 (1999): 1–18.
19. Stuart Hall, 'Black Britons', *Community* 1/2/3 (1970).
20. Stuart Hall, 'Politics, Contingency, Strategy', 157.
21. I leave open at this point the question of whether Hall is more or less faithful to Derrida's sense of the project than others.
22. Stuart Hall, 'Thinking the Diaspora'.
23. Ibid.
24. Stuart Hall, 'Not a postmodern nomad', 55.
25. Ibid., 61.
26. More broadly, this is a promising attempt to retheorize the relation of identity and difference, offering a way to move beyond anti-essentialism to what Paul Gilroy calls anti-anti-essentialism. It may also help to explain the difference between Hall and Gilroy over the saliency of race itself as an identity.
27. Stuart Hall, personal conversation, April 10, 2005.
28. Ibid.
29. Stuart Hall, 'Race, Articulation and Societies Structured in Dominance', in *Sociological Theories: Race and Colonialism,* ed. UNESCO (Paris: UNESCO, 1980), 336.
30. Stuart Hall, 'Racism and Reaction', *Five Views of Multi-Racial Britain: Talks on Race Relations* broadcast by BBC TV (London: Commission for Racial Equality, 1978), 26.
31. Stuart Hall, 'Race, Articulation and Societies', 337.
32. Ibid., 338.

33. Stuart Hall, 'What is this "Black" in Black Popular Culture?', in *Black Popular Culture*, ed. Gina Dent (Seattle: Bay Press, 1992), 21.
34. Stuart Hall, personal conversation, April 10, 2005.
35. Stuart Hall, 'Notes on "Deconstructuring the Popular"', in *Cultural Resistance: A Reader*, ed. S. Duncombe (London: Verso, 2002).
36. David Bailey and Stuart Hall, 'The Vertigo of Displacement', *The Critical Decade Ten-8* 2, no. 3 (1992): 15.
37. Quoted in Kobena Mercer, 'Back to My Routes', *The Critical Decade, Ten-8* 2, no. 3 (1992): 37.
38. Stuart Hall, 'Gramsci's Relevance for the Study of Race and Ethnicity', in *Stuart Hall: Critical Dialogues in Cultural Studies*, 435.
39. Stuart Hall, 'Race, Articulation and Societies', 330.
40. Stuart Hall, 'Subjects in History', 294.
41. Stuart Hall, personal conversation, April 10, 2005.
42. I must add that too often, Foucault is read without the key concept of articulation (and as a corollary, the differentiated unity [or totality]. See Gilles Deleuze, *Foucault* (Minneapolis: University of Minnesota Press, 1988); and Michel Foucault, *Society, Must be Defended* (New York: Picador, 2003).
43. Stuart Hall, 'Cultural Studies', 277–94.
44. Ibid.
45. Stuart Hall, (interviewed by Julie Drew) 'Cultural Composition: Stuart Hall on Ethnicity and the Discursive Turn', *Journal of Composition Theory* 18, no. 2 (1998): 192.
46. Stuart Hall with Bill Schwarz, *Conversations with Stuart Hall*.
47. Ibid.
48. John Frow and Meaghan Morris, 'Introduction' to *Australian Cultural Studies: A Reader* (Urbana: University of Illinois Press, 1993).
49. Stuart Hall, *The Hard Road to Renewal: Thatcherism and the Crisis of the Left* (London: Verso, 1988), 127.
50. Theories, like conjuncturalism, which assume a fractured sociality, have to face, it seems to me, the question — explicit in Marx, Weber, Durkheim, et cetera — of how society is possible without the assumed unity guaranteed through notions such as mechanical solidarity or the commonality assumed in images of community. How is society possible if one assumes difference, dissensus and even a certain limited relativism. Presumably one would want to avoid both the violent revolutionary utopianism of certain readings of Marx, and the self-legitimating narratives of organic solidarity (the contractual basis of social relations) or bureaucracy. How is a society built on dissensus without perpetual violence, possible?
51. Stuart Hall with Bill Schwarz, *Conversations with Stuart Hall*.
52. Ibid.
53. This offers the possibility of conjuncturally rethinking the particular/universal dichotomy.
54. We need to investigate the emerging form of what Carl Schmitt called the 'nomos' of the world. See Paul Gilroy, *Postcolonial Melancholia* (New York: Columbia University Press, 2004).
55. See Stuart Hall, *The Hard Road to Renewal*; Paul Gilroy, *There Ain't No Black in the Union Jack* (London: Hutchinson, 1987); John Clarke, *New Times and Old Enemies* (London: Harper Collins, 1991); Stuart Hall, Tony Critcher, Tony Jefferson, John Clarke and Brian Roberts, *Policing the Crisis: 'Mugging', the State and Law and Order* (London: Macmillan, 1978); Centre for Contemporary Cultural Studies, *The Empire Strikes Back: Race and Racism in 1970s Britain* (London: Hutchinson, 1982).

56.   See Paul Gilroy, *There Ain't No Black in the Union Jack* and Stuart Hall, 'Race, Articulation and Societies'.

57.   This may be slightly different than Foucault's notion of the relations of a non-relation.

58.   Antonio Gramsci, *Essential Classics in Politics: Antonio Gramsci*, DVD (n.d.)

59.   Roger Simon, 'Gramsci's Political Thought: An Introduction', *Essential Classics in Politics: Antonio Gramsci*, DVD.

60.   There is good reason to assume that the USA, similarly, at least since the mid-1970s, has been in a somewhat similar series of organic crises, and that we too do not have an adequate conjunctural analysis on which to build a critical diagnoses and strategy. See Stuart Hall, Tony Critcher, Tony Jefferson, John Clarke and Brian Roberts, *Policing the Crisis: 'Mugging', the State and Law and Order*, 218.

61.   Stuart Hall, 'Who Needs Identity?', in *Questions of Cultural Identity*, eds. S. Hall and Paul du Gay (London: Sage, 1996).

62.   Stuart Hall, 'Negotiating Caribbean Identities', *New Left Review* 209 (1995): 3–14.

63.   Michel Foucault, 'The Subject and Power', in *Michel Foucault: Beyond Structuralism and Hermeneutics* (Chicago: University of Chicago Press, 1983), 212.

64.   Ibid.

65.   Stuart Hall, 'The Multicultural Question', in *Un/settled Multiculturalisms*, ed. Barnor Hesse (London: Zed, 2000), 209–41.

66.   Stuart Hall, 'Aspiration and Attitude: Reflections on Black Britons in the Nineties', 39–40, 42.

67.   Ibid., 42.

68.   Ibid.

69.   Stuart Hall, 'Negotiating Caribbean Identities'.

70.   Ibid.

71.   Stuart Hall, 'Aspiration and Attitude'.

72.   If cultural studies is to move into the complexities of the current conjuncture, we have to find ways to bring the political, economic and cultural together in their conjunctural specificity. I do not think this can be accomplished by following the path of political economy, even when it tries to take the cultural turn seriously, which is rare enough. In the end, it sees culture as a medium into which the economy is translated and through which it moves, but which has no real effects of its own. Hence, political economy always assumes a universal privilege of the economy over politics and culture. Nor do I think this project can be realized through the notion of 'governmentality', where economic forces have no determining power but are merely the background to governmental shifts and where culture is merely assimilated into the political. Even more importantly, if, as I have argued elsewhere, the contemporary conjuncture cannot be understood simply as a struggle with or within capitalism, but requires us to approach it as a struggle over the specificities and configuration of modernity itself, then our historically constituted assumptions about the social formation — whether as an organic unity or a structure in dominance — have to be deconstructed and reconstructed. We have to face the radical challenge of thinking overdetermination, totality and difference together. Althusser's solution — the concept of the relative autonomy of the levels — too quickly leaves the levels in tact, each with its own specificity that transcends the particular conjuncture. In this way, Althusser reinscribes the very fracturing of the social totality and the reification of its parts that North Atlantic

modernity itself produced. Instead these distinctions — and the specificities they carry with them implicitly — have to be understood conjuncturally. Not only is the establishment of a distinction between economics, politics and culture conjunctural, but also what it means for a practice to be economic (and hence where any practice might be located in the social totality) is itself also conjuncturally defined. This requires us to rethink categories like economies, and cultures, and states, in radically contextual and discursive ways. I want to thank John Clarke for helping me to formulate these thoughts. See my *Caught in the Crossfire: Kids, Politics and America's Future* (Boulder: Paradigm, 2005).

7 | *Stuart Hall's Changing Representations of 'Race'*

Charles W. Mills

For radical social and political theorists over the last century, the task of accurately representing 'race' in its manifold dimensions — subjective and objective, phenomenological and social-structural, labile and enduring, oppressive and emancipatory — has been and continues to be a perennial challenge. In opposition to mainstream theorists who have framed racism in terms of natural dispositions, primordial tribal sentiments, or individualized prejudice, radical theorists have emphasized its contingency, historicity, and link with larger environing structures of a supra-individual nature. And in opposition to those in the orthodox white Left who have either ignored race altogether, or treated it as a residual category to be assimilated or reduced to some element of a class, theorists of colour in particular have insisted on its importance and specificity. In this chapter, I want to look at Stuart Hall's changing theorizations of race over the years and its relation to different bodies of radical theory, specifically Marxism and postmodernism. I will try to bring out some of the crucial continuities and discontinuities in his representations of race, and raise some questions and misgivings I have about these changes.

Hall on Race, 1977–1997

In attempting to track the evolution of Hall's views, one is, inevitably, handicapped from the very start by the size of his corpus — an impressive body of work that now stretches back over half a century.[1] Most of these pieces do not deal with race, of course, but the number that do, whether directly or indirectly, is still intimidating, and certainly there is no question of essaying a comprehensive treatment in the limited space available to me, especially given the additional qualitative obstacles of the complexity and nuance of his appropriation of various theorists. What I have chosen to do is to look at nine representative articles and talks, covering a 20-year span from 1977 to 1997, and also three interviews over this same time period, in 1985, 1992, and 1996.[2] In my opinion, these nine pieces, especially read in conjunction with his own retrospective characterization in the interviews of his intellectual development, give a good sense of the evolution of Hall's theoretical position on race, which as a first approximation can be summed up as a transition (related to larger theoretical shifts in his outlook) from Marxism to postmodernism. I emphasize 'as a first approximation' because Hall's relation to orthodox Marxism has always been ambivalent, and in fact although, as Chris Rojek comments in the introduction to his book-length study of Hall, 'he evidently found much in the Marxist tradition to be formative and congenial to his outlook',[3] he was never an orthodox Marxist. Thus in Hall's 1996 interview with David Scott, looking back at his experiences with fellow-Caribbean students and the anti-Stalinist Left in England in the 1950s, he reminisces:

> [My] relation to Marxism is very long and tortuous and complicated. . . . In relation to that first generation of West Indian intellectuals who were my reference point when I went to England, there is one difference between me and them and that is that I am not an economist. They are all economists. I am a student of literature. So I was always more interested in cultural questions. . . . [T]here is therefore initiated from then onwards a conversation in my head between my interest in culture and orthodox Marxism. Even though the two don't fit? So even though I am extremely interested and go through many variations of an intimate inside conversation with Marxism, I was never an economic reductionist. Never. I was never an orthodox Marxist. I was always a heterodox Marxist.[4]

On the other hand, as we will see, he has remained dubious about many postmodernist claims as well, so perhaps he cannot be categorized as an orthodox postmodernist either (if this category is not in any case intrinsically oxymoronic). Moreover, a further complication, of course, is that neither of these terms is univocal or monolithic. Apart from geographical markers — Eastern and Western, First World and Third World — Marxism can be further subdivided into Hegelian and analytic, structuralist and existentialist/humanist, 'white' and 'black', and so forth, while postmodernism is a very broad umbrella raised over theorists like Michel Foucault, Jacques Derrida, Jean Baudrillard,

Julia Kristeva et al., who have very significant differences amongst themselves as thinkers. Nonetheless, insofar as key concepts and key figures from one or the other tradition have been more salient in Hall's writings and theoretical assumptions at one time as compared to another, it does not seem unreasonable to conclude that — as a second approximation, say — Hall's representations of race are more clearly linked to classic Marxist themes and ideas at the start of the trajectory I am demarcating, and more clearly linked to classic postmodernist themes and ideas by the end. If nothing else, then, there is at least a major shift in emphases.

The starting point I have chosen is his 1977 and 1980 UNESCO articles, 'Pluralism, Race and Class in Caribbean Society', and 'Race, Articulation and Societies Structured in Dominance'. In contrast to the more culturalist turn of the later writings, these essays are centrally located in dialogue with classic sociological literature. Indeed the first includes various diagrams of class and colour stratification in the region, some adapted from the pioneering work of L.E.S. Braithwaite on Trinidad. The first essay addresses the obviously crucial question of the origins and evolutionary dynamic of the class/colour systems of the non-Hispanic Caribbean. Hall begins by critiquing M.G. Smith's famous 'plural society' thesis of discrete white/brown/black 'cultural' sections.[5] He argues that (i) the 'over-determined' overlap of race, colour, cultural and occupational stratification precludes singling out culture as determinative; (ii) the vertical/hierarchical (rather than horizontal/parallel) segmentation of these societies in 'a single pyramid of domination' makes the 'pluralist' thesis particularly implausible; (iii) Smith's one-dimensional emphasis on coercion misses the role of hegemony in legitimating the structure.[6] He goes on to emphasize that '[h]istory has been absolutely decisive in constructing the "modal type" of Caribbean social structure', and that 'Fundamentally, it is economic production which draws these two groups [whites and blacks] into a relation of domination/subordination'.[7] Clearly, then, we are on conceptual territory here that is completely congenial to the Marxist Left, and in fact at one point, rebuking Smith, Hall writes

> Thus all class societies exhibit enormous cultural complexity as between the class segments and fractions. . . . So the Caribbean example is distinct, not because there is class-cultural

differentiation, but because (a) this class-cultural differentiation is peculiarly sharp, and because (b) it is coincident to a high degree with race/colour stratification.[8]

The overarching category is therefore unequivocally 'class society', albeit one of a particular type. Hall tracks the development of these societies from slavery to Crown Colony, from caste to class, admitting the 'enormous territorial variation' within this 'basic paradigm', and the complications for social structure of variations in colour and phenotype.[9] Nonetheless, he insists that in the 'stratification matrix' of race, colour, and status: 'We would argue that this is not, usefully, considered as an ethnic or race-based or even race-colour based social system, but a social class stratification system in which the race-colour elements in the stratification matrix constitute the visible index of a more complex structure.'[10]

So at this stage, Marxist class categories are obviously theoretically crucial for Hall. In his closing pages, he warns against a 'crude' and 'mechanistic' application of class analysis, which would seek in a reductionist way to derive consciousness from 'objective economic position'. One needs to take account of 'ideology and of political class practices', of 'ethnic, cultural and ideological factors'.[11] But it is still the case, he claims, that what is called for is a 'sophisticated contemporary application of a Marxist class analysis' rather than 'less powerful' pluralist or ethnic models.[12]

His lengthy, wide-ranging, and highly theoretical 1980 essay, 'Race, Articulation, and Societies Structured in Dominance', can be read as his most elaborated statement of this position. Hall starts by demarcating and comparing two broad tendencies in the theorization of race, which he dubs the 'economic' and the 'sociological'. The economic approach, which for Hall includes both internalist and externalist accounts (for example, dependency theory), explains racial and ethnic division 'principally with reference to economic structures and processes', and thus 'tends to be monocausal in form'.[13] The sociological approach, on the other hand, emphasizes 'the autonomy, the non-reductiveness, of race and ethnicity as social features' and so 'tends to be pluralist'.[14] Hall regards both as expressing a partial truth (the 'historical specificity of race' and its link with 'economic processes'; the 'specificity of those social formations which exhibit distinctive racial or ethnic characteristics'), but he also sees them as both ultimately deficient.[15] Citing John Rex's work on South Africa as scoring valid Weberian points 'against a too-simple Marxism',[16] and referring to the famous debate between Andre Gunder Frank and Ernesto Laclau on the question of the historically capitalist nature of Latin America,[17] Hall salutes the emergence of a more sophisticated Marxism to theorize these issues: Louis Althusser's structuralism.[18] Through such concepts as the 'articulation' of different modes of production, 'relative autonomy', and 'overdetermination', structuralist Marxism will, Hall believes, be able to overcome the economically-reductionist tendencies in a Marxism innocent of the methodological prescriptions of the *Grundrisse*,[19] which had recently been translated and published in English for the first time.[20] Hall regards Antonio Gramsci's work as crucial for such an elaboration (though in some tension with Althusserian structuralism),[21] because of Gramsci's militant anti-economism, and his development of the concept of 'hegemony' in a framework that stresses the active intellectual and political labour required to achieve it.[22] So there is no automatic, economically-guaranteed relation between classes and their ideologies.

For Hall, then, this emergent new anti-reductionist Marxist paradigm has the potential to avoid the theoretical errors of both economic and sociological approaches, since it can register the historical specificity of racism as an ideology articulated to particular social formations while maintaining the link (necessary but not sufficient) to economic structures. Racism as a concept is a 'rational abstraction' (here he is citing Marx's methodological passages in the *Grundrisse* on abstractions), but one cannot extrapolate it without qualification. Instead, one must be sensitive to the differences between, say, the racism of plantation slavery in the American South and the varieties affecting nominally free black labour in the North. Moreover, since, in Althusserian language, racial ideologies 'interpellate' individuals as subjects, the experiential/phenomenological dimension of race, which tends to suffer in Marxist accounts, can be given its place also. Race and class can be reconciled:

> In each case, in specific social formations, racism as an ideological configuration has been reconstituted by the dominant class relations, and thoroughly reworked. It translates "classes" into

"blacks" and "whites," economic groups into "peoples," solid forces into "races". This is the process of constituting new "historical subjects" for ideological discourses — the mechanism we encountered earlier, of forming new interpellative structures. It produces, as the natural and given "authors" of a spontaneous form of racial perception, the naturalised "racist subject" . . . and yet these processes are themselves never exempted from the ideological class struggle.[23]

Race, racism, and anti-racism are thus being conceptualized in the terms of a Marxist conceptual apparatus, if one that is somewhat modified from the original (or at least what the original was thought to be), and explicitly located in relation to class forces and class struggle. So even if a greater theoretical distance is being taken from economism, and from the 'base/superstructure' metaphor that Hall had always found deeply problematic — with correspondingly highlighted emphases on ideology and interpellation — Hall is still located on recognizably Marxist terrain, if perhaps closer to its borders than before. As he says in the 1996 David Scott interview, looking back at the period:

> In the time of Althusser in the 70s I am very Marxist. But why? Because Althusser's problematic is a counter-reductionist Marxism. So of course I'm an Althusserian. . . . [Althusserianism] doesn't make ideology dependent on the economic. So it gives space to the things I am interested in. But it calls that instance the ideological instance rather than the cultural instance. Ideology in my work is still thinking about culture, and the work I do on ideology is to kind of bring it more in touch with how I understand culture . . . . So I can say I am a Marxist in the Althusserian moment because Althusser suggests that there is always an economic instance, a political instance, and an ideological instance. . . . So he gives me a Marxism I can assent to. If that is Marxism I can begin to live with it.[24]

Similarly, in 1986 — six years after the Althusserian race essay, with not just Althusserianism in particular in demise, but also Marxism in general on the decline — Hall's clarification of his position to an interviewer, while obviously reflecting his ongoing and perhaps exacerbated ambivalence, still maintains his Marxist commitments, albeit qualified. Thus, when asked to describe his relation to the recently emergent categories of 'post-Marxism' and 'postmodernism', he replies:

> I am a "post-Marxist" only in the sense that I recognise the necessity to move beyond orthodox Marxism, beyond the notion of Marxism guaranteed by the laws of history. But I still operate somewhere within what I understand to be the discursive limits of a Marxist position. And I feel the same way about structuralism. My work is neither a refusal nor an apologia of Althusser's position. I refuse certain of his positions, but Althusser certainly has had an enormous influence on my thinking, in many positive ways that I continue to acknowledge, even after he has gone out of fashion. So 'post' means, for me, going on thinking on the ground of a set of established problems, a problematic. It doesn't mean deserting that terrain but rather, using it as one's reference point. So I am, only in that sense, a post-Marxist and a poststructuralist, because those are the only two discourses I feel most constantly engaged with. They are central to my formation.[25]

As late as 1986, then, Hall is still identifying with a Marxist problematic. At the same time, he is simultaneously 'engaged' with poststructuralism, in an intellectual period (mid-1980s) of what would turn out to be — though not recognized at the time — an epochal transition between dominant social paradigms in the radical academy, with the collapse of 'actually existing socialism' only a few years away. When asked to locate himself with respect to Ernesto Laclau and Chantal Mouffe's recently published *Hegemony and Socialist Strategy*,[26] he carefully distances himself from one of their key moves: 'I would put it polemically in the following form: the last book thinks that the world, social practice, is language, whereas I want to say that the social operates *like* a language.'[27] So while he concedes the 'enormously generative' significance of the discursive turn, and its implications for re-theorizing subjectivity and the self, he remains sufficiently materialist to have reservations about 'the notion of society as a totally open discursive field':

> I would say that the fully discursive position is a reductionism upward, rather than a reductionism downward, as economism was. What seems to happen is that, in the reaction against a crude materialism, the metaphor of x operates like y is reduced to x = y. . . . We can't be

materialists in that way any longer. But I do think that we are still required to think about the way in which ideological/cultural/discursive practices continue to exist within the determining lines of force of material relations, and the expropriation of nature, which is a very different question. Material conditions are the necessary but not sufficient condition of all historical practice . . . . I think the discursive position is often in danger of losing its reference to material practice and historical conditions.[28]

Accordingly, an article published the same year as the interview, 'Gramsci's Relevance for the Study of Race and Ethnicity', continues to strike Marxist notes, though Althusser is put in the background, and the focus is now on Gramsci. Most of the paper is in fact an exposition of Gramsci's key ideas, with their application to race only being discussed in the last few pages. Hall begins by emphasizing that Gramsci was not trying to develop 'a *general* social science'; rather he was working within a historical materialist framework, and trying to revise and sophisticate it.[29] Whereas Marx's concepts tend to be 'epochal', ordered at a high level of abstraction, Gramsci was seeking to develop a conceptual apparatus appropriate for more concrete study, focused on specific historical conjunctures.[30] Although he did not write about colonialism and racism, his background in the under-developed Italian 'South' oriented him to issues of regionalism and uneven development that make his work applicable to the subject of race.[31] Above all, as we have seen, he was opposed to economism, the view that so-called superstructural features and events 'mirrored' the economic base, as manifested in his sharp critique of Nikolai Bukharin.[32] Toward the goal of providing a more adequate representation of this relationship, he developed various crucial concepts, for example, hegemony, the historical bloc, and the 'war of position' appropriate in the West (and representing the trend of the future) as against the 'war of manoeuvre' appropriate in the East, where civil society was 'primordial'.[33] Correspondingly, Gramsci argues for a rethinking of the narrow Marxist vision of the state as merely 'administrative and coercive'; instead, its educational, moral, and cultural role in exercising hegemony needs to be recognized.[34] Ideology is crucial to this process, understood above all as imbricated with popular thought and common sense, not 'false consciousness' but 'contradictory consciousness', composite and complex.[35]

In Hall's opinion, Gramsci's insights are illuminating for the study of racism in at least eight ways: (i) the need for historical specificity and the periodization of different forms of racism (ii) the emphasis on national characteristics and regional unevenness; (iii) non-reductionism about the race/class relationship and attention to the 'culturally specific quality of class formations'; (iv) the recognition that the class subject is not homogeneous; (v) the imperative of studying actual class behaviour, as against imputing particular traits to classes on the basis of abstract and a priori theoretical principles; (vi) the need for appreciating the educative/ideological role of the state and civil society in reproducing race; (vii) the centrality of cultural factors and the 'national-popular' as the site of struggle for hegemony; (viii) the concession of the ideological dimensions of racism, and the related fact that 'the so-called "self" which underpins these ideological formations is not a unified but a contradictory subject and a social construction'.[36]

Consider now Hall's two short papers from 1987, 'Minimal Selves' and 'New Ethnicities', both seen as landmarks and frequently cited in the secondary literature. As transcribed talks, admittedly, the first-person singular is necessarily more salient in both of them. Thus he begins 'Minimal Selves' as follows: 'A few adjectival thoughts only. . . . Thinking about my own sense of identity, I realise.'[37] But I would contend that although Hall is speaking here very much in the personal voice, drawing on his own individual history as an immigrant to Britain, this heightened aura of the 'subjective' is more than just a matter of format and grammar. What we have here, I suggest, is something of a shift in perspective. Hall goes on to locate himself as an individual in 'the postmodern age', and asks whether 'this centring of marginality [is] really *the* representative postmodern experience?'[38] Using immigration as his central trope, he argues that in a sense the rest of the world is only now catching up with the migrant experience of marginality and fragmentation. The migrant experience is a 'narrative', a 'story', but always a 'fiction':

> Who I am — the 'real' me — was formed in relation to a whole set of other narratives. I was aware of the fact that identity is an invention from the very beginning, long before I understood any of this theoretically. Identity is formed at the unstable point where the

"unspeakable" stories of subjectivity meet the narratives of history, of a culture.[39]

Obviously, then, we are on somewhat different theoretical terrain here. The use of the word 'narrative', with its distinctively postmodernist associations, contrasts with the language of orthodox social science of the earlier essays. Moreover, while the 1986 Gramsci essay does talk about the self as a social construction, it is still contextualized within specific historical conjunctures. Here, by contrast, the emphasis is on the subjectivizing of identity formation. The Althusserian structures, with their links, even if somewhat mediated, to specific objective determining and constraining social formations, are gone. It is not a matter of a self interpellated by the ideologies of class forces, but of a self that is constituted by narratives.

What he says about blackness also reflects this theoretical dividedness:

> "Black" has never been just there either. It has always been an unstable identity, psychically, culturally, and politically. It, too, is a narrative, a story, a history. Something constructed, told, spoken, not simply found. . . . Black is an identity which had to be learned and could only be learned in a certain moment. In Jamaica that moment is the 1970s. [40]

The emphasis on construction and the created character of racial identity coexists with the (arguably still somewhat 'materialist') insistence that this construction would not have been possible in a previous time period. Moreover, Hall explicitly rejects some of the assumptions of postmodernism. At one point, for example, he refers negatively to 'the [solipsism] of much postmodern discourse', warns that '[t]he politics of infinite dispersal is the politics of no action at all. . . . So one has to reckon with the consequences of where that absolutist discourse of postmodernism is pushing one'[41] and argues that even if the self is a fiction, an 'arbitrary closure', it is a necessary one if political action is to be possible:

> Is it possible for there to be action or identity in the world without arbitrary closure. . . ? Potentially, discourse is endless: the infinite semiosis of meaning. But to say anything at all in particular, you do have to stop talking. . . . So what is this "ending"? It's a kind of stake,

a kind of wager. . . . Politics, without the arbitrary interposition of power in language, the cut of ideology, the positioning, the crossing of lines, the rupture, is impossible. I don't understand political action without that moment.[42]

So the commitment to the necessity of political change remains (and there are still echoes of the language of the earlier work: for example, he also speaks of '*a politics of articulation* — politics as a hegemonic project'), but the framing assumptions are somewhat different. Hall still wants to hold on to the need for activism, the repudiation of the quietism that many have seen to follow from postmodernist assumptions. As he points out: this is going to be a 'politics of difference, the politics of self-reflexivity, a politics that is open to contingency but still able to act'.[43] Socialist politics was, of course, predicated on the assumptions of the centrality of class, the importance (if too often exaggerated into the all-purpose determinant) of the economic, and the agency of the class subject. What by contrast would be the guiding principle of this 'politics of difference'?

'New Ethnicities', the other short 1987 piece, provides some guidelines in its discussion of black cultural politics in Britain. Hall argues that in this politics, two (concurrent rather than sequential) phases are discernible. The first one involved the coining of 'black' as an umbrella identity for 'a new politics of resistance, among groups and communities with, in fact, very different histories, traditions, and ethnic identities'. This cultural politics sought to change the 'relations of representation', insisting on rights of access to representation and the challenge to black marginalization and stereotyping in these images.[44] The new phase, by contrast (though Hall emphasizes that it by no means replaces the first), is a 'politics of representation itself'. Blackness and the black subject then need to be seen as politically and culturally constructed, with 'no guarantees in nature', and subject to 'immense diversity and differentiation'. There is no essential black subject, and race always appears 'historically in articulation, in a formation, with other categories and divisions', of class, gender and ethnicity.[45] Questions of gender and sexuality thus need to be raised, and Hall praises the 1985 Stephen Frears film 'My Beautiful Laundrette' for its transgressive refusal of the monolithic and virtuous black subject.[46] His discussion here broaches what in the USA is called the issue of 'intersectionality', the need to theorize the multiple identities, particularly of the subordinated, that result when race, gender, class, sexual orientation, and so forth, come together.

However, what is really important is the 'culturalizing' of the political. It is not merely that Hall is advocating a cultural politics as one component of an overall progressive anti-racist struggle, which would obviously be completely unexceptionable. Rather, I would suggest that what is striking is the extent to which the cultural has now assumed overwhelming significance in itself. The following passage is crucial to understanding Hall's shift away from Marxism:

> My own view is that events, relations, structures do have conditions of existence and real effects, outside the sphere of the discursive; but that it is only within the discursive, and subject to its specific conditions, limits and modalities, do they have or can they be constructed within meaning. Thus, while not wanting to expand the territorial claims of the discursive infinitely, how things are represented and the 'machineries' and regimes of representation in a culture do play a *constitutive*, and not merely a reflexive, after-the-event, role. This gives questions of culture and ideology, and the scenarios of representation — subjectivity, identity, politics — a formative, not merely an expressive, place in the constitution of social and political life.[47]

So if the original objection was to a Marxist materialism that was too often reductionist, denying the relative autonomy of superstructural levels, Hall's more radical objection now is directed against this whole way of conceiving things, insofar as what would once have been thought of as 'material', determining, is now claimed to have its effects only within a discursive field that itself 'determines' how these effects will be thought of. Whatever his other reservations and caveats, this repudiation shifts Hall more clearly on to classic postmodernist territory. Correspondingly, for him, cultural politics, the politics of the discursive, of representation, should be seen as central to social transformation. Two linked papers presented at a 1989 conference, 'The Local and the Global' and 'Old and New Identities, Old and New Ethnicities', further develop these themes, analysing ethnicity in the context of globalization, with the focus on cultural politics (Hall uses the term 'ethnicity' somewhat more broadly than would be standard in the US context, referring generally to the various ways in which subjects are historically, culturally, and politically constructed). Yet at the same time Hall continues to strike notes with more Marxist overtones, describing macro-historical processes and citing Gramsci as well as Marx himself.

In the first talk, Hall points out that, from the perspective of England, globalization is an old story, though in this case, of course, globalization really means imperialism. English identity was then constituted in relation to inferior colonized 'others', in a Manichean world, an ethnicity that did not represent itself as such, but as natural, despite being negotiated against difference not merely externally but internally.[48] Britain's decline in the international system, Third World migration to the First World, the growth of supranational organizations, and planetary ecological interdependence have eroded national identities and the significance of the nation state, in a world increasingly dominated in the cultural sphere by a global mass culture, which is centred in the West.[49] Hall argues that a sensitive reading of *Capital* should remind us that Marx anticipated that capital's logic would manifest itself in the selective reinforcement of particularity as well as a commodifying homogenization, so that we should not be surprised to find nationalism and gender differentiation being strengthened in certain spheres. Thus it is a mistake to see globalization as a non-contradictory and unproblematic process.[50] Hall then turns to the local, arguing that paradoxically, 'marginality has become a powerful space' as manifested in the 'emergence of new subjects, new genders, new ethnicities . . . hitherto excluded from the major forms of cultural representation'.[51] He suggests that ethnicities can 'go in both an expansive and a defensive way', engaging with the metropolis from their own distinctive perspective, or retreating into a defensive and dangerous fundamentalism.[52]

In his second talk, 'Old and New Identities', Hall argues that the question of identity has again become crucial, but it cannot be in the form of old identity politics, which has been undermined by Marx's insights on historical constraint, Freud's work on the unconscious, and Saussure's linguistics, not to mention the relativization of the Western episteme and feminism. The 'great collective social identities of class, of race, of nation, of gender, and of the West' have been fragmented and cannot function theoretically for us as we thought they could, as 'master concepts'.[53] Identity needs to be thought of 'as contradictory, as composed of more than one discourse, as composed always across the silences of the other' rather than as 'a sealed or closed totality'.[54] Hall pays tribute to Derrida's insights on *différance*, but, as before, distances himself from American professorial appropriations that turn deconstruction into an 'endless academic game', 'mere playfulness', in which 'everybody has a great time' but which is uncoupled from politics.[55]

What would the cultural politics of the local be, given this new sense of identity? The original kind of identity politics 'had to do with the constitution of some defensive collective identity against the practices of [British] racist society', involving the search for roots, and the production of 'blackness' as a political and cultural category that people identified with, which would not have been the case before. He repeats his earlier claim that only in the 1970s did Jamaicans start to think of themselves as black. In Hall's opinion, this was 'the most profound cultural revolution in the Caribbean, much greater than any political revolution they have ever had'.[56] In Britain, this category provided a useful umbrella for non-white immigrants from South Asia as well as Africa and the Caribbean, in a political struggle against multiculturalism and exoticism. But it also obfuscated some of the specific experiences of Asians, as well as black women and blacks in the underclass.[57] In general, we need to recognize that 'the politics of living identity through difference' requires a realization of our multiple identities, our complex construction, engaged in a Gramscian 'war of position'. The 'politics of manoeuvre' that unites all the locals into one global struggle as the composite revolutionary subject will never happen. Hall refers again to 'My Beautiful Laundrette' as an exemplar of a cultural statement of this multiplicity, complexity, and contradictoriness of the new identity politics.[58] In the question and answer session afterwards, he points out that one day you realize that 'history' or the 'economy' are not going to step in at the last minute and solve your problems, and if you wait for that, you will be waiting forever. 'If you lose enough battles that way, you just do not play that game any more.'[59] But Hall thinks that the Left is 'still waiting for the old identities to return to the stage. It does not recognise that it is in a different political game'.[60]

The Marxist positing of class as central and as able to constitute a 'master-narrative' is thus clearly rejected, while Hall simultaneously draws on *Capital* to explain why we should anticipate that capitalist globalization and market commodification will have contradictory effects. Derrida is cited approvingly, if with some qualifications, while at the same time Gramsci's claims about hegemony and a counter-hegemonic 'war of position' are endorsed. Indeed on the final page Hall suddenly and startlingly declares: 'I remain Marxist.'[61] Moreover, as noted, he distances himself from the excesses and political quietism of much academic postmodernism, and tacitly continues to invoke a meta-narrative, that of imperialism and post-imperialism. So his position is a remarkably eclectic one, and the question obviously raised is the extent to which it is going to be possible to reconcile what must surely in some respects be conflicting theoretical commitments.

His 1991 paper, 'What is this "Black" in Black Popular Culture?' delivered at a conference at the Studio Museum in Harlem, begins with an enthusiastic endorsement of Cornel West's genealogy of the (then) present moment, which Hall sees as significantly convergent with his own analysis. The 'three general coordinates' are the 'displacement of European models of high culture', the 'emergence of the United States as world power and, consequently, as the centre of global cultural production and circulation', and the 'decolonisation of the third world'.[62] He invokes, albeit with major reservations, the idea of the 'global postmodern', which shifts culture towards the popular and is fascinated with exoticized difference, and which has enabled hitherto marginal cultural spaces to become more central. But he warns of the likely backlash in terms of anti-multiculturalism, reaffirmation of the grand narratives, and a resurgence of racism and xenophobia.[63] As with his earlier points about the global and the local, he argues that black popular culture too is necessarily drawn into commodifying processes, but remains nonetheless a site of 'strategic contestation', manifested in style as the subject, the preference for music as against logocentrism, and the use of the body itself as a canvas.[64] Hall asks whether what Gayatri Spivak called 'strategic essentialism' is still appropriate as a strategy, and lists what he sees as several weaknesses: the refusal of dialogic forms and hybridity, the tendency to naturalize and dehistoricize difference, and the naïve privileging of experience as being able to speak for itself, without representation. So it is crucial to recognize the differences within difference, of gender, class, and sexuality, and not endorse monolithic essentialized identities that privilege some blacks over others.[65]

Finally, in his 1997 paper, 'Subjects in History: Making Diasporic Identities', delivered at a conference at Princeton, Hall makes a point of referring to an earlier polemical exchange at the conference between Stephen Steinberg and Cornel West. (Steinberg had accused West of ignoring structural factors in his analysis of underclass problems.) For the benefit of those who had missed it, he repeats his intervention: 'Please remember that questions of culture are not superstructural to the problems of economic and political change; they are constitutive of them!'[66] He goes on to say that 'questions of culture and of representation, of cultural productions, and of aesthetics, politics, and power are of absolute centrality'. Race is best thought of as a Foucauldian discourse and in that capacity it 'organises, regulates, and gives meaning to social practices through the distribution of symbolic and material resources between different groups and the establishment of racial hierarchy'.[67] Meaning is produced through the 'movement of signifiers', so that culture becomes 'absolutely central' because it is on the terrain of culture that identity is produced and social subjects are constituted. One does not appeal to a pre-existing identity, for there are none; rather one struggles to create subjects out of this cultural terrain. 'It isn't that the subjects are there and we just can't get to them. It is that they don't know yet that they are subjects of a possible discourse.'[68] But the danger with race is that the suppressed biological referent is always waiting there beneath the analysis in terms of socio-historical forces, so that when mobilizing for an anti-racist politics, the essentialized black subject tends to raise its head. Though tradition exists as the legacy of a racist history, it has to be reworked to produce black subjects, as in the United States civil rights movement, and as in Jamaica. He refers again to the British experience, and the moment, now past, when 'black' was developed to include non-whites in general, and repeats the points about the world-historical significance of migration patterns and its transformative effect on the First World.[69] He concludes with the following warning:

> It is not, I warn you, because things are going through a little postmodern shake, and then they're going to settle down; then we're going back to the stabilised, well-organised, clearly demarcated frontiers of the past. We are in a new political conjuncture not without racism, not a conjuncture without

difference; it is not a conjuncture without poverty and deprivation and marginalisation on a world scale. But it is one in which the marking of difference, the careful and over-latticed marking of finely drawn distinction, can't be easily convened under a single political roof and fought in a simple battle. It is a much more differentiated, sophisticated, positional kind of battle that has to be developed, to be conducted, if we are serious about refusing its human cost. . . . Words can always be transcoded against you, identity can turn against you, race can turn against you, difference can turn against you, diaspora can turn against you because that is the nature of the discursive. I am trying to persuade you that the word is the medium in which power works.[70]

This could be taken, appropriately, as the last word.

Continuities and Discontinuities

Let us now try to track the continuities and discontinuities in Hall's thought on race over this 20-year period.

First, though it presumably goes without saying, his commitment to the struggle against racist oppression and its legacies obviously remains unaltered and undiminished throughout, whatever his shifting analysis of what the most efficacious forms of that struggle may be. From his early essays onward, Hall's interest in representing race is not an academic one, but linked to the prescriptive: the question is what the best optic is (if there is one) for understanding race so that racism can be combated and a more racially just society brought about. Hall's experience of growing-up as a (darker-skinned) 'brown man' in the class- and colour-structured Jamaica of the 1930s and 1940s, and his later experience of racism as a black man in the England of the 1950s and 1960s, naturally sensitized him directly and personally to these issues, even if they were not a central theme of his work. So there is always a politics of one kind or another implicit or explicit in these writings. The subject of that politics may have changed over the years — may indeed have become a subject yet to be constituted — but the emancipatory purpose has always been the same. So even when he shows himself most sympathetic to postmodernist claims and strategies, he is wary, if not dismissive, of the self-indulgences and academic language-games of university postmodernism. Hall was a prominent signatory of the 2000 Parekh Report on racism in Britain, and, according to Chris Rojek, 'the influence of his ideas on race and identity permeate many of the central recommendations', in what was a 'landmark contribution to the debate on multicultural/multi-ethnic society'.[71]

Relatedly, Hall continues to emphasize the connection between race and broader socio-historical factors and forces, even if the presumed connection between them is now conceived of significantly different in the later writings. Race is not biology, race is not transhistorical, race is not an essence outside of social dynamics and representations, but a social creation, whatever the particular sociological account of those dynamics may be. In his high Althusserian period, race is linked as an interpellating ideology to societies articulated in dominance. In his later, more Derridaean or Foucauldian phase, race is linked with language and discourse. But the reference to European imperialism, to a world constituted through the confrontation between the West and its 'others', to macro changes of immigration and globalization, remains a common note throughout.

Even when, in the early writings, he was closest to Marxism, Hall was emphatic that a crude reductionist Marxism needed to be repudiated: economism was the main target of his critical fire from the start. His enthusiastic endorsement of Althusser's structuralist Marxism was motivated by his conviction that a conception of historical materialism was necessary which would register the distinctive causal efficacy of what were called superstructural regions, and his embrace of Gramsci (perhaps his most consistent reference point over the years) is based on the Italian theorist's unwavering opposition to mechanical Marxism, and insistence on the need for understanding the ideational and cultural realms in their own terms. Thus in the 1996 Scott interview he continues to endorse a Gramscianism of some kind:

> I may be closer to being wholly a Gramscian than anything else, but that is because . . . we have re-invented Gramsci. I have re-invented a kind of non-reductionist, non-Leninist Gramsci . . . a Gramsci that is in touch with Marx's questions but gives culture more seriousness.[72]

To a greater or lesser extent, then, concerns about identity and subjectivity have always been present in his analysis along with the socio-historical claims about environing 'objective' structures, though their salience has obviously become far greater in the later work, and their logic arguably rethought. In the original, more Marxist essays, these concerns are conceptualized through Althusserian interpellation, the ideology that calls to the subject and makes him a subject, identifies him as a being of a certain kind. In the later, more postmodernist essays, these concerns are conceptualized through post-structuralist notions of difference and discourse. But from the start, it has been clear that subjectivity and lived experience are crucial to the theorization of race.

Finally, it should be noted that from beginning to end — and this is a general point, not limited to his work on race — Hall's theoretical perspectives have been marked by an eclecticism, a willingness to draw from a wide range of theorists. Thus in the original essays, as seen, he writes approvingly of John Rex's attempt to synthesize Marx with Weber. In the 1992 interview, he describes how in the early days of the Centre for Contemporary Cultural Studies (CCCS) 'we actually went round the houses to avoid reductionist Marxism. We read Weber, we read German idealism, we read Benjamin, Lukacs. . . . We read ethnomethodology, conversational analysis, Hegelian idealism, iconographic studies in art history, Mannheim; we were reading all of these'.[73] In the later work, this theoretical diversity continues to be manifest, in that he holds on to Gramsci's 'hegemony' and 'war of position' while simultaneously drawing on Derrida and Foucault, and even, as cited earlier, claiming at one stage that he is still a Marxist. So as emphasized in the opening comments, it is less a matter of going from Marxism to postmodernism than of going from one kind of eclecticism to another, with differing elements in the mix being more prominent at different stages.

Let me now turn to what I would see as the crucial differences. Though hedged and qualified in the ways indicated, in the early writings Hall is insistent on the centrality of class, and the characterization of Caribbean societies as class societies. The quote cited previously critiquing M.G. Smith makes this clear. Class is still at this stage a strategic identity for Hall, a master concept that is part of a grand narrative, even if it is not to be thought of in a crude way. In the more recent writings, by contrast, as will have become evident, class, and all other such categorical pretenders, are denied this status. To the extent that class figures in the later writings, it is largely as a factor that needs not to be neglected (for example, the 'underclass') in the conceptualization of black identities, lest a monolithic — and in effect privileged — specifically middle-class black oppositional identity be posited as globally representative of the group. Nor is it the case that the idea of a capitalist class, a bourgeoisie with differential power over Althusser's 'ideological state apparatuses', seems to play any crucial role in overall patterns of social causality. Originally, following Gramsci, this would have been part of a reconceptualization of society in terms of a historical bloc and hegemony rather than in terms of simple overt ruling-class domination. But in the later work, differential capitalist class power as active agency is scarcely mentioned, if it even exists. In terms of a transformative praxis, as Hall emphasizes, waiting for the revolutionary proletariat will be like waiting for Godot.

The commitment to materialism, in the sense of the differential causal significance of economic forces and group interests, is also gone. Whatever its cruder manifestations and vulgarizations, the base/ superstructure relationship is, above all, a representation of causal asymmetry, of the claim that in the overall social picture some varieties of causation are more important than others. In the 1980 essay on societies structured in dominance, Hall rejects as clearly deficient what he sees as the 'monocausality' of economic theories of race, but affirms nonetheless that this school 'is surely correct when it insists that racial structures cannot be understood adequately outside the framework of quite specific sets of economic relations'.[74] Althusserian over- determination was theoretically attractive precisely because it claimed to be able to reconcile multiple social causality with differential economic efficaciousness. But the later Hall no longer has such commitments. Certainly it is not the case that we hear much about economic interests in understanding the logic, the dynamics of construction, of race. Indeed, from an orthodox Marxist perspective (but not only from an orthodox Marxist perspective), many of the postmodernist claims to which Hall is sympathetic would be seen as classically idealist, as attributing to subjectivity and ideation, a causal influence that they do not in fact have. But from a postmodernist view, of course, this very way of putting things, this very 'binary opposition', needs to be transcended, and postmodernists would typically deny that it makes sense to think of things in these terms. Hall's statement that while the extra-discursive exists, it has its meaning only through the discursive, as I earlier suggested, an affirmation of this crucial postmodernist move.

More broadly — though this might just be another way of saying the same thing (depending on how you interpret 'materialism' and 'base') — his present approach is antithetical to structuralist accounts in general. By 'structural' here I do not mean to refer to (long dead) Althusserian structuralist Marxism, but to theories which focus differentially on social institutions, group interests, legal limitations, economic constraints on opportunities, and so forth, in analysing the social dynamic. Hall's emphasis on culture and identity as the Archimedean points of leverage, as manifested in his West-Steinberg intervention, and underwritten by his postmodernist sympathies, preclude such an analysis. So though, as noted, he continues to invoke global social processes, the connection between them and group identity, agency, and political movements is now much looser — has much more 'slack', so to speak — than for more traditional accounts.

The later writings are far more sensitive to the multiplicity of identities within racial identity, which Hall conceptualizes in terms of 'ethnicity'. Of course, even in the earlier essays there is an awareness that 'race' is intertwined with class and colour. But the emphasis on diversity, and on the always-qualified, partial, and conjunctural nature of all identity, is now much more salient.

Finally, though the commitment to radical anti-racist political change remains, the nature of the emancipatory politics involved is, of necessity, now much more fuzzy. This problem is not peculiar to Hall's work, of course, but is rather a general problem for all those who still think of themselves as radicals, but, with the apparent collapse of the socialist ideal, are no longer sure which way is the way forward. Hall's cultural politics of difference is based on the claim that it is on the terrain of subjectivity and the discursive that identities are constructed in the first place.

Problems and Misgivings

I would now like to raise some questions and express some misgivings, which are inevitably shaped to a certain extent by my own experience of having lived for the past 18 years in the United States, and of working for the past ten years or so on race in that particular context.

First, there is Hall's theoretical eclecticism, which is perhaps the single most frequently made point of criticism by commentators in the secondary literature, and which is conceded by Hall himself:

> [S]ome people think it is a problem with me and some people think it is a great merit of mine. I don't think it's either; I think [it's] just how I am — I never have been wholly anything. . . . I use theory in strategic ways. I am not afraid to borrow this idea and try to match it up with this idea borrowed from another paradigm. I am aware of all the dangers of eclecticism and lack of rigour, which there is in my work. My work is open to both those criticisms. But on the other hand it's because I think my object is to think the concreteness of the object in its many different relations.[75]

A principled openness to insights from more than one theoretical tradition bespeaks a commendable open-mindedness. But at what stage does it cease to be a matter of remedying gaps and deficiencies in complementary bodies of thought, and become the taking on of incompatible and contradictory sets of framing assumptions? Is it possible to reconcile Gramscian hegemony, linked to the concept of a historical bloc of classes in dominance, with the Foucauldian notion of an ubiquitous dispersed power? Or to continue to insist on the central role of imperialism in shaping the West versus the Rest while affirming the end of all meta-narratives? Or to invoke as explanatory the commodifying tendencies of global capitalism and simultaneously theoretically marginalize the significance of economic trends and shifting class interests? Or, finally, to claim to be a Marxist in even the weakest sense and yet make so much discursive? How would it ever be possible to operationalize, or to test and verify or falsify, a theoretical mélange with so many conflicting components? Moreover, can the theoretical implications many have seen in post-structuralist claims really be severed from its praxis? As noted above, Hall explicitly distances himself from the excesses of academic postmodernism, and continues to assert the need for an emancipatory anti-racist politics. But are these really 'excesses', or are they natural corollaries of a theory which makes language foundational, which is famous for declaring that there is nothing outside the text, which undercuts the positive agency of the subordinated by its claims about the vanishing of the subject, and which, through its Nietzschean repudiation of classic liberal humanist values, in effect reduces the affirmation of the personhood of the oppressed and their demands for racial justice to no more than the will to power of another discourse? Classic Left politics has certainly proved itself deficient — no argument necessary there — but can you really get any positive reconstructive (as against simply negative and deconstructive) politics out of theorists like Derrida and Foucault, or do their very assumptions lead to the frivolous and sterile academic language-games that Hall decries, and which are so prevalent on the American campus scene?

Hall's 1977 essay is sharply critical of M.G. Smith's plural society thesis for, among other things, placing such explanatory weight on culture. But one might ask whether, a quarter-century later, Hall himself does not over-culturalize social theory. Admittedly, 'culture' is now being conceptualized somewhat differently than in the earlier writings. But it seems to me that in his repudiation of vulgar Marxism and economism, Hall has gone way too far in the opposite direction. In the 1986 interview cited above he warned against 'a [discursive] reductionism upward' that is 'in danger of losing its reference to material practice and historical conditions'.[76] But has he himself not eventually fallen prey to this very 'upward' cultural reductionism? One gets little sense in the later essays of the extent to which race continues to be tied up with unreconstructedly old-fashioned matters of economic privilege and disadvantage, of access to and exclusion from job opportunities and wealth creation, of class mobility and class stasis. In the USA, for example, the creation of a seemingly permanent black 'underclass', with all its predictable consequences for the reinforcement in the white mind of negative racial imagery, has to be understood in the historical context of urban segregation and recent deindustrialization.[77] Although cultural representations of blacks undoubtedly played a role in these processes, their dynamic lies elsewhere, in the evolution of a white supremacist polity in a period of US manufacturing decline. Correspondingly, what is arguably required for social justice is a 'politics of representation' of the old-fashioned kind, demanding not (primarily) cultural change but rather that the state fulfil its obligations as a representative democracy to its non-white citizenry, including the equal protection of their interests and rights so flagrantly denied to blacks throughout US history.

Moreover, the anti-reductivist disconnection of the cultural from the economic on which Hall is so insistent cuts both ways, raising the question of whether a cultural politics aimed at transforming representations, even if successful, will translate into socioeconomic and political equality. After all, US popular culture, and to a significant extent global popular culture, is now to a high degree 'black'. But this striking spread of African-American cultural influence has not meant equal political representation in governing bodies and equal access to opportunities for the black population as a whole. Apart from the inevitable commodification of hip-hop by market forces and corporate interests (an enduring economic connection not so readily severed!), a central cause for this continuing marginalization is that contemporary white racial ideology in the USA is now organized centrally around the concept of 'colour-blindness'. In contrast to the straightforward racist exclusionary biologistic representations of the past, blacks are now conceptually assimilated to the white population, thereby pre-empting the need for any reparative measures to redress their situation. So it is possible for whites, without any sense of contradiction, or any uneasiness of conscience, to think of themselves as anti-racist and dance to hip-hop at night while denying systemic black handicap and holding on to their white privilege by day. The main ideological battle is no longer over putative black inferiority but over the claim that a historically racialized economy continues to reproduce unfair advantage and disadvantage. But that is a battle to be fought in the arenas of sociology, economics, and public policy.[78] Obviously it will involve 'representation' in some sense, in that concepts, claims, and arguments about race will be deployed by both sides, but does it make sense to think of this as primarily a cultural dispute?

Finally, and relatedly, it needs to be remembered that the social constructionist insight of the non-natural character of race does not *ipso facto* imply its volatility. This is an additional claim that only follows from specific supplementary assumptions about what the dynamics of the social are. In other words, the choice is not between biologistic essentialism about race and an unqualified social constructionist lability, since social constructionism itself comes in different varieties, and a materialist — nay, even Marxist! — version of the thesis is possible. In the US context, for example, materialist constructionism would advert to the role of enduring material group interests, for example the startling fact that from 1863 to 1990 black ownership of US wealth rose only from 0.5 per cent to 1 per cent, or that the net worth of the median white household is now an astonishing 14 times the net worth of the median black household.[79] Such huge discrepancies in wealth and resulting life-chances embed racial identities in structures of privilege and disadvantage, generating group-based motivations and attitudes, which are not to be willed away through subjective whim and individual choice. To use lamentably old-fashioned left-wing language, it seems to me that there is often a kind of voluntarism about the way postmodernists represent racial identity creation and choice, ignoring the determining 'weight' of these structures. The language standardly employed of 'contingency' and 'negotiation' exaggerates the space available for genuine options. If it is a contingent historical fact that the country we now know as the USA developed as a white supremacist state, it is not equally contingent that — given this background sociopolitical reality — the choice of racial identities is then constrained in key ways. Certainly (with the minor exception of 'passing') blacks cannot in general choose to be white, given the policing of these boundaries by the racially privileged population. Hall's work is not focused on the black American experience as such, but insofar as his approach is supposed to be generally applicable, I wonder if the emphasis in the later work on 'narratives' and 'subjectivity' does not overstate the extent to which different patterns of racialization are really possible.

Or consider the example he does actually and repeatedly give, that of Jamaica's only having become black, as a positively affirmed identity, in the 1970s. This demonstrates the constructed nature of racial identity, to be sure. But it also indicates, by its timing and incompleteness, the objective basis and objective limits of that construction. To the extent that such a revaluation took place in the period, it is surely linked to larger enabling global historic shifts like post-war decolonization, the (partial) discrediting of racist ideology by the experience of Nazism and the revelations of the death camps, and the influence of the black civil rights struggle in the USA from the 1950s onward. Locally, as Deborah Thomas has recently argued in her fine book on what she calls 'modern blackness' in Jamaica, it was tied (in the 1970s) to a specific political project, viz. the People's National Party's 'more general attempt to position Jamaica's "blackness" and African heritage as bases for new kinds of mobilisation' and thus challenge the previously hegemonic 'creole multiracial nationalism' ('Out of Many, One People') endorsed by the brown elite as the appropriate ideology for independence.[80] Moreover, Thomas emphasizes that this newly affirmed 'blackness' was limited in its scope ('this new focus was not explicitly a black nationalist one'), and was in any case defeated because of the PNP's inability 'to transform the economy' and crushing 1980 electoral rout at the hands of the local elite and their foreign backers.[81] Only in the 1990s, Thomas suggests, has a 'modern blackness' established itself, as a result of 'a confluence of factors', including 'a significant decline in the influence' of middle-class cultural and political brokers, the racial agenda of the black Prime Minister, P.J. Patterson, the growing impact of a diasporic black consciousness, and the displacement by the USA of the lingering 'British colonial class and colour hierarchies'.[82] Thus in Thomas's own summary of her work, she sees her approach as 'situated in relation to a historical political economy of race and nation that is contextualised by changing transnational circuits of ideas, opportunities, and constraints'.[83]

Speaking for myself, I find such an approach, with its reference to socioeconomic changes, group interests (class and race), ideological frameworks, and specific political projects far more congenial and illuminating than a hyper-culturalist post-structuralism. If a class-reductionist political economy has proven itself clearly inadequate to the theorization of the logic of race, it does not follow that a political economy that recognizes racial domination as a system in itself, whether in the USA or in the postcolonial world, is not possible. So from the fact that racial identities are constructed, necessarily involving representation, it does not follow that their evolution cannot be related to legal, political, and economic structures that tend to hold these identities in place, with openings for change created by particular objective conjunctures.

Let me end on a note of appreciation. We are currently in a difficult political period for those seeking a more egalitarian social order, a time of defeat for the Left, with widespread uncertainty about appropriate models for theoretical understanding and emancipatory political practice. Stuart Hall has been grappling courageously with these issues for half a century and we have all benefited from his insights. I hope that my comments will be taken in the spirit both of a tribute to the significance of his work and, where I have been critical, of the need for a principled engagement with it — a testimony to my great respect for his intellectual achievement and major contribution to radical theory.

Notes

1. The bibliography of Hall's work listed in *Stuart Hall: Critical Dialogues in Cultural Studies*, eds. David Morley and Kuan-Hsing Chen (New York: Routledge, 1996), begins with a 1958 article from *Universities* and *Left Review*. However, this listing is apparently only partial, since in David Scott's 1996 interview with Hall, published in *Small Axe* in 1997, Scott refers to articles by Hall on West Indian literature that appeared in *Bim* 'in the middle '50s', and which are not cited by Morley and Chen. See 'Politics, Contingency, Strategy: An Interview with Stuart Hall by David Scott', *Small Axe: A Journal of Criticism*, no. 1 (1997).

2. In chronological order, the nine articles and talks are: 'Pluralism, Race and Class in Caribbean Society', in *Race and Class in Post-Colonial Society: A Study of Ethnic Group Relations in the English-speaking Caribbean, Bolivia, Chile and Mexico*, ed. UNESCO (Paris: UNESCO Publishing, 1977); 'Race, Articulation and Societies Structured in Dominance', in *Sociological Theories: Race and Colonialism*, ed. UNESCO (Paris: UNESCO Publishing, 1980); 'Gramsci's Relevance for the Study of Race and Ethnicity' (1986), reprinted in *Stuart Hall*, eds. Morley and Chen; 'Minimal Selves' (1987), reprinted in *Black British Cultural Studies: A Reader*, eds. Houston A. Baker, Jr., Manthia Diawara, and Ruth H. Lindeborg (Chicago: The University of Chicago Press, 1996); 'New Ethnicities' (1987), reprinted in *Stuart Hall*, eds. Morley and Chen; 'The Local and the Global: Globalisation and Ethnicity' (1989), in *Culture, Globalisation and the World-System: Contemporary Conditions for the Representation of Identity*, ed. Anthony D. King (London: Macmillan, 1991); 'Old and New Identities, Old and New Ethnicities' (1989), in *Culture, Globalisation and the World-System*, ed. A. King; 'What is this "Black" in Black Popular Culture?' (1991), reprinted in *Stuart Hall*, eds. Morley and Chen; 'Subjects in History: Making Diasporic Identities', in *The House that Race Built: Black Americans, U.S. Terrain*, ed. Wahneema Lubiano, (New York: Pantheon Books, 1997). The three interviews are: 'On Postmodernism and Articulation: An Interview with Stuart Hall' (1986), ed. Lawrence Grossberg, reprinted in *Stuart Hall*, eds. Morley and Chen; 'The Formation of a Diasporic Intellectual: An Interview with Stuart Hall by Kuan-Hsing Chen' (1992), in *Stuart Hall*, eds. Morley and Chen; 'Politics, Contingency, Strategy' (1996), *Small Axe*.

3. Chris Rojek, *Stuart Hall* (Malden, Mass: Polity Press/Blackwell Publishing, 2003), 5.

4. Hall, 'Politics, Contingency, Strategy', 143, 146–47.

5. M.G. Smith, *The Plural Society in the British West Indies* [1965] (Reprint, Berkeley and Los Angeles: University of California Press, 1974).

6. Hall, 'Pluralism, Race and Class', 152–59.

7. Ibid., 160.

8.   Ibid., 154.
9.   Ibid., 167.
10.   Ibid., 171.
11.   Ibid., 177, 180.
12.   Ibid.,180.
13.   Hall, *'Race, Articulation and Societies'*, 17–18.
14.   Ibid., 18.
15.   Ibid., 19–20.
16.   Ibid., 20–29.
17.   Ibid., 30–34.
18.   See, for example: Louis Althusser, *For Marx*, trans. Ben Brewster [1969] (Reprint, New York: Verso, 1996); Louis Althusser, *Lenin and Philosophy, and Other Essays*, trans. Ben Brewster [1971] (Reprint, New York: Monthly Review Press, 2001); Louis Althusser and Etienne Balibar, *Reading Capital*, trans. Ben Brewster [1970] (Reprint, New York: Verso, 1997).
19.   Hall, *'Race, Articulation and Societies'*, 35–43.
20.   Karl Marx, *Grundrisse: Foundations of the Critique of Political Economy*, trans. Ben Brewster [1973] (Reprint, New York: Penguin Classics, 1993).
21.   Hall, *Race, Articulation and Societies'*, 45–48.
22.   Antonio Gramsci, *Selections from the Prison Notebooks*, ed. and trans. Quintin Hoare and Geoffrey Nowell Smith [1971] (Reprint, New York: International Publishers, 1999).
23.   Hall, *Race, Articulation and Societies'*, 56–57.
24.   Hall, 'Politics, Contingency, Strategy', 147, 149–50, 151–52.
25.   Hall, 'On Postmodernism and Articulation', 148–49.
26.   Ernesto Laclau and Chantal Mouffe, *Hegemony and Socialist Strategy: Towards a Radical Democratic Politics*, trans. Winston Moore and Paul Commack (London: Verso, 1985).
27.   Hall, 'On Postmodernism and Articulation', 146.
28.   Ibid., 145–47.
29.   Hall, 'Gramsci's Relevance', 411–12.
30.   Ibid., 413–15.
31.   Ibid., 415–17.
32.   Ibid., 417–20.
33.   Ibid., 420–28.
34.   Ibid., 428–30.
35.   Ibid., 430–34.
36.   Ibid., 435–40.
37.   Hall, 'Minimal Selves', 114.
38.   Ibid., 115.
39.   Ibid.
40.   Ibid., 116.
41.   Ibid., 118.
42.   Ibid., 117.
43.   Ibid., 118.
44.   Hall, 'New Ethnicities', 441–42.
45.   Ibid., 442–44.
46.   Ibid., 449.
47.   Ibid., 443.
48.   Hall, 'The Local and the Global', 20–22.
49.   Ibid., 23–28.
50.   Ibid., 29–32.
51.   Ibid., 33–34.

52. Ibid., 35–39.
53. Hall, 'Old and New Identities', 42–44.
54. Ibid., 49.
55. Ibid., 50.
56. Ibid., 52–54.
57. Ibid., 55–57.
58. Ibid., 57–60.
59. Ibid., 63–64.
60. Ibid., 64–65.
61. Ibid., 68.
62. Hall, 'What is this "Black" in Black Popular Culture?', 465.
63. Ibid., 466–69.
64. Ibid., 469–70.
65. Ibid., 472–74.
66. Hall, 'Subjects in History', 289.
67. Ibid., 290.
68. Ibid., 291.
69. Ibid., 292–96.
70. Ibid., 298–99.
71. Chris Rojek, Stuart Hall, 48–59, 182, 196.
72. Hall, 'Politics, Contingency, Strategy', 151.
73. Hall, 'The Formation of a Diasporic Intellectual', 499.
74. Hall, 'Race, Articulation and Societies', 19.
75. Hall, 'Politics, Contingency, Strategy', 151–52.
76. Hall, 'On Postmodernism and Articulation', 145–47.
77. See, for example, Douglas S. Massey and Nancy A. Denton, *American Apartheid: Segregation and the Making of the Underclass* (Cambridge, Mass: Harvard University Press, 1993).
78. See, for example: Melvin L. Oliver and Thomas M. Shapiro, *Black Wealth/ White Wealth: A New Perspective on Racial Inequality* (New York: Routledge, 1995); Eduardo Bonilla-Silva, *Racism without Racists: Color-Blind Racism and the Persistence of Racial Inequality in the United States* (Lanham, Md: Rowman & Littlefield, 2003); Ashley W. Doane and Eduardo Bonilla-Silva, eds., *White Out: The Continuing Significance of Racism* (New York: Routledge, 2003); Michael K. Brown, Martin Carnoy, Elliott Currie, Troy Duster, David B. Oppenheimer, Marjorie M. Shultz, and David Wellman, *Whitewashing Race: The Myth of a Color-Blind Society* (Berkeley and Los Angeles: University of California Press, 2003).
79. Dalton J. Conley, *Being Black, Living in the Red: Race, Wealth, and Social Policy in America* (Berkeley and Los Angeles: University of California Press, 1999), 25; 'Study Says White Families' Wealth Advantage Has Grown', *New York Times* (October 18, 2004): A13.
80. Deborah A. Thomas, *Modern Blackness: Nationalism, Globalisation, and the Politics of Culture in Jamaica* (Durham, NC: Duke University Press, 2004), 77, 11.
81. Ibid., 77–78.
82 Ibid., 12.
83. Ibid., 8.

PART III

Caribbean Contingencies

8 | Unspeakable Worlds and Muffled Voices: Thomas Thistlewood as Agent and Medium of Eighteenth-Century Jamaican Society[1]

Cecilia Green

Introduction

The approach to history has tended to be bimodal — imposition from above or resistance from below, hegemony and oppression or autonomy and resistance. This is not to deny that many historians, perhaps most nowadays, have abandoned the either/or approach for a more fruitful both/and framework. Rather, the point is that even the both/and approach has too often fallen into a pattern of expository juxtaposition or side-by-side narration, and has not adequately pursued efforts to weave a more complex tapestry constituted by analytical and sociohistorical mediation and relationality. Of course, because of the longstanding bias towards History of and by Great, Powerful, and/or Evil Men, there has been a concerted counter-assertion of histories, with a small 'h', of the subaltern, who both resists and evinces relative ontological, cultural and even economic autonomy. However, the latter corrective has been itself sometimes unable to avoid falling into the all-or-nothing trap, going too singlemindedly in the direction of voluntarism, autonomy and resistance. Such an overemphasis eventually begins to negate the very basis of the concepts of power and domination and therefore of resistance itself. Why, if s/he were so self-determined, would the energies of the 'subaltern' be so taken up with resistance?

The study of slavery has been beset by all these problems, now emphasizing hegemony/erasure/social death (and totality), now insisting on the transcendence of resilience/retention/resistance (and plurality). In an early and brilliant sociological analysis that addresses the dialectic between centripetal and centrifugal forces dynamizing Caribbean social structure, Stuart Hall points out that the 'plural society' model of M.G. Smith, despite the promise inherent in its recognition of diversity, fails to account for hegemonic unity or the 'structure in dominance'. The model essentializes, absolutizes and freezes difference, and (therefore) can secure unity only through naked instrumental force. But, Hall reminds us, '[m]ost societies with complex social structures achieve their "unity" via the relations of domination/ subordination between culturally different and class differential strata.'[2] The plural model is devoid of the critical (and particular, Gramscian) concept of hegemony, 'which secures the unity, cohesion and stability of [the] social order in and through (not despite) its "differences"'.[3] Even the violently assembled systems of West Indian slavery, therefore resulted in societies which cohered on the basis of 'complexity-and-unity' mechanisms: 'To put it crudely, the "world" of the slave house and the village and the "world" of the plantation great house are two socio-cultural "worlds" which form differentiated parts of a single socioeconomic system: they are not plural segments of parallel but distinct cultures.' After all, '[w]hat matters is not simply the plurality of their internal structures, but the articulated relation between their differences'.[4]

Just as Hall 'puts it crudely' in thinking broadly — and abstractly — about slave societies, he cannot deny that the crudely empiricist Smithian plural society model has great resonance in its empirical details. He does allow that 'the Caribbean example is distinct, not because there is class-cultural differentiation, but because (a) this class-cultural differentiation is peculiarly sharp, and because (b) it is coincident to a high degree with race/colour stratification'. However, despite the enduring brilliance of Hall's judicious critique of the plural model,[5] he never really resolves this matter of the Caribbean's distinctiveness or 'difference' or 'peculiarity'. In his discussion of Caribbean slave societies he quotes approvingly Lowenthal's statement that 'creolisation' was essentially a bastardization (my word) of European culture; that, having been stripped of their ethnic identities, African slaves 'were forced to undergo creolisation', so that '[s]lave culture became in large measure a creolised form of European culture'.[6] This is where Hall's broad sweep begins to ride roughshod over the complexities of colonial slave systems and the dialectical cultural processes on the ground, and does so despite his claims regarding 'a complexly structured social formation, rather than a simple, unitary, expressive totality'.[7] He fails to heed his own indispensable advice that

> [i]t does not help, here, to depress some factors of this matrix, e.g. race/colour, class, in favour of others, e.g. culture, and then, analytically, to subsume the former into the latter, since it is precisely the generative specificity of each, plus the over-determined complexity of the whole, which is the problem.[8]

Where Smith depresses race and class in favour of culture (and subsumes the former into the latter), Hall seems to depress culture/ethnicity in favour of race and class and to subsume the former into the latter. Hall seems considerably less interested in the relative autonomy of these differentiated class/ethnic cultures than in the question of unidirectional 'cultural power', 'hegemony', and 'legitimation'.

His paradigm begs several questions. What is this 'European culture' of which he and Lowenthal speak (that is, what are the circumstances of its transplantation and functional transformation in an entirely new social order)? What about the dislocations and spatial rupture of, not just African, but also European cultures? What about the (vast majority of) enslaved Africans as themselves agents of creolization? What are the implications of the difference (and dislocation) between institutional/formal culture and expressive/informal culture? And what about 'inter/culturation'[9] or the reciprocal action of European and African cultures upon one other? Is the Gramscian concept of hegemony, superbly mobilized by Hall at the broader theoretical level (the level of the totality), well served by his apparent unidirectional thrust at the level of cultural process on the ground?

This structuralist flattening on the part of Hall — so effective as critique — seems to be at odds with his later poststructuralist incursions into the unsettled question of identity or identities, especially in an age of globalization. But is it? Hall's entry point into the conversation about identities of postmodernity has been very much from the location that has served as the authoritative source or point of reference for the formation of those assumed stable identities of modernity and the nation state whose more recent decentring and destabilization have been the occasion for the launching of the conversation in the first place. Of course, as Hall himself is the first to point out, this stability and supreme self-certainty had always been sustained (indeed, had been founded in large part) on the basis of the violent and traumatic displacement and decentring of the Other, both internally and externally. It is within this larger framework of the more recently experienced dislocations of contemporary globalization that Hall has returned to 'address questions of Caribbean culture'.[10] Like C.L.R. James and Sidney Mintz before him, he suggests that the Caribbean was present at the birth of modernity, as both modernity's other and as the other modern or 'another kind of modernity'. For Hall, '[t]he Caribbean is the first, the original and the purest Diaspora.'[11] Others have named it the earliest laboratory of so-called postcolonial hybridity or the first postmodern social formation. Hall's idea that the destabilization of the nation state has led to identities that are at once global and local[12] strikes a chord with those familiar with Caribbean history, so deeply implicated in the core processes of globalization, yet so trivialized by sojourners from the privileged centre as mere 'local colour'.

But that is just the point. While this destabilization is hailed for 'real' societies as their grand postmodern moment, it is vaguely evoked for the Caribbean as its enduring and ahistorical condition. It seems to me that despite the powerful insights of both Hall's earlier and more structuralist take on the Caribbean and his later more poststructuralist musings, the Caribbean qua Caribbean continues to evade our understanding, lost somewhere between the immeasurable global and the quaint local and lacking its own mediated solidity. In the end, the Caribbean is summoned up as a ghost-like impression that is compelling only because it provides an amenable historical symbol for the violent rupture of modernity and the recombinant fragmentation of postmodernity. Hall is far too sophisticated and careful to be guilty of this, but his generalizations sometimes seem to provide an opening for this kind of intellectual practice. In his discussion of Caribbean identities, for example, Hall sees the Caribbean mainly through the (masculinist) eyes of those who project their own identities as mediated through an existential-intellectual process of metaphorization writ large, like Fanon, like Césaire, like the Rastafarians, and like Hall himself.[13] The point, of course, is not to deny the tremendous insight contained therein.

It has been too easy, therefore, to see the Caribbean as a metaphor for something else, for angst-ridden 'global' processes rather than as its own specific historical and social formation. The Caribbean as metaphor, the Caribbean as myth: in the long run this becomes a sanitized version of reality and a way of avoiding the tough, messy, painful task of understanding and sociologically constructing the Caribbean as a set of 'real' societies, instead of somebody else's fantasy, somebody else's playground or production platform, or everybody's favourite metaphor. I believe that, at the very point where many in the privileged centre are inclined to eschew history, the Caribbean needs to find its feet, to understand what structures have sustained it, both to figure out where to go from here and to resist with all the 'secrets' of its pent-up and sometimes unspeakable past the pervasive and terroristic amnesia of imperialism. I suspect that Hall would agree with me.

In this chapter, as part of an exercise in sociohistorical grounding, I consider the case of Thomas Thistlewood (T), whose prodigious eighteenth-century daily journals, recorded over a span of 30-plus years, have provided us with unique insight into the inner world of plantation Jamaica.[14] The journals offer the self-recorded life of one embedded deep within the entrails of that society, and whose biographical zenith synchronized almost perfectly with Jamaica's period of colonial pre-eminence. The other reason Thistlewood's journal is especially significant and fascinating has to do with his particular location within the social and spatial circuits making up the complex cartography of empire and colony, the global and the local. Moreover, the journal is unique in the subject position(s) to which it gives expression and in its recording of a central agency or firsthand role in the daily enactment and reproduction of white Creole (sub-) hegemony and local plantation society.

A study of Thistlewood's role allows one to both tap into Hall's penetrating sociological and proto-sociological insights and do the kind of reconstruction which is suggested but not attempted, and not fully addressed, in his work. This kind of study, which is only preliminarily tackled here, might contribute to both a grounded sociohistorical construction of Caribbean society as 'mediated solidity' and a better understanding of embedded hegemony as part of the formation of neoteric West Indian societies. The figure of Thistlewood (and his kind) defies the either/or approach which sees West Indian history as either remote and untouchable European imposition or local enslaved

African resistance. Despite his unflagging attachment to an imagined England, he represents a rupture with the Motherland in a different but no less certain way than that in which the enslaved and creolized Africans represent a rupture with Mother Africa. He is also a key agent in the domiciling or embedding or internalizing of colonialism in West Indian social structures, so that colonialism can never be thereafter something 'out there'. Moreover, it is not just the process of deracination, transplantation and functional displacement that creolizes him, but the fact that his encounter with the New World of Jamaica is mediated by his dependence upon and acculturation by enslaved Africans and the web that is woven by his subsequent brutal and intimate relations with them.

Beyond studying Thistlewood as master, disciplinarian, patriarch, and sexual predator, this chapter shifts its attention to the female protagonists of Thistlewood's black domestic network, centred on Phibbah, his slave 'wife'. As such, I am concerned to show how Phibbah is both object and re-agent of hegemony, and how she humanizes Thistlewood, as well as is dehumanized by him. Finally, Thistlewood's patronage and Afro-Caribbean women's ingenuity, agency, and deployment of Africanist cultural resources help to generate an entire subaltern economy upon which the local centre comes to depend. I suggest that this (among other things) demonstrates how intimacy is both predatory/parasitic and productive/creative of new forms of power. In the end, I want to insist that it would be as much a mistake to underestimate the role of Thistlewood (and his kind) — as master and intimate, and a key vector of localized and creolized hegemony — as it would be to forget the unremitting resistance particularly of those most marginalized and whose voices are most muffled in Thistlewood's text.

Distance and Intimacy in the Production of Empire

Even if one forces Thistlewood's diaries into a more general genre of testimonial texts, I see all varieties of those not just as sources of information, however dangerously biased, but also as excavated fragments of the social relations of the societies they capture in text. In other words, these testimonials not only furnish salvageable evidentiary details of the day-to-day life processes of plantation society at the time, but, as hegemonic or sub-hegemonic frames — as exhumed social constructions of knowledge, so to speak — they also represent and embody aspects of the contemporary relations of race, class, patriarchy, and empire. But of course not all testimonials are the same, and one of the key things I want to establish here is Thistlewood's difference, as the postmodernists would have it, or his historical and social specificity, in older Marxist parlance.

It is important to make a distinction and maintain a dialogue between those who officially authorize social relations and those who intimately 'author' them. There are also those who wishfully or ideologically imagine them, sometimes with neither authority nor direct participation, but from safe and sanitized distances. The British Empire, in its metropole-colony configuration, comprised a complex circuitry of serially interlinked, crosscutting sets of relations which operated at a variety of spatial scales, from the most intimate to the most remote. It was constituted through a variable set of encounters among metropolitans, locals (including transplants), and translocals, these encounters usually tracked within distinct and intersecting socio-spatial circuits and niches. At the same time that we maintain a distinction (though not an absolute one) between the official story line or other forms of wishful metropolitan thinking and the intimate enactment of warm-bodied colonial life on the ground, we want to understand how the intimate is itself thoroughly imbricated in the production of a hegemonic regime, or how it becomes the theatre for the enactment of hegemony and the normalization and routinization of violence and brutality. Simply put, how does intimacy localize empire and help reproduce historically unique West Indian Creole societies? The idea therefore is to understand how the local is produced, and how the dialectic of brutality and intimacy by which it is configured becomes normalized and shaped into its own historic form — one which is typically unimaginable on its own terms by the metropolitan mind, either of the pro-slavery or anti-slavery variety.

An example may suffice. Adam Smith, who never set foot in the West Indies, placed the enslaved African female, as brute agent, at the generative core of the alleged moral chaos and widespread sexual promiscuity of West Indian slave society. At the height of the plantocratic regime of slavery in the Caribbean, he asserted with absolute proprietary confidence: 'Among our slaves in the West Indies there is no such thing as a lasting union. The female slaves are all prostitutes and suffer no degradation by it.'[15] Writing in the years after slavery, whose demise he had witnessed first-hand in Jamaica, the British Baptist missionary James Phillippo judges that society through a very different moral and discursive lens. He avers that '[c]oncubinage was almost universal, embracing nine-tenths of the male inhabitants'. Moreover, nowhere in his account does he leave room for doubt that the 'unblushing licentiousness' which pervaded the colony was centred in the white male group, following a chain of command 'from the Governor downwards throughout all the intermediate ranks of society'. Indeed, '[n]early every one down to the lowest white servant had his native female companion'.[16] It is white men who suffered no social degradation as a consequence of their blatant transgressions of the most dearly held tenets of respectable European society. For Phillippo, the painstakingly slow moral reformation that became evident in the post-emancipation period was marked most significantly by the decline in cross-racial concubinage and the increase in (endogamous) marriage among various sectors of the population. James Phillippo and Adam Smith brought to bear two different and somewhat contradictory traditions in the making of Western society: impassioned Christian enlightenment and universalist humanism (with an anesthetized homo Europus at the epicentre of humanity) on the one hand and ruthless (that is, rational) and impersonal capitalist logic based on the imperatives of an international and interracial division of labour on the other. But while these were critical ingredients at the fluid intersection of the local and the global, always available (in varying degrees of force) in the ongoing work of the reconstruction of the local, they obviously did not comprehend the core of local subject formation and the lived dialectic of local social relations. So one might ask, how did people negotiate on the ground the relentless inevitability of imperial political economy on the one hand and the promise of Christian fraternity on the other? But, even more critically, how did local life take shape in ways altogether unimagined by these two grand visions and imperializing projects? How did the actuality of local life subvert the paradigmatic constructs of the African-Caribbean woman as 'natural' prostitute and beast of burden on the one hand and innocent and helpless victim on the other?

Between the outerworlds of Adam Smith and James Phillippo, therefore, a number of more or less submerged and spatially dislocated innerworlds await discovery: those of Thomas Thistlewood — son of the middling yeomanry, a casualty of the law of primogeniture in his native Lincolnshire, denied the respectability of a proper/tied match — who reinvents himself as a petty colonial overlord in the violently racialized new world of Jamaica; of Phibbah, his slave 'wife' for over 30 years, who humanizes him — somewhat — and becomes herself an important mediating link in a complex network of inter- and intra-class transactions and subaltern economy; of Coobah, her daughter, who travels to England with her mistress and is christened Jenny Young, introducing obscure, groping aspirations towards half-baked versions of Christianity and western respectability (and systems of signification) among eighteenth-century enslaved Africans still grounded in relatively autonomous Africanist cultural practices; of their son, Mulatto John, who receives the twin privileges of freedom and schooling, but resists the prison of his in-betweenness and his father's determination to discipline him into that unfamiliar and ill-fitting frame. Indeed, there is also Susannah Strickland, white British author and abolitionist sympathizer, transcriber and ghost writer of Mary Prince's story (as told to her in London), who edits out of the script — exquisitely honed to middle-class British sensibilities — the contaminating revelations 'about living for seven years with a Captain Abbott prior to her marriage, about whipping another woman she found in bed with the captain, and about living with another man out of wedlock'.[17] Then there is the private agony of Mary Prince herself, caught between the searing loneliness of a double transatlantic displacement and the symbolic sacrifice of her life as a public abolitionist mascot.

Thistlewood's Jamaica

Thistlewood arrived in a Jamaica that was at the height of its profitability and profligacy. In fact, the first 25 years of his 36-year sojourn in Jamaica overlapped exactly with the third quarter of the eighteenth century, considered to be Jamaica's 'Golden Age of Sugar', and described by Craton and Walvin[18] as a time of 'fantastic prosperity'. It was also a time of unrestrained white Creole hegemony and a relatively impermeable and autonomous local despotism as yet unassailed by the barely nascent transatlantic discourses of pragmatic amelioration, religious and secular humanism, abolitionism, and free trade. The wealth of the upper strata of the Jamaican plantocracy was phenomenal. Burnard, in his recent book on Thistlewood, has provided us with some eye-popping figures which (despite obfuscating mathematical 'averaging') easily put our protagonist Thistlewood in perspective and infuse the term 'lesser white' with new meaning:

> On the eve of the American Revolution, white Jamaicans were among the wealthiest subjects in the British Empire. In 1774, per capita white wealth was £2,201, with white men having average wealth amounting to £4,403. By contrast, wealth per free white was £42.1 sterling in England and Wales, £60.2 in the thirteen colonies, and just £38.2 in New England. The average white in Jamaica was 36.6 times as wealthy as the average white in the thirteen colonies, 52.3 times as wealthy as the average white in New England. The richest Jamaicans had holdings that would have been emulated only by the wealthiest London merchants and English aristocrats.[19]

During Thistlewood's time, whites accounted for between six and eight per cent of the total population. Moreover, this group was predominantly male, young, and migrant, adult men outnumbering adult women by over two to one.[20] The white population was skewed towards immigrant single male subalterns partly as a result of absenteeism among the upper ranks of the plantocracy and the tendency to recruit, prefer or require unmarried men as overseers and other lesser plantation surrogates. The demographic structure of Britain's West Indian colonies can primarily be explained by their classification as non-residentiary colonies of exploitation and their economic administration through surrogacy. In 1730 in Jamaica, according to one source, 76.2 per cent of the white population, which itself comprised only 6.6 per cent of the entire population of the island, were servants, 'usually working as bookkeepers or overseers on plantations'.[21] Thistlewood, a fortune-seeking and unattached 29-year-old, seemed a perfect candidate for the role he was about to occupy.

The social space of the West Indian planter class was therefore transnationally split. In one recurring version, the transnational split was accommodated entirely by proxy, with the proprietors remaining in the metropole and their second-class surrogates presiding over their plantations and replicating the dualism of the system on their behalf. Overseers on absentee-owned plantations were 'master[s] of the place',[22] whereas bookkeepers, in spite of the authority of immediate, everyday tyranny they sometimes held over blacks, were typically among the poorest and least powerful whites. As pointed out before, single status was usually stipulated as a condition of employment in the contracts of the white overseers and bookkeepers, for whom these positions were expected to act as stepping stones to bigger and better things. This (or, frequently, the absence of the resident proprietor's wife), in conjunction with the rigid taboo on interracial marriage and the ready availability of exploitable slave women in predominantly black surroundings, practically ensured the proliferation of a system of concubinage, whereby a selected slave — or a free coloured — woman was brought into the (real or surrogate) master's house as a live-in 'housekeeper' and mistress. The 'housekeeper system' was so common that it was euphemistically referred to as the 'custom of the country'.

But even where white wives were present, the system of concubinage flourished. White planters often became the mediating biological link between two (or more) sets of families, helping to reproduce two different classes either simultaneously (usually, but not always, involving multiple residences) or sequentially (perhaps beginning — or resuming — their legal marital careers after going 'home' to England). R.T. Smith refers to this as the 'dual marriage system', noting that '[from] the beginning of the development of the slave regime, a marriage system was in place that included both legal marriage and concubinage, a system in which the elements were mutually and reciprocally defining and which articulated with the racial hierarchy'.[23] The 'dual marriage system' racialized the age-old pattern of sexualization of the class hierarchy (or class-based ranking of sexuality) within gender groups, so that the madonna/whore ideological dichotomy of feudal Europe gave way in the Caribbean to the symbolism of the White Madonna and the Black whore, placing the ideological correlation between race and sexuality on an enduring footing.

The so-called 'dual marriage system' potentially or actually generated two race/class lines — one legitimate, the other illegitimate — with the white master as common genitor (reproducing white paterfamilial propriety on the one hand, Afro-Creole matrifocality on the other).

Just as marriage came to be an exclusive property of the very wealthy and a mechanism for the transnational reproduction of the Euro-Creole upper class, concubinage came to be the means by which a 'bastard' intermediate class was bequeathed to the societies of the West Indies by the planters and their surrogates as the social superiors of the slaves and, later, of the black working class. But 'dual marriage', involving simultaneous access to white wives and black concubines, was not an option for subaltern white men, and, indeed, not all the liaisons that produced these 'bastard scions' had the same social standing. Thistlewood himself became the protagonist of two other informally institutionalized or normalized forms of master–slave sexual encounters: those involving the almost routine and often random selecting and summoning of different enslaved women at different times to the beds of Thistlewood and his overseer or planter colleagues, depending on their sexual appetites of the moment. And those involving a more permanent and potentially life-long relationship with a favoured slave mistress, like the one into which Thistlewood eventually settled with Phibbah. Both types of liaison were fraught with danger for enslaved women and involved varying levels of compulsion and humiliation, but the latter type could go beyond the resigned and strategically accommodative participation of the chosen mate to engage elements of productive initiative, encouragement, manipulation, and desire on her part.

Thistlewood's first appointment in Jamaica is as overseer of Vineyard Pen, a livestock farm, in St. Elizabeth. He remains there from July 1750 to July 1751. Thistlewood is the only supervisory white over a workforce of 40 enslaved Africans. Conditions there are modest and the Africans teach Thistlewood about the local flora and fauna, fruit, foodstuff and cuisine. Marina, a field slave, becomes his slave wife, completing his initiation into Jamaican society. For one year Thistlewood lives in a completely black world, depending on the slaves for his everyday physical needs and knowledge of the Jamaican landscape, labour culture, and a firsthand introduction to African and Afro-Caribbean customs. Weeks went by without sight of another white person. In his chronicles, Thistlewood emerges as a kind of déclassé self-invented character, moving intimately — and increasingly with the power of a petty patriarch — abroad in the social underworld, both in London and in Jamaica.

Next he accepts the position of overseer on William Dorrill's struggling sugar plantation, Egypt, at a salary of £60 per annum. He starts September 1751. This offer came just in time because he was planning to go to Hispaniola with Captain Riviere de la Bruce to learn how to make indigo. (22) At Egypt, Thistlewood wastes no time in claiming his at-large *droit de seigneur* with regard to the hapless female slaves. He gets his first dose of the clap (in his own words) at the end of his first month at Egypt. After several months of availing himself of his pick of the sexual labour force, he appears to abandon all pretensions and dreams of ever attaining wedded respectability or a sentimental love match with a European woman when he gets rid of a small memento of his unsuccessful suit prior to his departure from London. He throws away the ivory fish, a small gift, given to him by Elizabeth ('Bett') Mitchell. He also records a growing infatuation with Jenny, one of the slaves, on whom he had already begun showering gifts. His fondness for Jenny does not stop him from crudely gratifying his sexual urges with random others that are forced to render anonymous, short and brutish sexual service. These encounters — or ambushes — are obsessively reported in terse one-liners. The women are typically given two bitts for their troubles, although some favoured women received more and those less favoured, less.

With Jenny, as later with Phibbah, his words reveal the much more nuanced complexity of a kind of courtship, complete with the ritualistic and volatile swings of deepening emotional and sexual tension, as well as glimmers of rough tenderness. There is a suggestion that Jenny has a son by Thistlewood, for whom he does not evince any paternal feeling, as he does, in his usual minimalist style, for 'Phibbah's son' later.

Here I want to interrupt the early chronology of Thistlewood's life in Jamaica to turn to the socially inflected biography(ies) elliptically captured in his dense, voluminous journals. Generally, the latter speak to us of two worlds: the predominantly homosocial world of dominant (both 'greater' and 'lesser') white men and the overwhelmingly African world over which he presides with routine and unremitting brutality, but which he also shares, however unevenly, in an intimate and sometimes startlingly mundane domestic arrangement with Phibbah, an Afro-Creole house slave. How does Thistlewood reinvent himself as a white Creole, thereby carrying out the performative requirements of localized empire — the purveyance of tenaciously imagined

Englishness, dislocated hybridity, and near absolute local hegemony? How does he morph into a white West Indian and what kind of white West Indian does he become? How does he (help to) produce a hybridic new world while simultaneously reproducing the British empire at large?

Thistlewood could be described as a naturalized local or localized transplant. He becomes a key vector of the social order, occupying a place at the crossroads of several socio-spatial circuits and comprising — through his various practices and the paths that he cuts through relatively uncharted territory — a link between different segments of the social structure. In his unsentimental and unblinking way, he appears to make himself up as he goes along, and in so doing helps to construct, routinize, and normalize the deeply traumatic social structure. Lest I appear to be attributing too much agency or too much uniqueness to Thistlewood, I want to stress that it is his complex and heterogeneous status as a lesser or 'not quite' social white/local master/intimate of black slave elite/producer of domestic economy and facilitator of subaltern economy — combining ultimate dominion, ultimate prohibitions, and an autonomous and creative local life force — that makes his life such an illuminating one for our purposes. The process of negotiation through which he painstakingly accomplishes (some) social mobility also sheds light on the social structural components that are being manoeuvred, or that work in his favour.

Master and Patriarch: Reproducing White/Black Subalternity

Thistlewood thus acts as a mediator/link and traverser between two worlds, the predominantly homosocial world of white men without, or unaccompanied by, white wives and the world of enslaved and sexualized black men and women. His role in each world is contradictory and complex. He is a lesser white but he is at the same time socially respected (because of his skills and, presumably, his robust sense of self), socially aspirant, and slowly socially mobile. He is in great demand as a superior sort of overseer, and even before becoming a proprietor himself, he is entrusted with the responsibilities of attorney for the estate of a temporarily absent proprietor, one of the most lucrative and sought after appointments among resident whites. (133) Having accumulated a small force of slaves and capital while still an overseer, he eventually becomes proprietor of a small non-sugar property — a 'pen', which reproduces a genuinely domestic sub-economy in the interstices of the dominant colonial-export economy. For the upper plantocracy, this kind of enterprise is merely ancillary to their great sugar estates, but Thistlewood is able to transcend the stigma of subsidiarity through the skilful cultivation of his farm into a much admired horticultural showpiece and paying local concern. As a successful horticulturalist and pen-keeper he supplies vegetables, flowers, livestock and game for grand social occasions, at most of which he is not himself among the invited guests.

Perhaps one of the more surprising things we learn from Thistlewood's diary is how much authority is exercised by the overseer, as resident master, over the white subordinates below him. Thistlewood's management authority in this regard extends not just to the strict terms of their employment but to their moral and sexual conduct as well, especially in relation to the estate slave labour force, the most precious of estate property. He wields the ultimate power of patriarchal arbitration over both the white underlings and the male and female slaves. He approves, makes, and breaks matches (including both white/black and black/black couplings), arbitrates sexual conflicts between male rivals over women, upholds the sexual and conjugal claims of one against the other(s), settles sexual grievances, denies predatory sexual rights over the female slaves to certain white subordinates, sets and polices the boundaries of mate selection or sexual pursuit, punishes women who cuckold their mates, punishes men who beat women beyond acceptable limits, and women who beat other women in contests over men, settles conjugal conflicts between opposite-sex mates, and of course reserves to himself the absolute right of access to any female slave, unmitigated by prior claims, including claims freshly upheld by him in favour of a successful claimant against interlopers.

Over the course of his tenure at Egypt, he has cause to either approve or thwart the designs of members of his white staff regarding both transient sexual opportunities and more lasting 'housekeeper' relationships with enslaved women. Given the high turnover of estate staff most of the relationships turn out to be transient (but not necessarily un-reproductive, potentially expanding the master's property and reinforcing in yet another way the matrifocality of the slaves' niche).

Sometimes his authority derives more clearly from direct ownership of the slave in question. In late 1762, he gives his assent to the partnering of the new driver, Robert Gibbs, a Barbadian, with his slave Nanny. (127) On December 1, a second white driver, an Irishman, Christopher White, was hired. He 'makes a match' with Egypt Susanah. Nanny's next 'keeper', another white man, Patrick May, stayed only six days. He came home drunk on the evening of May 23, 1763, 'quarrelled with Nanny whom he kept, and shot her with small shot, one of which struck her head near the top, and the other her ankle, both these shots seem to be lodged'. (128) T dismisses him. A previous employee, James Rogers, leaves after being reprimanded for assaulting the slaves in the field while drunk. (124) All this happens while Thistlewood is overseer at Egypt. He mentions without comment other bids by white workers to take enslaved 'wives'. But sometimes he steps in to prevent what he sees as inappropriate or injurious couplings. He is particularly averse to the risk posed by white drunkenness — an endemic feature of plantation life — to slave property and to his own authority. He denies the right of certain white underlings to prey upon the female slaves at will. For example, he 'reprimanded Henry MacCormick for frequenting the Negro houses in the night'. (140) But his objections might be much more focused and specific. His nephew John Thistlewood, who has joined him from England in early February 1764, has made himself unpopular by pursuing Little Mimber, the wife of the driver Johnnie. Hall comments that this liaison 'was strongly resented by her "husband" driver Johnnie. Thomas Thistlewood also raised objections, seemingly unwilling to allow Johnnie to be deprived of his woman. Several times he warned his nephew to keep away, and on each such occasion he severely punished Little Mimber'. (132)

Tragedy strikes John Thistlewood, and, though neither Hall nor Thistlewood himself speculates on the matter, one wonders whether foul play was involved. He goes off by himself on a shooting trip up the river and is found drowned a day later. That same evening, Thistlewood hears the sounds of guns being fired in a celebratory salute in the slave quarters and assumes it is 'for joy that my Kinsman is dead'. 'Strange impudence,' he observes. (133) In establishing his authority and superior sense of self over white subordinates (many of whom are, to compound matters, Irish or non-English British), Thistlewood implicitly holds up a particular standard of robust white manhood —

sober, industrious, and in control — that the latter are incapable of meeting given the desperation of their lives and circumstances. This generates continuous systemic friction above which Thistlewood can then (appear to) masterfully rise, and which therefore sustains and enhances his superiority. He is in a position to authorize and police the boundaries between legitimate and non-legitimate violence. Thus, the brutal punishments he metes out to — and the brutish sexual gratification he routinely demands from — the plantation slaves, as resident and later proprietary master, are legitimate; drunken or arbitrary individual assaults upon slaves by white underlings are not. The unremitting punitive and extractive violence against slaves in the context of the plantation's political economy becomes institutionalized, normalized, and rational, with Thistlewood as duly authorized administrator, while all irrational, disruptive, and chaotic violence is attributed to drunken, sexually desperate white subalterns and savage blacks. Not even Cope holds up under scrutiny because he lacks self-control, he is incompetent as a planter (a status he holds courtesy of his wife's properties), and his depraved abusiveness towards the sympathetic figure of his long suffering wife as well as other victims exceeds the limits of acceptable male behaviour.

Other white men also violate the standards of robust white manhood, for example, by allowing themselves to become besotted with a particular slave lover. William Crookshanks is a case in point. Mirtilla, his slave mistress, whom he has hired for £20 a year and re-hires out to earn her expenses, completely manipulates him (according to Thistlewood), refusing to work, feigning illness, 'only resolved to put William through a needless charge through spite'. (70) 'William cries sadly, the more fool he, as it is probably for Salt River Long Quaw,' (68) T comments, regarding a miscarriage Mirtilla suffers early in their relationship. The love-crazed William curses her owners when they punish her for some misdeed. He attends her in the labour of the birth of their child. 'W.C. came home and cried', overwhelmed by the experience. T clearly regards W.C.'s softness for Mirtilla as excessive and foolish, and a dangerous embarrassment to the standards of potent and inscrutable white manhood.[24] In contrast to Cope and Crookshanks, Thistlewood lives comfortably in the Creole style (or in accordance with the 'custom of the country'); he endorses (as far as practicable) the exclusive sexual rights of some black and white subaltern men to particular enslaved women; he patronizes a black slave elite networked around his 'wife' Phibbah, fathers mulatto children exclusively, and facilitates and exploits a black informal economy. As hands-on master, I would argue, he is much more significant than someone like Cope in localizing empire, patriarchy, and class and in incorporating subaltern social strata into their intricate web.

Thistlewood intervenes to uphold the exclusive sexual and conjugal claims of particular male slaves against those of others. In many of these situations, as we have seen above, the woman is both denied human agency or independent personhood and punished as the transgressor. Thus in December 1765, 'he flogged Egypt Lucy for leaving Daniel and going to Quashie'. Quashie in turn defends his own aggrieved masculinity and rival claims to Egypt Lucy by beating Daniel. (134) We find Thistlewood again, in November 1773 — this time as owner of his own estate — flogging Maria 'for cuckolding Solon at the Retrieve, and stirring up quarrels'. (189) One year later, Maria is still sneaking off to see her lover, prompting another flogging from Thistlewood, no doubt on the basis of Solon's complaints. (196)

At yet other times, however, Thistlewood metes out severe justice to male slaves who physically assault females. For beating Sukey so badly that she was robbed of speech, Lincoln is flogged, pickled and then put in the 'bilboes'. despite an intercessionary letter on his behalf from Mr Hayward. (144) Sukey herself receives immediate and thorough medical attention. She regains her speech later in the day after various forms of therapy to alleviate her physical and emotional trauma. The care exercised on this occasion was no doubt a reflection of the extent to which Thistlewood, still overseer at Egypt, was moved to protect and maintain his own property, as Sukey belonged to him. Moreover, she is prone to fits.

On a more mundane level, Thistlewood regularly polices and manages the reproductive and sexual lives of the enslaved. The slaves come to him to settle sexual and conjugal conflicts and disputes. Slaves could only press contingent and de facto claims against interlopers. Thistlewood was called upon to adjudicate disputes between men over women, between women over men, and between women and men over conjugal and domestic matters. On Monday, March 16, 1752, Thistlewood settled a complaint by Sancho that he had found Morris sleeping with his wife Quasheba by advising the couple to split up, which they did. (44) And there were those disputes that the slaves settled themselves, without the interference of the master. T reports the beating of one female slave by another over the attentions of a male slave. The aggressor beat the other so badly 'we were forced to have her carried home'. (75) Thinking she had killed her victim, she goes to the river with the clothes of her lover that she retrieved from her rival's home, and drowns herself. (75) The object of contention between the two women was Cobenna, perhaps the same Cobenna who is himself cuckolded the following year when he finds London and Rosanna, his current wife, together in his bed. 'London got a good thumping as I hear,' reports T, with obvious relish. (77)

What recourse did aggrieved female slaves have when their aggressor was the resident master himself? Despite the risk, especially given the expectations of uncomplaining sexual service on the part of the master, there was often fierce resistance from both assaulted female slaves and wronged male conjugal partners or kin. Hall notes:

> As one would expect, there was resistance. Slave women occasionally braved resistance to the sexual demands of their masters, and were usually punished for their "impudence". Slave men sometimes made clear their disapproval of the master's assaults on slave women. Quashe, the Egypt slave driver, more than once made threatening remarks occasioned by Thistlewood's favouring Jenny with gifts and lighter tasks. Individual slaves assaulted their masters, sometimes in offensive attack, sometimes in self-defence against assault. Usually they suffered dire consequences, but not always. (50)

Women often ignored or rejected the presumption of ownership over them by slave men. Despite the adjudications of the master and the pretensions of the informal patriarchy, enslaved women on the whole were not under any rigid sanction of (in-group) monogamy and many of them left unsatisfactory relationships for more desirable ones. It is here, however, that we are faced with our greatest challenge of interpretation, since we cannot be sure to what complex distillation of forces, to what multi-stranded story, the evidence bears witness. At what intersections of residual autonomy and the double oppression of absence — of a self-determined historical community of order, sanction, protection, and tradition — and presence — of a compulsive regime of corporeal and psychic objectification — does the subjectivity of enslaved women emerge? The more anonymously embedded in Thistlewood's text, the less we are able to determine.

We do know that not all female slaves were cowed into thinking that white men had an automatic right to their bodies. On January 11, 1766, Thistlewood overhears Margaritta in the trash-house expressing indignation that 'Buckrah wanted her to go in the bush with him near the Styx bridge.' She repeats her rejoinder to her audience, 'Me bin say, heh, no me go, bin say warrah.' (138) Slaves could refuse to prostitute themselves with strangers if they were not being compelled in this regard by their owners. Refusing the resident or proprietary master, however, posed far greater dangers.

While Thistlewood upheld exclusive conjugal rights of certain male slaves against others, he completely exempted himself from this restriction. He regularly exacts his seigneurial dues from those female slaves whose slave husbands' conjugal rights he has adjudicated even moments before, or whom he has personally matched up. This was evident in his frequenting of Sukey, the wife of Lincoln, his one-time driver and otherwise close domestic assistant; Abba, his chief domestic slave, a laundress, and one of his favourites, whose match with Cudjoe he had consented to; Mirtilla, whose husband Johnie (sic) was the driver at Egypt (previously matched with Little Mimber). In fact, Thistlewood freely availed himself of all his female slaves, showing little regard for conjugal, reproductive, or generational status. He is a consistent, compulsive, and lifelong sexual opportunist and potentate, but this prerogative which he seems to invoke on the slightest impulse, and which surely wreaks untold havoc on the psyches and bodies of his victims, is thoroughly domesticated and normalized within the boundaries of the total institution of the plantation. In his sixties, just months before his death we find him still exercising his sexual dominium over the daughters of his original slaves and other enslaved young women. On November 18, 1779, he has sexual intercourse with Mulatto Sukey Crookshank, the daughter of Mirtilla and William Crookshank, whom we have met before. He gives her a dollar. (269) On Friday, March 8, 1784, it is Abba's daughter Mary, blinded by smallpox at one and a half years old, and now 22 and six months' pregnant, who renders sexual service. She is given four bitts. (298) He is a little over 40 years her senior. He is undeterred by even the most advanced stages of pregnancy. He takes Phoebe on April 18, 1781; she gives birth five days later, on the 23rd. (283)

There is evidence of Thistlewood mellowing through time, but also, it appears, through the agency of Phibbah. The gruesome excesses of his punishments of absconding slaves may be seen in direct contrast to his growing tenderness towards Phibbah. Here I do not want to be misunderstood. The dialectic and simultaneity of brutality and intimacy, of sadism and desire, comprise an integral feature of the moral economy and disciplinary regime of absenteeist West Indian slave plantation societies, as I have tried to show. Much is known, after all, about the relationship between sadism and desire. However, it is possible to read beyond this story, without erasing or downplaying it, to a less acknowledged script about the core humanization (relatively speaking) of some European settlers like Thistlewood by enslaved Africans like Phibbah, the focus here being on the effective agency of the latter and her co-agents. While Thistlewood plays a key role in the institutional and moral normalization of corporal, sexual and psychic violence, and while he continues to be a direct agent in the dialectical simultaneity of brutality and intimacy, it is possible to trace an expansion of his capacity for complex affective human relationships within the realm of his domestic and extended familial network. This process begins with Phibbah's resistance against objectification and her insistence on being respected. It is also true that part of Thistlewood's 'mellowing' is a diminishing of his capacity to perform the full range of requirements for robust white manhood and an increasing retreat into the private and the opportunistic sexual exploitation of the weakest and most vulnerable (for example, blind, pregnant Mary).

Master and Intimate: Mediating Afro-Caribbean Community

Can the subaltern speak through the master's text? There is no doubt that echoes of the voices of the enslaved, though muffled, resound throughout Thistlewood's text. This is as much a result of the resistance and defiance[25] they so palpably express — and which he disdainfully records — as it is of his intimate engagement with and direct participation in parts of their world. Thistlewood's personal reproductive niche is located within the small overlap between the socio-spatial circuit of a predominantly black (and, in some ways, predominantly female) world and the socio-spatial circuit of a predominantly homosocial white world. In ideal-type 'modern' wage-labour regimes, race/class socio-spatial niches converge only at the point of production or in the public sphere; their reproductive niches tend to be separate and largely endogamous. Here, Thistlewood is bodily and affectively 'reproduced' in a predominantly black female domestic, emotional and cultural economy, and he is also a participant in and facilitator of their extended extra-domestic informal economic and social networks. With respect to this scenario, I want to look briefly at a number of things: Phibbah's role and his relationship with her (and with Mulatto John);[26] the extended domestic network of a small coterie of Creole household slaves connected by occupation, status, friendship, fictive and real kinship, and a variety of monetary and non-monetary exchange transactions; the wider informal slave economy; and evidence of (aspirations to) social mobility among the enslaved, which occurs most cogently with Coobah/Jenny Young, Phibbah's daughter.

We have witnessed Thistlewood ache with loneliness for Phibbah when he temporarily leaves Egypt in 1756 for another position. 'I wish they would sell her to me.... Tonight very lonely and melancholy again. No person sleep in the house but myself, and Phibbah's being gone this morning still fresh in my mind.' (80) They exchange gifts. Phibbah sends him fruits and vegetables, fish, crabs, land turtles, biscuits, cashews. 'God bless her!' he says. Thistlewood is informed that Phibbah is sick, 'for which I am really very sorry.' And he despairs, 'Poor girl, I pity her, she is in miserable slavery.' (80) Apart from these rare poignant, soul-baring moments, the entries on Phibbah switch throughout from stark reminders of her subordinate status to accounting records of an economic partnership of sorts, from expressions of disapproval over some sexual indiscretion or over-indulgence (particularly in relation to their son John) to routine domestic details of unremarkable and even cozy conjugal cohabitation. They look over the land that T is proposing to buy, and, later, together identify a suitable spot for the Negro provision grounds. Phibbah goes on ahead, in June 1767, before the move, to plant yams and plantains, 'and "many things" besides, in the Negro ground'. (145) And, on Tuesday, July 14, 1768, T records in his diary that 'Phibbah and me sat up till past 10 o'clock, to see the moon totally eclipsed'. (166) Some years later, on June 1, 1775, Phibbah is ill, and T writes to Mrs Cope to send Phibbah's daughter, the christened Jenny Young, to come to nurse Phibbah. (238)

Phibbah and Thistlewood regularly exchange gifts through the periods of their 'courtship' and beyond. While still an overseer at Egypt, Thistlewood supplied the labour services of his slaves for the maintenance of her house and gardens. On Tuesday, August 19, 1766, his 'girls' were weeding Phibbah's garden and his men were thatching her house. (141) By this time, their son, John ('Little Mulatto John'), was six years old. Later, his domestic enterprise is even more clearly merged with hers, and he is firmly entrenched in the role of protector and provider. During the threat of war and rumours of a Spanish invasion in March 1782, he gives his own Franke a 'ticket' (a pass for travelling), 'and sent her with Phib's trunk, of her most valuable clothes, &c. to Jenny Young in the mountain, as a place of greater safety than here'. (289) In December 1783, it is noted that her ground has been prepared, fenced in, and a gate put up. (296)

Phibbah is a seamstress, manager of the plantation cookhouse, and a favoured domestic slave, enjoying an unusually warm and close relationship with her owner, Mrs Cope (Mary Dorrill). She is also 'a woman of some property', as Hall points out. (94) On January 27, 1760 she sells her filly for £4 10s to William Rickett's slave, Coffee. Some weeks later she sells 'her mare Patience to the Negro man of Col Barclay's named Crossley for seven pounds. He paid her £5 10s down, and is to pay the remaining 30s in three months'. (94) On Sunday, May 17, 1772, she sells another filly 'to long Pond Melia for £5 13s 9d cash, and delivered her'. (230) She receives a gift of a 'Negro wench name Bess' from (free coloured) Mrs Bennett, the woman who later sells her pen to Thistlewood and Say and boards 'Little Mulatto John' during the week while he attends Mr Hugh's school in the Savanna. (134) Bess has to be registered as Thistlewood's because, as a slave, Phibbah cannot own another slave.[27]

One of the ways in which Phibbah humanizes Thistlewood, even against his better judgement, is by her intercessionary and mitigating role on behalf of the other slaves. He sometimes admonishes her for interfering in his management of the slaves, but he also concedes some authority to her in this regard. In one instance we are startled by Phibbah's uncharacteristically fierce punishment of Sally, who steals compulsively from the cookroom and has no doubt pushed Phibbah's patience beyond its limits. (198) More often, however, Thistlewood complains of Phibbah's leniency and indulgence towards the other slaves and her constant protection of them. He thinks Jimmy 'makes a fool of Phib. just as he pleases, and so do they all'. (205) He is particularly unhappy about what he sees as her over-indulgence of their son John and her interference with his development into manhood. In an early pronouncement he fears '[h]is mother promotes his ruin by excessive indulgence and humouring him beyond all bounds'. (231)[28]

Phibbah is part of a network of relatively privileged house slaves who have specialized domestic skills in sewing, culinary and healing arts; own livestock and trade goods, in the sale of which they conduct a lively business; host relatively large entertainments and ritual events in the community;[29] join together in informal credit associations; perform important supervisory and management functions; and usually serve as 'housekeepers' or 'wives' to white men, elite male slaves or free men of colour, placing them at a relative distance from the casual sexual reserve force. They are able to deploy the services of other slaves (through privileged allocation, direct hire, or even informal lifetime 'ownership' as in the case of Phibbah's Bess), sometimes discipline other slaves, claim superior provision grounds, parlay their influence among whites and blacks of both genders, intercede with the master on the behalf of lesser plantation slaves, and serve as cultural mediums and gathering posts for the community. They provide the kernel of Thistlewood's and Phibbah's shared friendships and community, with Phibbah (of the two) as the centre from which the network radiates and interconnects. The other core members of this close group are House Franke, Egypt Lucy, Vine, Phibbah's sister Nancy and her daughter Coobah/Jenny Young. In some respects the sorority extends outside and upwards of the circle to include Mrs Cope, Mrs Bennett and a few other free coloured women.

A close-up of one of this group illustrates their remarkable personalities. Vine, a close friend of Phibbah's and Thistlewood's, belongs to or is hired by Samuel Say, who jointly purchased Paradise Pen with Thistlewood, and operates his portion as a separate enterprise. She is clearly his 'housekeeper', with all that this implies. When Say accepts an offer from Martin Williams to be overseer of Old Hope

Estate, he goes to live there and leaves his pen, which he visits from time to time, in her care. The responsibility is a major one. She quarrels with '[Thistlewood's] Negroes for taking dry wood from off Mr Say's land'. (226) On other occasions, she becomes the object of complaint for allowing her hogs to run amok in the provision grounds of Thistlewood's slaves. On July 21, 1772, T calls her in to show her the errant hogs, since she has taken offence at previous complaints. Three days later he is asked to witness the sale of her horse to Mr Hughes for £17. (228) Vine has a series of relationships with white men, although one of her earliest reported relationships is with 'Mrs Bennett's driver, Sam, a Negro'. (129) She has played an active role as daughter to both her parents and she gets some medication from Thistlewood for her father who is ill. She gives him a 'fine musk melon' as a token of gratitude. (227) She is an important purveyor of Afro-Caribbean healing and cultural arts, being, among other things, a master storyteller. Between Sunday, September 17 and Tuesday, September 27, 1768, she keeps Thistlewood's Breadnut Island Pen household enthralled with nightly Anansi storytelling sessions, during an extended period of relaxation and entertainment. (160)

During his early acquaintance with Jamaican life, Thistlewood learns from William Dorrill that 'by a very good computation, the Negroes in this Parish lay out near 20 thousand pounds per annum'. (54) Before long, Thistlewood himself becomes directly involved in this thriving subsidiary economy. While he dispatches his slaves on higglering missions on his own behalf, he also engenders and patronizes their proto-peasant and trading activities on their own account, and does so more particularly within the closer circle of Phibbah's associates. On Sunday, September 3, 1769, Thistlewood '[returns] to Phibbah £27 2s 6d, money I borrowed of her in crop time, out of her own, House Franke's and Egypt Lucy's money' (219), suggesting their participation in a type of Yoruba-origin savings institution known variously as sou sou, 'partner', or 'meeting turn'. In addition to occasionally borrowing money and buying goods from these and other individuals, he sells them goods that allow them to improve their subsistence capability, and advances them credit or capital to buy trade goods. On Friday, March 14, 1760, he sells Old Sharper 'the gun I bought from driver Quashe many years ago. He gave me only 10s. for her but paid ready money. He will soon shoot alligators &c. enough at Hill'. (96) On

Sunday, January 23,1774, Egypt Maria comes to visit; at least part of the purpose of her visit is business: 'Gave Egypt Maria an order, or letter, to Mr Abraham Tavarez, Snr to let her have what she wanted, as far as 40 shillings. (She took up £2 1s 3d.).' (233) On Sunday, August 9, 1778, he '[b]ought a young horse of Egypt House Franke, for which I paid her £12 cash down. Salt River smith, Charles, present'. (258) Two months later he buys another filly from Egypt House Franke, this one for £6. 'Paid her in cash.' (259) On Saturday, July 21, 1781, he records that 'Damsel killed her hog & made me a present of the head. Bought a leg of her, 4 1/2 lb at 5 bitts. Now sold at 10d per lb. The whole, 50 lb weight in 12 small pieces comes to 63 bitts, which she received'. (284–85)

Finally we consider the case of the socially mobile, border-crossing Coobah/Jenny Young. Coobah's life is archetypal for pressing the full range of the extremely limited trajectory of social mobility that is possible for a black (racially unmixed) female slave. She is Phibbah's (pre-Thistlewood) daughter, and if that were not enough to confer a relatively privileged status upon her, she is also Mrs Cope's personal waiting maid and a skilled seamstress. Like her mother and Egypt Franke, she owns chattel property and engages in lucrative trading activity. Most of her lovers appear to be privileged in at least two of the following three criteria for higher social status: race/colour, occupation, and civil status. The list includes Mulatto Davie; Nagua, 'a free man'; John Hartnole, white driver; Limburner, white overseer; Jimmy Stewart, a relatively privileged mulatto slave who is also something of a dandy. Most of her pregnancies, of which those reported all appear to be mixed-race, end up in miscarriage (including the one suspected to be by Mr Cope), though she does have one daughter, Nancy (mulatto). She finally has another successful pregnancy by Jimmy Stewart, her most enduring conjugal partner. Sadly, Little Jimmy Stewart dies of a fever when he is almost eight years old. (305)

Coobah/Jenny Young's potential for bearing mulatto children becomes an occasion for social strategizing when she is pregnant with Limburner's child. Limburner, Jenny Young, House Franke and Phibbah get together to make plans for the manumission of little Nancy and 'the child Jenny Young is now big of, if a Mulatto, &c'. (240) Unfortunately, on April 16, 1776 she miscarries and any immediate hopes of having another mulatto child dies with Limburner, who passes away in late June. (245)

There have been other strategies. She travels to England with her mistress and mistress' family on two occasions, once in 1767–78 and the second time in 1771–72.[30] As reported previously, she is christened and converted to 'Jenny Young' on the second occasion. While there is no reference to Christianity, in either substantive or nominal form, as the basis for this conversion (although it is, nominally), the assumption of a new double-monikered persona is unmistakable.

After returning from England the first time, Coobah settles back into a predominantly Africanist (and decidedly pre-Christian) cultural setting. Some months later, she hosts two or more Myal dances at her house, for which she gets a tongue-lashing from Thistlewood when she comes to visit. Myalism might be seen as an exorcism of European influence. Schuler describes it as 'the first documented Jamaican religion cast in the "classical" African mold.... It emerged in the 1760s as a pan-African religious society to protect slaves against European sorcery.' It is not until the early nineteenth century that the adoption of Christian elements becomes evident in the syncretic constitution of the religion.[31]

The path from the socially risky engagement in practices of Myalism to the socially enhancing adoption of a thin veneer of nominal Christianity and European respectability surely is not fortuitous, especially given Thistlewood's obtrusive and aggressive intervention. Indeed, while Thistlewood appears to take just fleeting note of the circumstances surrounding 'Phibbah's Coobah['s christening] at home' (227), her new name is firmly etched in all his subsequent references to her. She is no longer Phibbah's Coobah; she is now Jenny Young, prefiguring the long process of renaming (from crudely functional and oftentimes African-inflected slave appellations to 'proper' two-part Euro-Christian slave names) that would pick up speed in the decades ahead. Jenny Young is ahead of her time. There is also evidence that she is lettered (an extremely rare condition, therefore, enjoyed by both of Phibbah's children), however rudimentarily, but it is never made clear how she came by that condition. (159) Finally, her apparently conventional but strategic adoption of European form turns out to be not so safe and conventional after all. In post-Thistlewood Jamaica, whites would increasingly find the idea of converted, literate — and 'properly' married — slaves to be offensive and dangerous. It eroded and contaminated the exclusivity and sacrosanctity of European privilege and identity by allowing slaves to partake of them, if only distantly and symbolically; it weakened the availability of the slaves as objects of unmitigated exploitation and of the murky colonial underside of European 'civilization' and fantasy; and it potentially threatened the physical security of the whites and their property by inciting the slaves to visions of total freedom. Manyoni[32] cites a contemporary observation that 'when coloured concubines adopted Christianity, "their renunciation of base connections gave the greatest offence to the white community".' It occurred to whites that 'uppity' black people who went to the great lengths required to become literate, convert to Christianity or obtain a clerical marriage, might have pretensions to being something other than their sexual and economic tools. In the overwhelming black majority situations of the Caribbean, such pretensions were extremely threatening to the planters' race/class niche.

Some Tentative Conclusions

I want to sum up by reviewing once more (a) the particular significance of Thistlewood and his journal and (b) the scope and nature of the evidence of enslaved black subjectivity submerged within it. As was pointed out earlier in this chapter, Thistlewood's journal has particular significance because of the conjuncture it occupies — the heyday or 'high noon' of Jamaican slave society — and the position Thistlewood himself occupies in the social structure, to which it bears witness. He is a naturalized local/socially mobile lesser white/bachelor/master and intimate of blacks. As such, he is called upon to negotiate in person the entire race/class/gender spectrum of the social structure, and his diary reflects this. It runs the gamut of the local social hierarchy through the palpable medium of direct authorial participation and 'insidership'.

Apart from the more obvious difference in textual form and frame, it is clearly distinct from other known journals in this more substantive regard. For example, Matthew 'Monk' Lewis,[33] as visiting 'ameliorating' proprietor, can maintain throughout a quixotic, ironic, and sometimes parodic distance from both the black and white elements of the society, although he too is a sojourner in a mostly black world. The policies of amelioration to which all the major planters ultimately acquiesced, though mostly unsuccessfully, were chiefly concerned with stemming the inexorable tide of demographic failure that had been a long-standing structural feature of the plantation system, particularly in view of the imminence and, later, the aftermath of the 1807 abolition of the slave trade. Adherence to a policy of amelioration did not require any essential belief in the humanity or spiritual worthiness of the slaves; it was primarily a system of good husbandry, a system for 'making the Negroes healthier and happier and inducing them to breed'.[34] Of course this pragmatic preoccupation is mostly submerged in Lewis's sophisticated and literarily inflected tale of which he emerges the (rescuing) hero, the Great and Wise White Father. His account is mediated throughout, but subtly so, by the self-congratulatory, self-flattering largesse of a benign but detached and passing-through paternalism. Against the crudity, parochialism, and short-sightedness of the white Creole and even the authoritarian proselytism of the missionaries, he presents himself as the advanced champion of enslaved black welfare, as the quintessence of Euro-cosmopolitan civility and as purveyor of an enlightened, flexible, even indulgent paternalism, having a superior insight into and appreciation for 'his Negroes" native and positional intelligence and wit, as well as the proper recipe for their health and happiness (always as slaves). Indeed, his keen visitor's eye and liberal bent yield a rich portrait and evidentiary cache of intra- and inter-plantation relations of early nineteenth-century Jamaica, although, to repeat, it does so from a discreet and ironic distance and within protected socio-spatial limits, beyond which he does not venture and against which he does not push. The point is not that Thistlewood's account is not ideologically mediated — indeed, I hope I have provided some insight in this chapter on how it is so — but that it is unmindful, for a variety of reasons to do with textual medium and socio-historical position, of the need to justify itself to or conceal itself from an anti-slavery audience lurking in the shadows, and it narrates a first person agency in the wide swathe of social relations, activities, processes, and actions it records. Slavery is the utterly taken for granted context from which Thistlewood speaks, as a fully embedded dominant insider. This very unselfconsciousness speaks volumes, even as it muffles countless other voices.

Thistlewood is also critical in helping us to pose and answer the following pair of questions. How is the hegemonic local intimately produced, in distinction from (though not, strictly speaking, in opposition to) being distantly or officially authorized, wishfully imagined, or phantasmagorially conjured up from grotesque stereotypes? How does intimacy (help to) reproduce race/class and patriarchal hegemony and normalize corporeal, sexual, and psychic violence? How is intimacy both predatory/parasitic and productive/creative of new forms of power (in the Foucauldian sense)?

The journal helps to answer the question asked in the beginning section of this chapter: How did the actuality of local life subvert the paradigmatic constructs of the African-Caribbean woman as 'natural' prostitute and beast of burden on the one hand and innocent and helpless victim on the other? It helps us to go beyond merely settling the clash between discourses of natural racial destiny and those of historical causality and culpability to understand how the top-down instrumentation of hegemony becomes a structural and cultural condition permeating the entire social order, in a series of interlinked and gradient social relations. We get a better idea of how hegemony is transmitted through the connective tissues of society, and how it is lived by those constituted as its objects. Hegemony appears to be accommodated through contradictory processes of internalization, strategic deployment, resistance, and rejection. As such, we get some indication of how enslaved black women and men who are vested with certain (relative) advantages by the system might have helped to normalize its violence, even as they were victimized by and operated against and in spite of it. This is not a novel discovery. Subaltern societies do not have a choice about hierarchies of incorporation and hegemonic accommodation. However, we learn specific, everyday details about some of the survivalist strategies and forms of self-empowerment through which they invent and practice alternative, subsidiary, and sub-hegemonic folkways of life.

The journal also shows us the white Creole subject as split, inhabiting (in different social modalities of outsider/insider) multiple racialized socio-spatial niches locally and still connected through ties of extended kinship, systems of property devolution, import/export activity, and reservoirs of identity to England, the motherland. At the same time, it would be a mistake to see Thistlewood's lesser-white creolized masculinity as sourced only from a European imagination, as his oblique admiration of Maroon virility might remind us. Colonialism produces a peculiarly fractured subject, and this fracturing occurs in different forms throughout the social structure, manifested, for example, in a black domestic 'elite' socio-spatial niche which is caught between white patronage, African cultural and spiritual practices, and the authoring of (relatively) independent subsidiary networks on which the local centre becomes dependent. This last observation should be qualified by my gendered focus on enslaved women in relation to the variously delimited discussion of enslaved subjects taken up in this chapter. Obviously, this discussion can only be extended and given flesh in another context.

Beyond the partially discernible figures of the core network of black women referred to, the terrorized and defiant subaltern cannot take on a distinct subjectivity in Thistlewood's text. However, in his routine reporting of everyday life, the persistence of terror is equally matched by the persistence of resistance, especially through the act of running away. Certain personalities do emerge in connection with this practice and as symbols of the consistently lived refusal of slavery within the community of the enslaved. A brief example will have to suffice here. Mary is one of the most successful Breadnut Island Pen runaways. On September 24, 1781, she had absented herself from the pen to go 'up on the mountain to see Robin'. (286) She had failed to return, prompting a search for her. She did not come back until the first week of October, when Thistlewood had her flogged, 'put her on a steel collar with a few links of chain to it', branded her on her left cheek, and let her go. She was soon off to the mountain again. Four days later she was brought in by Strap, and given another flogging. (286) In one long absence, she manages to escape seizure from May 20, 1782 to January 1784, a period of more than one and a half years. (290) She is finally retrieved when T finds out that she is in the Lucea gaol, probably on account of being a runaway. He sends Mr Hayward's Coffee for her. (297) However, she soon runs off again. (298) She is brought back on March 27 and put in irons until April 6 when she is released and sent into the field 'under charge'. (298)

It is perhaps fitting, therefore, to end on a reminder of both the unspeakable suffering and the unremittingly defiant intractability of those most deeply submerged and silenced within Thistlewood's script, those who occupy the polar extreme of the process of 'othering' that underlies the construction of European empire.

Notes

1. I wish to gratefully acknowledge the three following fellowships or grants which have allowed me to work on this and other papers related to a larger project entitled, 'Between Respectability and Self-Respect: Colonialism, Moral Regimes and Afro-Caribbean Subalternity' — 2000–2001 NEH-Schomburg Scholars-in-Residence Fellowship, Schomburg Center for Research in Black Culture, New York; 2001–2002 Henry Charles Chapman Research Fellowship, Institute of Commonwealth Studies, School of Advanced Study, University of London; and a 2002–2003 Faculty Research Grant from the Center for Latin American Studies (CLAS), University of Pittsburgh. All references to Thistlewood's Diary are taken from the 1999 Douglas Hall volume *In Miserable Slavery: Thomas Thistlewood in Jamaica, 1750–86*.

2. Stuart Hall, 'Pluralism, Race and Class in Caribbean Society', in *Race and Class in Post-Colonial Society*, ed. UNESCO (Paris: UNESCO, 1977), 158.

3. Ibid.

4. Ibid., 162.

5. I consider it to be a classic of Caribbean sociology.

6. Stuart Hall, 'Pluralism, Race and Class', 162.

7. Ibid.

8. Ibid., 154.

9. Edward Kamau Brathwaite, *Contradictory Omens: Cultural Diversity and Integration in the Caribbean*, Savacou monograph, no. 1 (1974).

10. Stuart Hall, 'Negotiating Caribbean Identities', in *New Caribbean Thought: A Reader*, eds. Brian Meeks and Folke Lindahl (Jamaica, Barbados, Trinidad and Tobago: the University of the West Indies Press, 2004), 24.

11. Ibid., 28, 34.

12. Stuart Hall, 'Ethnicity: Identity and Difference', *Radical America* 23, no. 4 (1989): 9–20.

13. Stuart Hall, 'Negotiating Caribbean Identities'.

14. Douglas Hall, *In Miserable Slavery: Thomas Thistlewood in Jamaica, 1750–86*. (Kingston: the University of the West Indies Press, 1999); Trevor Burnard, *Mastery, Tyranny, and Desire: Thomas Thistlewood and his Slaves in the Anglo-Jamaican World* (Chapel Hill and London: the University of North Carolina Press, 2004).

15. Adam Smith, *Lectures on Jurisprudence*, eds. R.L. Meek, D.D. Raphael, and P.G. Stein (Oxford: Clarendon Press, 1978), 451.

16. James M. Phillippo, *Jamaica: Its Past and Present State* (Westport, CT: Negro Universities Press, [1843] 1970), 123.

17. Clare Midgley, *Women Against Slavery: The British Campaigns, 1780–1870* (London and New York: Routledge, 1992), 91.

18. Michael Craton and James Walvin, *A Jamaican Plantation: A History of Worthy Park 1670–1970* (Toronto and Buffalo: University of Toronto Press, 1970), 46.

19. Trevor Burnard, *Mastery, Tyranny, and Desire*, 15.

20. Ibid., 17–18.

21. Trevor Burnard, 'Inheritance, and Independence: Women's Status in Early Colonial Jamaica', *William and Mary Quarterly* 48, no. 1 (1991): 93–114.
22. Edward Kamau Brathwaite, *The Development of Creole Society in Jamaica 1770–1820* (Oxford: Clarendon Press, 1971), 142.
23. Raymond T. Smith, 'Hierarchy and the Dual Marriage System in West Indian Society', in *Gender and Kinship*, eds. J.F. Collier and S. Yanagisako (Stanford: Stanford University Press, 1987), 167.
24. In fact, it might be argued that, for Thistlewood, the Maroon leaders — Colonel Cudjoe, Captain Accompong (accompanied by '[m]any of his wives, and his son'), Captain Cuffee *et al.*, who dine regularly at Egypt during Tacky's Rebellion, and who strike a posture of manhood and virility that he clearly admires — fit the image of proper masculinity far more convincingly than Crookshanks or Cope. Their military prowess, apparent control of women-as-wives, autonomy, and collaboration with colonialism make them a worthy symbol.
25. This includes both armed insurrection (like Tacky's Rebellion) and everyday forms of resistance, which is of greater concern here. Everyday resistance took many forms, including sabotage of plantation operations and destruction of property, aggressive and defensive modes of physical and verbal assault, stealing, lying and dissembling, poisoning, and running away. Running away, which will be briefly re-addressed in my concluding remarks, constitutes a constantly recurring and routine entry in Thistlewood's compendium of daily events.
26. See note 28 below.
27. In his last will and testament, Thistlewood orders his executors to purchase Phibbah's manumission and leaves 'Bess and her Child Sam together with her future issue and increase' to Phibbah conditional upon said manumission. (313)
28. Nevertheless fatherhood becomes a critical part of the process of Thistlewood's humanization. He becomes an active father to John after a period of referring to him anonymously as 'Phibbah's child'. John is manumitted by the Copes, ostensibly through purchase by his father, at the age of two. Thistlewood puts great hope in his intellectual development, buys children's books and tries to cultivate in him a habit of reading. He sends him to school and supplements this with home schooling. He does not neglect other initiation rites, teaching him to shoot and passing on to him precious mementos of childhood and tokens to mark his coming of age (232, 275). Having apparently failed to make an intellectual out of him, Thistlewood arranges an apprenticeship with a master carpenter. The tug-of-war that ensues between father and son is fought over discipline, identity, status, and the growing demands of manhood. The two are just beginning to find common ground when John is tragically struck down by a fatal illness.
29. They appear to get special concessions in this regard, since other slaves get punished for drumming, 'loud entertainments', and 'plays', African-derived extended- or post-funerary ancestral celebrations.
30. She prefigures today's informal commercial importer when she brings with her from England goods that she sells upon arrival. She sells '24 yards of coarse sheeting' to Thistlewood at a price of 60 bitts. (158)
31. Monica Schuler, 'Myalism and the African Religious Tradition in Jamaica', in *Caribbean Slave Society and Economy*, eds. Hilary Beckles and Verene Shepherd (Kingston: Ian Randle Publishers; London: James Currey Publishers, 1991), 295.

32. Joseph R. Manyoni, 'Extra-Marital Mating Patterns in Caribbean Family Studies: A Methodological Excursus', *Anthropologica* 22, no. 1 (1980): 85–118.

33. Matthew 'Monk' Lewis, *Journal of a West India Proprietor; Kept during a Residence in the Island of Jamaica*, edited with an Introduction and Notes by Judith Terry (Oxford and New York: Oxford University Press, [1834] 1999).

34. J. Harry Bennett, Jr., *Bondsmen and Bishops: Slavery and Apprenticeship on the Codrington Plantations of Barbados, 1710–1838* (Berkeley and Los Angeles: University of California Press, 1958), 91.

9 | Civic Politics in Jamaica: New Populism or Political Breakthrough?[1]

Obika Gray

The turn to governance and to the effective management of public affairs is now a fairly entrenched process in Jamaica and in the wider Caribbean.[2] More specifically, state and non-state actors' recent affirmation of a civic politics in Jamaica, their summoning of civic identities rather than partisan ones, and their efforts to make the Jamaican citizen an empowered political actor, all point to interesting developments in the character and tone of Jamaican politics.[3]

The evidence for this change is apparent from key development over the last 15 years or so.[4] They include:

- the hasty retreat of politicians and the repudiation of political gunmen and the state's evasion of greedy, supplicant clients;
- the parties' ideological demobilization of supporters and their return to a centrist, pragmatic politics;
- the shift to a consensus model of policy formulation and decision making between state and society;
- the passage of legislation to restrain state power; make public policy more transparent and public officials more accountable;
- the adoption of Citizen Charters in the Office of the Prime Minister and in a variety of public agencies with the purpose of affirming the public's right to the efficient receipt of state services;
- the signing of memorandums of understanding between the state, the private sector and trade unions;
- a retreat from base partisanship in making public decisions and adoption of a technocratic style in making public policy;
- a resort to enunciations that seem to privilege the 'national interest' and the 'public interest' over narrowly partisan and expedient interests, the rights of the citizens against the prerogatives of the state, and the recuperation of civil society

and its autonomy from a hitherto debased relationship to Jamaica's parasitic and warlordist state.

These developments represent an important nuance in the etiquette of Jamaican statecraft, and in the opposition to it. They also point to a potential sea change not so much in mass political values, as in a gradual transformation of elite political culture. This cultural shift is evident among change-oriented elements of the liberal political class. Why this should be happening should come as no surprise. Given Jamaica's decades-long crisis that saw the collapse of state authority, the jettisoning of conventional morality and the massive accumulation of an insolent and uncivil social power by a rebellious counter-society, these elites' embrace of political reform is quite understandable. Caught in the throes of a great crisis, the political class appears to be moving away from predation to civism as a form of rule. I have commented elsewhere on the destructive consequences that a noxious statecraft has had on Jamaican politics and society since the 1960s. This form of political rule wedded violent factionalism and destructive clientelism to the social mobilization and cultural solicitation of the militant urban poor. The outcome was predictable. It produced carnage and death, damaged already weak democratic norms, corrupted the political culture and undermined the legitimacy of public institutions. Indeed, the Jamaican drive for national development, as elsewhere in other parts of the periphery, took an unfortunate turn. It fostered overpoliticized notions of development and encouraged debased forms of political participation.

Political Parasitism: A Noxious Model of Power

One consequence of this debased politics was that the Jamaican civic public realm, so lively and vigorous as political independence neared, grew more and more stunted in the aftermath of that independence. This was so much the case that since the 1970s this realm was effectively emptied of both civic content and civil politics.

This emptying occurred because a motley crew of criminal gunmen, populist middle-class politicians, greedy supplicants and armed 'political contractors' seized this public space for their base designs. The consequence was a debased public realm, a corrupted political culture, and Jamaicans' increasing flight from politics.

These outcomes were not accidental. Rather, they came as a consequence of politicians' inventive construction of a unique repertoire of power in Jamaica that I call political parasitism. The identity of Jamaican political power is its parasitism.

By that I mean a form of power that exercises its sway not so much by the expulsion of hostile ideologies and contrary sociopolitical tendencies, but by the harnessing and feeding on the antinomies found in these clashing, contradictory tendencies.

For instance, in the quest for political dominance, Jamaican state actors embraced democratic norms and practices but joined them to their polar opposites. So for example, at one moment politicians developed enunciations that decried criminality, affirmed the rule of law and championed the value of public morality. This rhetoric was backed by legislation and the active interdiction of criminals. This fitted quite nicely with the obligations appropriate to a democratic society governed by the rule of law. At another moment, however, these same politicians, driven by political necessities, showered politically protected criminals and supplicant clients with warm accolades, handed them favours, and supported their claims on the political parties. Where the rebellious poor received no party protection and challenged the state outside the clientelist structure, the police mowed them down.

Complicit politicians abetted these extra-judicial murders. This resort to outlawry fitted equally nice with a key aspect of Jamaican political culture: its capacity for moral boundary-crossing. In a context of weak public opinion and absence of effective countervailing institutions, this orientation accommodated not just extra-judicial murder but also extra-constitutional practices. The combination of outlawry and constitutionalism disclosed this moral ridge-riding and political border-crossing as political actors joined constitutionalism to the informality of discretionary politics. This same moral dilation and political border-crossing is also apparent in the state's posture toward settlers' unlawful capturing of land, in the government's response to incidents of police brutality, and in state agents' stance on the appropriation of public funds to satisfy the demands of favoured political clients.

In each case, Jamaican statecraft was capable of condemning the morality associated with these events at one moment in time, while valorizing them at the next.

Witnessing this shifting definition of propriety, morality and law a political gunman or a ghetto client seeking the spoils of politics, could be forgiven for wondering out loud: 'Why the rass dem man deh caan mek up dem mind and stick wid one ting?'

The issue, however, was not the state's political indirection and uncertainty, as it was political dilation and moral border-crossing as statecraft. As I have observed elsewhere:

> As the Jamaican state moves back and forth across the border between the legal and the illegal, between the shadow economy and the formal economy, and between reliance on constitutionally mandated security forces and dependence on private, party-linked militias, it becomes something new in the process.[5]

This new identity is its parasitism. Yet the exercise of parasitic rule is neither essentially for the benefit of the rich nor unalterably against the poor. Similarly, parasitic rule does not employ state power in favour of order against disorder; it does not valorize legal-democratic measures over illegal mercenary tactics in political contestations, nor is it reluctant to embrace both the rule of law and the subversion of that law in making public policy.

The point here is that this dilating state power with its flexible morality and shifting definition of the politically permissible is a unique method of political management.

It draws on strong traditions not just of liberal political pluralism and political freedom, but also on a Jamaican culture of political outlawry, informality and guile, as well as base criminality. The Jamaican state summoned and assimilated these two aspects of Jamaican political culture — the formal constitutional and the informal illegal — the better to exercise its sway. This authority, it should be noted, is not wholly tyrannical. On the contrary, it pays substantial respect to constitutional norms, shares power with the poor, and exhibits a communications politics that is redolent with popular values. Those values with their ambiguous combination of militancy for black freedom and contingent propensity for social outlawry, piracy and crime, find in the ontological life of Jamaican state power a culturally familiar politics.

Selective violence against rebel cultures of the urban poor and warm solicitation of the antinomy in their cultural values — along with gestures to constitutional norms — have kept the Afro-Jamaican majority spellbound. Parasitic rule, then, is a means of social cohesion and political control. Moreover, in contexts of economic dependence and because of weak and uneven class formation in Jamaica, both by-the-book constitutionalism and off-the-books official outlawry become repertoires of this culturally familiar power.

Counter-Elite Civism: Horizontal Challenge to Power

How then to make sense of the seeming political shift away from this predation politics to civism? How to assess the move from the post-independence pattern of 'stop-go' policy making to technocratic governance?

Turning first to civism and its recuperation, it is clear that this is less the project of a weakened and embattled political class, than it is the agenda of emboldened civic groups, crusading journalists, notable political figures, and embryonic third-party formations. These latter spoke up in defence of human rights, called for the public accountability of politicians, and demanded clean government. What is remarkable about such groups is not so much the demands made of weakened politicians, as these groups' bid to rescue the idea of the public interest, to restore the category of the citizen, and to promote the norm of civism as an autonomous citizen-based activity for the common good. This development is apparent from various forms of political activism. They include media-inspired 'vox pop' call-in radio programmes that allowed citizens to vent their rage against political power as well as human rights groups' summoning of international watchdog agencies like Amnesty International.

Such initiatives testify to the reinvigoration of a stunted public opinion, the recuperation of a near-dormant civil society, and the new authority of citizen politics. The achievements and effectiveness of civic groups such as Citizens Action for Free and Fair Elections (CAFFE), Jamaicans for Justice (JFJ), and Families against State Terrorism (FAST) confirm renewed interest in civism. At the same time, these initiatives show the ability of the non-partisan civic groups to prevail against a reluctant state, particularly when these civic groups focus and sharply define their concerns.

Compared to the collapse of third-party political formations in recent years, the entry of these civic groups into the political arena produced modest, but better results. CAFFE, for example, earned public respect for its work in cleaning up electoral practices, while Jamaicans for Justice effectively denounced police brutality, criticized the law's disregard for the rights of the accused, and successfully pressed for international scrutiny of police killings. There can be little doubt that these are worthwhile achievements. Still, the modesty of these outcomes, continuing state hostility to human rights claims, as well as the public's ambiguous stance concerning the merits of human rights in a high-crime society with spiralling murder rates, point up difficulties and constraints associated with this form of civism. Moreover, it is no secret that JFJ, no matter its principled defence of the black poor, is a brown middle-class formation headed by a few notable personalities without any real social connection to the Afro-Jamaican majority. Thus far, and mostly for the worse, only the two dominant political parties have established these enduring and affectionate ties to the Jamaican people.

The point is not that the JFJ can establish no gainful connection with the poor on discrete issues of importance to them. Rather, it is that JFJ civism is problematic. Confined as it is to mostly brown middle- and upper-middle-class elite circles, and to complex legal arguments and petitioning over the constitutional exercise of power or lack thereof, JFJ civism reveals ongoing divisions and power contestations between weakened politicians and their new middle-class challengers. This contestation seems more akin to a family quarrel over who gets to speak for the poor and who sets the terms of their social domination than to a new politics that mobilizes the popular classes and links their social justice ideologies to either JFJ or state-led civism.

In sum, it appears that this elite form of civism, though well-meaning, is not really transformative of class and social relations in Jamaica as it is constrained by the impediments of class leadership, the dynamics of its kin politics and the fetters of liberalism. In these circumstances citizen politics rather than realizing its radical potential of challenging dominant class power in ways that empower the whole subordinate class of Afro-Jamaican poor, merely falls back into the recurring middle-class default mode. This is the well-known pattern of seeking reforms on the basis of elite agreements struck from on high and without the people's input and participation.

Rather surprising, therefore, is that while the crisis of predation politics encouraged the formation of new centres of political opposition and power beyond the state, these middle-class poles of opposition in summoning the citizen, failed to invest this supra-identity with the subversive content drawn from black popular militancy.

If in the name of reform, social groups such as JFJ found in civism a means of challenging power, albeit in limited ways, then given the identity of state power sketched above, it is not surprising that the Jamaican state also found in civism's universalist identity a means for recovering some of its lost legitimacy.

Under pressure from detractors at home and abroad, Jamaican political leaders also embraced this notion of citizen politics. These leaders also moved from a 'stop-go' approach to policymaking to more technocratic modes of political management.

With respect to state support for civic politics, it is the incumbent PNP which has moved significantly along this road — certainly much more so than the conservative and cautious JLP.

Citizen or Loyalist: Jamaican Statecraft in Transition

In the last decade, the PNP has encouraged some forms of citizen participation that do not threaten its power. It has put in place citizen charters, encouraged the development of parish development committees, and backed local government reform. These and the roster of measures identified above indicate the extent to which the PNP has strengthened society against the historic dominance of the Jamaican state. What is interesting about state-driven support for civic politics, on the one hand, is its apparent conformity with known patterns of Jamaican statecraft: resort to symbolic manipulation and cooptation of often antagonistic sociopolitical tendencies without fulfilling their radical potential. Hence in the narrative of the Jamaican state, the summoning of civic politics becomes a basis for extending the state's ideological authority. Moving away from predation politics into civism allows the state to associate itself with newer forms of dissent now rooted in claims to political empowerment and mobilization of the citizen, rather than the political loyalist.

In an age where both confiscatory socialism and developmental populism are politically discredited, state-driven civic populism may well offer a new basis for political legitimacy beyond the traditional political categories. After all, in this form of civic populism political actors are recruited not on the basis of class, ethnic, or cultural belonging, but rather on the basis of a common, supra-identity beyond confining political partisanships.

In the hands of anti-system actors that are committed to social transformation, this form of civic mobilization possesses a radical potential because it opens up a new social space that is universalist and transnational. The subversive content of this form of civic mobilization should therefore not be devalued. Again, the radical potential was achieved when a local human rights group challenged a stubborn Jamaican state by successfully inviting international human rights agencies to look into incidents of police brutality. By internationalizing the issue, and by appealing to the non-partisan supra-identity of Jamaican citizens' human rights, local actors bypassed divisive political relations tied to older forms of partisanship on the local scene. When taken up by embattled state elites in a neo-liberal world, however, their defense of civism is at best ambiguous. In Jamaica, the embrace of civism by elites of the state is contingent and uncertain — they are always on the look-out for new ways to recuperate power. Still, this state's flirtation with civism could threaten and even undermine for good, the old parasitism and its exclusionary politics.

Like the contributions of its civic group rivals, state-led initiatives that restrain state power and enhance popular needs do make a big difference. When backed by effective implementation and surveillance to entrench citizen-enhancing measures, this endorsement of citizen politics is more than meaningful — it is deeply subversive of older forms of exercising power and can provoke a nasty civil war within the party that champions this initiative. This does not mean, of course, that the alternative form it adopts is necessarily transformative much less revolutionary. It is merely to say that in moving away from predation politics, this later politics creates a contested space for the realization of radical possibilities. After all, in state-driven forms of civism, its popular appeal is its claim to empower the citizen and its promise is to deliver public goods in a non-partisan way. When this happens, as it now does in limited ways in Jamaica, the state gains some legitimacy and wins a modicum of popular support. That unfolding process of favouring society over the prerogatives of the state, however fragile and uncertain, is now more than a decade old. It is gaining ground in elite political culture, and it seems unstoppable as various formations contest for public influence and political support. Where a hitherto violently partisan state summons its supporters not on the basis of their partisan ties, but on their presumed rights as citizens, this is not just good news. It is also disruptive of the conventional wisdom and is subversive of the political status quo. I do not believe that this particular antinomy in which popular claims anchored in universalist and transnational values that challenge state power, as opposed to securing narrowly partisan causes, can be absorbed without significant ruptures and division within the state and among its personnel. Unlike earlier Third World mobilizing ideologies that invoked 'the popular' against some narrow dominant class interest, civism-as-ideology does not easily lend itself to the kind of manipulation, debasement and social polarization associated with quarrels over redistributive populism, revolutionary socialism, or neoliberal capitalism.

While the approach to citizen politics by small civic groups may be compromised by class association and blunted in their political reach, state-driven citizen politics that speaks in the name of citizens' presumptive rights against those of the state, is a very destabilizing move indeed. It is bound to create problems for Jamaica's politically weakened governors who must operate in a society where democratic values are deeply entrenched and a rich associational life beyond the state is jealously guarded.

I think, then, that the turn of the Jamaican state to what I shall call 'civic populism' can be destabilizing of predation politics. Civic populism, no matter how weak, is likely to create turbulence and ruptures in Jamaican statecraft. And this disturbance can only embolden already alienated constituencies nursing historic grievances rooted in denial of their rights as citizens. It should also encourage social movements to see the radical potential of displacing this liberal civism with something else that links citizen politics to wider issues of class, race, culture, and inequality in Jamaica. Barring this development current PNP enunciation of citizen politics is likely to pit PNP personnel accustomed to doing things in the old ways against their colleagues who are experimenting with new approaches to power. I need only cite rumblings inside the PNP that seem to confirm this clash, as cabinet members prepared to violate civism, war with those who find in embracing civism a way to gain political advantage while securing popular support. Thus we heard the Minister of National Security, Peter Phillips, utter his *mea culpa* for having attended a PNP gunman's funeral in 2004, even as he warned his colleagues against consorting with criminals. Similarly, in 2005, Prime Minister Portia Simpson-Miller, then the Minister of Local Government, broke party lines and abstained from voting against an Opposition resolution that criticized the PNP's budgetary allocation for the fire department. The harsh manner with which her PNP colleagues, both male and female, denounced her indicates something of the danger of toying with civism. Both incidents that found PNP leaders at odds with colleagues accustomed to the old way of doing things, confirm the ongoing embattled restoration of the public interest and the sharpening of inner-party strife as this nettle of the public good pricks the fingers of the PNP brass.

Civism's Dark Side

This paean to the liberating potential of civic politics need not ignore civism's dark side. It is expressed in a variety of contrary tendencies that take the following forms:

- civic groups and the insistence of notable personalities on the suspension of the civil liberties of Afro-Jamaicans in the interest of recovering a civil, democratic politics;
- the discontinuity between politicians' bracing calls for civic empowerment and their deafening silence and inaction on the dismantling of political garrisons;
- failure to connect the narrative of citizen politics to the ethnic and class-driven narratives of black popular militancy;

- the compromising of commitment to citizen politics by the countervailing shift to technocratic and managerial enunciations and practices that privilege the party managerial elite;
- the refusal of elites of the state to countenance mass involvement in this renewal of citizen politics.

Conclusion

The revival of citizen politics marks the latest phase in the ideological and political evolution of the Jamaican political class. Civic politics and its celebration is the new project over which different sections of the politicized middle class are contending in the aftermath of the breakdown of predation politics. This contention is apparent from the clashes and flare-ups within the parties and between the state and presumptive middle-class champions of the poor. Summoning the citizen to exercise presumed rights and politicians' willingness to countenance the trimming of their own prerogatives — along with their readiness to clip the wings of state — highlight the new direction of Jamaican statecraft. I have argued that this modality is ambiguous and problematic. It is entangled in the old politics of predation and cooptation, even as it moves to create new bases of legitimization. Confined as it is within the framework of liberal dispensation, the Jamaican state's encouragement of citizen politics — for all its destabilizing potential — actually summons a puny subjectivity. That is, state-sponsored and lobby group civism tend to hail the citizen as consumer of public goods in a market economy and as dissatisfied individuals in a politically liberal setting. Rather than tapping into a subjectivity that connects the call for citizens' rights vis-à-vis the state, to forms of black militancy that are persistently questioning the structure of inequality and the character of power at home and abroad, liberal civism arrests the radical promise of citizen politics. The development of this latter project, this other citizen politics, in which 'raced' Afro-Jamaican subjects are summoned awaits its inventive social movement.

Notes

1. A version of this article was published in *Ideaz* 3, nos. 1–2 (2004).
2. For a discussion of governance in the Caribbean, see *Governance in the Age of Globalisation: Caribbean Perspectives*, eds. Kenneth O. Hall and Denis Benn (Kingston: Ian Randle Publishers, 2003).
3. For an example of the turn to civic politics even among former detractors of the Jamaican political system, see Trevor Munroe, *For a New Beginning* (Kingston: CARICOM Publishers, 1994).
4. The changing face of Jamaican democracy is reviewed in Trevor Munroe's 'Transforming Jamaican Democracy through Transparency: A Framework for Action', in *Fostering Transparency and Preventing Corruption in Jamaica*, ed. Laura Nelson (Atlanta: The Carter Center, Emory University, 2002).
5. Obika Gray, *Demeaned But Empowered: The Social Power of the Urban Poor in Jamaica* (Kingston: the University of the West Indies Press, 2004), 8.

10 | *The Politics of Power and Violence: Rethinking the Political in the Caribbean[1]*

Anthony Bogues

*Look into my eyes, tell me what you see
Can you feel my pain, am I your enemy.
Give us a better way, things are really bad
The only friend I know is this gun I have.
Listen to my voice this is not a threat, but
now you see the nine are you worried yet ...
I make up my mind to end up in the morgue
I know I rather die than live like dog.*

– Bounti Killa

*Do not be deceived by the multiplicity of sounds that ring and jingle like
laughter.... Death speaks with a thousand whispers, but a single voice.*

– Roger Mais

Introduction

There can be no disagreement that violence is perhaps the single most discussed and vexing issue in many Caribbean societies today. The number of individuals killed in Jamaica and Saint Lucia, the bomb attacks in Trinidad, and the growing number of people violently killed in Guyana, speak not of a mundane crisis in the Caribbean postcolony, but of a crisis we have perhaps yet to name. This is not a crisis of hegemony,[2] the end of the Bandung project,[3] nor even as I suggested a few years ago, one of 'language, life and labour'. Crisis as phenomenon morphs and when not resolved takes on new life, reproducing itself into different forms. In such contexts, one element of a conjunctural crisis can become a long-term feature of a society, shifting some of the central grounds and practices through which a human community reproduces itself. Such a condition not only produces what Walter Benjamin calls 'states of emergency' which becomes a temporary rule, but instead seeks to consolidate that rule as a norm, and eventually a way of life. When this happens the conventional ways and conceptual frames in which thinkers and scholars have grappled with the different modalities of both examining and understanding these societies, perhaps no longer obtain. I would suggest that such is the current case of some Caribbean nation states.

Currently within the 'English-Speaking' Caribbean, there is the absence of radical political will, political imagination and of any mass progressive and radical agenda. All three elements play some role in the current crisis but do not offer by themselves or combined an adequate explanation. To grapple with the current crisis we might be required to critically examine different objects and forms. This means shifting some of our intellectual labour into understanding a new set of relationships and subjectivities — death, power, violence and how the perennial quest of freedom in the Caribbean is being played out. I am not suggesting here a focus on 'political culture' nor do I wish to engage in what I consider sometimes to be an unproductive debate about the relationship between politics and culture. Instead, in this essay, I undertake a different task. I want to think about the relationship of power in its 'capillary forms of existence', how power as a field of force exists in other ways than its conventional state forms and how in these ways, it becomes productive creating geographical spaces of violence and death while re-mapping sovereignty.

The construction of these geographical spaces not only sustains subjectivities but does three other things. First, it forces us to rethink the relationship between violence and power. Secondly, it cracks open homogenous conceptions about subaltern counter-hegemonic practices. Finally, it may posit another way of thinking about the history of the region since the 1838 slave emancipation. In this regard rather than thinking that the nineteenth-century Caribbean was either marked by the failure of slave revolution to achieve full freedom from racial chattel bondage or by the consolidation of colonial reform, it may be more useful to reconceptualize that history as one shaped by incessant contestation between different force fields of power, jockeying for dominance and hegemony.[4] This reconceptualization might prove fruitful and certainly could be a prelude to thinking about our present. Such a perspective is necessary since I am not positing any essential permanent structural or cultural features of Jamaican society, but rather engaging in an historical analysis while wrestling with the 'angels of theory', to glimpse how the present is constructed. There are two other consequences of this move. Rethinking both the arc and direction of the Jamaican historical narrative also requires us to re-examine the historical experiences of Jamaican radical politics. As well, it may allow us to interrogate the nation state in its postcolony iteration while thinking differently about the meaning of the political and sovereignty. If this is so then it is appropriate to begin our journey in the nineteenth century.

Power, Coercion and Hegemony: From Racial Slavery to Tutelage

It is neither the intention nor purpose of this essay to engage in extensive historical unpeeling of nineteenth-century Jamaica. However, since my arguments about the relationship of power to violence suggest a series of shifts in how Jamaican society is conventionally studied it is perhaps important to rehearse a few critical elements about the historical construction of power in Jamaican society. The abolition of racial slavery in colonial Jamaica was a watershed for the forms of rule deployed by British colonial power. Racial slavery under British colonialism combined four kinds of violence. Achille Mbembe has observed that colonial sovereignty 'rested on three sorts of violence … the founding violence … the second [a violence of] legitimation …[and] the third form of violence …, falling well short of … "war" , [recurring] again and again in the most banal and ordinary situations'.[5] However, in instances where racial slavery was combined with colonial power, power also rested on a fourth leg of violence. If colonial power ruled through projects of civilization, violence of conquest, tutelage or assimilation, then racial slavery required a kind of absolute domination over the body of the slave. This means that the slave was not only property but a *res,* a thing that was excluded from the social and political mechanisms of the community. The enslaved existed in what Orlando Patterson has called a state of 'social death'. In this condition the slave's human life was reduced. It was not reduction to 'bare life',[6] but rather it was life made superfluous. W.E.B. Du Bois in *Black Reconstruction* sums up very well this type of domination when he notes that Atlantic slavery represented a form of domination which rested on the 'submergence below the arbitrary will of any sort of individual'.[7] Thomas Thistlewood, the well-known English planter records in his diaries incidents on Jamaican slave plantations that were illustrative of this kind of power and domination. He notes:

> — Wednesday, 28th January, 1756 — Had Derby well whipped, and made Egypt shit in his mouth.

> — Flogged … Quacoo well, and then washed and rubbed in salt pickle, lime juice and bird pepper; also whipped Hector for losing his hoe; made Negro Joe piss in his eyes and mouth.

> — End of October 1776 — a Stout Negro man of Dr. Lock's is now gibbeted alive in the Square.[8]

Racial slavery was a form of domination in which power deployed technologies of rule that targeted the slave body. The objective of this kind of power was not to turn human beings into subjects but into objects and things. In this context violence was deployed to break and destroy, to remove possibilities and act immediately upon the person through the body. It was power over the flesh. The abolition of racial slavery shifted this kind of power in the colonial Caribbean changing its terrain from a singular focus on the body to the art of creating subjects. Although, it should be noted as Diana Paton has pointed out that this shift did not mean the end of certain kinds of punishment since flogging was reintroduced in the 1850s and the treadmill became a common feature of plantation life in the post-emancipation Caribbean.[9] There was however a general shift and one that was not welcomed by all elements of British colonial power, a fact illustrated by the events and debates surrounding what became known as the 'Jamaica Affair', after the 1865 Morant Bay Rebellion.[10] However, it was not just the terrain of colonial power that shifted. Abolition created new spaces for the ex-slave to begin a series of historic confrontations with the technologies of colonial rule. There were two other primary technologies of colonial rule in the post-emancipation period other than colonial violence. The first was that of Christianity (hence the heavy deployment of Christian Missionaries) and the second was the vigorous attempt to turn the ex-slave into a wage labourer. Combined these two forms of rule sought to create a moral culture that was modelled in part on an imaginary Victorian male respectability, what Horace Russell has so felicitously called, the 'Christian black'.[11] The creation of this subject provided the ground for power to act outside of naked violence. In this instance, in the words of Michel Foucault, power becomes a condition for the 'management of possibilities'. It is of course very well documented that the ex-slaves captured the Christianity of the missionaries and wrought a number of Afro-Christian religious practices.[12] The emergence of the religious practices of Myalism and Zionism, what Curtin described as the Africanization of the 1861 Christian Revival, was a process in which Afro-Jamaican subaltern subjects staked out a new ground for fashioning their own humanness. Central to this process was the emergence of what Diane Austin-Broos has called a 'logic of affliction'. Writing about Revivalism she observes that it was:

> not simply a "mixing" of elements but rather a redefinition of the form of Christianity that the missionaries had brought to Jamaica … [it] was not simply a nativistic movement … it was rather a complex of rite and belief that sought to sustain the *logic of affliction* by assimilating elements of Christianity to it.[13] (emphasis added)

There are two critical things about this 'logic of affliction'. Over time it would become an integral part of a series of narratives about the meanings of 'black suffering' in the New World and construct meanings that would eventually be bolstered by a reinterpretation of the biblical Exodus story.[14] Secondly, it would re-merge in the political language of the Jamaican subaltern in various periods as 'sufferers' (both noun and adjective). At this point we are running ahead of our story, but we should note that perhaps one of the main features of the present is the erosion and aggressive rejection of this logic by many young males. Today, I would argue that the 'logic of affliction' has been superseded by a different understanding of the Afro-Jamaican subaltern self. It is perhaps one dimension of the crisis.

If late nineteenth-century Jamaican society was marked by the vibrant emergence of Afro-religious practices then one element of the early twentieth century was the way in which these religious practices merged with an international African diasporic strain of Ethiopianism. We know of course that twentieth-century Jamaica society was marked by the 1938 labour rebellion; the consolidation of a Creole nationalist movement and the establishment of the formal two-party political system. The common radical conceptual frame for thinking about these events is that the struggles of the labour movement were mediated or deflected into the two-party political systems; that the 1938 rebellion was a high secular moment in the island's history from which emerged a small Marxist Left organization signifying the political modernity of the urban, and rural agricultural proletariat.[15] The structure of this historical narrative transforms the Jamaican 'Christian black' into a sugar factory proletariat, banana plantation worker or small farmer. Typically this narrative then generalizes 1938 as the moment of inauguration of Jamaica's modernity. I do not wish to spend time demonstrating the conceptual flaws of this perspective but rather only to note its embeddedness in a developmentalist modernization paradigm which in turn enacts a series of studies on Jamaican society that have erased and then silenced complex actions and practices of the subaltern Afro-Jamaican.

The emergence of so-called 'modern' political moment in Jamaica did create the Creole nationalist movement. As this movement reached for the 'political kingdom' it sought to construct new grounds of subject formation, tell an alternative story of Jamaica's history, and implement new norms for citizenship. The strivings of Creole nationalism culminated in the island's political and constitutional independence in 1962. However, I think that it is critical to observe that at the level of the Afro-Jamaican subaltern, while Creole nationalism was being consolidated into a national state form, and proclaiming national sovereignty, the politico-religious doctrines and practices of Rastafari offered an alternative. Rastafari emerged from three sources.[16] An international diasporic black religious tradition; a series of contestations between elements of Revivalism and early black religious doctrines which reread the bible in attempts to answer the causes and meanings of 'black suffering' in the New World; and finally a growing gender conflict between females who joined Pentecostalism and Revivalism.[17] Given all of the above it should not be surprising that the major conflict on the eve of political independence was the Henry Rebellion and that in the early postcolonial period, Rastafari was to play an important role in the radicalization of the early postcolonial moment. As well Rastafari became the central yeast for the cultural forms which made attempts to refashion popular culture. But Rastafari was not the only source of subaltern rebellion because alongside it emerged the figure of the *Rude Bwoy*.

The Rudie

Partha Chatterjee has noted that the 'history of nationalism as a political movement tends to focus primarily on its contest with the colonial power in the domain of the outside, that is the material domain of the state'.[18] In the Jamaican case this preoccupation resulted in the creation of a nation state that modelled itself on the Westminster system and the construction of a hegemony that was both Creole nationalist and masculine. The consolidation of local political power in the forms of Creole nationalism excluded other terrains that black Jamaicans had struggled upon. At the level of hegemonic discourse masculinity was understood as a dichotomy between ambitious male quests centred on the achievements of education, and female strivings for so-called respectability that centred on legal marriage and domesticity. However, at the level of urban subaltern groups, masculinity was not always constructed around male educational ambition but instead was sometimes driven by a desire to challenge and shake postcolonial norms. The Rude Bwoy was the exemplar of this desire.

Garth White in his seminal essay on this figure observes that,

> Rude Bwoy is that person, native, who is totally disenchanted with the ruling system; who generally descended from the "African" in the lower class and who is now armed with ratchets, other cutting instruments and with increasing frequency nowadays, with guns and explosives.[19]

David Scott in a reading of both White and the Rude Bwoy suggests that this figure is at 'once a figure of intense fascination and mortal dread … at once an emblematic Fanonian figure of internalised violence and rituals of embodied resistance, and the incarnation of a desperate, even pathological, criminality and lawlessness'.[20] Perry Henzell's film,

'The Harder They Come' allows us a visual representation of this figure. The film puts together, the two male subaltern exemplars of early postcolonial resistance, Rastafari in the figure of Ras Daniel Heartman and Ivan in the person of Jimmy Cliff. Both are rebellious, but the terms of their rebellion are different.[21] For Ivan rebellion is captured in the song, 'You Can Get It If You Really Want', while for Rastafari, rebellion is captured by the stoicism of the plaintive song 'Many Rivers to Cross'.

It is accurate to point out that violence was part of the repertoire of rebellion of the Rude Bwoy, however I want to suggest that this was not the violence of the lumpenproletariat preying upon itself and its community, but rather that violence was a strategic instrument deployed as an end. Fanon in *The Wretched of the Earth* notes that violence is a force that makes the 'native' 'fearless and restores self-respect'.[22] In other words for the Rude Bwoy violence was often a means of creating and safeguarding zones of black masculinity which were at odds with the hegemonic conceptions of the Jamaican nation state. It was deployed to construct what George Beckford calls 'a mode of life'.[23] It marked out a different set of normative terms for this subaltern group's self-conception, in particular that of the profound notion of respect.

Over time the Rude Bwoy developed into gang formations and many of them become attached to the Jamaican two-party political system. However, there was no easy slide from rebellion to accommodation, incorporation and eventual transformation. In the initial stages of the courting by the political parties many Rude Bwoys expressed ideas which drew both from Rastafari doctrine and in some instances the Cuban Revolution. For example the posters and iconography which decorated many of their small dwelling places ranged from pictures of Haile Selassie I, Che Guevara, Fidel Castro and icons of the American Black Power Movement as well as the hammer and sickle symbol. As gang members of this group became integrated into the two-party systems, they initially saw themselves as warriors, or soldiers. Integration into the two-party system was done at two levels. At the first level they became a protective force for communities that waged political war against each other, becoming political enforcers. Secondly, over time these enforcers became the central figures who would be responsible for the distribution of patronage benefits. When this happened the transformation of the Rude Bwoy from rebellious figures into political enforcers became complete.

However, I want to advise caution. While there was a general drift into the political parties, many figures resisted or kept their distance, or worked through ambiguous relationships to the political parties, trying to keep alive a radical masculinity that was hostile to neocolonialism. Some of these people made links with radical urban youth groups and others sought out relationships with members of the radical middle-class intelligentsia. In some instances a couple of individuals independently developed their own ideology of urban warfare that called for attacking banks, the island's race track, and the known police officers who consistently brutalized the communities of the urban poor. Obika Gray has recently observed that some of these figures such as Dennis 'Cooper' Barth

> were neither a common criminal devoid of political ideology nor a revolutionary prophet from the slums. Rather he was a combination of the avenging criminal gunman with a band of men.... He was both patron and feared avenger to the Rennock lumpenproletariat and a dangerous competitor who challenged the state's grip on the desperate poor.[24]

Never mind the moralizing tone of this interpretation, what we should be aware of is how this tone misunderstands one important thing — what such a figure like Barth represented to subaltern Afro-Jamaican communities.[25]

In general is it safe to say that over time, the Rude Bwoy was transformed into a political party warrior. It is at this point that we should turn to how political violence was understood from the perspective of one urban community.

War, Violence and Party Politics

Terry Lacy's 1977 study on violence and politics in Jamaican society argues that one of the critical issues facing the society in the 1960s and early 1970s was an 'internal security situation'. He posed this dilemma as central to any prospects for political change. Lacy documents how the new ruling Jamaican elite denounced 'the general attitude of lawlessness; maintained armed vigil; called for flogging in schools'.[26] Lacy then suggests that the group who were responsible for violence and created disquiet amongst the new ruling elite was the lumpenproletariat. He notes:

> This was what the national bourgeoisie called "criminal" or "hooligan element". Trench Town, Denham Town, Back O' Wall, Moonlight City — these names of parts of Western Kingston conveyed images of youth gangs, political gangs, Rastafarians, of Prince Henry's gang, The Max gang, the Blue Mafia, The Dunkirk gang ... the Vikings or the Roughest and the Toughest.[27]

Lacy ends his argument on violence by stating that the 'lumpenproletariat were the primary source of violence against the whole political system whereas over the decade other social classes were the primary source within the system'.[28] There is not enough space here in this essay to be engaged in arguments about the radical or revolutionary agency of the so-called lumpenproletariat or the relevance of such a designation for the Jamaican urban poor in a postcolonial economy. Instead, I want to focus on violence from a different angle — not violence as an incipient force of insurgency but rather violence as a way of constructing a form of rule in local communities, violence as a form of disorder deployed to produce and create order.

There is no longer any argument about the historic links between the Jamaican two-party political system and the emergence of political war and a politics of violence. The current debate instead is about the degree of continuing links. Historically, several questions perplexed many commentators and radical activists, amongst them is this: how was it possible for urban and rural oppressed groups to be so divided that they would end up engaging in violence against each other? How is it that class solidarity has been so lacking and seemingly impossible to construct? There are many possible answers to this but one I think resides in the ways the two-party system was able to construct not just clientelisim as a 'mechanism by which to institutionalise a power structure',[29] and alongside it a politics of 'scarce benefits', but how the system constructed and maintained a politics of difference based upon one of the oldest political stratagems — the division between friends and enemies.

The conservative German legal and political theorist, Carl Schmitt in developing a conception of the political from a conservative stance, drawing from Machiavellian notions of the political order argued that, 'the specific political distinction to which political actions and motives can be reduced is that between friend and enemy'.[30] Schmitt continues, 'the political enemy need not be morally evil nor aesthetically ugly.... But he is nevertheless, the other, the stranger; and it is sufficient for his nature that he is, in a special intense way, existentially something different and alien.'[31] Of course this definition of the political eschews conceptions of common humanity as espoused by humanism in African political thought as well as that of Western liberal notions of a political community rooted in Aristotle's claim of man as a political animal. It is certain that the enactment of politics based upon the dichotomy between friend and foe which organizes itself into difference is required for contexts where violence is a necessary feature of political life. What is particularly intriguing in the Jamaican case is the ability of the Jamaican two-party system to construct difference — friend/foe into localized geographical spaces. It is also critical to observe that these constructions were consistently reinforced by notions of belonging and enacted through political dramaturgy of songs, colour, party conferences, dances, popular music and the appropriation of the religious symbology both of Rastafari and other Afro-Jamaican religious practices. For many who engaged in Jamaican political wars the political rationale offered was one primarily based on the politics of friend/foe. I now wish to empirically illustrate this by briefly reporting on a series of research findings.

In a community we will call Cascade Gardens, extensive interviews conducted with individuals who themselves had been part of warfare and with those who supported it would dovetail with the remark of Nigel (not his real name) who said:

> The rationale behind it is that if we kill off one set then there won't be any votes.... Individuals growing up learned that the person who were [sic] fighting against you and you were fire shot at were our enemy. So if they saw us anywhere and hear where we stay they will kill us.[32]

Another person pointed out that the enemy (who lived a few blocks away) would behave similarly. Thomas (not his real name) states that,

'Anybody who dem catch…. Have to dead. You naw mek you enemy live. At that time I shared the same sentiment.'[33] In these contexts difference was re-articulated into reasons and rationales of war. Nobody admitted that they were fighting for a job, a house or for any scarce benefit. Instead those interviewed spoke about party, community, self-defence and being a warrior. According to one person, 'from you hear stone a lick pon you fence you know say you have fi bleach. A de same youth wah you cook with and you know and ting. So you go pon the corner.'[34] The construction of difference organized around practices of friend or foe, the reinscribing of this difference by rituals of belonging, meant in the words of one resident, 'we now become instead of natural African people, labourites and PNP.'[35]

Currently there are three forms of violence in Jamaica, and I will focus only on two. One is political violence which reached its peak in the 1980 general election where over 800 people died. The second is violence which links itself to the operation of power in small geographical spaces, (lanes, streets, small communities divided into areas). Both kinds of violence are sometimes linked but they must be distinguished. What I would argue is that the practices of political violence engendered the other form of violence. I want to now turn to a discussion on violence and its relationship to power and death.

Violence, Death and the Making of Duppies

Violence is both a difficult and slippery subject. Its primary enactment in terms of physicality and the infliction of pain involves assaults on personhood. As a practice violence is also about spectacle. To be effective as order it must first awe then create fear. Even though it kills or maims, the logic of violence is not about death per se but about its use in the production of order. This is the commonplace understanding of violence and its separation from power. Hannah Arendt suggests that violence is 'ruled by the means–end category'.[36] She also argues that there is an element of 'arbitrariness' to violence and that it interrupts routine processes. As a consequence she observes, 'power and violence are opposites; where one rules absolutely, the other is absent. Violence appears where power is in jeopardy, but left to its own course it ends in power's disappearance.'[37] Of course, Arendt is proposing a conception of power in which political authority rules the roost. In such a framework, violence is instrumental and only when it becomes war does it impact on power.

However, following Foucault, if we rethink power and begin to see it as one of 'capacity', of designating a relationship, rooted in the network of the social,[38] then violence is not a means–end instrumental but a logic which accompanies power. In other words, violence is a technology of power and not a pre-modern instrument which is negated with the creation of a disciplinary liberal society. How does this function in the Jamaican postcolony and what is its relationship to death? At this point we confront not only power but sovereignty. Achille Mbembe has suggested that the expression of 'sovereignty resides, to a large degree, in the power and the capacity to dictate who may live and who must die'.[39] Of course Mbembe is pointing us to the chief feature of sovereignty, its finality. In much of political philosophy we have become accustomed to speaking about sovereignty as a form of rule, a power that is the final 'arbitral agent', independent from external influences. This was the great political call of anti-colonial movements and subsequent demands for other forms of decolonization. In many ways the anti-colonial movement's political claim of nation and history was a claim to national sovereignty. I want to complicate this conventional understanding by shifting away from our justified fierce claims for national and cultural sovereignties. In other words, I want to remove sovereignty from the domain of rule which is constructed primarily around national state making, and bring it to the local and therefore to methods of human self-fashioning. In doing this, I suggest that rule can be constructed on the micro level rather than on the national level. I think that this is an important shift particularly for a postcolony since historically these sites were first colonial states before they became nation states.

In making this shift I want to suggest that sovereignty need not be on a large scale. Secondly, since integral to rule are notions of belonging, that in some circumstances the enactment of belonging operates at a micro level. In this regard, I want to argue that in many Jamaican urban communities, there has been a shift in the grounds of belonging. One resident of Cascade Gardens puts it well:

> There was no money, there was no food, there was no hope. Politicians had failed. They don't see nobody to look up to, because

as far as it go dem no cater for nobody ... everything drop, every man fe himself, everybody fe dem food. So everybody pon dem own.[40]

I do not mean to suggest by this citation that the political parties have lost complete political control over communities, but rather that another logic may now be at work in communities, one which seeks to break the absolute dominance of the two-party system. It is within this space that the Rude Bwoy re-emerges as another figure, the area leader.

Sovereignty as I have noted before does not have to operate on a large scale. In the Jamaican postcolony there were already active subaltern currents operating in opposition to creole state sovereignty. These forces did not engage in huge rebellions, but practised a form of cultural guerilla warfare, seeking to challenge the norms of citizenship and its values, what Rex Nettleford has called the 'battle for space'. In this situation the Creole nation state was never able to fully establish its hegemony.[41] A consequence of this failure was its inability to establish hegemonic notions of citizenship to which all classes could adhere. This meant that instead of a narrative of citizenship and its rituals of belongings practised through different performances of citizenship, the rituals of belonging and solidarity were practised through community linkages within politically controlled parameters. In turn, these practices were shaped by a master class language and discourse which emphasized 'outside' and 'inside' and continually positioned the urban poor as 'dem de people down there'. In the present shift of political control belonging occupies mirco spaces within communities. It is within these micro spaces that the area leader rules. There are many features about the area leader but two I think are critical for our current discussion.[42] The first is that, as they emerged many area leaders mixed Rastafari symbols with black nationalism. The base of the area leader is typically organized around some economic venture, for example a small shop. On many of these bases (and they are called bases in popular discourse), murals of Marcus Garvey, Bob Marley, Malcolm X adorn the walls. Dances are frequently held at such spots, where people from neighbouring opposite and sometimes hostile political communities are often welcomed. The second feature of note is that the rule of the area leader functions through a set of community codes which are enforced primarily by male individuals. Within this context I want to suggest that violence operates in two ways. In the first the enforcement of the code can be violent.[43] Secondly, once war breaks out between communities warriors then take up their guns and engage in fire fights often to the death. So how does death function in these operations?

One of the striking features of young men who engage in violence is their conversations amongst each other in which they often ask — 'how many duppies you mek?'

If as Bataille argues, death is a form of destruction and a sacrifice which is irreversible, as well as a spectacle which haunts life itself, then for many males involved in violence, death is a spectacle which affirms their life. This is so since in the middle of war/violence, other life affirming activities are not common. A resident of Cascade Gardens had this to say:

> Yu have time when every Sunday, every Saturday, you have funeral inside ya. For years you don't have a wedding, because it is like a trend. This week Tom going bury, next week is John, so we making preparation for that funeral. People just dead, and some of we just take it like joke, and we dress up and go a de funeral. The funeral is like a fashion show. And the latest fashion go a funeral.[44]

In such communities young males expect death as an affirmation that they have lived and the ritual of burial is marked not only by fashion but by gun salutes at the graveside. It should be observed that this is not the general view of the community even for those who have engaged in violence. As one young man, Marcus (not his real name) puts it, over time, as he became more involved, he had 'no feelings at all' and 'had to turn to God to seek answer due to vibes and tension'. Residents in Cascade Gardens often commented that they would begin to panic if they heard no gunshots for any extended period. They said that this panic was due to the fact that the silence of guns might mean that new strategies were being developed for war. Many residents stated that they were more relaxed when they heard gun fire since they were able to determine its direction.[45]

It would therefore seem that any radical transformation of Jamaica has to begin with the recognition that not only has Creole state hegemony collapsed but that there is a new form of politics in which organized communities operate outside the constitutional and juridical norms of the nation state. This is not a situation of dual power nor a prelude to revolution because, I would argue, what has also collapsed is the radical subaltern self-fashioning which extensively drew from Rastafari and a politics of radical black nationalism. This collapse within subaltern geographical spaces means that the area leader is rapidly losing his dominance and is being replaced by the 'shotta don'.

From Rude Bwoy to 'Shotta Don'

Bounti Killa's recent remarkable commentary on urban Jamaican life, in a song titled 'Petty Thief', observes how the petty thief is a predatory figure upon the urban community and not a Rude Bwoy. It is a song which marks the complete transition of a postcolonial rebel figure into a commanding figure of vengeance. This vengeance seeks both to destroy while searching for ways to enter into the mainstream of Jamaican society. I want to suggest that two episodes were central to the formation of this figure of the 'shotta don'. This is important because the conventional story suggests that it is drug runnings, the emergence of posses and deportees that are the primary explanations for the emergence of 'shottas dons'. The two episodes are the two peace processes, one that was attempted in the 1970s and the other in 1999 and their subsequent failure.

In the aftermath of the Green Bay massacre of 1978, political enforcers from both political parties organized a peace treaty. The ambush killing of political enforcers by the Jamaican military shook many enforcers' political ties. The two major figures in this peace effort were Claude Massop from Tivoli Gardens, the main JLP stronghold in the western end of Kingston and Aston 'Buckie' Thompson from the PNP. The peace treaty was warmly welcomed by many of the political enforcers and had the backing of prominent individuals notably Bob Marley. The peace process was organized and managed by a council that met regularly at the Ambassador Theatre in West Kingston. Its advocates demanded a programme of public works for the unemployed male youths of urban Kingston. At one of the rallies held to support the peace treaty, Buckie Thompson in an outspoken speech declared: 'After peace now, we want to see improvement in living conditions. We want work in general and government must put more in youth programmes.' Echoing this call another individual stated, 'Unity wonderful but we want better housing, better living standard for all people whether JLP or PNP. We cannot allow politicians to come into West Kingston and divide the youths anymore. The situation must remedy.'[46] Individuals close to the process have pointed out that many of the discussions at the Ambassador Theatre circled around the possibility of a new political party of Rastafari that would be funded with Marley's money. Here it should be noted that the financial management of the council resided in the hands of Bob Marley's lawyer, Diane Jobson, as well as an administrator of the Ethiopian Orthodox Church. The peace process did not last and was buried with the killing of Massop in Jamaica and Thompson in New York.

Some of the individuals who attended the various peace council meetings recalled in interviews with this author both the promise and its example. In 1999, 21 years later, some of these figures made a second attempt. However, if the first peace treaty was driven by a desire for unity in the face of certain death by the state forces, the second one was driven by two elements: economic activities of individuals who had used their position as political enforcers to garner state resources and secondly, a growing feeling in many urban communities that violence had taken its toll.

The second peace process was not as centralized as the first. There was no central advisory council although various attempts were made to pull the leadership of communities together into a combined peace movement. However, it was clear that in the 21 years many urban communities had become balkanized. Wherever peace was declared because of the exhaustion of a community, criminal activity like rape and petty thieving declined.[47] In community spaces where peace was enacted there emerged forums of community justice. These forums were sometimes organized to include individuals in communities who were seen as either elders or having some amount of respect. Again, elements of black nationalist ideas and Rastafari were used to undergrid declarations of unity and peace. In one community the peace process allowed for the emergence of classes in black radical history and the development of a literacy programme. However, in all communities peace was unstable. Peter Tosh had long declared at the peace concert in 1978 that there would be no peace without justice. The second effort at peace collapsed because of two things. The first was the inability of the peace makers to provide economic development in the communities. The second was the emergence of a generation of young males called 'shottas', who did not buy into any of the two central ideological forces of radical subaltern Afro-Jamaica, Rastafari or radical black nationalism. These 'shottas' challenged many area leaders, themselves became dons and engaged in predatory activity. It is the emergence of this avenging figure that is the main sign of the crisis. This is a figure who does not seek to explain and understand his social location by references to any logic of 'black suffering'. For this figure the Jamaican postcolony is itself a predatory state, the ways of contesting it rooted in subaltern rebellious cultures have all failed. There is only one way out, garner enough capital through extortions, government contracts, and haulage business and then use these resources to influence the formal two-party system.

The Jamaican postcolony therefore faces a unique situation. Not only has the formal creole nationalist hegemony collapsed, but the historical forms of radical counter-hegemony are in decline. In such a context politics takes on different dimensions. In the first, the 'shotta', who becomes the area leader, is a figure in which rule in communities is established by the force of death. In such circumstances death is not a rupture but a norm to be deployed, violence becomes the foreclosure of possibilities and is arbitrary, as targets are no longer specified. Rule therefore is about the absolute power of death. Violence must now be brutal in a special sense and it is significant that rape becomes a regular feature of violent attacks. The split between 'shottas' and those figures who although involved in criminality live their lives through a nostalgia of Rastafari was recently illustrated with the widespread beating in the Jamaican prisons of persons who were jailed for rape that accompanied their criminal activity. In the second instance the 'shotta dons' make efforts to replace the clientelism of the political parties in the community that they rule.

Conclusion

The contemporary nature of violence in Jamaican society is a mark of a profound crisis in the Jamaican postcolony. It is not a crisis which can be named by recourse to discourses about lack of values and attitudes or by nostalgic musings about return to British colonialism. For us to grasp the complexities of the crisis and its qualities two things are required. The first is a genealogy of the male rebellious subaltern figure, a gaze which allows us to trace how the contestation of power in the spheres outside of formal institutional political authority and upon different terrains operates. We also need to begin to grapple with violence and its relationships to power and the meanings of death. These turns will allow us to make sense out of what seems to be a strange situation, one in which practices of sovereignty and belonging operate on a micro level. The situation seems strange as well since, as Martin Heiddeger once pointed out, one possible dimension of human freedom is our own death wish. For many Jamaican males involved in violence this 'death wish' is their own claim and the parameters of their lives change from 'tek life' to 'tek death'. In doing this new work, our genealogy rethinks domination and the spaces between its formal enactment and the population it must rule. From this perspective the current Jamaican crisis points to the idea that the political can be a nebulous site and that power walks in many guises.

Notes

1. Thanks to Geri Augusto, George Lamming and David Scott for critical comments on this essay. A version of this essay was read at a conference on Caribbean Studies held at Yale University in 2005. I want to thank in particular Hazel Carby for inviting me and all the participants who commented on the paper.
2. Brian Meeks has argued that the current crisis in the Caribbean is in part the result of the dissolution of hegemony. See Brian Meeks, *Narratives of Resistance* (Kingston: the University of the West Indies Press, 2000).
3. David Scott has consistently argued this position. See in particular David Scott, *Refashioning Futures: Criticism After Postcoloniality* (New Jersey: Princeton University Press, 1999).
4. This work is already being done to some degree, see for example, Brian L. Moore and Michele A. Johnson, *Neither Led nor Driven: Contesting British Cultural Imperialism in Jamaica, 1865–1920*, (Kingston: the University of the West Indies Press, 2004). See as well Catherine Hall, *Civilising Subjects: Metropole and Colony in the English Imagination, 1830–1867* (London: Polity, 2002).
5. Achille Mbembe, *On the postcolony* (Berkley: University of California Press, 2001), 25.
6. The term 'bare life' has become popular in contemporary Western political philosophy. It connotes a life that is limited to biological reproduction and is distinguishable from the end of politics which is about human capacity and the structuring of common life. For the enslaved in Atlantic slave societies very often not even bare life was permitted. For a discussion of 'bare life' see Andrew Norris, 'Giorgio Agamben and the 'Politics of the Living Dead', in *Politics, Metaphysics and Death*, ed. Andrew Norris (Durham: Duke University Press, 2005).
7. W.E.B. Du Bois, *Black Reconstruction* (New York: Atheneum, 1962), 9.

8. Cited in Hilary Beckles, 'Black Masculinity in Caribbean Slavery', in *Interrogating Caribbean Masculinities,* ed. Rhoda E. Reddock (Kingston: the University of West Indies Press, 2004), 234.

9. See Diana Paton, *No Bond but the Law: Punishment, Race and Gender in Jamaican State Formation, 1780–1870* (Durham: Duke University Press, 2004).

10. See for an extensive discussion of this Anthony Bogues, 'J.S. Mill. "The Negro Question" Race, Colonialism and the Ladder of Civilisation', in *Race and Racism in Modern Philosophy,* ed. Andrew Valls (Ithaca: Cornell University Press, 2005), 217–34.

11. Horace Russell, 'The Emergence of the Christian Black: The Making of a Stereotype', *Jamaica Journal* 16, no. 1 (1983): 51–71.

12. This process is described in many texts but see Philip Curtin, *Two Jamaicas: The Role of Ideas in a Tropical Colony, 1830–1865* (New York: Antheneum, 1970).

13. Cited in *Neither Led nor Driven,* 53.

14. Of course this reinterpretation belongs to two segments of Afro-Jamaican religious practices, Rastafari and native Baptist.

15. See of course Ken Post's remarkable book, *Arise Ye Starvelings* (The Hague: Martinus Nijhoff, 1978). The narrative is often recounted and in the Marxist Left during the 1970s it was widely reproduced. The most popular Left political education pamphlet along these lines was Don Robotham, *Our Struggles* (Kingston: Workers Liberation League, 1975).

16. See of course Barry Chevannes's important study on Rastafari, Barry Chevannes, *Rastafari: Roots and Ideology* (Kingston: the University of the West Indies Press, 1995).

17. See Diane J. Austin Broos, *Jamaica Genesis: Religion and the Politics of Moral Orders* (Kingston: Ian Randle Publishers, 1997).

18. Partha Chatterjee, *The Nation and its Fragments: Colonial and Postcolonial Histories* (New Jersey: Princeton University Press, 1993), 9.

19. Cited in Anthony Bogues, *Black Heretics, Black Prophets: Radical Political Intellectuals* (New York: Routledge, 2003), 191.

20. David Scott, *Refashioning Futures: Criticism after Postcoloniality* (New Jersey: Princeton University Press, 1999), 209.

21. Of course the figure of Ivan is based on the Jamaican folklore character Rhyging.

22. Frantz Fanon, *The Wretched of the Earth* (New York: Grove Press, 1963), 94.

23. George Beckford, 'Introduction' to Erna Brodber, *Standing Tall: Affirmations of the Jamaican Male* (Kingston: Sir Arthur Lewis Institute of Social and Economic Studies (SALISES), 2003), xxix.

24. Obika Gray, *Demeaned But Empowered, The Social Power of the Urban Poor in Jamaica* (Kingston: the University of the West Indies Press, 2004), 204.

25. In a series of interviews I conducted for a research project done on violence in urban Kingston, the majority of the participants made a very sharp distinction between the exploits of Cooper and those of the political enforcer. He was called the 'original rebel' and remembered as someone who did not engage in what was called, unnecessary violence. The general feeling was that if he was alive then the peace process which emerged in the late 1970s would have had a better chance of success, and war and violence in the poor urban communities minimized.

26. Terry Lacy, *Violence and Politics in Jamaica, 1960–1970* (Manchester: Manchester University Press, 1977), 28.

27. Ibid., 32.

28. Ibid., 33.

29. This is Carl Stone's definition of the relationship between clientelisim and political power. Cited in David Scott, 'Rationalities of the Jamaican Modern', *Small Axe*, no. 14 (September 2003): 1.

30. Carl Schmitt, *The Concept of the Political* (Chicago: the University of Chicago Press, 1996), 26.

31. Ibid., 27.

32. The interviews from which this citation is taken were done in 1999 in an urban community which we will call Cascade Gardens. This community is an urban inner-city community which has had an extensive history of political violence and warfare. I want to thank the entire 1999 graduate class in Caribbean politics for agreeing to do this project. Many of the interviews were conducted by them. Also thanks to Judith Wedderburn, Veraldo Barnett and Sharene McKenzie all of whom worked with the project and made it possible.

33. Interview in Cascade Gardens, 1999.

34. Ibid.

35. Ibid.

36. Hannah Arendt, *On Violence* (New York: Harvest, 1970), 4.

37. Ibid., 56.

38. See Michel Foucault, 'Subject and Power', in Michel Foucault, *Power* (New York: The New Press, 2000), 326–48.

39. Achille Mbembe, 'Necropolitics', *Public Culture* 151 (2003): 11.

40. Interview in Cascade Gardens.

41. The closest the Jamaican state perhaps arrived at this hegemony was in the period between 1972–77 during the regime of Michael Manley and the PNP government.

42. There are two types of area leaders in many communities. One type is deeply connected to the two-party political system while the other is a semi-independent figure. It is the latter that I am concerned with.

43. Diana Paton observes how in nineteenth-century Jamaica the existence of alternative justice systems depended upon the headman. See, *No Bond but the Law* (Durham: Duke University Press, 2004).

44. Interview in Cascade Gardens, 1999.

45. Ibid.

46. Obika Gray, *Demeaned But Empowered, The Social Power of the Urban Poor in Jamaica*, 244.

47. For a discussion of this and two case studies, particularly one in the community of August Town, see Horace Levy, 'Peace in August Town', unpublished paper.

11 | Canvasses of Representation: Stuart Hall, the Body and Dancehall Performance

Sonjah Stanley Niaah and Donna P. Hope

Introduction

Since the 1980s, the body — individual and collective, social and natural, symbolic and real — has received great focus. It was finally understood that

> the relationship between the human body and the social collectivity is a critical dimension of consciousness in all societies.... It is a truism that the body is the tangible frame of selfhood in individual and collective experience providing a constellation of physical signs with the potential for signifying the relations of persons to their contexts. The body mediates all action upon the world and simultaneously constitutes both the self and the universe of social and natural relations of which it is a part.... The logic of that universe is itself written into the 'natural' symbols that the body affords.[1]

The growing literature and scholarly inquiry on the body as a space and in space in fields such as cultural studies, performance studies and geography within and outside the growing gender discourses is evident. Many pointed to the importance of acknowledging the body, dispensing with Cartesian logic to theorize the body in its own right on its own terms, through its specific size, class and racial dimensions in disciplines such as gender studies, performance and dance studies, sociology, cultural studies, and anthropology. From understanding of embodied bodies in an African sense,[2] bodies as sites[3] of battle,[4] the body in dance,[5] body as pleasure zone,[6] the body and the city,[7] to politicized, racialized[8] and gendered bodies, the map of the body in society has expanded with each passing year.

What is Hall's contribution? This paper is not intended to historicize Hall's contribution to the body project; rather, it is intended to look critically at the contribution and its pointers for close scrutiny of New

World performance practices such as dancehall. Stuart Hall in his plenary address at the Third International Crossroads in Cultural Studies conference,[9] puts the body in the context of postcolonial power, that is, as a central warfare weapon. The power of the idea of the body he says is seen in, for example, the way that race as a notion derived from biology or nature has been powerfully used to interrupt, displace, exclude and include for centuries of Western history in particular, the transfer of religious ideas, wealth, and ideology under the (race) banner. Hall was speaking of the black bodies that had been denied presence, voice and place in the schema of world politics. In earlier work, Hall spoke to the meaning of this 'black' in popular culture. He highlighted style as an important dimension of agency for Diasporans much in the same way that Lamming[10] in his tribute to Mittlehozer did.

A most interesting dimension, and this, where the inspiration for this paper comes from, is the way Hall contextualizes black bodies as 'canvasses of representation' — 'these cultures have used the body — as if it was, and it often was, the only cultural capital we had. We have worked on ourselves as the canvasses of representation'.[11]

With the physical body and its style as a central part of the 'black repertoire',[12] Hall underscores a representational dimension of the body here. Representation is the 'production of meaning through language, discourse and image'.[13] Being about how we construct meaning then, representation is itself a language system which is integrated into everyday life to create identity, rules, norms, stories, and conventions in social life.[14] There are various languages and the body is also one of them, using instead of the spoken word, gestures. Like other representational systems, the body is mediated by power, difference, sexual politics, ideology, practice, time, and space. What are these symbols, constellations of signs that bodies offer for our scrutiny? Beyond race, politics, and ideology, what dimensions of the body are explored, or under-explored in Cultural Studies? Are there non-representational systems that are yet to be fleshed out in relation to the body? For example, recent research shows that even the body has its own spatiality. It is not just flesh and blood, it has shape, size, and definitions of its structure, social utility and symbolic value vary from place to place. In other words the body has maps and there is a geography of embodiment.[15] In a recent study, Thomas[16] in what was described by Bryan Turner as an 'intellectual coup', affirmed that 'human bodies have been invested with a wide range of shifting and unstable meanings' and rarely have these bodies been interpreted on their own terms, allowed to speak for themselves. Given the opportunity, 'the mindful body' then, [17] defined by 'consciousness, intentions and language' can speak for itself through its own performance acts.

In the long and winding discourse on the body, Hall's contextualization of 'black' popular culture highlights some crucial elements for the study of the body. Black bodies in particular have been silenced, defined through 'ethnic hierarchies' even as black bodies within American culture broadly have defined key traditions of selfhood and nation in the face of fascination and 'fetishization' of male and female black bodies. In referring to black bodies as 'canvasses of representation', Hall highlights what is a representational dimension, a dimension thought to be inadequate to explain the complexity of black psychology and ecology, that is, the black body in social contexts, but we cannot assume that Hall falls into the trap that writers such as Thrift[18] was seen to be guilty of. Research in the interstices of Cultural Geography and Cultural Studies, includes especially Nash's[19] review of moves toward a non-representational analysis to that of analysing practices. She noted that performativity seen through embodied practices such as dance opens spaces for new theoretical, imaginative and material understanding. While she cautions against the irreverent migrations of performance and dance studies beyond their original academic agendas and boundaries, Nash points to the way in which 'work on cultural histories and geographies of specific dance forms offer alternative directions for thinking about practices and performance'.[20] Examples of this (what she calls choreocriticism) embraces questions such as those about who could dance 'where, with whom, for what audiences and how, tell of contests over culture, masculinity, class and nationhood, the legitimate, the civilised, the respectable, the primitive, the authentic and the exotic' in various local, national and global sites.[21]

We cannot assume, and this is where the strategy of the racial category takes over, that Hall was oblivious of the feel of his own black body, the knowledge of his own discrimination in the British context, the understanding that black bodies are more than what they represent, more than what they signify, that they can speak on their own terms beyond and before signification, speaking other kinds of politics, strategies, and memories. In other words, Hall is not Thrift. Hall's starting point is different because he has danced the black dance, walked the black walk and talked the black talk both in the symbolic representational sense and in the sense of the lived experience. He acknowledges the insufficiency of the racial category,[22] as much as he acknowledges that bodies are about desire and fantasy. Through Hall's contribution therefore, there is space for other questions to emerge — what lies beneath the display of the body through dance in particular locations, that is, beyond colonial, gendered, resistance, beyond eroticism or fleshly pursuit? This is where discourse on dancehall dance and deejay performance can enter.

Dancehall Dance: Representing Past and Present

Dancehall is Jamaica's premiere popular street theatre which first flourished around the 1950s. Its antecedents are popular sacred and secular forms such as the slave ship *Limbo, Jonkonnu, Dinki Mini, Gereh, Revival* and *Brukins Party*, among others. There is something very old therefore, and simultaneously new and renewing about Jamaica's dancehall. As it draws on the old, so it invents and reinvents itself. Dancehall occupies a tenuous place, a war zone[23] in Jamaican society. It is marginal, yet central to national identity. In real and symbolic terms, everyday dancehall occupies shrubs, streets, yards, the cracks and margins but yields (/wields) tremendous power in philosophy, transcendence, and transformation of space. As the progeny of world renowned Reggae music, dancehall is music, space, attitude, fashion, dance, life/style, economic tool, institution, stage, social mirror, ritual, social movement, profile, profession, brand name, community, and tool of articulation especially for inner-city dwellers who continually respond to the vibe expressed through the words:

Without the Dancehall a wha wi woulda do?
Reggae music call you must answer to,
Wine up, jump up, when you hear sweet reggae
Buju Banton, Beres Hammond affi tell them go deh ...
Everywhere I look is pure skanking
I see no statue around ...

I see girls a get wild, selector a spin music versatile
Dem waan tu'n down wi sound an' bruk wi vibes down
A who dem a try turn inna clown.[24]

– Buju Banton/Beres Hammond

Two important performance acts of the dancehall are those of the dancers and deejays. Let us examine the performing acts, the first being dance, what it signifies and symbolizes. What are these bodies, these dancing bodies telling us of what is venerated, fetishized or discriminated in Jamaican culture? Staying aware of cautionary notes from dance and performance scholars that some text-based descriptions have produced characterizations of dance as a 'metaphor for spontaneity, frivolity, and the inexpressible, as mad, transient and unanalyzable performance', [25] we engage the dance as a primary signifier of the body in dancehall. Dancehall style revolves around and is expressed by the body. In particular, the dancing body embodies dancehall style and becomes a crucial site of articulation at the individual, community and national levels. The transformation of tried and tested drum rhythms to mass-produced and patented digital drum rhythms highlights the maturation of a musical experience and form of production which attracts increasingly mature and unique bodily expressions. Through bodily movement, social identities are signalled, formed and negotiated, [26] and class, ethnicity, cultural continuity, identity, difference, affiliation, nationhood, gender, and race are transmitted. Movement is therefore a primary social text as it is complex, dynamic, and signals group affiliation and difference. Dance is a language, [27] 'a mode of expression and representation … a form of cultural knowledge'.[28] Specifically, dancehall dance offers a vision of its actors' identity/survival discourses that are revealed through a constellation of location, history, adornment, imagining, the imaginary, gestural patterns, play, codes and rules, and therapeutic devices.

Brathwaite[29] in his poem 'Didn't He Ramble' stated that 'what the heart lacked we supplied with our hips and the art of our shuffle shoes', in speaking of the Harlem Renaissance and African-American experience broadly.[30] These 'shuffle shoes' became the voices, whips and means of transgression for many disenfranchised in the debilitating postcolonial condition, especially inner-city dwellers. Dance moves such as the Yanga (Mento dance), and Ska movements that emphasize domestic activity (washing clothes, bathing), recreation (horse racing, cricket) or anything that appealed to the ska dancer,[31] are antecedents of popular dancehall moves such as the Butterfly and Log on. So are moves such as 'legs', performed by such famous dancers as Pam Pam and Baskin of the early years,[32] the 'Chucky', and 'Horseman scabby'.

An assessment of dancehall dance reveals the dynamic nature of dance creation and naming in the contemporary years especially throughout 1990 to 1994 and 1999 to 2004. Like the musical rhythms — 'punawny', 'taxi', 'sleng ting', 'rampage', 'old dawg', 'diwali',[33] 'fiesta', 'wicked', 'nine night' and 'tai chi' — that have maintained a dynamic naming system, dance moves have names which tell stories. These include stories of cross-fertilization, identification with/of characters, vibes, phenomena or body parts. For example, the 'Jerry Springer' and 'Erkle' present interesting names for an analysis of dancehall within the text of two television characters originating within the social milieu/melee displayed in America's visual scape. *Jerry Springer* is a talk show named after its host. It is known for the high levels of controversy and public display of interpersonal feuding. The Erkle, on the other hand, is named after a nerd from the series *Family Matters*.

As descendants of African movement and aesthetics, dancehall moves convey continuities such as the emphasis on 'the beat' documented in various African performance practices as the Ugandan Bongo and the 'natural bends' — elbow, head, pelvis, torso and knee bends[34] in the movement pattern. Welsh Asante[35] recognized that commonalities in all African dances have an inherent connection to ancestral Africa 'through epic memory and oral tradition, even though these dances represent different languages, people, geographies, and cultures.'[36] Following from this she identified seven foundations or senses in African dance: polyrhythm, polycentrism, curvy linearity, multi-dimensionality, epic memory, repetition, and holism which are all evident in contemporary dancehall moves.

Closer to home, specific aesthetic qualities have been isolated. Ryman[37] discusses the connection to ancestral rhythms and moves through an explanation of the characteristic 'wining' of the hips, the bounce (facilitated by natural bends) and S-shaped stance in both male and female dance. The 'S-90 skank' (1970s), mimicking the actions of the Rudie on his motorcycle is an early example, as well as traditional movement forms such as in Revival, Gereh, Bruckins, and Mento.

Ryman discussed the seeming preoccupation with sexual (hip-centred) movements within the context of African principles.

> If we understand that procreation was/is considered vital to the African's survival in life and death, in Africa as well as the Diaspora, then we can perhaps understand their apparent preoccupation with 'sexual' movements. Further, it is not unusual, as in Jonkonnu, for the traditional treatment within the context of the dance to be such as to allow for what the folk themselves define as 'sexual play'. It is simply a representation in dance-movement.[38]

Importantly, the characteristics pervade traditional and contemporary movement, and they have utility outside the dance. The agile pelvic movements help with uphill walks especially with heavy contents on the head. In this sense it acts as a 'shock absorber'.[39] Other characteristics such as bent knees, grounding of the body rather than lifts, rhythmic complexity and parallel feet have also been documented. Apart from interpretations by Ryman[40] and White,[41] public debate about dancehall moves has revolved around evaluative judgements rather than understanding generated from the dancer's discourse and practice. Therefore, the discussion of dance moves below has been generated primarily from the dancers as key informants and the movement as key texts. What is the general character of these dance moves? At what periods have they been most prolific? Are there identifiable gender demarcations? Can kinaesthetic genres be mapped? Do the dances reveal insights about recruitment patterns or the politics of location? First, dance movements are more fluid or easy going when tensions are less.[42] From my research, preliminary observations suggest that the highpoints of increased dance creations, events and spread of dancehall have been periods in which there were no general elections with attendant political tensions. Secondly, dances can be classified according to the sex for which they are intended. Bogle, a major dancehall dance master or ethno-choreographer, acknowledged that the 'Bogle' dance is really for men while the 'Butterfly'[43] is for women.[44] While many dances are performed by women, those such as the 'One foot skank', 'Legs', 'Cool an' Deadly', 'Get flat' and more recently the 'Chaplin' are performed mostly by men. On the other hand, the 'Head top', 'Body basics', 'Sketel', 'Bike back', 'Position', and the various 'wines' — 'Wine an' go down', 'Go go wine', and 'Bruk wine' — have mostly been performed by women. A larger number of the dance moves, especially the more recent ones, are performed by both sexes: the 'World dance', 'Bogle', 'Tatti', 'Screetchie', 'Angel', 'Tall up Tall up', 'Higher level', 'Curfew', 'Log on', 'Row like a boat', 'Wave', 'Parachute', 'Blase', 'Signal di plane' and 'Shankle dip'. The stylization of the everyday is particularly pronounced in this proliferation of movement patterns. Where dance moves like Erkle, Acapella, and Bogle in the early 1990s depicted characters and aspects of life, dance moves during the current highpoint have served to magnify Jamaican style of life. In other words, everyday acts are more visible, and have taken on new expressive proportions through dance. Such practices as 'burn a spliff' or 'give dem a drape', as the police are well known to do to dance patrons, are enacted through dance. Similarly, 'Row like a boat', 'Fan dem off', 'Thunder clap', and 'Fall the rain' are other examples. As has been said of the Blues, for example, dancehall movement went back 'to the individual, to his completely personal life and death' for its 'impetus and emotional meaning'.[45] It issued directly from the individual 'social and psychological environment'.[46]

Female dances are generally those where the essential point of articulation is the rotation/thrust of the pelvic girdle, male dances emphasize complex leg- and hand-coordinated movements, and moves performed by both sexes are multi-dimensional in nature. The latter are not centred on the pelvic girdle or hand/leg coordination, they emphasize individual memory rather than dance skills and the entire community can execute these moves. In other words the criteria for recruitment are significantly less for unisex dance moves, which ensures continuity of the characteristic sociality in the dancehall space. Everyone can participate.

At the individual level, Stacey as self-proclaimed dancehall diva has a definitive style. Her performances often involve mounting a tower of speakers, humping the ground, or hanging from a nearby roof to perform sexually provocative moves which rely on complex hip movements and strength. Examples of such performances are the X-News Anniversary party on August 8, 2003 in Spanish Town or the British Dance 2002 at Rainbow Lawn, where Stacey entertained the audience with gyrating hip movements while hanging upside down from the roof's edge. In such a case, all patrons and dancers at the event are rendered spectators. The dance that is the norm for Stacey is not for most patrons and therefore the recruitment criteria would be very high.

We want to now look specifically at the movement pattern of the most popular female dance steps. The 'Butterfly' reigned supreme in 1992. With the hands and spread legs, the life force of a butterfly is depicted. The 'Butterfly' is danced with the knees bent, a characteristic feature of African and Diasporic movement patterns, the feet flat which supports the dynamic displacement of the hip, shoulder girdle, and legs while the fluid rotation of the knees laterally on a horizontal axis is achieved like the flapping of the butterfly's wings in flight. While the Butterfly has clear connections with its North Atlantic cousin the 'Charleston' (Ashanti ancestor dance), with its quick spreading and crossing of hands on the knees, [47] there are differences. For example, the forward and backward thrust of the hip which supports the opening and closing of the legs allows for increased degrees of variation on the movement style. Importantly, the 'Butterfly' might present not only a dance, but also a dancehall philosophy, of an ethos of struggle, freedom, creativity, celebration, and beauty. The dancer's/dancing body is a frontier occupying space and time and its field of performance implies fields of time and space. Like the slave ship *Limbo*, there is an inherent passage through several real and psychic states of being. First there is the fact of releasing one state of being or point of origin to embrace another (voluntary or involuntary). In the case of the enslaved it was an African origin, in the case of the butterfly it is the state of caterpillar, and in the dance it is the release of a passive state into an active performance. Inherent struggles give way to triumph at the end of the passage when the dancer and audience are finally fulfilled, the enslaved arrives in the New World, and the butterfly engages in flight. There is a narrative here that transcends movement from-one-point-to-another to embrace a philosophy of how to dance, how to undertake the passage.

There are other kinds of messages to be read from the dance moves. Tangible sociocultural and anatomical scripting is evident. For example, dances that comment on social ills include the 'Curfew' and 'Drive by'. The movement in 'Curfew' represents policemen carrying guns while searching for criminal elements in inner-city communities that come under attack from gang warfare or warring political factions. With the characteristic bent knees, sometimes to the *demi* and *grand pliéi* levels (very low bends), the dancer walks in a forward motion with hands mimicking the shape of a rifle while the dancer is looking forward and backwards. The 'Get flat' dance popularized by the Bloodfire Posse band through a song of the same name is an early replica of the curfew.

The 'Drive by' represents two things. First it comes into common Jamaican usage because of the 'importation' of drive-by shootings from North America, as a sign of more complex criminal activity in Jamaica. Added to this however, is the representation of the actions involved in driving a car. The dance moves through a sequence of actions such as steering, gearing down, turning left, indicating, braking, and parking. With increased access to cars by a wider cross section of the middle and lower classes, since the influx of reconditioned cars in the late 1990s, one could argue that the 'Drive by' also represents the 'coming of age' of car culture in Jamaica.

Alongside such imports as cars, and technological advancements as it were, there are others such as the internet and the concept of 'logging on' which are reflected in the 'Internet' and 'Log on' dance names. In the case of the 'Log on' dance however, its movement and description in song are unrelated to information technology strictly. The lyrics by Elephant Man instruct the dancer to 'Log on an' step pon chi chi man, dance we a dance an' a bu'n out a freakie man, log on an' step pon chi chi man' with a lift of the leg followed by a twist to the side before stepping down. Apart from the reference to the 'chi chi bus' (popular 1970's Jamaican public transportation) popularized by Jamaican poet Louise Bennett, there is the reference to homosexuality which the dancehall moral code denounces as a social ill. In the late 1990s, the meaning of 'chi chi' transformed to refer primarily to a homosexual male rather than the transportation mode. There are also explicit spiritual themes in the dance. The 'Poco man jam', and 'Angel' are examples. The 'Poco man jam' highlights the movement of a Pocomania (also known as Pukkumina and closely related to the Revival religious group) dancer who is possessed or on the verge of possession. The head, hands and feet are the central points of articulation. The dancer's head moves (sometimes erratically) from side to side with sharp jerky movements and forward thrusts on the right foot while the body is propelled forward with rhythmic thrusts of the right hand. This movement pattern is characteristic of the Revival religious groups and is described as the 'trumping' step.[48] The 'Angel' is characterized by a side shuffle which moves the body to the left and to the right. In Harry Toddler's song 'Dance the Angel', the dancer is instructed to 'dance the Angel, hail up Moses ... move to left, move to the right' in what Toddler describes as a salute to the angels: 'if you are not saluting the angels you are up with the devil angels.'[49]

Then there are dances that require the skill of 'wining': the smooth, generic 'bubble' or rotation of the hips, 'wining' like a go-go dancer (exotic dancer), or 'wining' on the top of the head. There are various songs that encourage 'wining' and a developed 'wining' skill: Elephant Man's 'Wining Queen'[50] asks the question — 'who is going to be the next "wining" queen, the next "wining" machine?' His 'Fan Dem Off'[51] encourages the dancer to 'fan them off 'cause them a fly...trample them with yuh dancing cause them bad mind, don't stop wine up your body like a snake in the vine, wine it up 'cause you inna you prime'. Captain Barkey's[52] song 'Go Go Wine' sings of the dancer 'wining' their waistline, their chest, and their rumps because they have no problem: they have fed their children, and they are hotter than the competition. Patra's 'Bruk Wine', Admiral Bailey's 'Stuck', Shabba Ranks's 'Girls Wine' are all similar 'wining' incantations to the dancer.

A crucial component of the 'wining' capacity that dancers must have is the placement of the buttocks. In various body positions, the dancer's buttock can shimmy, thrust, rotate, release and contract, push, press and pump, in a light, heavy, frantic, sharp, fluid or jerky manner. Moves such as the 'Bike back', 'Position', and 'Sidung pon it' are examples: not only do they require fluid movement of the hips; they also feature a particular aesthetic of the buttock. Johnny P's recording of the 'Bike Back' move is captured in a song of the same name in which he described the movement of the experienced female bike rider/dancer. He explained:

Cock up yuh bumpa when yuh deh 'pon di bike back
Mek dem know gal pickney you a shock, shock
Cau' dem know gal seh you hot
All a di gal dem 'pon di bike back
when dem a ride dem a wine an' flash
If you ever see how dem bum it just cock
Round a back an' it a lick an' it a shock an' it a ...

Yuh just hunk yuh knee an bend you back
An' go down gal an' yuh get flat
An' set you'self like yuh deh pon bike back
An' show di gal dem dat you know dat
Becau' Honda it nah run 'tings again
An' Suzuki nah run again
An' Yahama it nah run 'tings again
An' mi ago start up all di gal dem
A Kawasaki fi dem, saki fi dem
An' if its not di saki di Ninja fi dem ...
Watch her pon di Ninja, whoaa, she a spowler!
An, a mogel, Lord, 'pon di bus driver!
Watch yah now she a move like di bubbler!
Whoooaa, watch her nuh, Lord she get inna fever!
A wha' she have, nuh di Ninja fever!
Whooaa, watch di rider as di owner
Hol' di bike an' lick it roun' di corner
'Pon di side mi t'ink it tu'n over
Watch di gal how she sidung a di 'pellar
Whooaa flash up her spoiler
A a a at, she a hot number'[53]

Essentially, as the dancer hoisted her derriere, with bent knees facilitating rotating and flashing movements, perfect balance and control was mastered and maintained on the highly fashionable Kawasaki motorbike, so much so, she upstaged the competition and passers-by. Obviously, the large derriere which is celebrated in dancehall and Jamaican culture more widely matters in such a move. It is the dancer with a buttock that is visible and can be manipulated that will command attention. As Johnny P explains, such a movement is best executed with a large, but flexible, derriere because girls with flat bums cannot effectively ride the bike back.

It is important to note that, as with the post-1960s deejay music where songs were recorded with their versions, dances have versions as well. A dance such as the 'Imitation Bogle' and 'Soca Bogle' are versions of the 'Bogle'. There are also unnamed or more informal versions seen within the context of individual interpretations or improvisations on specific dance steps. This 'versioning' in the dance/music nexus is an important continuity within African performance aesthetics.[54]

Finally, the 'Blase' is a dance which is popularly performed through a sequence of moves because of deejay Elephant Man's[55] song of the same name. The dance is performed by both sexes and moves through six steps: 'Propellar', 'Hand cart', 'Shake dem off', 'Elbow dem', 'Rock away', and 'Wi head gone'. Besides these, there are two important steps that were the original before the song. Developed by Blase, a youth of the same name from the Arnett Gardens area, the dance is similar to the 'Drive by' because it is characterized by several named steps and not just individual creativity.

Dance moves are created overnight and in a similar vein, those created can disappear. In spite of power plays within the space and from external forces, they exist on every street corner and are accessible to each citizen, among them 'the blind, the dumb, the deaf and the cripple':[56]

> A wan new dance weh Beenie fin' again
> Around di Street and di lane an' 'round di bend
> World dance is the name and the title
> The blind the dumb di deaf di blind an di cripple an
> I don't know why Black Roses love it sooo.[57]
>
> – Beenie Man

The documentation of these moves has primarily been undertaken (consciously or unconsciously) by videographers since the early 1990s. What is contributed here is a record of the dynamic creation of dance moves within a cultural system of embodied elocution that holds dance as a sixth sense. It is by this sixth sense that many key participants articulate their likes, dislikes, loves, burdens, prejudices and ultimately, their identities. The celebratory ethos of the dancehall culminates in the dance events around dancers and dance acts. The consistent urban self-fashioning embodied within performance and ultimately strategies of survival, undoubtedly places the female dancer at the centre of some of the most important innovations in the space and its general appeal. Dancehall queens such as Stacey and Carlene have made indelible marks on the practice and standard of dance, criteria for engagement, hierarchies established, and the democratization of dance. Numerous protégés have emerged and the queens as well as kings continue to inspire, groom, and create heirs to their thrones.

Representations of Masculinities in Dancehall Culture

Stuart Hall's concept of representation is particularly relevant to current work on the gendered representations of identity in the dancehall; and even more so for an examination of the movement of these gendered representations through the realm of the discursive into the political where the 'politics' of representation becomes critical when these images affect/effect the gendered structures of power that they obtain in Jamaica. His approach provides a conceptual framework for the articulation of discourses within a historically specific moment where, through the use of gendered/diasporic identity-stories, particular groups of Jamaican men work out their fantasies of masculinity on the dancehall stage. Here we examine and analyse how these men produce, articulate and represent gendered meanings using narrative, discourse and image while simultaneously grounding these masculine fantasies, the gendered structures of power in Jamaica and play into, with and against these structures. This results in very ambivalent forms of masculine discourse in the dancehall.

This work locates dancehall culture in a particular historical context marked by the political, social and economic transformations of 1980's Jamaica. The factors at work included the fall-out of structural adjustment; the rise of the market capitalism; the explosion of Jamaica's informal economy; increasing urbanization; rising political violence; and a growing ideological convergence between the People's National Party and the Jamaica Labour Party.

During this intense period of flux the new cultural griots that emerged in dancehall music and culture appropriated the power to name, and call into being, from their Rastafari-influenced predecessors. There is no clear evidence that the music deliberately sought to ignore the Marley-type refrain of black pride, race consciousness and social commentary. It is arguable that those who rose to prominence in the 1980's dancehall exhibited no clear attachment to the ideals/ideology of Rastafari and African pride because the ideology of capitalism encapsulated its own ideals — individualism, materialism and its attendant moral values. This does not discount the emergence of Rastafari artistes like Capleton, Sizzla and Anthony B within the dancehall genre. However, the hybrid 'Dancehall Rasta' that this group represents cannot be adequately discussed and analysed within this paper.

While it may be affected by and encapsulate elements of earlier forms of Jamaican music (for example, mento, ska, dub, roots rock and reggae), the music culture labelled 'dancehall' occupies a late twentieth-century cultural, political, ideological and economic space in Jamaica, and has a definite point of disjuncture with preceding manifestations of popular Jamaican music culture. As Hall notes:

> These moments are always conjunctural. They have their historical specificity; and although they always exhibit similarities and continuities with the other moments in which we pose a question like this, they are never the same moment. [58]

Therefore, dancehall music and culture utilized extreme manifestations of social, cultural, political and economic issues that were particular only to the late twentieth century (and now the twenty-first century), and remains simultaneously linked to but critically exiled from all preceding genres of Jamaican music culture.

The cultural vacuum created by Bob Marley's death in 1981 was filled with the cacophony of griots from Kingston's inner cities. This use of the power to name and call into being, using dynamic and transient inner-city slang grounded in Jamaica patois, signalled new powers of representation similar to that appropriated by Rastafari in the foregoing era. The griots of the dancehall disseminated their lyrics in hard, 'vulgar' dancehall slang and spoke of the poverty and deprivation, urban and political violence, police brutality, sex and sexuality and other factors that characterized life for Kingston's urban poor. This represented a shift in the terrain of culture 'towards popular, everyday practices and local narratives; and towards the decentring of old hierarchies and grand narratives'. [59] Aided by digitization, the market and the rise and proliferation of new media, dancehall deejays were able to articulate their narrative discourses and project their images and representations across and beyond the inner cities of Kingston and St. Andrew into the national spaces of Jamaica outwards to the global spaces of the Jamaican and African Diaspora. Although popular Queens like Carlene, deejays like Lady Saw and Dancers like Stacey and Keva have gained prominence and social power in the dancehall, it evolved as a predominantly masculine space under masculine power and control. It created a stage where men use/d lyrical narratives, performances and embodied representations to articulate the plural masculinities that are radically intertwined with other social and political factors. The siting of this discourse in the popular space of dancehall music/culture means that this dialogue of masculinities is grounded in historical specificity. It is a late twentieth- and early twenty-first-century patriarchal phenomenon in a predominantly black, postcolonial society that is rigidly structured by class.

The Hegemonic Standard

Masculinity is neither a fixed category nor a biological given. It is a social and cultural construction that accretes a variety of different meanings and different ways of 'being' or 'becoming masculine' in different historical contexts. Contemporary dancehall culture is an ideal space within which one can examine the multiple representations of contemporary masculinities that inform and reaffirm the identity structures of some Jamaican men, particularly those from the poverty-stricken inner cities of Kingston, St. Andrew and more recently, Portmore in St. Catherine. It is where these men articulate their narrative conceptions of masculinities; it is the arena where popular and legitimated images of 'real Jamaican men' are parodied and performed. It is 'where we discover and play with the identifications of ourselves, where we are imagined, where we are represented, not only to the audiences out there who do not get the message, but to ourselves for the first time'.[60] It is the popular space where deejays, dancers and other male adherents of the dancehall act out their masculine fantasies as they strive towards the superordinate standard of Jamaican masculinity.

The hegemonic ideal of masculinity[61] that is set up as the standard is one that men in their respective societies (are expected to) strive to attain. In Jamaica, male and female gender roles are rigidly demarcated with the early socialization of boys and girls being severely gendered.[62] Jamaica's hegemonic masculinity is defined by key elements which include but are not limited to middle-class background/status; tertiary education; white collar career; economic wealth; high social status; ability to provide for/control immediate family; (polygamous) heterosexuality; and access to leisure, expensive cars, and women. Men who fall short of the often unattainable elements that complete this ultimate standard are often labelled as deviant or are placed lower down on the hierarchy of manhood and power. These include homosexual men; feminized men; undereducated men; economically deprived men. Some of these men overcompensate for their perceived lack in different areas by inflating and excessively performing particular masculine characteristics that are deemed legitimate. These include promiscuous heterosexuality; misogyny; homophobia; conspicuous consumption ('bling bling'); and aggression and violence. In postcolonial Jamaica, the extreme male-centred practices and rituals which underpin these concepts become preferred masculine roles that are articulated across the bodies of men. These roles gain primacy in defining masculinities and bestowing status to 'deserving' men. In this paper we briefly speak to masculine representations that are underwritten by promiscuous heterosexuality; aggression/violence; and 'bling bling' or conspicuous consumption.

'Ole Dawg' with 'Nuff Gyal': Promiscuous/Polygamous Masculinity

Promiscuous/polygamous heterosexuality is one route to masculine status that is produced and re-produced in dancehall music and culture in what we label the 'Ole Dawg/Nuff Gyal' discourse. Despite public protestations to the contrary, this performance of male heterosexuality is one of the most socially accepted discourses of masculinity that exists across all classes in Jamaica where public moralizing often gives way to hidden dalliances with multiple partners. Dancehall discourse and worldview re-produce and extrapolate this patriarchal tenet that gives men power over (their) women. It is encoded in the lyrical output and performed and parodied in an almost grotesque aberration that denotes high levels of masculinity to men (particularly from the lower-classes and inner cities) who can claim to be an Ole Dawg with 'nuff gyal inna bungle' (an Old Dog with many women). In his hit song 'Nuff Gyal', ace dancehall deejay, Beenie Man exhorts 'ghetto youts' to see him as a role model in this quest for masculinity:

> Man fi have nuff gyal an gyal inna bungle,
> Gyal from Rema, gyal from Jungle
> Man fi have nuff gyal an none ah dem nuffi grumble,
> All ghetto youts oonu fi tek mi example ...

Di one burna business nah work agen, caw one man fi have all fifty gyal fren

If yuh stop drink roots start drink it agen, we haffi have di stamina fi service dem

When mi talk bout nuff gyal just undastan wheh mi mean,

Suppose mi waan fi line up all a netball team

One gyal cyaan mek mi team nieda, two gyal cyaan fulfill mi dream

So mi haffi tek a walk ova Portmore scheme

Gyal ah gi mi money, gyal ah kip mi clothes clean,

Gyal fi cook gyal fi clean, gyal fi stitch mi gabardine.[63]

– Beenie Man

Beenie Man continues his exhortations to encourage men to give in to their urges and engage in multiple sexual liaisons, thus legitimizing their status as 'Ole Dawgs':

Ole Dawg like we, wi haffi have dem inna twos an trees

An everybody know wi wile aready,

Believe you me, wi navel string cut unda pum pum (vagina) tree

From mi see ah gyal weh look good mi haffi fool har an get weh mi want

Caw mi nuh live outa Shortwood so mi haffi bunks har mek she drop inna mi paw

Ah nuff gyal wi ah go pass trough like Patra an di one Lady Saw

An mi deh hear bout di Ouch Crew wheh have them gyal x-rated an raw

Dat mean mi ah go want dem an mi haffi get dem an nu tell mi say mi cyaaan.[64]

– Beenie Man

These exhortations for promiscuous/polygamous heterosexual lifestyles are underwritten by masculine codes that depend on feminine sexual conquest. Consequently, the practising Ole Dawg with Nuff Gyal often becomes a father in multiples. The man who can produce evidence of his sexual prowess is often rewarded with high levels of masculine status as a potent and virile man. The pride in this monumental achievement reflects the patriarchal impetus to have ultimate control and unlimited sway over the feminine body. It is also underpinned by a driving productive ethos — the masculine urge to produce which is forced into regression by high rates of unemployment;

diminishing marketability and economic poverty. The authority/control and productive ethos are played out on the terrain of promiscuous sexual relations and multiple pregnancies. Though some men may be concerned about the economic and emotional welfare and upbringing of the children who spring from their multiple unisons, these concerns are often suppressed in the face of higher levels of masculine status that other men bestow on them. The often economically-deprived 'babyfather' plants and fertilizes the seed and abandons the seedling to grow and mature on its own; to weather the perils of childhood, adolescence, adulthood and maturity without the necessary paternal support. The young banana shoot cannot stand without the parent plant, it bends, falls and often breaks. The society is burdened with fatherless children, many of whom become young men who are webbed in a paternal legacy of poverty, promiscuity and posturing masculinity as Merciless notes in his song Ole Gallis, 'Mi puppa was a gyallis, same way mi come. Mi granfaada alone get fifteen son.'

Aggression and Violence: Ninja Man

The articulation and embodiment of aggression and violence in the dancehall also feeds into the masculine discourses that underwrite Jamaican patriarchy. The costuming, bodily movement, menacing presence and aggressive performances of particular male artistes in the dancehall like Ninja Man, SuperCat, Josey Wales and Bounti Killa, are extremes of traditional Jamaican masculinist discourse which these men represent through violent performative styles and use of imagery in the lyrical narratives that they articulate across the body of the dancehall.

> Some ah rally back an some ah dem tan so back
> Wi a rude bwoy yute an wi nuh tek back nuh chat ...
>
> Wheh dem deh when di ghetto run hot;
> When wi looking di food fi wi pot
> Man have him 16 ova him back;
> 45 an wi have it ram pack
> Carry Bazooka an nah lef eh Glock;
> When wi moving wi move compack.[65]

>   – Supercat

While violence cannot be viewed as an entirely masculine purview, aggression, force and violence have often been defined as masculine traits. The association of violence with lower/working-class men in Jamaica can often be attributed to high levels of insecurity and low self-esteem that accompany their positioning at the lowest reaches of the socioeconomic ladder. Men from poor families in the inner cities are more likely to adopt aggressive, violent masculine styles and values that confer higher levels of status and masculinity. The gun as a symbol of phallic and social power holds a primary position in dancehall discourses of masculinity. In the dancehall and in ghetto culture, the Shotta and Don are the ultimate signifiers of this illegal/extra-legal gun-toting status.

Some popular dancehall artistes like Supercat, Josey Wales, Bounti Killer and Ninja Man adopted monikers and on- and off-stage performance and lifestyles that feed into and reproduce this masculine discourse of (gun) violence. The clash of dancehall culture and masculine status is played out *ad extremis* in the performative spaces of the dancehall; within the habitus of dancehall adherents; and within the wider Jamaican society. Many times these three stages are one and the same. Dancehall deejay, ghetto griot and 'real badman', Ninja Man can be analysed as an arbiter and incarnation of the aggression and (gun) violence that underpins some Jamaican masculinities:

> From you si pon di Ninja Man yuh see seh mi ah gunslinger
> Yuh look pon di face of di Ninja Man mi say mi fava ah Lone Ranger.
> My weapon, my weapon tell dem Ninja Man nah go leff mi weapon
> My weapon my weapon tell dem Spanglers nah go leff dem weapon
> Dis is something whey yuh muss undastan
> From mi born outa mi modda reach di age of one
> Pity yuh nuh know mi ah sling ah M-1
> At the age of 2 mi kill five policeman.[66]
>
> – Ninja Man

Since his entry into the dancehall in the early 1980s, Ninja Man has been noted for his aggressive, stuttering, vocal style, confrontational lyrics and extreme dalliance with violent, gun-filled imagery. He is famous for his flashy dressing (from full ninja suits to fatigues with gas masks) and his ability to compose lyrics on the spur of the moment. Some of his more popular dancehall songs include 'One Worl' ah Gun'; 'Murder Dem'; 'Border Clash'; 'Renkin' Meat'; 'Married to mi Gun'; and 'Ten Gun a Buss'. Ninja Man has gained significant popularity for his involvement in violent interaction both on and off stage where personal tensions brewing within the dancehall are fought out lyrically and physically at the performative event. His spectacular lyrical 'murderation' of Shabba Ranks at Sting 1990 and Supercat at Sting 1991 resulted in his being crowned as the ultimate lyrical gladiator in the dancehall. Both events remain immortalized in dancehall legend as an eternal reminder to the dancehall body of Ninja Man's undying lyrical prowess. Despite ongoing challenges, for example, from deejay Merciless at Sting 2001 and Vybz Kartel at Sting 2003, Ninja Man remains the true lyrical gladiator of the dancehall and his name has become synonymous with lyrical combat — epitomized in the verbal clash between rival deejays. The competitive nature of the dancehall means that Ninja Man remains positioned as a lodestone against which aspirants and rising stars like Vybz Kartel must measure their skills and battle for supremacy in the famed 'clash'. Any artiste who wishes to claim Ninja Man's position as ultimate lyrical gladiator of the dancehall must lyrically 'battle' with and unseat Ninja Man from his throne. This was parodied in the lyrical/real clash between veteran Ninja Man and newcomer Vybz Kartel at Sting 2003.

At Sting 2003 Ninja Man's costume of a full length graduation gown, complete with mortarboard and tassel, symbolized both his graduation to a higher level and his seniority within the ranks of dancehall artistes. However, the final lyrical parody on stage between Ninja Man and Vybz Kartel broke the boundaries of dancehall performance and developed into a melee of fists and feet on stage between Ninja Man, Vybz Kartel and his supporters. During this debacle, members of the audience who supported either (or both) Ninja Man and Vybz Kartel also flung bottles on stage. The tension broke into a violent riot when the crowd realized that, after waiting all night, headline act, Bounty Killer had decided not to perform.

Ninja Man's overt aggressiveness, publicized preening and lyrical/symbolic/real dalliances with the gun and violence position him as a signifier of one extreme type of masculinity that exists within the gendered structures of power in Jamaica. His moniker, 'the Original

Front Teeth, Gold Teeth Gun Pon Teeth Don Gorgon' symbolizes his prowess as the ultimate don of all dons. The term don encodes social, economic and political power and the use of violence. 'Don' is a title of distinction afforded to men who are considered to be of high social, political and economic status in Jamaica. It is particularly used to denote status among men from the lower socioeconomic levels and in the inner-city context and is commonly used in dancehall slang. The Jamaican definition of Don draws significantly from the distinctive label given to Mafia overlords of the kind immortalized in the movie *The Godfather*; however it is oriented around indigenous symbols. Dons are community overlords who generally rule over particular garrison communities in Jamaica. They are usually affiliated to one of the two major political parties in Jamaica (the ruling People's National Party or the opposition Jamaica Labour Party). Many Dons have been accused of illegal or extra-legal activities including extortion and drug-running. The shotta (shooter) refers to the 'ghetto gunman' who may sometimes have political or narco-political linkages. Shottas may act as independent gunmen or may be under the rule of particular dons.[67]

Consequently, for some Jamaican men, particularly those from the lower, working class or inner cities, aggression, forcefulness, violence and phallic imagery are valued markers of masculine status as they negotiate the treacherous spaces between their marginalized lives and the often unattainable images of hegemonic masculinity. In the inner cities of Kingston and St. Andrew, this aggression and (gun) violence is idealized and incarnated in the don and the shotta. The don and shotta as lyrical and embodied beings represent a masculine standard that uses the adoption of aggression and violence to signify high levels of power and to denote correspondingly high masculine status. This dependence on aggression and violence as a means of expressing masculinity is related to the 'provider' impetus where men are expected to be breadwinners; and the control impetus where men exercise control over their lives and the lives of their families and peers. The don and shotta are praised in dancehall music culture; revered in inner city and garrison culture and often act as role models for some young men from within and beyond these communities where aggression, violence and 'badmanism' are deemed as positive norms of socialization (among others) for young men in Jamaican inner cities.[68] Ninja Man's extreme dalliance with gun-talk, gunplay and violent lyrics and his success in embodying and performing violent, gun lyrics and representing an extreme form of aggressive/violent masculinity for nearly two decades speaks to the gendered and political spaces that exist in Jamaica for a hyper-masculine discourse.

Bling Bling and Conspicuous Consumption: British Link Up

Fashion, adornment, spectacle and sartorial excess play an important role in dancehall culture. Women's sartorial practices have been a site of vigorous debate on morality and sexuality and the Dancehall Queens have been immortalized in discourses on dancehall dress and female sexuality.[69] Men in the dancehall have also used fashion, style, spectacular costuming and adornment in their representations within and beyond the space of the dancehall.

Moving from an early (1980s/1990s) dalliance with multiple and heavy gold necklaces to the current platinum and 'ice' (diamond) craze, the dancehall 'modeler' complements his jewellery with expensive brand-name clothing; the latest model SUV or sports car; the latest model cellular phone; and a taste for expensive wines and liqueurs. The popular lyrics and styles of dancehall creators continue to encourage and promote this culture of 'bling bling' and 'bashment' that, in reality seeks to approximate the lifestyles of the educated/monied middle and upper classes. The men who can afford to parade in these status-generating costumes are elevated to high levels of masculine status in the dancehall habitus.

In the dancehall, groups, sects and crews like the Black Roses Crew, Higglers Crew, Ouch Crew, Scare Dem Crew, Diplomat Crew and British Link Up Crew represent collective embodiments of overlapping and competing discourses.[70] The British Link-Up Crew incarnates a discourse that represents a truly consumptive and glocalized masculine identity. This crew is a diasporan group of male actors in the dancehall whose staged presentations of conspicuous consumption project them as an important example of the masculine hype and consumption. Through the use of 'bling bling', sartorial excess, cool pose and conspicuous consumption, the men of British Link Up work out practices to garner masculine status within/beyond the dancehall stage. Their consumptive practices represent ways of fulfilling desires that are identified with highly valued lifestyles in Jamaica and Britain, and project an attempted realization of the image of the good life. This includes the conspicuous display of expensive brand-name fashion, jewellery, clothing, the latest model cellular phones, and cars and public displays of wealth and largesse. Expensive, well-tailored, formal suits with matching jackets and pants are imported directly from Paris with fashion from Moschino and Versace complemented with 'ice' (diamond) and platinum jewellery and the omnipresent Rolex watch — a universal symbol of great personal wealth. British Link Up represents a glocalized[71] impulse that converges with competing sociopolitical and gendered discourses operating in the dancehall. The resulting costume reveals the colonial impetus for the former Motherland, Britain, and the postcolonial thrust for the contemporary superpower, the USA. Ultimately, the fantastic elaboration of the British Link Up costume and its attendant masquerade of elegance and overt consumption is the primary strategy that these men use to attain higher levels of masculine status in the dancehall.

British Link Up's sartorial representations of the male body on the overlapping stages of the dancehall, Jamaica and the Diaspora is a multilayered discourse that creates and projects an identity/product that incorporates some agency, however limited, for a marginalized group in the subaltern spaces of Jamaica and its Diaspora. Nevertheless, it also replicates the tensions and contradictions that characterize the global capitalist arena in its convergence with the vibrant and pervasive cultural, social and political mores from lesser developed societies like Jamaica. Many men from the inner cities may never truly inhabit this space. However, the identity incarnated in the British Link Up Crew and performed in dancehall culture provides an alternative model of social mobility and masculinity for some Afro-Jamaican men who are denied any real access to resources and power via the traditional sociopolitical and gendered structures of power in Jamaica. Consequently, the embodied practices of British Link Up represent a competing discourse of masculinity that strikes at the core of the structures of power that operate in Jamaica. The discourse, practices and representation of this group of men empower a new and different set of actors by appropriating and re-scripting the norms and boundaries set by bourgeois society, while foregrounding a vulgar parody of 'respectable bourgeois masculinity' among its peers and power brokers in the spaces of the dancehall.

The fantasized masculinity represented by British Link Up remains transient and illusory. Indeed, to maintain this illusory ideal, men like Father Roy Fowl, founder and premier Crew member, often engage in illegal practices that work against the maintenance of a stable identity. Many ultimately pay the real price of their masculine performance and lavish lifestyles. The June 12, 2004 *Guardian* headline announced 'Head of crack cocaine empire convicted' and reported the conviction of 'a flamboyant international drug baron who ran a multi-million-pound crack cocaine empire spanning five countries and supplying every major city in the UK'. This international drug baron, Owen 'Roy Fowl' Clarke, reportedly lived in a modest two bedroom bungalow in South London but led a fantastic lifestyle on the international stage of dancehall and narco-culture, throwing lavish parties and owning several luxurious homes in Jamaica. In July 2004, Owen Clarke was convicted on drug-related charges in the UK and sentenced to 13 years in prison.

How do we conceptualize the articulation of these masculine fantasies across the bodies of individual Jamaican men? How does the sexually promiscuous and carefree Ole Dawgs with Nuff Gal who become Best Babyfaadas; the nihilistic, menacing, urban aggressive don/shotta performed/parodied by a genre of artistes like Ninja Man; and the sartorial spectacle of bling bling, bashment and conspicuous consumption of men like those of the British Link Up Crew move from fantasized image to practice?

Foucault's notion of 'techniques of the self' provides a historical and dynamic conceptual framework for the articulation of these gendered representations across the body of black, lower-class or urban Jamaican men. These narratives, embodiments and representations are operationalized in the adoration that surrounds legacies of promiscuous heterosexuality and irresponsible fatherhood that is passed on to man-children who strive to become ole dawgs with nuff gyal inna bungle and best babyfaadas with multiple offspring. The representations of don/shotta parodied by artistes like Ninja Man are appropriated in the techniques of performance, glamourized nihilism and violence, aggressive facial contortions; body language; ritualistic slang; narratives and activities of gun violence and criminal/illegal/extra-legal activities that become the chosen lifestyle of individual men. The popularity of the urban don/shotta and his embodiment in dancehall narratives represent a hardened kind of masculinity that is often equated with inner-city masculinity. It is defined in dancehall culture by urban life, rampant materialism, fatalistic attitudes, physical strength and the acquisition of respect through violence or the implicit threat of violence and the ever-threatening spectacle of the gun. The discourses encoded in the image of men like British Link Up are incarnated in the mimicry of the techniques/practices of care, bodily aesthetics and grooming, leisure, shopping, preen, posture, pose and conspicuous display of wealth in the lives of many men, some of whom reputedly engage in questionable activities to fund their ostentatious lifestyles. The urge to create living, breathing fantasies of masculine being that reflect these embodied narratives is grounded and operationalized in the daily lives and real practices of men who exist within and beyond the spaces of Jamaica's inner cities and dancehall music and culture. These embodied representations of masculinity are energized and mimicked. They live.

The pervasive class/colour(race) hierarchy in Jamaica that denies real power to many men from the poorest social groups works concurrently with the patriarchal hierarchy to proffer power to these same men, if only in the most perverse representations of masculine status. These representations feed on the patriarchal legacies to breach the cultural boundaries of coded imagery and narrative discourse and enter the realm of possibility. They confront us as underperforming boys and failing men whose confusion penetrates the public discourse in the traditional spaces of middle-class debates. Today, these debates coalesce around underperforming boys failing into men; increasing levels of men involved in criminal activities; growing under-representation of men in tertiary-level institutions and the overwhelming need to create man-spaces within which to craft strategies to resolve the corrupting discourses of masculinity.

Conclusion

Hall's work remains critical to the body project in Jamaican popular dancehall culture as scholars seek to deconstruct the 'canvasses of representation' on which contemporary cultural griots, dancers and actors paint and project their identity-stories. The dancehall body remains organically tied to ghetto livity and Jamaican society. Its stylistic contortions replicate multiple spatial, social, political and gendered tensions in a consistent self-fashioning of plural identities. These representations are encoded in dancehall narratives and performed in the urban spaces of dance events, dance performances and styles. And they are articulated in the gendered narratives that are parodied across the dancehall stage. Through the popular performances of deejays, dancers, fans and the wider dancehall audience, these bodies signify and symbolize philosophies of space; memorializing strategies; gendered identities, and histories of survival in the African Diaspora and postcolonial Jamaica.

Notes

1. Jean Comaroff, *Body of Power, Spirit of Resistance: The Culture and History of a South African People* (Chicago: University of Chicago Press, 1985), 6.
2. Omofolabo Ajayi, *Yoruba Dance: The Semiotics of Movement and Body Attitude in a Nigerian Culture* (Eritrea and Trenton: Africa World Press, 1998), 1–6.
3. Heidi Nast and Steve Pile, *Places Through the Body* (New York and London: Routledge, 1998).
4. Rex Nettleford, *Inward Stretch Outward Reach* (London: Macmillan Press, 1993), 86; Stuart Hall, 'Multi-culturalism, Equality and Difference', (Keynote Address, Third Crossroads in Cultural Studies Conference, University of Birmingham, UK, June 21–25 2000); Barbara Browning, *Infectious Rhythm: Metaphors of Contagion and the Spread of African Culture* (New York and London: Routledge, 1997).
5. Helen Thomas, *The Body, Dance and Cultural Theory* (UK: Palgrave Macmillan, 2003).
6. David Bell and Gill Valentine, *Mapping Desire: Geographies of Sexualities* (London: Routledge, 1995); David Bell, 'Fragments of a Queer City', in D. Bell, J. Binnie, R. Holliday, R. Longhurst and R. Peace, *Pleasure Zones: Bodies, Cities, Spaces* (New York: Syracuse University Press, 1995); Jon Binnie, 'The Erotic Possibilities of the City', in D. Bell, J. Binnie, R. Holliday, R. Longhurst and R. Peace, *Pleasure Zones*; Robyn Longhurst, 'Trim, Taut, Terrific, and Pregnant', in D. Bell, J. Binnie, R. Holliday, R. Longhurst and R. Peace, *Pleasure Zones*.
7. Richard Sennett, *Flesh and Stone: The Body and the City in Western Civilization* (London: W.W. Norton and Co., 1994).
8. Radhika Mohanram, *Black Body: Women, Colonialism and Space* (London: Allen and Unwin, 1999).

9. Stuart Hall, 'Multi-culturalism, Equality and Difference', (Keynote Address, Third Crossroads in Cultural Studies Conference, University of Birmingham, UK, June 21–25, 2000).

10. George Lamming, *Conversations. George Lamming: Essays, Addresses and Interviews 1953–1990*, eds. Richard Drayton and Andaiye (London: Karia Press, 1992), 34.

11. Stuart Hall, 'What is this "Black" in Black Popular Culture?', in *Stuart Hall: Critical Dialogues in Cultural Studies*, eds. David Morley and Kuan-Hsing Chen (London and New York: Routledge, 1996), 470.

12. Ibid.

13. Stuart Hall, 'The Spectacle of the "Other"', in *Representation: Cultural Representations and Signifying Practices*, ed. S. Hall (UK and USA: The Open University and Sage, 2002, [1997]), 1.

14. Ibid., 3.

15. Ruth Butler, 'The Body', in *Introducing Human Geographies*, eds. P. Cloke, P. Crang and M. Goodwin (London: Arnold, 1999).

16. Helen Thomas, *The Body, Dance and Cultural Theory*.

17. Chris Shilling, *The Body and Social Theory* (London: Sage, 1993); Helen Thomas, *The Body, Dance and Cultural Theory*, 46.

18. Nigel Thrift, 'The Still Point: Resistance, Expressive Embodiment and Dance', in *Geographies of Resistance*, eds. S. Pile and M. Keith (London: Routledge, 1997).

19. Catherine Nash, 'Performativity in Practice: Some Recent Work in Cultural Geography', *Progress in Human Geography* 24, no. 4 (2000): 653–64.

20. Ibid., 658.

21. Ibid.

22. Stuart Hall, 'What is this "Black" in Black Popular Culture?', 474.

23. Browning, Barbara. *Infectious Rhythm*, 1–6.

24. Buju Banton feat. Beres Hammond, 'Pull it up', *Unchained Spirit*, Anti Inc, 1999.

25. Catherine Nash, 'Performativity in Practice: Some Recent Work in Cultural Geography', 657.

26. Susan Reed, 'The Politics and Poetics of Dance', *Annual Review of Anthropology* 27 (1998): 503–32.

27. Kariamu Welsh Asante, 'Commonalities in African Dance: An Aesthetic Foundation', in *African Culture: The Rhythms of Unity*, eds. M. Asante and K. Welsh Asante (Westport Connecticut: Greenwood, 1985); Jane Desmond, 'Embodying Difference: Issues in Dance and Cultural Studies', in *Meaning in Motion: New Cultural Studies of Dance*, eds. J. Desmond (Durham: Duke University Press, 1997); Omofolabo Ajayi, *Yoruba Dance*.

28. Helen Thomas, *The Body, Dance and Cultural Theory*, 215.

29. Edward Brathwaite, *The Arrivants: A New World Trilogy* (UK: Oxford University Press, 1973), 22.

30. Leroi Jones, *Blues People: Negro Experience in White America and the Music that Developed From it* (New York: William Morrow and Co., 1968 [1963]), 74, noted that this was a popular tune played by marching bands at funerals.

31. Verena Reckord, 'Reggae, Rastafarianism and Cultural Identity', in *Reggae, Rasta, Revolution: Jamaican Music From Ska to Dub*, ed. Chris Potash (New York and London: Schirmer Books and Prentice Hall International, 1997), 6–7.

32. Garth White, 'The Development of Jamaican Popular Music, Part 2. Urbanization of the Folk, the Merger of Traditional and the Popular in Jamaican Music', *ACIJ Research Review*, no. 1 (1984).

33. It should be noted that the 'diwali' rhythm could be seen as a major factor in the emergence of the second dancehall highpoint between 1999 and 2003. It introduced a 'party' vibe into what had become a static moment in dancehall.

34. See Esther A. Dagan, ed., *The Spirit's Dance in Africa: Evolution, Transformation and Continuity in Sub-Sahara* (Canada: Galerie Amrad African Arts Publications, 1997).

35. Kariamu Welsh Asante, 'Commonalities in African Dance: An Aesthetic Foundation'.

36. Ibid., 71.

37. Cheryl Ryman, in *Tapestry of Jamaica: The Best of Skywritings, Air Jamaica's Inflight Magazine*, ed. Linda Gambrill (Kingston and Oxford: Macmillan Caribbean, 2003), 170–71.

38. Cheryl Ryman, 'The Jamaican Heritage in Dance', *Jamaica Journal* no. 44 (1980): 4.

39. Kees Eskamp and Frank de Geus, 'The Pelvis as Shock Absorber: Modern and African Dance', *Journal of Popular Culture* 27, no.1 (1997): 55–65.

40. Cheryl Ryman, 'Jamaican Body Moves: Source and Continuity of Jamaican Movement'; 'Bouyaka Boo-ya`h-kah: A Salute to Dancehall', unpublished paper, author's personal papers, 1993.

41. Garth White, 'The Development of Jamaican Popular Music, Part 2. Urbanization of the Folk, the Merger of Traditional and the Popular in Jamaican Music'.

42. Ibid.

43. Of note, in an interview with Carlene Smith, the first and most popular dancehall Queen, May 5, 2000, revealed that she takes credit for the development of this dance. In an interview with Bogle, June 7, 2002, he stated that he created the Butterfly.

44. Carla Reyes, 'Investigation into Dancehall' (Research Paper in Dance and Theatre Production, Jamaica School of Dance, Edna Manley College for the Visual and Performing Arts, Jamaica, 1993).

45. Leroi Jones, *Blues People*, 67.

46. Ibid., 65.

47. Leroi Jones, *Blues People*; Kees Eskamp and Frank de Geus, 'The Pelvis as Shock Absorber: Modern and African Dance', 60.

48. See George E. Simpson, 'Jamaican Revivalist Cults', *Social and Economic Studies* 5, no. 4 (December, 1956): 354; Hilary Carty, *Folk Dances of Jamaica: An Insight* (London: Dance Books, 1988), 68–74; Ivy Baxter, *The Arts of an Island* (New Jersey: Scarecrow Press, 1970), 142.

49. Interview with Harry Toddler, 'The Party' (CVM TV, Kingston, Jamaica, May 25, 2002).

50. Elephant Man, 'Wining Queen', Studio 2000 single, 2002.

51. Elephant Man, 'Fan dem off', *Good 2 Go*. Atlantic Records, 2003.

52. Captain Barkey, 'Go Go Wine', *Strictly the Best* vol. 17, VP Records, 1996.

53. Johnny P. 'Bike Back', *Punanny*. New York and UK: Greensleeves Records, 2000 [1991].

54. Kariamu Welsh Asante, 'Commonalities in African Dance: An Aesthetic Foundation'.

55. Elephant Man, 'Blasé', *Good 2 Go*, Atlantic Records, 2003.

56. Beenie Man, 'World Dance', *Strictly the Best*, vol. 13, New York: VP Records, 1994.

57. Ibid.

58. Stuart Hall, 'What is this "Black" in Black Popular Culture?' 466.

59. Ibid., 466.
60. Ibid., 474.
61. The concept of hegemonic masculinity [R.W. Connell, *Masculinities* (Berkeley and Los Angeles: University of California Press, 1995); R. Hanke, 'Hegemonic Masculinity', in *Thirtysomething: Critical Studies in Communications*, vol. 7 (1990): 231–48] draws on Gramsci's notion of hegemony and 'spontaneous consent' where individuals participate in their own domination without necessary resort to coercion or violence. Connell argues that at any given time, one form of masculinity rather than others is culturally exalted. He defines hegemonic masculinity as 'the configuration of gender practice which embodies the currently accepted answer to the problem of the legitimacy of patriarchy, which guarantees (or is taken to guarantee) the dominant position of men and the subordination of women'. See, in particular, Connell, 77–78, for a discussion of hegemonic masculinity.
62. See for example Barry Chevannes, *Learning To be a Man: Culture, Socialization and Gender Identity in Five Caribbean Communities* (Barbados: the University of the West Indies Press, 2001) whose qualitative study in three Caribbean countries revealed that despite some minor differences that are related to ethnic and class background, boys and girls undergo highly gendered socialization, for example with relation to types of household chores, degree of parental supervision and social expectations related to sex and sexuality.
63. Beenie Man, 'Nuff Gal', *Best of Beenie Man*, VP Records, 2000.
64. Beenie Man, 'Ole Dawg', *Best Of Beenie Man*, VP Records, 2000.
65. SuperCat, 'Ghetto Red Hot', *Don Dada*, Sony, 1992.
66. Ninja Man, *My Weapon. Anything Test Dead.* Reggae Anthology – Ninjaman. VP Records, 2001.
67. See Charles Price, 'What the Zeeks Uprising Reveals: Development Issues, Moral Economy and the Urban Lumpenproletariat in Jamaica', *Urban Anthropology* 33, no. 1, (Spring 2004): 73–113; Christopher Charles, 'Garrison Communities as Counter Societies: The Case of the 1998 Zeeks Riot in Jamaica', *Ideaz* 1, no. 1 (2002): 29–43, for a discussion on Jamaican garrison communities and dons.
68. Carolyn Cooper's ('"Lyrical Gun": Metaphor and Role Play in Jamaican Dancehall Culture', *The Massachusetts Review* 35, Iss. 3–4, (1994): 429–447) discussion on lyrical and metaphorical gun play in dancehall culture also tackles this point, noting that 'badmanism' is a theatrical pose that has been refined in the complicated socialization processes of Jamaican ghetto youth who learn to imitate the sartorial and ideological style of the heroes and villains of imported American films. See also recent discussions in the Jamaican *Daily* and *Sunday Gleaner* about the 'crisis of Jamaican masculinity', in particular Kevin Chang, 'The dominant sex', *Sunday Gleaner* (June 6, 2004); Melville Cooke, 'The "babyfather" privilege – Me a de bes' babyfaada inna Jamaica', *Daily Gleaner* (June 3, 2004); Claude Mills, 'Ex-Jesuit Ruffles Male feathers', *Sunday Gleaner* (May 30, 2004); Damion Mitchell, 'Rescue the Boys! — Special Intervention Mooted for Schools', *Sunday Gleaner* (May 30, 2004); and Glenda Simms, 'Winds of Change, or Cool Breeze', *Sunday Gleaner* (June 6, 2004).
69. Some works which examine the feminine space of dancehall costuming, dance and/or sexuality include: Carolyn Cooper, 'Erotic Play in the Dancehall', *Jamaica Journal* 22, no. 4 & vol. 23, no. 1 (1990): 14–50; Cooper, 'Slackness hiding from Culture: Erotic Play in the Dancehall', in *Noises in the Blood: Orality, Gender and the 'Vulgar' Body of Jamaican Popular Culture* (London: Macmillan, 1993); Cooper, 'Punany Power', *Black Media Journal* 2 (2000):

50–52; Kezia Page, 'Dancehall Feminisms: Jamaican Female Deejays and the Politics of the "Big Ninja Bike"', unpublished paper presented at the Borders, Boundaries and the Global in Caribbean Studies conference (Bowdoin College, New Brunswick, Maine, 2003); Tracey Skelton, '"I sing dirty reality. I am out there for the ladies". Lady Saw: Women and Jamaican ragga music resisting patriarchy', *Phoebe* 7, nos.1 & 2 (1995): 86–104; Imani Tafari, 'Lady Saw … Dancehall donette', *Sistren* 16 ½ (1994).

70. See Donna P. Hope, 'The British Link Up Crew — Consumption Masquerading as Masculinity in the Dancehall', *Interventions: International Journal of Postcolonial Studies* 6, no. 1 (April): 101–17. Special Issue on Jamaican Popular Culture, for an in-depth discussion of the British Link Up Crew.

71. 'Glocal' is the term used by Arturo Escobar (1995) to describe the intersections between local and global cultures in the global marketplace.

12 | *Diaspora, Globalization and the Politics of Identity*

Percy C. Hintzen

Now one of the main reactions against the politics of racism in Britain was what I would call "Identity Politics One", the first form of identity politics. It had to do with the constitution of some defensive collective identity against the practices of racist society. It had to do with the fact that people were being blocked out of and refused an identity and identification within the majority nation, having to find some other roots on which to stand. Because people have to find some ground, some place, some position on which to stand. Blocked out of any access to an English or British identity, people had to try to discover who they were. It is the crucial moment of the rediscovery or the search for roots.[1]

Diaspora and Modernity

There is an ineluctable association between capitalism and race that emerged in the formation of the nation state. This relationship is not merely inevitable but necessary as a condition of modernity. It has produced what sociologist Paul Gilroy calls 'a distinctive ecology of belonging'[2] that links territory to identity and, relatedly, sovereignty to belonging.[3] As such, under the modern condition, citizenship has become the basis of claims to rights and of assertions of privilege.

The link between identity and the modern state emerged in the crucible of contradictions produced out of increasing heterogeneity. This occurred in the wake of an intensification of migratory flows of people as technical and social conditions experienced rapid changes in the transformation to capitalism. From such changes emerged a need for new conceptions of belonging that moulded disparate populations into a unified, homogeneous, national peoplehood. The changes also necessitated a need to make distinctions among those who could claim the rights and privileges of belonging as 'citizens' and those who could not. These were integrally related to the division of labour as an imperative of capitalist accumulation.[4] Thus, the development of the nation state was characterized by the development of racial regimes of inclusion and exclusion.[5] Diasporic consciousness emerged as a necessary condition for accommodation, in particular national spaces of those who are denied the right to national belonging, or whose rights to such are curtailed and compromised.

Diasporic identity was historically produced, particularly, in the wake of the trans-oceanic movement of people in service of the colonial project. Under colonialism 'stateless' territories came under the dominion of colonizing 'civilized' states. Regions of the world outside 'civilized' Europe were organized into bounded territories for European conquest and jurisdiction. An integral link developed between civilization and sovereign power: only the civilized could exercise sovereignty. Relatedly, only the civilized could make claims of belonging to the modern state. This explains, for example, the exclusion of the indigenous populations of the Americas from national imaginations. Thus, modernity implies a conjoining of the nation and the civilized. The latter is racially inscribed.

Racial belonging was produced and imposed by the technologies and apparatus of the state. The former refers to the imposed categorizations of the population through censuses, for example. It also refers, *inter alia*, to 'invented histories and traditions, ceremonies, and cultural imaginings' that are integral to the power of the state to include and exclude. By the apparatus of the state, I refer to its instrumentalities and institutions of power organized for jurisdictional deployment over territory. These include law and policymaking as well as bureaucracies.[6] State technologies and apparatus function for the production of peoplehood. The latter identifies those with legitimate claims of belonging. It also forms the basis for legitimate exclusion from the materialities of the nation of those who cannot make such claims. Inevitably, this produces a cultural politics of sameness necessary for the homogenizing project of the state.[7] This politics of inclusion is challenged, rejected, or ignored by the racially excluded in a 'cultural politics of difference, of struggles around difference, of the production of new identities, of the appearance of new subjects on the political and cultural stage'.[8]

Thus, residence in the jurisdictional space of the state does not necessarily come with claims of belonging and with contingent rights of citizenship that legitimize access to the deserved materialities of the nation. It does not lead, necessarily, to participation in the performative imageries and the poetics and aesthetics of national identification. The tension this produces is played out around the cultural politics of inclusion and exclusion that, in the final analysis, is racialized. Diasporic imagination is organized materially around, in response to, and participates in the cultural politics of exclusion. This raises the need for considerable modification in the analytics of Diaspora. Because diasporic identity is organized around notions of origin and of longings for return, the ideas of displacement, dislocation, and uprootedness have become its dominant themes. They have acted to reify and territorialize imaginary 'homelands'.[9] Such objectification is problematic on both empirical and analytical grounds. There is no Africa, or East Asia, or South Asia, or Arabia, or America to which most diasporic subjects can return. For most who participate in diasporic imaginaries, the possibility of return is foreclosed. This has less to do with generations of residence in their host countries and more with the constructed and imaginary nature of their originary homelands. The West Indies, for example, has no concrete existence. While the Diasporas of St. Kitts or Jamaica may have meaning in these two countries, they become meaningless in the diasporic construction of the societies that host their emigrants. Both become absorbed into a 'West Indian' Diaspora with a 'homeland' that can exist only in the imagination. Thus, for many, homeland has no concrete existence. This prompted Stuart Hall to make a distinction between 'open' and 'closed' Diasporas. The former refers to 'diasporic communities, with no possibility or desire for return'.[10] It does not resolve the problem. Disporic imagination is constitutive of the cultural politics of place deployed against nationalist imaginaries and its material implications of exclusion.[11] Its contingent representations and practices are shifting signifiers that respond to the material particularities of place. They are conditioned and framed by discourses of belonging and exclusion in national locations of residence. However, they respond to differences in the social geography of locality. Diaspora is therefore the cultural politics of the un-included and non-included deployed in highly localized arenas. In this sense, diasporic imagination is organized around structural notions of difference. But structural understandings are and can never be fixed. Rather, they emerge dialogically out of conjunctural processes that are always changing. They are reflexive of the changing positionalities of individuals and collectives across time, space, and institutional formation. This is what is entailed in social mobility. In the mobile subject is found a rejection of the Cartesian self as fixed and unchanging in time and over time. The self is revealed as a product of the moment created out of conjunctural processes that are constantly in flux.

What is universal and fixed in all of this, at least in the modern condition, is the relationship between race, territory, and belonging. This relationship refers, not to national but to racial identity. In the final analysis, Diaspora reveals the inevitable link between race and conceptions of origin because the latter is racially marked. This is notwithstanding the reorganization of the racial imaginary in the nineteenth century. The scientific fixing of race around biology obscured the integral association between race and territory. It did not, however, displace the relationship between racial identity and myths of origin.[12] This is the challenge that hybridity offers up to modernity by dislodging subjectivity from racially inscribed origin myths. The biologism introduced to racial discourse by scientific racism came without the refutation of Africa as the source of blackness in the racially constructed discourse of origins. It also deepened the signification of blackness as the embodiment of the uncivilized. In this imaginary construction, black bodies are denied the capacities (understood as rationality and reason) for full belonging in the spaces of civilized modernity. This denial applies even in the territorialized locations of Africa organized under statist jurisdiction.[13] The state and nation are markers of civilization. And blackness, understood as uncivilized, becomes ascribed to their constitutive outsides. At the same time, blackness becomes the object of state regulation, control, and jurisdiction. Diasporic identity emerges in the contradiction of exclusion and inclusion that this implies. Blackness cannot be accommodated within the national space because of its negation of civilization. At the same time, the imperative of its management demands inclusion under the jurisdiction of the state. It is therefore an intrusive and undesirable, even though necessary and unavoidable, presence in national spaces where civilization is imaginatively constructed and where its materialities are deployed. Its inclusion in national peoplehood is foreclosed.

Diasporic imagination is produced out of the cultural politics of exclusion. It is shaped by the contradictions that emerge from the concreteness of participation in the project of modernity by those symbolically excluded on racial grounds. Participation comes in the form of contributions, achievements, and access to the materialities of modernity. Race is not the only structural determinant of positionality or the sole imaginary around which claims of belonging can be made. It is not always and singularly the basis of legitimate access to the economic, political, social, and cultural materialities of modernity. In other words, it is not the only basis upon which the rights of citizenship are conferred. Claims to national belonging can also be made by birthright and positionality derived from social, economic, cultural and symbolic capital.[14] For the diasporic subject, the 'cultural politics of difference' is complicated by possibilities for inclusion provided on account of acquisition of these attributes of belonging. Such acquisition can either be denied or can be shorn of racial signification. The entanglements of the racially excluded with modernity and the possibilities they produce are what make diasporic identity ambiguous, contradictory, polysemous, and multivalent.

Diasporic identity must also respond contextually to differences in possibilities for acquisition of the attributes of modernity over time, social geography, and social positioning. Acquisition of such attributes does not always provide access to citizenship. Birth is not always a guarantor of such access even under conditions of juridical and constitutional sanction. Wealth and cultural attributes may guarantee full claims of belonging to those born outside the jurisdictional space of the state even while continuing to exclude those with claims based on birthright. Thus, diasporic imagination responds to the realities of time, locality, and positionality. This does not mean that it is inchoate. Rather, as more or less well formed, it is available to be recalled, interpreted, and reinterpreted in keeping with the conjunctures of the moment, either by the individual or by collectivities. But there is no singularity in its deployment. Within the limits imposed by racialized construction, there is neither a single diasporic imagination nor universality in its interpretation. There are multiple diasporic imaginaries available for recall even under the single rubric of racial identity. Each becomes available in the cultural politics of difference under conditions of nationalist exclusion or ambiguous inclusion. The unifying theme of any particular diasporic imagination is the collective memory of homeland. However, there is no single corpus of memory, and no single imaginary of homeland, even for those identified singularly in ideologies of racialized inclusion and exclusion. An individual can have many claims to homeland and many diasporic imaginaries to call upon at a particular moment of racial challenge.

Diaspora functions to bridge the gap between the imperative of national belonging imposed by the modern state, on the one hand, and the discourses, aesthetics and poetics of exclusion on the other. It preserves the link between identity and territory while acknowledging, even in their contestation, the exclusionary practices of the state. Since race is integrally linked to territorial origins, then Diaspora, in the final analysis, must be conceptualized racially. One may argue that whites, understood as those with originary claims to Europe, belong everywhere as the bearers of civilization and as the nation's protectors from crisis and threat.[15] This point receives added importance because it allows for the inclusion of continental Africans in black diasporic imagination. In racial terms, the African continent is cast as uncivilized hinterland territories with the state as a civilizing outpost for containment, management, and tutelage of its populations. In the discourse of modernity, continental Africans are understood to be the objects of state control and management. Even when Africans control the apparatus of the state, they continue to be seen in historicist terms of immaturity, in continual need of the civilizing tutelages of the North. Thus, the technologies of state power in Africa remain embedded in relations of coloniality because of the persistence of relations of imperialism after the end of formal colonial governance.[16] African states also retain relations of dependency characterized by forms of exploitation, subordination, and expropriation constitutive of colonialism. As a result they continue to suffer the consequences of persistent underdevelopment.[17] As such, the incorporation of continental Africans into the modern state is just as ambiguous as, for example, black populations in what is conventionally understood as the African Diaspora. It is this ambiguity of (un)belonging that connects African subjectivity on the continent to black diasporic consciousness organized around notions of universal black intimacy.

Whiteness eviscerates the ambiguity of belonging that is at the critical centre of Diasporic identity. European immigrants to the United States could retain claims to their national spaces of origin while participating equally in American peoplehood. They become 'ethnicized' Americans.

Or they pass easily into the group of Americans whose associations with origins disappear completely in the construction of their identities. They become absorbed into the unambiguous peoplehood of the USA. African Americans, as blacks, cannot make these claims to unambiguous belonging, even against European immigrants whose presence they preceded in the territorial and jurisdictional space of the American state. Nor can Native Americans.

The role of Africa in the African Diasporic imaginary raises interesting questions. These revolve around the links among civilization, the state, and the nation. In its naturalist conception, the Africa that exists in the racialized imagery of modernity cannot be civilized. In its historicist version, the African represents the 'historical immaturity' of the colonial subject. This calls forth a pervasive and continuing necessity for white supremacy exercised through the instrumentalities of the 'postcolonial' state. This is where the idea of the 'outpost' receives its analytic power. In the final analysis, racialized discourses of inclusion and exclusion, even though organized around national imageries, refer inevitably to distinctions between the civilized and the uncivilized. These determine who, deservedly, can make claims to the material benefits of modernity. If we accept the idea of Diaspora as the cultural politics of difference formed and fashioned in the crucible of racialized exclusion from modernity, then we can locate the continental 'African' firmly within the African diasporic imagination. This is because of the latter's centrality to the cultural politics of difference, marked by its notions of originary claims to Africa itself.[18] African nationalism and African nationhood have all emerged from the cultural politics of difference from which Africa gets its diasporic character.

Diasporic identity connects persons of African descent in a global web of racial intimacy. It occupies the sentimental centre in black transnational political alliances employed so successfully in the various nationalist struggles against colonialism and racial segregation. In the USA, it was the cement that tied black immigrants and African Americans together in a political alliance aimed at breaking the strictures of white exclusivity and privilege. It was the justification for black insistence on US intervention in the British West Indies during the 1930s in support of the region's nationalist anticolonial campaign.[19] And diasporic imagination occupied the critical centre in the challenges mounted against racial supremacy at least from the second decade of the twentieth century onwards. This period of struggle was ushered in by the 'Back to Africa Movement' of the United Negro Improvement Association (UNIA) headed by Jamaican Marcus Garvey. It continued with the black nationalist struggle for civil rights during the 1960s and 1970s.

Diasporic identity needs to be distinguished from ethnicization, which is the process of heterogeneous cultural accommodation. It emerges out of the cultural politics of difference that responds to racial exclusion from the modern national space and from its material benefits. It is framed by memories of a collective history rooted in common origins. The form, nature, and intensity of exclusionary practices differ across space, time, and social position. This explains the lack of fixity in diasporic imagination. Diasporic identity has to respond to the conjunctures of time, place, and position. It is also conditioned by possibilities for inclusion in the racial state offered through acquisition of non-racialized attributes of belonging. Possession of these attributes is integral to the process of cultural and social hybridization that is at the root of modernity.[20] Blacks in the territorial space of Africa, the Caribbean, North America, and Europe can successfully make material, cultural, social and ideological claims to modernity through the acquisition of social, cultural, and economic capital. These are so integrally related to modernity, and are so constitutive of it, that they meliorate and even eviscerate representations and practices of racial exclusion for those who possess them. At the same time, racialized exclusion is indispensable to modernity because of its role in the organization of the division of labour. Claims for inclusion in the nation state made exclusively on grounds of racial accommodation can never be accommodated. This is true, particularly for those with originary claims to Africa, explaining the universality and pervasiveness of Black diasporic consciousness.[21]

Thus, hybridization can complicate racialized discourses of exclusion around which diasporic identity is organized. We may understand the material expressions of diaspora as the structural politics of race.[22] Possibilities for inclusion lend themselves to a politics of deconstruction where resources available to those who have acquired the non-racialized attributes of modernity are available to be deployed against racially constructed exclusionary practices. This deepens the ambiguities and contradictions. Diasporic identity can, at one and the same time, challenge and collude with the racial state. Such conflicting tendencies have increased significantly with the universalizing impetus of neo-globalization. By the latter, I refer to the most recent innovations in communication and organizational technology, the development of new transportation efficiencies, the emergence of seamless networks of global production, consumption, and finance, and the complex of legitimating ideologies that allow their dispersal, their application and their derivative institutionalized practices. In the merger of the global and the local, there is a withering away of the jurisdictional and legal power of the nation state. This is accompanied by the erosion of the latter's political, economic, and cultural integrity. Thus, neo-globalization contributes to an intensification and universalization of diasporic intimacy as collective identities are globalized with the weakening of national alternatives. Transnational strategies become increasingly imperative for survival and success. There is need for quick and easy accommodation to multiple locations.[23] This has exposed modernity's secret: its rootedness in the massive movement (mostly involuntary and coerced) of populations dispossessed of the rights of ownership, belonging, and self-determination. This is precisely the impetus for diasporic imagination.

Neo-globalization therefore intensifies the very contradictions of the modern racial state that have created in diasporic identity possibilities for both challenge and accommodation. It offers increasing opportunities for inclusion in the modern state through the acquisition of cultural capital. At the same time, it intensifies significantly the processes that produce dislocation from place. Social mobility and migration challenge the racial state by making racial exclusivity increasingly untenable. But dislocation intensifies the diasporic imagination as people turn increasingly to imaginary homelands in the formation of their identities. Thus, the weakening of the racial state has produced, ironically, an intensification of racially defined diasporic identity. This has to do with the integral relationship between race and conceptions of originary homelands.

For black immigrants to the industrialized North, globalization has brought possibilities for transformation from victim to agent. It has provided access to rights and opportunities previously foreclosed by racially exclusionary practices of modernity. As agents, immigrants can reverse the material outcomes of exclusion through imaginative reconstruction of their subjectivities, or through engagement with political struggles for inclusion. Diasporic identity facilitates both.

But neo-globalization comes with new complications for diasporic identity. Gilroy speaks of the 'ambivalence' that is produced out of the 'Diasporic yearnings' of those caught up in its transnational sojourns. He locates diasporic identity in the interstices between 'residence' and 'origin'. This is what produces its 'complex and ambivalent' character. At its base is a political culture that is 'remembered and remade'.[24] These memories and cultural reformulations (or remakes) respond, I would like to argue, to localized social geographies. The North Atlantic is the actual and desired destination for the vast majority of black immigrants. There, they become inserted into white national spaces constructed out of white imaginations of exclusive racial belonging. They join a growing number of black immigrants, some from their own countries, who, like themselves, are responding to the intensification of conditions of neo-globalization. Innovative developments in transportation and communication technologies greatly facilitate diasporic connections to other local and national locations, to their countries of origins, and to Africa. All these contribute to an intensification of diasporic imaginaries across fragmented geographies. At the same time, immigration deepens notions of essentialized racial difference. As immigrants with non-European origins become inserted into exclusively white national spaces, they join with those historically engaged in racial confrontation. This structural politics of race contributes to a heightened sense of racial consciousness. As diasporic intimacy increases, ambiguous national affinities that meliorate racial conflict give way to the cultural politics of transnational racial identity. Immigration also produces contradictory tendencies by the introduction of national distinctions into racially defined communities. This is occurring at a time of increasing social mobility. Successful challenges to the exclusionary practices of race and the presence of skilled and educated immigrants within racial communities open up opportunities that were previously foreclosed on racial grounds. These together can unleash centrifugal forces introduced by increasing diversification in socioeconomic status and by diffuse attachments to different nationally and culturally defined communities.

Such conflicting tendencies of diasporic identity have become evident in the collective self-representations of West Indian immigrants in the San Francisco Bay Area of Northern California. West Indian identity emerges as confrontation and negotiation of the racialized terrain of the USA. At the most basic level, West Indians are forced to define themselves, collectively and individually, in relation to and against the African-American community to which they are racially bound. Their social positioning circumscribes the choices of identity available to them. The social economics of the West Indian community have been shaped by what may be termed the materialities of location. Northern California provides abundant opportunities for successful absorption of the skilled and educated West Indian immigrant. There are very few opportunities for employment available to those among them with limited education and little skill. Because of this, the West Indian immigrant community is almost exclusively middle class. This has to do with the 'pull factors' of West Indian immigration that operate against the unskilled and low skilled in Northern California while favouring the qualified and educated. The overwhelming presence of Mexican, Latino, and Pacific Rim immigrants in the labour intensive and service sectors of the California economy has had the effect of shutting out the unskilled and low skilled West Indian. As a result, success and achievement have become central themes in West Indian diasporic identity. These are publicized in rituals and performances of West Indian identity and are inscribed in popular understandings of the West Indian Diaspora.[25] Those without the social and economic capital of the middle and professional classes are marginalized, isolated, and excluded. They become invisible in the public face of the West Indian community. In this way, diasporic identity imposes expectation of success and achievement that support practices of selective inclusion and exclusion in the community's social reproduction.

Achievement and success can signal insertion into the national space. For West Indians in the San Francisco Bay Area, such insertion is circumscribed by the exclusionary practices of race in the peoplehood of the USA. The contradiction is resolved through a cultural politics of difference that locates West Indians outside of the national terrain of the USA on nationalist and cultural, rather than racial grounds. In other words, the West Indian community responds to racial exclusion by fashioning its identity around notions of national origin and cultural difference. While diasporic identity emerges inevitably out of practices of racial exclusion, it can become organized around notions of belonging devoid of racial signification. In its national and cultural expression, West Indian identity becomes incompatible with notions of American belonging. This mitigates challenges to American discourses of racial exclusion. It serves also to differentiate West Indians from the racially defined identity of African Americans. Such differentiation is cast in cultural and national terms.

In their diasporic constructions, West Indians elicit popular essentialized imageries about the West Indies in the construction of their identity. They engage in symbolic displays, rituals, aesthetics and poetics that confirm and reinforce notions of their exotic foreignness. These accommodate American racist notions of the West Indian as exotic, hypersexual, fun loving, and given to bacchanalian excesses. Deracination provides access to the materialities of American modernity. It positions West Indians firmly within the group of permanent foreigners identified with California's technological and financial success.

Diaspora can act to manage the contradiction between the imperatives of heterogeneity on the one hand, and racial exclusion on the other. It does so through notions of transnational belonging. This delinks diasporic subjects from issues of nationalist concern. It creates predispositions for disengagement with racial challenges to the state. Identification as 'foreign' preserves the nativist myth of white racial purity by foregoing any claim to nationalist belonging. It blunts charges of discrimination by racially specified domestic minorities by creating conditions for upward mobility for these similarly racialized immigrants. In the final analysis, however, diasporic identity cannot escape racial characterization, West Indians are forced to accommodate themselves to white racist imageries of their exoticization.

There are also forces that impel immigrants to a racial identification with domestic minorities. This has to do with the ineluctable association between race and diasporic identity. The white racial imaginary is pervasive in the construction of American peoplehood and belonging. So are notions of racial inferiority tied to myths of origin outside of Europe. Immigrants to the USA cannot escape the inevitability of this racial identification. For this reason, West Indians in the USA are marked as black. They cannot escape the implications of racial identity.

So they are forced to participate in African-American material politics of difference and in the structural politics of race. In the process, they become inserted into alternative forms of diasporic consciousness that tie them to African Americans. The post-World War II successes of African-American challenges to exclusionary racial practices have opened up opportunities for upward mobility under the rubrics of 'affirmative action', 'civil rights', 'equal opportunity', 'voting rights' and so on. The West Indian middle class is particularly well placed to exploit these opportunities. This has become quite evident in California. West Indians make claims to these opportunities on racial grounds. They do so in order to exploit the significant political strength of the African-American community, particularly in Los Angeles and in the San Francisco Bay Area. Increased access to opportunity emerged in response to massive political mobilization during the civil rights era of the 1960s and 1970s.[26] Black political clout in California has brought with it considerable access to public and private sector resources. The black West Indian middle class has been able to insert itself into these racially defined spaces created by African-American political power. This is reflected in the growth of the West Indian population in Los Angeles from around 500 before 1950 to around 50,000 by the early 1990s. Much of this growth occurred after the mid-1960s. [27]

Race is the critical ingredient in gaining access to the opportunities created by African-American political mobilization. Because of this, West Indians are forced into racial identification with African Americans. In this way, they are assured protection against the exclusive claims of a white peoplehood. This complicates their diasporic identity. As model minority, they reject racial identification and engagement with American racial politics. But diasporic engagement with African Americans demands invocation of a black racial commonality. So West Indians accommodate themselves to two conflicting notions of diasporic consciousness. The first relates to their identities as West Indian, while, the second to their identities as black. The two are not compatible because West Indian identity functions to signify their separation from the racialized African American. While both subjectivities are deployed against the material implications of white exclusionary practices, West Indianness becomes a means of discursive separation from the cultural, social and nationalist politics of African Americans. Blackness, on the other hand, elicits identification with the latter's material politics. The distinction is important. While black identity is necessary for the contestation of white supremacy, West Indian identity is symbolically deployed in collusion with it.

West Indian immigrant presence in the USA provides a concrete example of the ambiguities and contradictions of diasporic imagination that have received attention from scholars like Paul Gilroy.[28] As West Indians, these San Francisco Bay Area immigrants symbolically reject racial identification with African Americans. They also relinquish claims to American peoplehood by accommodating to their roles as permanent foreigners. As non-racial, non-Americans their access to the materialities of success is considerably enhanced. At the same time, West Indians cannot escape the material consequences of their racialization. This impels them into political identification with African Americans under the broad rubric of black diasporic consciousness.

West Indian identity in the San Francisco Bay Area also highlights the relationship between social positionality and diasporic imagination. West Indian middle-class status precludes participation in the poetics and aesthetics of African-American black diasporic expression, given the latter's association with historicist understandings of racial inferiority. It also precludes originary claims to Africa, given the racial implications of these claims. Thus, West Indian black identity is confined to deployment in the materialities of institutional, local and national politics. By this, I mean that black (as opposed to West Indian) identity is deployed in the structural arena of political engagement with racial exclusion. West Indians join black professional organizations, support black causes nationally and internationally, and align with African Americans in local and national politics. They do not, however, engage in the social and cultural practices of African-American subjectivity. The point here is that, like all identities, diasporic identity has to be contextualized if its ambivalences and contradictions are to be understood and explained. West Indians are black in certain contexts, when they are engaged with the materialities of their American existence. In other contexts, they resist black and American identification altogether.

There is a profound relationship between identity and social geography. The West Indian immigrant community in the San Francisco Bay Area differs in important respects from the larger West Indian immigrant communities on the East Coast of North America. It is relatively small, numbering less than ten thousand. Its members are not concentrated in defined localities of homologous residential concentration. Rather, West Indians are spread throughout the region in San Francisco and Alameda counties, in the East Bay, in Peninsula counties and in the city of San Jose. Most came to the area from elsewhere in the West Indian Diaspora rather than directly from the West Indies. Decisions to relocate are made because of offers of jobs or because of company transfers. Some move after being stationed at military bases in the area. Others come as students, studying in one of the area's colleges or universities. Many come as dependent and non-dependent family or because they are able to use their friendship networks to secure jobs. In socioeconomic terms, many are middle to upper-middle class.

The San Francisco Bay Area is one of the most ethnically diverse regions in the USA and a prime location for immigrants, particularly from Asia and Latin America. Along with Los Angeles, it is the host community to a significant proportion of the eight million foreign-born residents in California's total population of 32.4 million (1996 figures). These immigrants comprise 33 per cent of all foreign-born residents in the USA and 25 per cent of all California residents. Because of their numbers, immigrants and their families enjoy a high degree of visibility. This lends itself to both positive and negative assessments of their desirability, worth, and merit in the cognitive constructions of 'mainstream' Americans, both white and black. These understandings apply differentially to immigrants based on their particular countries and regions of origin.

The historical construction of difference in California has produced three broad understandings of the diasporic populations from the global south. These understandings apply differentially to West Indians. Their blackness allows location in the racialized space of the African American. Their 'foreignness' supports location in two cognitively constructed spaces. The first is the one occupied by the 'undesirable' grouping of Mexican and Latino immigrants. The second is the diasporic space of the 'model minority' occupied by the 'Asian immigrant'. West Indian identity is organized around representations and practices of this model minority. Because of this, they are not associated in popular imagination with the 'undesirables'. At the same time, they have available to them a racialized black identity.

Pre-existing generalized notions of West Indianness inform West Indian diasporic identity in the San Francisco Bay Area . Unlike Latinos, West Indians are identified in popular consciousness as a 'model minority' characterized by ideals of success similar to the white mainstream population of the USA. This is notwithstanding the occupational similarities between the West Indian majority living mostly on the East Coast of the USA and Latino immigrants on the West Coast. Both are primarily low-wage service sector workers. As a diasporic construct, the model minority is disciplining, self regulating, and segregating. It is also racially specified since it refers only to immigrants from the global south. It is one element in the technology of American racial control. It applies the universalistic logic of merit in the service of racial segregation and regulation. Accordingly, different racial groups are understood to get what they earn and deserve. Model minorities are understood to have overcome obstacles of poverty and migratory disruption to achieve, on merit alone, middle and upper-middle-class socioeconomic status.[29] As a diasporic construction, the model minority receives its importance as a legitimizing trope of white supremacy because of its deployment in the structural politics of race against charges of racial (and racist) exclusivity. It highlights and celebrates possibilities for successful meritocratic incorporation of racial minorities into the exclusive social and economic preserves of whites. It serves as a negation of claims of racism. Thus, conservative scholars have used the putative success of West Indians to refute arguments that African-American poverty stems from the pervasive effects of racial discrimination.[30] The model minority requires deracination and rejection of claims to American belonging. Because the socioeconomic incorporation of the model minority is not understood symbolically as racially transgressive, in a way that it would be for national minorities, it leaves the racial order unchallenged.

Claims made about West Indian success are much more important for the part they play in the ideological terrain of race relations than for what they say about the material realities of the West Indian immigrant presence. West Indians, collectively, are not better off than African Americans.[31] They face the same barriers to racial inclusion. Evidence to the contrary notwithstanding, the myth of the model minority continues to persist in popular understandings of the West Indian immigrant. It receives constant reinforcement both from within and outside West Indian communities and is sustained by the practice of highlighting West Indians who have risen to positions of national prominence as examples of West Indian universal success.

Model minority can also highlight the potential for diasporic imagination to expose heterogeneity as the critical ingredient in the construction of modernity. It challenges and contests the racial exclusivity of the modern state and its homogeneous discourse. The racial link between immigrants and racial minorities intensifies this challenge on two counts. The first is through the links forged between the latter and the broader diaspora in ways that contest claims to national and racial exclusivity made by the nation state. The second is by the intensification of immigrant insertion into racially exclusive arenas on grounds other than race. These immigrants are accommodated because their identities are culturally and transnationally rather than racially defined. But the fact of their accommodation cannot but break the stranglehold of racial exclusivity. Moreover, opportunities for accommodation cannot be separated from successes in the struggle waged by national minorities against racial exclusivity.

At the same time, the model minority highlights the contradictions of diasporic identity. Diaspora can collude with the state to shore up its racial character by undermining challenges to its exclusionary practices. This opens the way for the masking of the state's practices of racial exclusivity that become hidden behind the trope of cultural inferiority applied to its racialized minorities.

In the final analysis, diasporic subjectivity bridges the gap between modernity's demands for racial heterogeneity and hybridity, on the one hand, and capitalism's demand for racial exclusivity to support its imperative of a racial division of labour, on the other. Neo-globalization has intensified this contradiction with a resultant deepening and widening of diasporic consciousness. But diaspora may very well be the Achilles heel of modernity. Its intensification comes with the possibility of undermining the racial state even while it continues to serve its purpose.

Notes

1. Stuart Hall, 'Old and new identities, Old and new ethnicities', in *Theories of Race and Racism*, eds. L. Black and J. Solomos (London and New York: Routledge, 2000), 148.
2. Paul Gilroy, 'Between Camps: Race and Culture in Postmodernity' (Inaugural Lecture, Goldsmiths College, University of London, March 4, 1997), 3.
3. Ibid., 10.
4. This argument is cogently made by D.T. Goldberg, *The Racial State* (Oxford: Blackwell, 2002), 14–35.
5. Anderson has proposed the idea of nations as 'imagined communities'. See B. Anderson, *Imagined Communities* (London: Verso, 1991).
6. D.T. Goldberg, *The Racial State*, 9.
7. Ibid., 15–16.
8. Stuart Hall, 'What is this "Black" in Black Popular Culture?', in *Stuart Hall: Critical Dialogues in Cultural Studies*, eds. D. Morley and C. Kuan-Hsing (London and New York: Routledge, 1996), 467.
9. See for example *Imagining Home: Class, Culture, and Nationalism in the African Diaspora*, eds. S. Lemelle and R. Kelly (New York: Verso, 1976).
10. Stuart Hall, 'Routes to Roots', in *An Introduction to Women's Studies: Gender in a Transnational World*, eds. I. Grewak and K. Kaplan (New York: McGraw Hill, 2002).
11. This is a complexity that is well recognized by Hall, ('Thinking the Diaspora: Home-Thoughts From Abroad', *Small Axe* 6 (1999): 1–18) who, with reference to the Caribbean, sees diasporic imagination as the vehicle of national inclusion because it challenges the very 'binary conception of difference' upon which depends 'the construction of an exclusionary frontier' (7).
12. The ambiguity and contradictory nature of hybrid subjectivity is well recognized, especially by those who study the Caribbean because of its history of both contesting and colluding with modernity. In the Caribbean and Latin America, hybridized practices have functioned, universally, as instruments of coloniality by naturalizing racialized hierarchies [S. Puri, *The Caribbean Postcolonial: Social Equality, Post-Nationalism and Cultural Hybridity* (New York: Palgrave Macmillan, 2004); A.W. Marx, *Making Race and Nation: A Comparison of the United States, South Africa, and Brazil* (Cambridge and New York: Cambridge University Press,1998)]. Its possibilities and its complexities are recognized by Hall, 'Thinking the Diaspora: Home-Thoughts From Abroad'; M.L. Pratt, *Imperial Eyes: Travel Writing and Transculturation* (London: Routledge, 1991); E.K. Brathwaite, *The Development of Creole Society in Jamaica, 1770–1820* (Oxford: Oxford University Press, 1971; Kingston: Ian Randle Publishers, 2005).
13. A distinction must be made here between 'naturalist' and 'historicist' understandings of black inferiority. The former assumes a 'prehistorical condition' that is 'naturally incapable of development and so historical progress' (Goldberg 2002, 43). This has been superceded by a 'historicist' discourse that relates to notions of 'historical immaturity' that can be overcome through contact with and tutelage by the civilized. This allows differential incorporation of those with demonstrated attributes of reason and rationality into the arena of modern statist belonging, however circumscribed (see Goldberg 2002, 36–80).

14. I use these dimensions of capital following Pierre Bourdieu [*Outline of a Theory of Practice* (Cambridge: Cambridge University Press, 1977); P. Bourdieu, *Distinction: A Social Critique of the Judgment of Taste* (Cambridge, Mass.: Harvard University Press, 1984); see also J. Turner, *The Structure of Sociological Theory* (Belmont, CA: Wadsworth, 1991), 512–18]. In his formulation, economic capital refers to the ownership and control of productive resources. Social capital refers to those prerequisites that determine location in the hierarchically organized status groups, aggregates and/or categories and the social networks associated with them. Cultural capital refers to those 'interpersonal skills, habits, manners, linguistic styles, educational credentials, tastes, and lifestyles' acquired by persons in their lifetime (Turner, 512). Symbolic capital has to do with the recognized forms of deployment of social, cultural, and economic capital through ritualized and symbolic displays.

15. D.T. Goldberg, *The Racial State*, 6.

16. R. Grosefoguel, *Colonial Subjects: Puerto Ricans in a Global Perspective* (Berkeley, Los Angeles, London: University of California Press, 2003), 6.

17. For the more orthodox formulations of dependency see, among others, George Beckford, *Persistent Poverty* (New York: Oxford University Press, 1972); S. Amin, *Accumulation on a World Scale* (New York: Monthly Review Press, 1975); S. Amin, *Unequal Development: An Essay on the Social Formations of Peripheral Capitalism*, trans. Brian Pearce (New York: Monthly Review Press, 1976); A.G. Frank, *Capitalism and Underdevelopment in Latin America* (New York: Monthly Review Press, 1967); I. Wallerstein, *The Modern World-System II* (New York: Academic Press, 1980); I. Wallerstein, *The Politics of World Economy* (Cambridge Mass.: Harvard University Press, 1984).

18. There is a seamless relationship between the political materialities of African nationalism (as anti-colonialism) on the continent, on the one hand, and the cultural politics of black nationalist expressions such as Pan-Africanism, Black Power and so on, occurring outside Africa. The latter, in turn, have informed the cultural politics of Africa such as, for example, Negritude associated particularly with French West Africa and black consciousness in South Africa.

19. See C. Fraser, *Ambivalent Anti-Colonialism: The United States and the Genesis of West Indian Independence, 1940–64* (London: Greenwood, 1994).

20. As a result, postmodern scholars propose hybridity as the inevitable challenge to the racial state and to modernity itself. See, for example Paul Gilroy, *The Black Atlantic* (Cambridge, Mass.: Harvard University Press, 1993); and H. Bhabba, *The Locations of Culture* (London and New York: Routledge, 1994).

21. The case of blackness is special because of Africa's role in trans-Atlantic slavery and in the production of modernity. Other racialized constructions, organized around originary myths of homelands located outside of Europe and Africa, come with different implications for positioning in the space of modernity.

22. These would include African nationalism, Pan-Africanism, Black Nationalism, Black Power, Black Consciousness and so on.

23. Gilroy ('Between Camps: Race and Culture in Postmodernity', 10–12) speaks somewhat pessimistically of the possibilities of this new diaspora with the nation state (national camp) representing its 'negation'. He sees in its 'ambivalence' the possible transformation into an 'unambiguous exile'. From my own perspective, it is integrally tied to neo-globalization as the logical trajectory of modernity. The possibility of its negation through absorption in the nation state does not rule out its transformative potential.

24. Paul Gilroy, 'Between Camps: Race and Culture in Postmodernity', 10.

25. For a fuller discussion of this see P. Hintzen, *West Indian in the West: Self Representations in an Immigrant Community* (New York: New York University Press, 2001). The material for the ensuing discussion of West Indians in the San Francisco Bay area is taken from this work.

26. See S. Fisher, *From Margin to Mainstream: The Social Progress of Black Americans*, 2nd ed. (Lanham, MD: Rowman and Littlefield, 1992); G. Horne, *Fire This Time: The Watts Uprising and the 1960s* (Charlottesville: University Press of Virginia, 1995); Mervyn Dymally, 'The Rise of Black Political Leadership in California', in *What Black Politicians are Saying?*, ed. Nathan Wright (New York: Hawthorn Books, 1972), 32–43; R. Sorenshein, *Politics in Black and White: Race and Power in Los Angeles* (Princeton: Princeton University Press, 1993); B. Wyman, 'Roots: The Origins of Black Politics in the East Bay', *Express* 9, no. 43 (August 1987).

27. J.B. Justus, 'Introduction', in *Imagining Home: Class, Culture, and Nationalism in the African Diaspora*, 131.

28. Paul Gilroy, 'Between Camps: Race and Culture in Postmodernity'.

29. See C.V. Fong, 'Tracing the Origins of a "Model Minority". A study of the Depictions of Chinese Americans in Popular Magazines' (PhD diss., Department of Sociology, University of Oregon,1989); W. Young-Jin, '"Model Minority" Strategy and Asian American Tactics', *Korea Journal* (Summer 1994): 57–66; S. Steinberg, *The Ethnic Myth: Race, Class and Ethnicity in America* (Boston: Beacon Press, 1981).

30. N. Glazer and P. Moynihan, *Beyond the Melting Pot* (Cambridge, Mass.: MIT Press, 1963); T. Sowell, 'Three Black Histories', in *American Ethnic Groups*, eds. T. Sowell and L.D. Collins (Washington, DC: Urban Institute, 1978), 41.

31. P. Kasinitz, 'From Ghetto Elite to Service Sector: A Comparison of Two Waves of West Indian Immigrants in New York City', *Ethnic Groups* no. 7 (1998): 173–204; R. Farley and W. Allen, *The Color Line and the Quality of Life in America* (New York: Russell Sage Foundation, 1987).

13 | *Epilogue: Through the Prism of an Intellectual Life*[1]

Stuart Hall

Thinking about Thinking

I cannot begin at this point to try to reply or respond in any detail to the many papers which have been presented, the important ideas which have been circulated and the points which have been raised. Since I cannot respond in detail, what on earth can I do? Perhaps I can start by trying to invoke a certain way of experiencing myself over the last two days of the conference. I keep looking around trying to discover this person 'Stuart Hall' that everybody is talking about. Occasionally I recognize him. I sort of know him. He has a certain familiarity every now and again. I am familiar with a lot of the ideas people are referring to. I recognize some of the quotes, though I have to confess, not all! There are one or two I am very grateful to have rediscovered, and I hope to get the references. But this experience of, as it were, experiencing oneself as both subject and object, of encountering oneself from the outside, as another — an *other* — sort of person next door, is uncanny. It is like being exposed to a serialized set of embarrassments. And I want just to draw from that experience a first thought about thought. I think theory — thinking, theorizing — is rather like that, in the sense that one confronts the absolute unknowingness, the opacity, the density, of reality, of the subject one is trying to understand. It presents itself, first, as both too multifarious and too complicated, with its patterns too hidden; its interconnections un-revealed. One needs the act of distancing oneself — as Lacan would say — 'from the place of the other'. Marx once suggested that one should use concepts like a scientist uses a microscope, to change the magnification, in order to 'see differently' — to penetrate the disorderly surface of things to another level of understanding. There is a sense in which one has to stand back, outside of oneself, in order to make *the detour through thought*; to approach what it is one is trying to think about indirectly, obliquely, in another way, another mode. I think the world is fundamentally resistant to thought. I think it is resistant to 'theory'. I do not think it likes to be thought. I do not think it wants to be understood. So inevitably, thinking is hard work, a kind of labour. It is not something that simply flows naturally from inside oneself. Thus, one of the perplexities about doing intellectual work is that, of course, to be any sort of intellectual is to attempt to raise one's self-reflexiveness to the highest maximum point of intensity. Someone — I think Mike Rustin[2] earlier on — referred to my early work, the subject of my putative D.Phil, on the novels of Henry James, and what a bizarre thing it is that this is where my academic career started. One of the things about James was of course his attempt to gain the maximum intensity of self-consciousness, to be as self-aware as possible about the finest movements of his own conscious thinking — as he said, 'to be someone on whom nothing is lost.' Yet to do that is to become instantly aware of the enormous *unconsciousness* of thinking, of thought; one simply cannot and will never be able to fully recuperate one's own processes of thought or creativity self-reflexively.

These provisional thoughts about thinking come from being present at a conference at which I am, somehow, both being discussed and also discussing! If I distance myself, see myself 'from the place of the other', I can see what James, in one of his finest short stories, called 'the figure in the carpet' that I could not see before. I was often tempted during these last two days to join in and speak of me in the third person! Now what I wanted to say about this strategy is that, of course, by taking the 'detour through thought', one sees all sorts of things about one's self and one's own thinking, connections in one's work, the patterns behind the patterns, which one could not possibly see for oneself in any other way. In that sense, one is always unconsciously escaping the attempt to self-knowledge, the attempt to become identical with myself. That is not possible. I cannot become identical with myself. That is the paradox of identity which I have tried to write about elsewhere — one can only think identity through difference. To think is to construct that inevitable distance between the subject that is thinking and the subject that is being thought about. That is just a condition of intellectual work.

Caribbean Formation

The second thought about thinking and about the 'thought' that we have been discussing these two days was my response to the invitation from Brian, Tony and Rupert, to, as it were, become, at this very late stage in my life, a Caribbean intellectual. In what sense could I possibly claim to be a Caribbean intellectual? Certainly, not in the most obvious sense of the term. My work has not been largely about the Caribbean. I have not been actively present in the enormously important work of trying to *write* the history of the Caribbean and Caribbean societies in the period of independence, including writing its past from the perspective of an independent nation. Of course, my hopes have been caught up with the fate of the nations of the region since decolonization. However, I have not been party in that deep way to the project of 'nationhood'. I am Caribbean in the most banal sense, in the sense that I was born here. But that accident of birth is not enough to justify owning up to the title. I have to confess, although they do not know it, that I did seriously think of saying to them, 'I am sorry, but I am not a Caribbean intellectual in the sense in which I think the Centre ought to be honouring people.' The reason I decided not to do that was because, reflecting on my own life and practice, I have to say that, although in many moments of my life I have been thinking about what many people in the Caribbean would think of as other problems, other places, other dilemmas, it seems to me I have always been doing so through what I can only call *the prism of my Caribbean formation*. In that sense I am committed to the idea of a politics of location. This does not mean all thought is necessarily limited and self-interested because of where it comes from, or anything like that. I mean something rather looser — that all thought is shaped by where it comes from, that knowledge is always to some degree 'positional'. One can never escape the way in which one's formation lays a kind of imprint on or template over what one is interested in, what kind of take one would have on any topic, what linkages one wants to make and so on. This is true even about so-called Cultural Studies, the field with which, inevitably, my work and my career have been identified, and for which I feel a certain responsibility. I have tried as far as possible to evade this 'burden of representation', and I sometimes make rude noises about it so people think 'oh well it does not really belong to him after all'. I deny paternity —

Cultural Studies had many origins, many 'fathers', but nevertheless, one feels a certain responsibility for it.

Well, Cultural Studies has its own internal history as a discipline, but when I think about why I ever got into it, I know it was because, before what is called Cultural Studies ever began at Birmingham in the early 1960s, I had to confront the problem of trying to understand what Caribbean culture was and what my relationship was to it. I put it that way because my relationship to it, in terms of a naturalistic logic — 'He was born here, so he must be a Caribbean intellectual' — does not work. My relationship to the Caribbean was one of dislocation, of displacement, literally and figuratively. My life as a young person, as a child, as an adolescent, was spent there. I left when I was 18 years old. Though I have never ceased to think of myself as in some way 'Jamaican', I have never lived for long periods in the Caribbean since then. A relationship then — a negative relationship, you would think — of displacement and dislocation. Dislocation in a deeper sense, too. The reason why I was so committed to leaving the Caribbean when I finished school at the end of the 1950s and the reason why in some ways I never returned to live here, had to do with my colonial formation, my formation and experience as *a colonial subject.* Because there are so many young people in the audience, I want to remind you that I am talking about something very specific, now more or less lost as an immediate experience to those who are not of or nearly my age. Most of you are children of the 'postcolonial'. I am talking about experiencing oneself, thinking about one's society and one's future, from the position of a colonial subject. I left for England 12 years before independence. My whole formation had been as a child of coloured middle-class Jamaican society. That is to experience oneself as 'colonized' — that is, fundamentally displaced from the centre of the world, which was always represented to me as 'elsewhere' and at the same time dislocated from the people and conditions around me. My relationship to that background, which I do not want to go into in a personal sense, was to make me feel (in the eloquent term which the great critic of Orientalism, Edward Said, used as the title of his memoir of a strikingly similar childhood half way around the world in another colonized space) 'out of place', both in relation to my family and my personal formation and in relation to the society into which I had been born. I hope it is not necessary to add that colonization, class, race and colour were intrinsic to that troubled story.

Up to the point where I left Jamaica in 1951, I did not understand what was the source of that dislocation. I thought it was a largely personal one. It was not until much later that I discovered that this was a feeling of dislocation experienced by a whole generation of intellectual Caribbean people at the end of Empire. When I went to London, there they all were, hiding out: all of them making some kind of escape attempt from colonial society. All of them in search for a way to become modern subjects, but with the bizarre thought that in order to do so, you had to leave the place of your birth — to go somewhere else — to become, borrowing the title of one of George Lamming's novels 'a native of my person'. Not anywhere else, of course, but right to the heart of the dislocation itself, to that which had, at a distance, dis-placed, un-homed you. And when I say 'dislocated', I am talking about serious stuff. I am talking about never feeling at one with the expectations my family had for me; of the sort of person I should become, of what I should do with my life. And of dislocation from the people themselves — from the mass of the Jamaican people: not at home 'in the castle of my skin'. Not being able to find myself 'at home' in the context in which I was born, brought up and lived. And I thought, this a recipe for disaster. The thing to do, I felt, is get out of there. There is a wonderful passage in Lamming's *The Pleasures of Exile*[3] — a book which I strongly recommend to you if you are interested in this period of Caribbean intellectual history, and especially if you can appreciate and enjoy the ironies of the word 'pleasures' in which Lamming, speaking of the West Indian writers who all found themselves living in London between 1948 and 1958 says, 'they simply wanted *to get out* of the place where they were born'. This is the decade which, as he says, 'witnessed the "emergence" of the novel as an imaginative interpretation of West Indian society by West Indians. And every one of them: Mittelholzer, Reid, Mais, Selvon, Hearne, Carew, Naipaul, Andrew Salkey, Neville Dawes, everyone has felt the need *to get out*.'[4] As an aspiring young writer, get out I did. However, what I soon discovered was that I had not and could never really 'get out' or be fully part of this 'elsewhere' that had simultaneously made and un-made me. To make the return journey: not literally, because for many, 'you can't go home again', but symbolically, in my head. I had no alternative but to come to terms with and try to understand the very culture from which I had felt distanced and, unsuccessfully, engineered an impossible escape. And when in the mid-1950s after the *Empire Windrush* and the beginning of mass migration to England from the Caribbean, I met black Caribbean men and women looking for work and a place to live in the grey, wet and inhospitable London streets — one more turn in the story of the Middle Passage and a critical moment in the formation of another displaced black diaspora — I resolved to go back, to read, read about, try to understand and to make a part of me the culture which had made me and from which I could never — and no longer wished — to escape. The central theme of *Pleasures of Exile*, Richard Drayton says in the preface to the new edition,[5] is 'the recovery of self' — even if it can only be recovered on the other side of the Black Atlantic. That was the personal origins, for me, of my own 'making' as a black intellectual (like many Jamaicans of my generation and class background, I had never until then thought of myself as 'black'); and also the first encounter with, what later came to be called Cultural Studies. All this no doubt explains how my perspective on 'being a Caribbean intellectual' and my conceptualization of 'culture' acquired from its earliest point so disrupted and *diasporic* an inflexion.

Subjectivity and Culture

What we think of as our individuality — something given before culture, which we possess as a subject just by being born, after which we learn to use the tools of culture — is quite the reverse. This is part of what I meant by saying that identity is not settled in the past but always also oriented towards the future. We enter culture, and by doing so, appropriate a language, a culture, which someone else — many other people — created for us, and only in that way gradually become subjects. Men and women make history, not on conditions of their own making, but with elements which are provided for them from the past, and which in some sense, are their conditions of existence, and they and shape and form them in ways that they have to live subjectively but for which they cannot be directly responsible. It is one of Michel Foucault's greatest insights that in order to become 'subjects' we must be 'subjected' to discourses which speak us, and without which we cannot speak. Of course, culture is also enabling as well as constraining,

274

disciplining. Within culture, we can form intentions, make purposes, create the most extraordinary intuitions into life. We can produce great works of philosophy, of painting, of literature; but only because we have already subjected ourselves to the laws and conventions and meanings of a language, the circumstances of history and culture, without which we could not have made ourselves. This process is called 'the decentring of the subject'. It represents the dislocation of the subject from the position of authorship and authority. It is the dislocation from that humanist dream which, I think, is really a humanist fantasy, that actually Man (sic) is the centre of the universe, it all proceeds from us and we are the origin. I could say more about how that figure of the displacement from the position of origin and identity has recurred in my own thinking but this is not the place or the time. However, it represents the end of a certain fantasy of romantic individualism to which I once subscribed (I went to England, after all, as a Romantic poet manqué), and the starting-point in my thinking of a profound belief that 'the social' is more than the sum of individuals, it is what the early sociologists — Marx, Weber, Durkheim — called 'society *sui generis*'. My critics would say this is how I fell prey to structuralism but it really preceded all that. It came in part from thinking about my own formation, my own subjecthood. I do not apply this insight substantively. It is not what I think about but rather what I think *with*. When I think about a problem, I realize retrospectively that I have done so by making this 'detour'. I am sure this 'methodological presupposition' of my thinking has something to do with my own personal 'displacement', but this is a connection I cannot spend time reflecting on — it is part of the unconsciousness of thought about which I was speaking earlier.

Trans-disciplinary Thought and Intellectual Activism

I am trying to now respond or refer to things which have been said in the last couple of days without actually being able to take on directly arguments which have been made. I am trying to share with you my thoughts, prompted by the last few days, about this strange object/subject — 'the thought of Stuart Hall'. I have been describing a kind of 'thinking under erasure'. What I mean by that is simply that in intellectual thought there are rarely absolutely new paradigms, which nobody has ever attended to before. We think within traditions and paradigms of thought — they think us — even when our intention is to break with and transcend them. But there are moments when the paradigms shift, when what David Scott calls 'the problem space' changes. We do live in a period when many of the existing paradigms established and developed within traditional intellectual disciplines either no longer in themselves adequately correspond to the problems that we have to resolve, or require supplementing from other disciplines with which they have not historically been directly connected. These are the openings for what is called a trans-disciplinary field of inquiry. And I speak about it because I have — once again somewhat unconsciously — found myself in a trans-disciplinary field. I have never been able to be satisfied with working from within a single discipline. It has nothing to do with not respecting what has gone on in the work of developing intellectual disciplines, but I am at the same time aware of the fact that the organization of modern knowledge into the disciplinary framework occurred at a specific historical moment. That historical moment may have passed, or may be passing, or 'on the wane'; or that particular way of organizing knowledge may no longer be adequate to the reality it is trying to analyse and describe. I feel a disjuncture between the disciplines, on the one hand, and the rapidly shifting and changing fragments of reality which confront us today. Again, I am not recommending to you an anti-disciplinary pathway, I am simply saying that I have not found it possible to think simply within the framework of the given disciplines. I started in literature and literary criticism but I never became a writer or a critic. I was a professor of sociology but I have no formal academic training in the field. Cultural Studies is a trans-disciplinary field of inquiry, not a discipline.

Now, that has had profound costs on my own thought. First of all, I really am not an academic in the traditional sense at all. I mean Barry Chevannes[6] was very kind to refer to me as a 'scholar', but I am not really in the true sense of the word a 'scholar'. That is not what I am. I have lived an academic life and earned my living — not terribly well — from doing academic work. I love to teach. I wanted to teach from the earliest point that I can remember. And teaching goes on in academic worlds. I respect and defend the academy to the hilt and the capacity it gives to transmit knowledge to future generations and to pursue knowledge for its own sake. One has to defend this arena of critical thought — especially these days when it is under such attack from so many quarters — with one's life. But it does not mean that I want to be or think of myself as having been an academic. I would claim, I would insist on, my right to the title of having done intellectual work. I am an intellectual. I am an intellectual in Gramsci's sense because I believe in the power and necessity of ideas. Of course, as a sort of materialist, I do not believe ideas alone make the world go round. And I certainly do not mean that I think my task is to produce theory. I would do without theory if I could! The problem is I cannot. You cannot. Because the world presents itself in the chaos of appearances, and the only way in which one can understand, break down, analyse, grasp, in order to do something about the present conjuncture that confronts one, is to break into that series of congealed and opaque appearances with the only tools you have: concepts, ideas and thoughts. To break into it and to come back to the surface of a situation or conjuncture one is trying to explain, having made 'the detour through theory'. Marx, in his 1857 Introduction, which is a wonderful methodological text about which I have written, as Larry Grossberg[7] remarked the other day, describes exactly this process. I am talking here about a working method of Marx. I am not talking about whether one subscribes to all the theories of Marxism or not. That is a different question. And what Marx says is you begin with an obvious fact: a social system is composed of people, and this gives us our first, what he calls 'chaotic' conception — the category of 'population'. How far can you take this category of population? Well, you can take it quite far. But really, you have to break with that descriptive approach at the moment when you understand that every population is always divided, it is not a homogeneous or multifarious single object. Always within that population are relations between capitalists and labour, men and women, masters and slaves. Relations of difference are what matters. The social categories into which people are inserted are more important than the sum of the humanity — the fact 'that we are all human under the skin' — which they constitute. And to make the move of analysing the population, as it were, into its particular categories, and the relations of similarity and difference between them, seems an abstract movement: the necessary moment of abstraction. However, as Marx says, you cannot stop there — which a great deal of theory does. You know, it is pleased to produce the categories and it proceeds to refine the abstractions, but, Marx says, far from it. You need to return then to the problem you really wanted to solve, but now understanding that it is the product of 'many determinations', not of one: not of a singular logic unfolding through history; not of a teleology, a deterministic circle which has its own end already inscribed in its beginning. Not Hegel's fantasy of the 'resolution of reason', the sub-sumption of the real and the rational, the dialectical resolution which is some moment when Thought and The Real — theory and historical reality — could be identically the same. None of that. Instead, you return to a world of many determinations, where the attempts to explain and understand are open and never ending — because the historical reality to be explained has no known or determined end. Well, some of the things that people have remarked on in my work arise from this method of thinking, which I am only addressing because you selected the absurd notion of spending two days thinking about the thought of Stuart Hall!

Studying the Conjuncture

So I have been thinking about the thought of Stuart Hall too, and I am telling you what I seem to have found out! Certain habits of thinking, certain ways of addressing a problem. If you are not interested in the disciplines, and if your subject is not given by the discipline, what is it are you trying to find out about? What is the object of your inquiry, what methods can you use, and most important of all, when does your object of inquiry — and thus the questions demanding answers — change, opening a new paradigm moment, a new 'problem space'? David Scott has done much, especially in his challenging new reading of C.L.R. James's *The Black Jacobins,* to make me think about this idea of a problem space and to relate it to what Althusser called 'a problematic' and Gramsci called 'the conjuncture'. Does this cluster of concepts refer to aspects of the same thing? (Incidentally, I nearly said when David had finished his wonderful paper[8] that we can go home now, because we now know all we ever need to know about the thought of Stuart Hall!) David said that the question I am addressing is what he called the 'contingency of the present'. Now actually, I would not quite put it that way myself, although I understand perfectly well why he did. I would say that the object of my intellectual work is 'the present conjuncture'. It is what Foucault called 'the history of the present'. It is, what are the circumstances in which we now find ourselves, how did they arise, what forces are sustaining them and what forces are available to us to change them? The 'history of the present', which is a kind of Foucaultian way of talking, brings together two rather contradictory ideas: history and the present. The present sounds as if it is very 'presentist' in its implication: right now, what is happening to us right now. What confronts us immediately now, which is certainly what he describes as 'dangerous and difficult times'. Yet the history of the present commits us to thinking of its anterior conditions of existence, what Foucault might have called its 'genealogies'. So the present, of course, is a force we have to now transform, but in the light of the conditions under which it came into existence: the history of the present. The question of the contingency of the history of the present is critically important because this is what I want to say about the present — that it is the product of 'many determinations' but that it remains an open horizon, fundamentally unresolved, and in that sense open to 'the play of contingency'.

Contingency and Identity

Here I am simply going to try to identify a number of ideas or themes which have emerged in the course of the last few days and make a few brief remarks about them before I pass on. Why contingency? What is it that I have been wanting to say about contingency? I do not want to say, of course, that the world has no pattern, no structure, no determinate shape, no determinacy. But I do want to say that its future is not already wrapped up in its past, that it is not part of an unfolding teleological narrative, whose end is known and given in its beginning. I do not believe, in that sense, in 'the laws of history'. There is no closure yet written into it. And to be absolutely honest, if you do not agree that there is a degree of openness or contingency to every historical conjuncture, you do not believe in politics, because you do not believe that anything can be done about it. If everything is already given, what is the point of exercising yourself or of trying to change it in a particular direction? This is a paradox which lies, of course, right at the heart of classical Marxism. If the laws of history are certain to unfold, who cares about the practice of the class struggle? Why not just let them unfold? There are a whole series of Marxisms which were precisely mechanistic and reductionist in that 'scientistic' way. Let the laws of capital unfold! Contingency does require you to say, 'of course, there are social forces at work here'. History is not infinitely open, without structure or pattern. The social forces at work in any particular conjuncture are not random. They are formed up out of history. They are quite particular and specific, and you have to understand what they are, how they work, what their limits and possibilities are, what they can and cannot accomplish. As Gramsci said, 'Pessimism of the intellect, optimism of the will'. But the outcome of the struggle between those different contending relations or forces is not 'given', known, predictable. It has everything to do with social practice, with how a particular contest or struggle is conducted. Even Marx, who was too inclined to subscribe to nineteenth-century scientific historical laws, thought the triumph of socialism which was supposed to be written in 'the logic of history', was not inevitable. He saw another alternative — one which unfortunately seems much closer in the days of the New World Order: 'socialism or barbarism,' he predicted, 'the ruin of the contending classes.'

My task has been to try to think what determinacy means — what I once called 'the contradictory, stony ground of the present conjuncture' — but without falling into absolute determinacy. I do not believe history is already determined. But I do believe that all the forces at work in a particular historical conjuncture or a situation one is trying to analyse, or a phase of history or development one is trying to unravel, are *determinate*. They do not arise out of nowhere. They have their own specific conditions of existence. So the conceptual issue is, is there a way of thinking determinateness which is not a closed determinacy? And contingency is the sign of this effort to think determinacy without a closed form of determination. In the same way, people say, 'you are a conjuncturalist. You want to analyse, not long epochal sweeps of history, but specific conjunctures'. Why the emphasis on the conjunctures? Why the emphasis on what is historically specific? Well, it has exactly to do with the conception of a conjuncture. The fact that very dissimilar currents, some of a long duration, some of a relatively short duration, tend to fuse or condense at particular moments, into a particular configuration. It is that configuration, with its balance of forces, which is the object of one's analysis or intellectual inquiry. The important thing about thinking conjuncturally is its historical specificity. So, for example, to put it very crudely, I am not as interested in racism as a single phenomenon marching unchanged through time, but in different racisms that arise in specific historical circumstances, and their effectiveness, their ways of operation. I am less interested in capital or capitalism from the seventeenth century to now than I am in different forms of capitalism. I am interested particularly, just now, in the enormously important shift in global capitalism which occurs in the 1970s. That represents the end of what I would call one conjuncture — the conjuncture of the period of the post-war settlement, dominated largely — especially in Europe — by a social democratic balance of forces and the welfare state, and the beginning of the rise of neoliberalism, of global capitalism, and the dominance of 'market forces', which constitutes the contradictory ground on which new interrelationships and interdependencies are being created across the boundaries of nationhood and region, with all the forms of trans-national globalization that have come to dominate the contemporary world. This is what is stamping a new rhythm on politics, in different ways, across the face of the globe. Nation states, national cultures, national economies, remain important, but these 'differences' are being condensed into a new, contradictory 'world system', which is what the term 'global' actually stands for. This is radically different from the world of decolonization — what David Scott has called 'the Bandung moment' — into which new nations, like Jamaica, emerged. This is a radically new historical moment, and sets us radically new questions, radically new political questions. That is all that is entailed in the move from one conjuncture to another. And the task of — as I once put it — 'Turning your face violently towards things as they really are', is what is required by 'thinking conjuncturally'.

I have also emphasized the question, 'why identity?' I am interested in identity because identity is a source of agency in action. It is impossible for people to work and move and struggle and survive without investing something of themselves, of who they are, in their practices and activities and building some shared project with others, around which collective social identities can cohere. This is precisely because, historically, there has been an enormous waning and weakening in the given collective identities of the past — of class and tribe and race and ethnic group and so on, precisely because the world has now become more pluralistic, more open-ended, though of course those collective identities have not disappeared in any sense. So those constraints are still on any identity formation. But to me there is a relatively greater degree of openness in the balance between the 'givenness' of an identity and the capacity to construct it or make it. That is all that I was trying to register in the new work on identity. I thought the greater global interdependence and interconnectedness would undermine strongly-centred but exclusive identities and open the possibility of more complex ways of individuals and groups positioning themselves in their own narratives. And I believed that the complexities of the black and 'creole' cultures of the Caribbean and the complexities of the 'hybrid' diaspora identities emerging in the wake of global migration had a great deal to teach us about the dynamics of this new process of identity-formation. Paradoxically, you might think that the revival of fundamentalisms of all kinds runs counter to this thesis. Actually, I believe that the pull of fundamentalism and all types of exclusive identities is a reaction to being marginalized or left out of the process of 'vernacular modernization' — the search everywhere for all peoples to have equal access to the means of becoming 'modern persons' and to live the technological possibilities of modern life, in their own ways, to the full, as it were, 'from the inside', which I think is hesitantly, also going on across the world — in the very teeth of the struggle by global capital to master and hegemonize historically constituted differences.

However, though I wrote a lot about 'identity', I always refused the notion that a whole politics could be identified with any single identity position. I have tried to say that identity is always the product of a process of identification. It is the product of taking a position, of staking a place in a certain discourse or practice. In other words, of saying, 'This is, for the moment where I am, who I am and where I stand'. This positional notion of identity enables one then to speak from that place, to act from that place, although sometime later in another set of conditions, one may want to modify oneself or who it is that is speaking. So in that sense, identity is not a closed book any more than history is a closed book, any more than subjectivity is a closed book, any more than culture is a closed book. It is always, as they say, in process. It is in the making. It is moving from a determinate past towards the horizon of a possible future, which is not yet fully known.

Globalization and Diaspora

I want to think of one more set of terms, which has arisen in the course of our discussion. These are around the terms diaspora and globalization. I was, as you can imagine, absolutely astonished to discover that the Jamaican government is this week having the very first conference on the diaspora. Since the *Empire Windrush*[9] landed in 1948, there has been a massive black diaspora in Britain, and I am not only thinking about the numbers of people from the Caribbean, Africa, India and elsewhere from the former colonial world, who have landed up in Britain and the other postcolonial metropolises since World War II. What is happening to the nation, here, cannot be insulated from the process of globalization and from the formation of diasporas elsewhere — which is, indeed, in my view, the 'dark side' of the globalization process. I do not have time to unravel this problem but I do want to say one or two things, rather dogmatically, about it. In this new awareness of 'the diasporic' dimension, something very important is happening to the idea of nations and nationhood, to nationalism, which was the driving force of decolonization, and to social identities. The nation cannot be taken unproblematically as the 'given' entity which social and historical explanation takes for granted. What's more, the nation cannot be any longer identified with its territorial boundaries. Further, the nation is a territorial entity and a political power, but it is also an 'imagined community', and so the questions about how the nation is constructed culturally and represented are part of its contemporary reality. These three dimensions interact, but they are not the same and do not always coincide. Now, the thinking so far in Jamaica about its diaspora is, of course, really just emerging — I think it is a sign of how slowly but irreversibly globalization is de-centring the experience of nation-building which focused our minds in the first stage of decolonization. I do think you largely think of Jamaicans living abroad as just like you, as belonging to you. I think you largely think, these are really Us — only, over there. When they come back, they will come back and rediscover their 'us-ness'. This is of course, partly true: of course, those connections are deep and long-lasting and are constantly re-forged. But don't you think about how they made any connections with *there* as well as with here? Do you think people live a whole life, survive in strange conditions, often of poverty, discrimination and certainly of institutional and informal racism in Britain — brought up children, schooled them, watched them grow up in the multicultural metropolis and it does not rub off in any way on them? Do you imagine their culture — their Jamaicanness — which they took with them just goes on throbbing, unchanged, untransformed, preserving their culture as a fixed umbilical cord? Of course, they have roots; but don't you think they also had to put down new roots? How otherwise did they survive? For Caribbean people — part of a colonial and pan-African Diaspora who, having emigrated again, have been twice 'diasporized' — who go on being 'translated' — their 'routes' are as critical to their identities as their 'roots'. Oh, they certainly survived by thinking about home. They planned from the beginning to go back home. They are a little disturbed, when they return, that everybody says, 'But you been in 'foreign'! 'Something about the way you stand, walk, talk, shift around, or as somebody said, can't move the hips, marks out the difference!

The problem of the diaspora is to think of it always and only in terms of its continuity, its persistence, the return to its place of origin, and not always and at the same time in terms of its scattering, its further going out, its dissemination. The impossibility of ever going home in exactly the same way as you left it. The diaspora is always going to be, in a certain way, lost to you. It has to be lost to you, because 'they' have a double stake, an investment in both here and elsewhere. It is not because they love us or because elsewhere has been good to them, but because the material conditions, the historical necessity, of having to 'make a life' means that they have to have ideas, investments, relationships with somewhere else as well. Now, my writing about the notion of the diaspora, about identity, even about the necessary 'hybridity' or creolization of all culture, has been shaped profoundly by reflecting on the Caribbean experience, even when I have not directly written about it. I have been trying to think about these very complicated processes of continuity and rupture, of the return to the old, of the imaginary recuperation or reconfiguring of the old, as well as the becoming — the opening to the new, to the future — and what is happening, concretely, on the ground, in everyday life, in changing the culture of those people who have been 'diasporized'. That is certainly one dimension of the work that I have been trying to do on the diaspora.

The second one is to remember that in the particular circumstances of the Caribbean, the people are themselves 'a diaspora'. We are ourselves the effect of the dislocation and displacement, of the dissemination from somewhere else: and of what then happens, culturally, as, out of the cauldron of colonization, enslavement and plantation society, something new, something genuinely novel, emerges. Does that mean that we do not have any connection with what went before? How could it possibly mean that? But it does mean that that connection is not something which can now be naturally summoned up as if it exists in all of us, somewhere down there, in our bodies, in our genes, as a force of nature. It has to be recreated, has to be sustained in the culture, reconfigured, in the new historical circumstances which confront us. It has to be sustained in the mind, or the connection cannot be made. We would be wrong to adopt a notion of tradition as something which does not change, which protects us against change. As I have had to say to people before, 'Africa is alive and well in the diaspora', but the Africa we left 400 years ago under the conditions of slavery, transportation and the Middle Passage has not been waiting for us — unchanged — to go back to, either in our heads or in our bodies. That Africa, far from being just the ancestral home, is the subject of the most brutal and devastating modern forms of exploitation. It is the subject and the object of the most vicious forms of contemporary neoliberalism, victim of the strategies of the new forms of geopolitical power, as well as ravaged by civil war, poverty, hunger, the rivalry of competing gangs and corrupt governing powers and elites. Long after we left it, even after the war, Africa was first of all inserted into a relationship with the West in the very moment of decolonization, in the relations of neocolonial subordination. In the second phase of the Cold War, all the difficulties of creating independent polities and independent national economies were overridden by the Cold War struggle between two competing world systems. All the difficulties of the emerging societies and the nascent postcolonial states were overridden by the struggle between the two world powers: a struggle which was then, paradoxically, fought out on postcolonial terrain. When next we invoke the problem of 'failed states' in Africa, let us remember the distortions that the Cold War imposed on the problems of the emerging postcolonial states. Remember who is implicated in the failure of the capacity of those states. Since the mid-1970s, those already failing states, states with the enormous difficulty — never resolved — of becoming postcolonial, like the Caribbean and elsewhere in the so-called Third World, have been enmeshed in new constitutive relations of geopolitical, economic, cultural and symbolic global power — the new system, the New World Order. That is what the signifier, 'Africa', so often bandied about in Western media and political discourse, means today. I do not need to unpack that story for you. Now of course there is the most profound connection between the African diasporas of the Caribbean, the US, of Brazil and Latin America and the diasporas of London or Paris, but these different 'Africas', though deeply interconnected, historically, cannot be 'the same' any longer. They are not the same. There are, of course, strong and deep persistent threads which connect them. At the same time, each has negotiated its relation to the West, to the surrounding world, differently. This is the complicated dialectic of 'sameness' and 'difference' which confronts us in today's globalizing world. So when one talks about the way in which identities of this kind have been ruptured by the different conjunctural breaks in post-war history, reorganized and reordered by them, yielding deep and concretely specific, differentiated formations, we know we have to, not discover, but *rediscover* what our connection now is with Africa. I believe this is the difference between a 'cultural nationalist' approach to our African connection, and the pan-African imaginary, which has done so much over the years to keep these connections alive. The concept of 'diaspora' is — for me — central to that imaginary.

So diaspora led me to think, first of all, about what is happening, and the complicated cultural processes going on, in the black diasporas of the metropole. Secondly, it led me to think about what exactly is meant by the 'diasporic' nature of Caribbean society and Caribbean culture. What exactly do we mean by that? And that led me to think about the diasporic nature of cultures themselves. I became aware of the fact that, discursively, cultures always represent themselves as fixed, exclusive, originary and unchanging: but, historically, when you look at them, that cannot be the case. Some change very slowly, some more rapidly: but they all change. They are all interrupted by movement, by conquest, by colonization, by trade, by migration, free and forced. They are disrupted by external influences, as well as evolving internally. Culture — the forms through which individuals and societies make sense of themselves and represent their real conditions of life, symbolically, to themselves — cannot be outside of history. Cultures are changed within and changed by history. So the broadly diasporic nature of Culture itself is a kind of conceptual model that I have derived, analogically, from thinking about a specific diaspora and reflecting on the diasporic nature of the culture which I thought I had left behind and had to rediscover in myself and come to terms with in a different way. This is my very long way of trying to answer the question, in what sense can I be 'a Caribbean intellectual'?

Just a final twist to that: under globalization, everywhere is becoming more 'diasporic'. It is not because people like to travel. It is because the very conditions under which the world now operates create what one can only call the astonishing late twentieth-century, early twenty-first-century movement of dispersed peoples. From that perspective, I go back and look at my own movement in 1951, the black migration and the migration from the Asian subcontinent to Britain in the 1950s and 1960s, as the beginning of an enormous historical tide. The disruption of people from their settled places, from their homes, from their familiar surrounding, their roots in the land and landscape, from their traditional ways of life, from their religions, from their familial connections — the uprooting that has become the history of modern 'global society'. The fact of the homeless, of what Negri and Hardt, in their book on *Empire*[10] call 'the multitudes'; of people who only survive by buying a ticket from some person who is trading in bodies; hanging out on the bottom of a train, crossing boundaries at the depth of night, running the gauntlet of surveillance cameras and border patrols, and disappearing into the depths of the cities. The economic migrants and the asylum-seekers, the illegal immigrants, the 'sans papieres' — the ones without proper papers. The ones driven into the camps across the borders by famine, civil war, environmental devastation or pandemic. A movement of people trying never to be 'there', crossing every boundary in the world. And think, though we did not know it at the time, we were the forerunners! Since then, into the UK alone, there have been — how many? Seven waves? Caribbean, Indians, Pakistanis, people from Bangladesh, West Africans, Cypriots, Chinese, then the people displaced from North Africa and the Middle East — from Afghanistan, Iraq; the people displaced from ethnic cleansing in the Balkans, now the people from Eastern Europe, from the former

Soviet empire. Wave after wave after wave of people living in the new multicultural metropole, presenting the question of how is it possible to make a life where people from very different historical backgrounds and bearing different cultural values and religious traditions are required to make some kind of common life. People attempting to negotiate the terms of some kind of tolerant life without either eating one another, shooting one another or separating out into warring tribal enmity.

That is what I call the multicultural question of modern times. And this globalization from below is occurring in the context of the globalization from above, which is of course the movement of every single thing, apart from people. The movement of capital, of technologies, the 'flow' of messages and images, the 'flow' of investment, the movement of entrepreneurs, of the executive corporate global class. Everybody is 'on the move' according to the logic of globalization, except the poor; except the poor. Labour — ordinary folks — is the only factor which is not supposed to move. Why? Because how can you take competitive advantage of the trans-location of production and consumption, if the one-dollar a day labourer in Latin America is going to be 'free' to move to the West Coast and claim advanced salaries? The function of the dispersal of capital around the globe, of the decentralization of capital in the modern global system, depends on the capacity to exploit labour, cheap labour, where it is! So the control on the movement of how many people are allowed to cross borders is absolutely central to the new constituent logic of contemporary globalization. The movement of peoples for economic purposes — escaping poverty, escaping ill health, escaping ecological devastation, escaping civil war, escaping ethnic cleansing, escaping rural depopulation, escaping over-urbanization, escaping a thousand and one problems — has become illegal. This is the underbelly of the contemporary globalization system. Therefore, our new diasporas are simply one part of this huge new historic movement, of a huge new geopolitical formation, which is creating the mixtures of cultures, and peoples and histories and backgrounds and religions, which is the contemporary problem of the modern world.

Speaking Truth to Power

So though I started with a question of diaspora in a rather limited empirical way, it has — here's my last reflection on the thought of Stuart Hall — in its usual way, undergone enormous conceptual expansion. It has illuminated something else of vital significance to the Caribbean. The idea of the diaspora now is obliterating, not nations and nationhood, but the moment of the nation state, the moment of nationalism. It is quietly subverting it. It is quietly transcending the project of one life in one nation, in one nation state, located in one national economy, and superintended by one national culture, attached to one national identity, which was for decades the driving vision of nationalism.

What the ultimate balance might be between globalization from above and globalization from below, whether there is any way of transforming that system, it is not my purpose at this stage to discuss. I am trying to suggest what it might mean to be riveted throughout my life by the phrase 'unravelling the present conjuncture', by being disturbed by, and trying to analyse so as to transform, systems and structures of power, of injustice, of inequality, which are generated by forces that one does not fully understand and whose consequences one therefore cannot fully estimate and whom one cannot therefore effectively resist. Well, I commend to you what I have to call the politics of intellectual life. David Scott quite rightly said that, though he would not subscribe to everything that Edward Said has said about the nature of intellectual life, there is a kind of vocation there which is similar to my own. I am honoured by the comparison, for Edward Said's life and practice has been exemplary for me and I mourn deeply and personally his recent death. I do think it is a requirement of intellectuals to speak a kind of truth. Maybe not truth with a capital T, but anyway, some kind of truth, the best truth they know or can discover — to speak that truth to power. To take responsibility — which can be unpleasant and is no recipe for success — for having spoken it. To take responsibility for speaking it to wider groups of people than are simply involved in the professional life of ideas. To speak it beyond the confines of the academy. To speak it, however, in its full complexity. Never to speak it in too simple a way, because 'the folks won't understand'. Because then they will understand, but they will get it wrong, which is much worse! So, to speak it in its full complexity, but to try to speak it in terms in which other people who, after all, can think and do have ideas in their heads, though they are not paid or paid-up intellectuals, need it. They need it like you and I need food. They need it in order to survive. I commend the vocation of the intellectual life in this sense to you. I remind you that the academy is one of the places in which it takes root. It is not the only place, and I do plead with you not to over-estimate its role or to get entrammeled in its internal rituals. Simply because one is on the site, you might be led to think that somehow, because you are there, you are therefore thinking. It does not absolutely follow, believe me! But I commend to you the duty to defend it and the other sites of critical thought. I commend you to defend it as a space of critical intellectual work; and that will always mean subverting the settled forms of knowledge, interrogating the disciplines in which you are trained; interrogating and questioning the paradigms in which you have to go on thinking. That is what I mean by borrowing Jacques Derrida's phrase, 'thinking under erasure'. No new language or theory is going to drop from the skies. There is no prophet who is going to deliver the sacred books, so that you can stop entirely thinking in the old way and start from year one. Remember that revolutionary dream? 'Year One'? 'From now on, socialist man'? This is when the new history begins! Today, the dawn of the realm of freedom! I am afraid the realm of freedom will look mostly like the old realm of servitude, with just a little opening here and there towards the horizon of freedom, justice and equality. It will not be all that different from the past; nevertheless, something will have happened. Something will have moved. You will be in a new moment, a new conjuncture: and there will be new relations of forces there to work with. There will be a new conjuncture to understand. There will be work for critical intellectuals to do. I commend that vocation to you, if you can manage to find it. I do not claim to have honoured that vocation fully in my life, but I say to you, that is kind of what I have been trying to do all this while.

Notes

1.   I want to thank Brian Meeks, Anthony Bogues, Rupert Lewis, Directors of the Centre for Caribbean Thought, University of the West Indies, Mona, for the enormous work which has gone into organizing and presenting this

conference and Rex Nettleford for his generosity. I also want to thank Adlyn Smith, Sonjah Stanley Niaah and others who worked with me to prepare for this conference and the University Library for its tremendous work of research and discovery.

2. See in this volume, Michael Rustin, 'Working from the Symptom: Stuart Hall's Political Writing'.

3. See George Lamming, *The Pleasures of Exile*, 2nd edition (London: Alison and Busby, 1984).

4. Ibid., 41.

5. See George Lamming *The Pleasures of Exile* (London: Pluto Press, 2005).

6. Barrington Chevannes, Dean of Social Sciences at the University of the West Indies, Mona, 2004 and Chair of Stuart Hall's address.

7. See, in this volume, Lawrence Grossberg, 'Stuart Hall on Race and Racism: Cultural Studies and the Practice of Contextualism'.

8. David Scott's paper which opened the conference was entitled 'Stuart Hall's Ethics'.

9. The *Empire Windrush* was the first ship to arrive in the United Kingdom from the West Indies bearing immigrants after the Second World War.

10. See Michael Hardt and Antonio Negri, *Empire* (Cambridge, Mass. and London: Harvard University Press, 2000).

Bibliography

Ajayi, Omofolabo. *Yoruba Dance: The Semiotics of Movement and Body Attitude in a Nigerian Culture*. Eritrea and Trenton: Africa World Press, 1998.

Althusser, Louis. *For Marx*. Trans. Ben Brewster [1969]. Reprint, New York: Verso, 1996.

———. *Lenin and Philosophy, and Other Essays*. Trans. Ben Brewster [1971]. Reprint, New York: Monthly Review Press, 2001.

Althusser, Louis and Etienne Balibar. *Reading Capital*. Trans. Ben Brewster [1970]. Reprint, New York: Verso, 1997.

Amin, S. *Accumulation on a World Scale*. New York: Monthly Review Press, 1975.

———. *Unequal Development: An Essay on the Social Formations of Peripheral Capitalism*, trans. Brian Pearce. New York: Monthly Review Press, 1976.

Anderson, B. *Imagined Communities*. London: Verso, 1991.

Anderson, P. 'Components of the National Culture'. *New Left Review* 50. (July–August 1969). Reprinted in P. Anderson, *English Questions*. London: Verso, 1992.

Arden, John. *Serjeant Musgrave's Dance*. London: Methuen, 1966.

Austin-Broos, Diane J. *Jamaica Genesis: Religion and the Politics of Moral Orders*. Kingston: Ian Randle Publishers, 1997.

Bailey, David and Stuart Hall. 'The Vertigo of Displacement.' *The Critical Decade, Ten*-8 2, no. 3 (1992): 14–23.

Baxter, Ivy. *The Arts of an Island*. New Jersey: Scarecrow Press, 1970.

Beckford, George. 'Introduction' to Erna Brodber, *Standing Tall: Affirmations of the Jamaican Male*. Kingston: Sir Arthur Lewis Institute of Social and Economic Studies, 2003.

Beckles, Hilary. 'Black Masculinity in Caribbean Slavery'. In *Interrogating Caribbean Masculinities*, ed. Rhoda E. Reddock. Kingston: University of theWest Indies Press, 2004.

Beer, Samuel. *Modern British Politics: A Study of Parties and Pressure Groups*. London: Faber and Faber, 1965.

———. *Britain Against Itself: The Political Contradictions of Collectivism*. London: Faber and Faber, 1982.

Bell, David and Gill Valentine. *Mapping Desire: Geographies of Sexualities*. London: Routledge, 1995.

Bell, David. 'Fragments of a Queer City'. In *Pleasure Zones: Bodies, Cities, Spaces*, eds. D. Bell, J. Binnie, R. Holliday, R. Longhurst and R. Peace. New York: Syracuse University Press, 2001.

Bennett, Jr., J. Harry. *Bondsmen and Bishops: Slavery and Apprenticeship on the Codrington Plantations of Barbados, 1710-1838*. Berkeley and Los Angeles: University of California Press, 1958.

Bhabba, H. *The Locations of Culture*. London and New York: Routledge, 1994.

Binnie, Jon. 'The Erotic Possibilities of the City'. In *Pleasure Zones: Bodies, Cities, Spaces*, eds. D. Bell, J. Binnie, R. Holliday, R. Longhurst and R. Peace. New York: Syracuse University Press, 2001.

Bogues, Anthony. *Black Heretics, Black Prophets: Radical Political Intellectuals.* New York: Routledge, 2003.
———. 'J.S. Mill. "The Negro Question" Race, Colonialism and the Ladder of Civilisation'. In *Race and Racism in Modern Philosophy*, ed. Andrew Valls. Ithaca: Cornell University Press, 2005.
Bonilla-Silva, Eduardo. *Racism without Racists: Color-Blind Racism and the Persistence of Racial Inequality in the United States.* Lanham, Md.: Rowman & Littlefield, 2003.
Bourdieu, P. *Outline of a Theory of Practice.* Cambridge: Cambridge University Press, 1977.
———. *Distinction: A Social Critique of the Judgment of Taste.* Cambridge, Mass.: Harvard University Press, 1984.
Brathwaite, Edward Kamau. *The Development of Creole Society in Jamaica 1770–1820.* Oxford: Clarendon Press, 1971.
———. *The Arrivants: A New World Trilogy.* Oxford: Oxford University Press, 1973.
———. *Contradictory Omens: Cultural Diversity and Integration in the Caribbean.* Savacou monograph, no. 1 (1974).
Brown, Michael K., Martin Carnoy, Elliott Currie, Troy Duster, David B. Oppenheimer, Marjorie M. Shultz, and David Wellman. *Whitewashing Race: The Myth of a Color-Blind Society.* Berkeley and Los Angeles: University of California Press, 2003.
Browning, Barbara. *Infectious Rhythm: Metaphors of Contagion and the Spread of African Culture.* New York and London: Routledge, 1997.
Bryce-Laporte, R.S. and D.M. Mortimer. *Caribbean Immigration to the USA.* Washington, DC: Research Institute on Immigration and Ethnic Studies, Smithsonian Institution, 1976.
Butcher, K.F. 'Black Immigrants in the United States: A Comparison with Native Blacks and Other Immigrants'. *Industrial and Labor Relations Review* 47 (1994): 265–85.
Butler, Judith. *Bodies that Matter.* London: Routledge, 1993.
Butler, Ruth. 'The Body'. In *Introducing Human Geographies*, eds. P. Cloke, P. Crang and M. Goodwin. London: Arnold, 1999.
Burnard, Trevor. 'Inheritance and Independence: Women's Status in Early Colonial Jamaica'. *William and Mary Quarterly* 48, no. 1 (1991): 93–114.
———. *Mastery, Tyranny, and Desire: Thomas Thistlewood and his Slaves in the Anglo-Jamaican World.* Chapel Hill and London: The University of North Carolina Press, 2004.
Carty, Hilary. *Folk Dances of Jamaica: An Insight.* London: Dance Books, 1988.
Centre for Contemporary Cultural Studies. *The Empire Strikes Back: Race and Racism in 1970s Britain.* London: Hutchinson, 1982.
Chang, Kevin. 'The dominant sex'. *Sunday Gleaner* (June 6, 2004).
Charles, Christopher. 'Garrison Communities as Counter Societies: The Case of the 1998 Zeeks Riot in Jamaica'. *Ideaz* 1, no. 1 (2002): 29–43.
Chatterjee, Partha. *The Nation and its Fragments: Colonial and Postcolonial Histories.* New Jersey: Princeton University Press, 1993.
Chevannes, Barry. *Rastafari: Roots and Ideology.* Kingston: the University of the West Indies Press, 1995.
———. *Learning To be a Man: Culture, Socialization and Gender Identity in Five Caribbean Communities.* Barbados: University of the West Indies Press, 2001.
Clarke, John. *New Times and Old Enemies.* London: Harper Collins, 1991.
Cohen, S. *Folk Devils and Moral Panics.* 3rd edition. London: Routledge, 2002.
Comaroff, Jean. *Body of Power, Spirit of Resistance: The Culture and History of a South African People.* Chicago: University of Chicago Press, 1985.

Conley, Dalton J. *Being Black, Living in the Red: Race, Wealth, and Social Policy in America*. Berkeley and Los Angeles: University of California Press, 1999.

Dahrendorf, R. *Class and Class Conflict in Industrial Society*. London: Routledge and Kegan Paul, 1959.

Connell, R.W. *Masculinities*. Berkeley and Los Angeles: University of California Press, 1995.

Cooke, Melville. The 'babyfather' privilege — Me a de bes' babyfaada inna Jamaica. *Daily Gleaner* (June 3, 2004).

Cooper, Carolyn. 'Erotic play in the Dancehall'. *Jamaica Journal* 22, no. 4 and vol. 23, no. 1, (1990): 14–50.

———. 'Slackness hiding from culture: Erotic play in the Dancehall'. In *Noises in the Blood: Orality, Gender and the 'Vulgar' Body of Jamaican Popular Culture*. London: Macmillan, 1993.

———. 'Lyrical Gun': Metaphor and Role Play in Jamaican Dancehall Culture. *The Massachusetts Review* 35, Iss. 3–4 (1994): 429–47.

———. 'Punany Power'. *Black Media Journal* 2 (2000): 50–52.

Craton, Michael and James Walvin. *A Jamaican Plantation: A History of Worthy Park 1670-1970*. Toronto and Buffalo: University of Toronto Press, 1970.

Curtin, Philip. *Two Jamaicas: The Role of Ideas in a Tropical Colony, 1830–1865*. New York: Antheneum, 1970.

Dagan, Esther A, ed. *The Spirit's Dance in Africa: Evolution, Transformation and Continuity in Sub-Sahara*. Canada: Galerie Amrad African Arts Publications, 1997.

Desmond, Jane. 'Embodying Difference: Issues in Dance and Cultural Studies.' In *Meaning in Motion: New Cultural Studies of Dance*, eds. J. Desmond. Durham: Duke University Press, 1997.

Doane, Ashley W. and Eduardo Bonilla-Silva, eds. *White Out: The Continuing Significance of Racism*. New York: Routledge, 2003.

Du Bois, W.E.B. *Black Reconstruction*. New York: Atheneum, 1962.

Eagleton, T. *Exiles and Emigres: Studies in Modern Literature*. London: Chatto and Windus, 1970.

Eskamp, Kees and Frank de Geus. 'The Pelvis as Shock Absorber: Modern and African Dance'. *Journal of Popular Culture* 27, no. 1 (1997): 55–65.

Fanon, Frantz. *The Wretched of the Earth*. Harmondsworth: Penguin, 1971.

Farley, R. and W. Allen. *The Color Line and the Quality of Life in America*. New York: Russell Sage Foundation, 1987.

Finlayson, A. *Making Sense of New Labour*. London: Lawrence and Wishart, 2003.

Fischman, Gustavo. 'Peter McLaren: A Call for a Multicultural Revolution'. Gustavo Fischman Interviews Peter McLaren. *Multicultural Education* 6, no. 4 (Summer 1999): 32–34.

Fisher, S. *From Margin to Mainstream: The Social Progress of Black Americans*. 2nd ed. Lanham, MD: Rowman and Littlefield, 1992.

Fong, C.V. 'Tracing the Origins of a "Model Minority" A study of the Depictions of Chinese Americans in Popular Magazines'. PhD. diss. Department of Sociology, University of Oregon, 1989.

Foucault, Michel. *Power/Knowledge: Selected Interviews and Other Writings 1972–1984*, ed. Colin Gordon. New York: Pantheon, 1980

———. *Power*. New York: The New Press, 2000.

Fraser, C. *Ambivalent Anti-Colonialism: The United States and the Genesis of West Indian Independence, 1940–64*. London: Greenwood, 1994.

Frow, John and Meaghan Morris. 'Introduction' to *Australian Cultural Studies: A Reader*. Urbana: University of Illinois Press, 1993.

Galbraith, J.K. *The Affluent Society.* London: Hamish Hamilton, 1958.

Gilroy, Paul. *There Ain't No Black in the Union Jack.* London: Hutchinson, 1987.

———. *The Black Atlantic.* Cambridge, Mass.: Harvard University Press, 1993.

———. 'Between Camps: Race and Culture in Postmodernity'. Inaugural lecture, Goldsmiths College, University of London, March 4, 1997.

Gilroy, P., L. Grossberg, and A. McRobbie. *Without Guarantees: In Honour of Stuart Hall.* London and New York: Verso, 2000.

Glazer, N. and P. Moynihan. *Beyond the Melting Pot.* Cambridge, Mass.: MIT Press, 1963.

Goldberg, David, ed. *Multiculturalism: A Critical* Reader. London: Blackwell, 1994.

———. *The Racial State.* London: Blackwell, 2002.

Gramsci, Antonio. *Selections From the Prison Notebooks.* London: Lawrence and Wishart, 1971.

———. 'Passive Revolution, Caesarism, Fascism'. In *A Gramsci Reader,* ed. David Forgacs. London: Lawrence and Wishart, 1988.

———. *Essential Classics in Politics: Antonio Gramsci.* DVD. n.d.

Gray, Obika. *Demeaned But Empowered, The Social Power of the Urban Poor in Jamaica.* Kingston: University of the West Indies Press, 2004.

Green, Cecilia.'Gender and Re/production in British West Indian Slave Societies.' *Against The Current,* Vol. VII, (Part 1) no. 4 (Sept./Oct. 1992): 31–38; (Part 2) no. 5 (Nov./Dec. 1992): 26–31; (Part 3) no. 6 (Jan./Feb. 1993): 29–36.

Grosefoguel, R. *Colonial Subjects: Puerto Ricans in a Global Perspective.* Berkeley, Los Angeles, London: University of California Press, 2003.

Grossberg, Lawrence, ed. 'On Postmodernism and Articulation: An Interview with Stuart Hall'. Reprinted in *Stuart Hall: Critical Dialogues in Cultural Studies,* eds. D. Morley and Kuan-Hsing Chen. London: Routledge, 1996.

———. *Caught in the Crossfire: Kids, Politics and America's Future.* Boulder: Paradigm, 2005.

Hall, A. 'Encoding/Decoding'. In *Culture, Media, Language,* eds. S. Hall., D. Hobson, A. Lowe, P. Willis. London: Hutchinson, 1980.

Hall, C. *Civilising Subjects: Metropole and Colony in the English Imagination, 1830-1867.* Cambridge: Polity Press/ London: Blackwell, 2000.

Hall, Douglas. *In Miserable Slavery: Thomas Thistlewood in Jamaica, 1750–86.* Kingston: The University of the West Indies Press, 1999.

Hall, Kenneth O. and Denis Benn, eds. *Governance in the Age of Globalisation: Caribbean Perspectives.* Kingston: Ian Randle Publishers, 2003.

Hall, Stuart. 'Lamming, Selvon and Some Trends in the W.I. Novel'. *Bim* 23 (1955).

———. 'The new Conservatism and the old'. *Universities* and *Left Review* 1 (1957).

———. 'The deep sleep of England'. *Universities* and *Left Review* 3 (1958).

———. 'Mr Raymond and the Dead Souls'. *Universities* and *Left Review* 4 (1958).

———. 'A sense of classlessness'. *Universities* and *Left Review* 5 (1958).

———. 'Taste of the real thing'. *Universities* and *Left Review* 6 (1959).

———. 'The politics of adolescence'. *Universities* and *Left Review* 6 (1959).

———. '*Roots*'. *Universities* and *Left Review* 7 (1959).

———. 'Absolute beginnings' and 'The big swipe'. *Universities* and *Left Review* 7 (1959).

———. '*Serjeant Musgrave*'. *New Left Review* 1 (1960).

———. 'Black Britons.' *Community* 1/2/3 (1970).

———. 'Pluralism, Race and Class in Caribbean Society'. In *Race and Class in Post-Colonial Society: A Study of Ethnic Group Relations in the English-Speaking Caribbean, Bolivia, Chile and Mexico,* ed. UNESCO. Paris: UNESCO Publishing, 1977.

————. 'Racism and Reaction'. In *Five Views of Multi-Racial Britain*. London: Commission on Racial Equality, 1978.

————. 'Race, Articulation and Societies Structured in Dominance'. In *Sociological Theories: Race and Colonialism*, ed. UNESCO. Paris: UNESCO, 1980.

————. 'New Ethnicities'. In *Black Film, British Cinema*, ed. K. Mercer. London: Institute of Contemporary Arts, 1988.

————. *The Hard Road to Renewal*. London: Verso, 1988.

————. 'Ethnicity: Identity and Difference.' *Radical America* 23, no. 4 (1989): 9–20.

————. 'Cultural Identity and Diaspora'. In *Identity: Community, Culture, Difference*, ed. J. Rutherford. London: Lawrence and Wishart, 1990.

————. 'The Local and the Global: Globalisation and Ethnicity'. In *Culture, Globalisation and the World System: Contemporary Conditions for the Representation of Identity*, ed. Anthony D. King, 19–40. London: Macmillan, 1991.

————. *Redemption Song*. London: BBC/Ambrose Video, 1991.

————. 'What is this "Black" in Black Popular Culture?' In *Black Popular Culture*, ed. Gina Dent. Seattle: Bay Press, 1992.

————. Interview by Les Terry. 'Not a postmodern nomad.' *Arena Journal* no. 5 (1995): 51–70.

————. 'Negotiating Caribbean Identities'. *New Left Review* 209 (1995): 3–14.

————. 'Gramsci's Relevance for the Study of Race and Ethnicity.' In *Stuart Hall: Critical Dialogues in Cultural Studies*, eds. David Morley and Kuan-Hsing Chen. London: Routledge, 1996.

————. 'Cultural Studies and its Theoretical Legacies'. In *Stuart Hall: Critical Dialogues in Cultural Studies*, eds. D. Morley and Kuan-Hsing Chen. London: Routledge, 1996.

————. 'The Formation of a Diasporic Intellectual'. In *Stuart Hall: Critical Dialogues in Cultural Studies*, eds. D. Morley and Kuan-Hsing Chen. London: Routledge, 1996.

————. 'New Ethnicities'.Reprinted in *Stuart Hall: Critical Dialogues in Cultural Studies*, eds. D. Morley and Kuan-Hsing Chen. London: Routledge, 1996.

————. 'Minimal Selves'. Reprinted in *Black British Cultural Studies: A Reader*, eds. Houston A. Baker, Jr., Manthia Diawara, and Ruth H. Lindeborg. Chicago: The University of Chicago Press, 1996.

————. 'Who Needs Identity?' In *Questions of Cultural Identity*, eds. S. Hall and P. du Gay. London: Sage, 1996.

————. Interview by David Scott. 'Politics, Contingency, Strategy.' *Small Axe* 1 (1997): 141–59.

————. 'Subjects in History: Making Diasporic Identities.' In *The House That Race Built*, ed. Wahneema Lubiano. New York: Pantheon, 1997.

————. Interview by Julie Drew. 'Cultural Composition: Stuart Hall on Ethnicity and the Discursive Turn.' *Journal of Composition Theory* 18, no. 2 (1998): 171–96.

————. 'Aspiration and Attitude: Reflections on Black Britons in the Nineties'. *New Formations* 33 (1998): 38–46.

————. 'Thinking the Diaspora: Home-Thoughts From Abroad'. *Small Axe* 6 (1999): 1–18.

————. 'Diasporas, or the Logics of Cultural Translation'. Keynote lecture at the VII Congresso da ABRALIC, Salvador Brazil, 2000.

————. 'The Multicultural Question.' In *Un/settled Multiculturalisms*, ed. Barnor Hesse. London: Zed, 2000.

————. 'Old and New Identities, Old and New Ethnicities'. In *Theories of Race and Racism*, eds. L. Black and J. Solomos. London and New York: Routledge, 2000.

————. 'Multi-Culturalism, Equality and Difference'. Keynote Address, Third Crossroads in Cultural Studies Conference. University of Birmingham, UK, June 21–25, 2000.

————. 'The Work of Representation'. In *Representation: Cultural Representations and Signifying Practices*, ed. S. Hall. London: Thousand Oaks; New Delhi: Sage Publications, 2000 [1997].

————.The Spectacle of the "Other". In *Representation: Cultural Representations and Signifying Practices*, ed. S. Hall. London: Thousand Oaks; New Delhi: Sage Publications, 2000 [1997].

————. 'Routes to Roots'. In *An Introduction to Women's Studies: Gender in a Transnational World*, eds. I. Grewark and K. Kaplan. New York: McGraw Hill, 2002.

————. 'Marx's Notes on Method: A "Reading" of the 1857 Introduction to the Grundrisse.' *Cultural Studies* 17, no.2 (2003): 113–49.

————. 'Museums of Modern Art and the End of History'. Keynote address, 'Museums of Modern Art and the End of History' conference. Tate Gallery, London, May 1999. Re-published in *Annotations 6: Modernity and Difference*, Stuart Hall and Sarat Maharaj. London: inIVA, 2001.

————. 'Modernity and Difference: A Conversation between Stuart Hall and Sarat Maharaj'. In *Annotations* 6: *Modernity and Difference*, Stuart Hall and Sarat Maharaj. London: inIVA, 2001.

————. 'New Labour's Double-Shuffle'. *Soundings* 24 (2003).

————. 'Maps of Emergency: Fault-lines and Tectonic Plates'. In *Fault-lines and Contemporary African Art and Shifting Landscapes*, eds. Gilane Tawadros and Sarah Campbell. Institute of International Visual Arts (inIVA), forum for African Arts. Prince Klaus Fund, London, 2003.

————. 'The Caribbean: A Quintessentially Modern Zone'. In *Changing States: Contemporary Art and Ideas in an Era of Globalisation*, ed. Gilane Tawadros. London: inIVA, 2004.

————. 'Negotiating Caribbean Identities'. In *New Caribbean Thought: A Reader*, eds. Brian Meeks and Folke Lindahl. Jamaica, Barbados, Trinidad and Tobago: University of the West Indies Press, 2004.

————. 'Assembling the 1980s: The Deluge – and After'. In *Shades of Black: Assembling Black Arts in 1980s Britain*, eds. David A. Bailey, Ian Baucom, Sonia Boyce. London: Duke University Press in collaboration with inIVA and Aavaa, 2005.

Hall, S., ed. *Representation: Cultural Representations and Signifying Practices*. London: Thousand Oaks; New Delhi: Sage Publications, 2000 [1997].

Hall, S. and P. Whannel. *The Popular Arts*. London: Hutchinson, 1964.

Hall, S. and T. Jefferson, eds. *Resistance through Rituals: Youth Subcultures in Post-War Britain*. London: Routledge, 1990. First published as Working Papers in Cultural Studies 7/8, 1975.

Hall. S., C. Critcher, T. Jefferson, J. Clarke and B. Roberts. *Policing the Crisis: 'Mugging', the State and Law and Order.* London: Macmillan, 1978.

Hall, S. and M. Jacques, eds. *The Politics of Thatcherism.* London: Lawrence and Wishart, 1983.

————. *New Times: the Changing Face of Politics in the 1990s*. London: Lawrence and Wishart, 1989.

Hall, S. and Bill Schwarz. 'State and Society, 1880–1930'. In *Crises in the British State, 1880–1930*, eds. Mary Langan and Bill Schwarz. London: Hutchinson, 1985. Republished in Stuart Hall, *The Hard Road to Renewal: Thatcherism and the Crisis of the British Left*. London: Verso, 1988.

Hall, S. with Bill Schwarz. *Conversations with Stuart Hall*. Cambridge: Polity Press, forthcoming.

Hanke, R. 'Hegemonic Masculinity'. *Thirtysomething: Critical Studies in Communications* 7 (1990): 231–48.

Hardt, Michael and Antonio Negri. *Empire*. Cambridge, Mass. and London: Harvard University Press, 2000.

'Head of Crack Cocaine Empire Convicted'. *Guardian Unlimited*. Special Reports (June 12, 2004).

Henry, Matthew. 'He is a bad mother *\$%@!#': Shaft and Contemporary Black Masculinity'. *Journal of Popular Film and Television* (Summer 2004): 114–19.

Hesse, Barnor. 'Stuart Hall and the De/colonial question'. Paper presented at the Stuart Hall Conference at the Centre for Caribbean Thought, University of the West Indies, Mona, 2004.

Hintzen, P. *West Indian in the West: Self Representations in an Immigrant Community*. New York: New York University Press, 2001.

Holland, Robert. *Britain and the Revolt in Cyprus, 1954–1959*. Oxford: Clarendon Press, 1998.

Hope, Donna P. '*Ninja Man* the Lyrical Don: Embodying Violent Masculinity in Jamaican Dancehall Culture'. Paper presented at Caribbean Soundscapes, a conference on Caribbean Musics and Culture, Tulane University, New Orleans, LA, March 12–13, 2004.

———. 'The British Link Up Crew — Consumption Masquerading as Masculinity in the Dancehall'. *Interventions: International Journal of Postcolonial Studies*. (April 2004): 101–17. Special Issue on Jamaican Popular Culture.

Horne, G. *Fire This Time: The Watts Uprising and the 1960s*. Charlottesville: University Press of Virginia, 1995.

James, C.L.R. *80th Birthday Lectures*. London: Race Today, 1981.

———. *Cricket*. London: Allison and Busby, 1989.

Jones, Leroi. *Blues People: Negro Experience in White America and the Music that Developed From it*. New York: William Morrow and Co., 1968 [1963].

Julien, Isaac and Mark Nash. 'Dialogues with Stuart Hall'. In *Stuart Hall: Critical Dialogues in Cultural Studies*, eds. D. Morley and Kuan-Hsing Chen. London: Routledge, 1996.

Justus, J.B. 'West Indians in Los Angeles: Community and Identity'. In *Imagining Home: Pan Africanism Revisited*, eds. S. Lemelle and R. Kelly. New York: Verso, 1994.

———.'Introduction'. In *Imagining Home: Class, Culture, and Nationalism in the African Diaspora*, eds. S. Lemelle and R. Kelly. New York: Verso, 1976.

Kasinitz, P. 'From Ghetto Elite to Service Sector: A Comparison of Two Waves of West Indian Immigrants in New York City'. *Ethnic Groups* no. 7 (1988): 173–204.

Laclau, Ernesto and Chantal Mouffe. *Hegemony and Socialist Strategy: Towards a Radical Democratic Politics*. Trans. Winston Moore and Paul Commack. London: Verso, 1985.

Lacy, Terry. *Violence and Politics in Jamaica, 1960–1970*. Manchester: Manchester University Press, 1977.

Lamming, George. *Conversations. George Lamming: Essays, Addresses and Interviews 1953–1990*, eds. Richard Drayton and Andaiye. London: Karia Press, 1992.

———. *The Pleasures of Exile*. 2nd edition. London: Alison and Busby, 1984.

———. *The Pleasures of Exile*. London: Pluto Press, 2005.

Leavis, F.R. *Revaluation: Tradition and Development in English Poetry*. London: Chatto and Windus; Toronto: Macmillan, 1936.

Lewis, Matthew 'Monk.' *Journal of a West India Proprietor; Kept during a Residence in the Island of Jamaica.* Edited with an Introduction and Notes by Judith Terry. Oxford and New York: Oxford University Press, [1834] 1999.

Longhurst, Robyn. 'Trim, Taut, Terrific, and Pregnant'. In *Pleasure Zones: Bodies, Cities, Spaces,* eds. D. Bell, J. Binnie, R. Holliday, R. Longhurst and R. Peace. New York: Syracuse University Press, 2001.

Lowenthal, David. *West Indian Societies.* London: Oxford University Press, 1972.

Manyoni, Joseph R. 'Extra-Marital Mating Patterns in Caribbean Family Studies: A Methodological Excursus'. *Anthropologica* 22, no. 1 (1980): 85–118.

Marquez, Roberto. 'Zombie to Synthesis — Notes on the Negro in Spanish-American Literature'. *Jamaica Journal* 11, nos.1 & 2 (1977).

Marx, A.W. *Making Race and Nation: A Comparison of the United States, South Africa, and Brazil.* Cambridge and New York: Cambridge University Press, 1998.

Marx, Karl. *Grundrisse: Foundations of the Critique of Political Economy.* Trans. Ben Brewster [1973]. Reprint, New York: Penguin Classics, 1993.

Massey, Douglas S. and Nancy A. Denton. *American Apartheid: Segregation and the Making of the Underclass.* Cambridge, Mass.: Harvard University Press, 1993.

Mbembe, Achille. *On the postcolony.* Berkley: University of California Press, 2001.

———. 'Necropolitics'. *Public Culture* 151 (2003).

McLaren, Peter. *Schooling as a Ritual Performance,* 3rd edition. Lanham, MD: Rowman and Littlefield, 1999.

Meeks, Brian. *Narratives of Resistance.* Kingston: University of the West Indies Press, 2000.

Mercer, Kobena. 'Back to My Routes'. *The Critical Decade, Ten-8* 2, no. 3 (1992): 32–39.

Midgley, Clare. *Women Against Slavery: The British Campaigns, 1780–1870.* London and New York: Routledge, 1992.

Mills, Claude. 'Ex-Jesuit Ruffles Male Feathers'. *Sunday Gleaner* (May 30, 2004).

Mintz, Sidney W. *Caribbean Transformations.* New York: Columbia University Press, 1974.

Mitchell, Damion. 'Rescue the Boys! — Special Intervention Mooted for Schools'. *Sunday Gleaner* (May 30, 2004).

Mohanram, Radhika. *Black Body: Women, Colonialism and Space.* London: Allen and Unwin, 1999.

Moore, Brian L. and Michele A. Johnson. *Neither Led nor Driven: Contesting British Cultural Imperialism in Jamaica, 1865–1920.* Kingston: University of West Indies Press, 2004.

Mulhern, Francis. *The Moment of 'Scrutiny'.* London: Verso, 1980.

Munroe, Trevor. *For a New Beginning.* Kingston: CARICOM Publishers, 1994.

———. 'Transforming Jamaican Democracy through Transparency: A Framework for Action'. In *Fostering Transparency and Preventing Corruption in Jamaica,* ed. Laura Nelson. Atlanta: The Carter Center, Emory University, 2002.

Naipaul, V.S. *The Mimic Men.* Harmondsworth: Penguin, 1969.

Nash, Catherine. 'Performativity in Practice: Some Recent Work in Cultural Geography'. *Progress in Human Geography* 24, no. 4 (2000): 653–64.

Nast, Heidi and Steve Pile. *Places Through the Body.* New York and London: Routledge, 1998.

Nettleford, Rex. *Inward Stretch Outward Reach.* London: Macmillan, 1993.

Nixon, Sean. 'Exhibiting Masculinity'. In *Representation: Cultural Representations and Signifying Practices,* ed. S. Hall. London: Thousand Oaks; New Delhi: Sage Publications, 2000 [1997].

Norris, Andrew. 'Giorgio Agamben and the Politics of the Living Dead'. In *Politics, Metaphysics and Death*, ed. Andrew Norris. Durham: Duke University Press, 2005.

Nunn, Heather. *Thatcher, Politics and Fantasy: The Political Culture of Gender and Nation*. London: Lawrence and Wishart, 2002.

Oliver, Melvin L. and Thomas M. Shapiro. *Black Wealth/White Wealth: A New Perspective on Racial Inequality*. New York: Routledge, 1995.

Page, Kezia. 'Dancehall Feminisms: Jamaican Female Deejays and the Politics of the "Big Ninja Bike"'. Unpublished paper presented at the Borders, Boundaries and the Global in Caribbean Studies Conference, Bowdoin College, New Brunswick, Maine, 2003.

Page, Malcolm. *Arden on File*. London: Methuen, 1966.

Paton, Diana. *No Bond but the Law: Punishment, Race and Gender in Jamaican State Formation, 1780–1870*. Durham: Duke University Press, 2004.

Peterson, W. 'Success Story, Japanese American Style'. *New York Times* (January 6, 1966).

Phillippo, James M. *Jamaica: Its Past and Present State*. Westport, Connecticut: Negro Universities Press, [1843] 1970.

Post, Ken. *Arise Ye Starvelings*. The Hague: Martinus Nijhoff, 1978.

Pratt, M.L. *Imperial Eyes: Travel Writing and Transculturation*. London: Routledge, 1991.

Price, Charles. 'What the Zeeks Uprising Reveals: Development Issues, Moral Economy and the Urban Lumpenproletariat in Jamaica'. *Urban Anthropology* 33, no. 1 (Spring 2004): 73–113.

Puri, S. *The Caribbean Postcolonial: Social Equality, Post-Nationalism and Cultural Hybridity*. New York: Palgrave Macmillan, 2004.

Reckord, Verena. 'Reggae, Rastafarianism and Cultural Identity.' In *Reggae, Rasta, Revolution: Jamaican Music From Ska to Dub*, ed. Chris Potash. New York and London: Schirmer Books and Prentice Hall International, 1997.

Reed, Susan. 'The Politics and Poetics of Dance'. *Annual Review of Anthropology* 27 (1998): 503–32.

Reyes, Carla. 'Investigation into Dancehall'. Research paper in Dance and Theatre Production, Edna Manley College for the Visual and Performing Arts, Jamaica School of Dance, Jamaica, 1993.

Robotham, Don. *Our Struggles*. Kingston: Workers Liberation League, 1975.

Rojek, Chris. *Stuart Hall*. Cambridge: Polity Press, 2003.

Rose, Jacqueline. 'Mrs Thatcher and Ruth Ellis'. In *Why War? Psychoanalysis, Politics and the Return to Melanie Klein*. Oxford: Blackwell 1993.

Russell, Horace. 'The Emergence of the Christian Black: The Making of a Stereotype'. *Jamaica Journal* 16, no. 1 (1983): 51–71.

Ryman, Cheryl. 'Bouyaka Boo-ya`h-kah: A Salute to Dancehall'. Unpublished paper, author's personal papers, 1993.

———. 'Jamaican Body Moves: Source and Continuity of Jamaican Movement'. In *Tapestry of Jamaica: The Best of Skywritings, Air Jamaica's In-flight Magazine*, ed. Linda Gambrill. Kingston and Oxford: Macmillan Caribbean, 2003.

———. 'The Jamaican Heritage in Dance'. *Jamaica Journal* no. 44 (1980): 2–13.

Saunders, Patricia J. 'Is not Everything Good to Eat, Good to Talk: Sexual Economy and Dancehall Music in the Global Marketplace'. *Small Axe* no. 13 (March 2003): 95-115.

Schmitt, Carl. *The Concept of the Political*. Chicago: the University of Chicago Press, 1996.

Schuler, Monica. 'Myalism and the African Religious Tradition in Jamaica'. In *Caribbean Slave Society and Economy*, eds. Hilary Beckles and Verene Shepherd. Kingston: Ian Randle Publishers; London: James Currey Publishers, 1991.

Schwarz, Bill. 'Becoming Postcolonial'. In *Without Guarantees. In Honour of Stuart Hall*, eds. Paul Gilroy, Lawrence Grossberg and Angela McRobbie. London: Verso, 2000.

———. 'Crossing the Seas'. In *West Indian Intellectuals in Britain*, ed. Bill Schwarz . Manchester: Manchester University Press, 2003.

———. 'Claudia Jones and the *West Indian Gazette*. Reflections on postcolonial Britain'. *Twentieth Century British History* 14, no. 3 (2003).

———. 'C.L.R. James, George Lamming and the Measure of Historical Time'. *Small Axe* 14 (2003).

———. 'Stuart Hall'. *Cultural Studies* 19, no. 2 (2005).

———. *Memories of Empire. Vol. III – Disorder.* Oxford: Oxford University Press, forthcoming 2008.

Scott, David. *Refashioning Futures: Criticism After Postcoloniality.* New Jersey: Princeton University Press, 1999.

———. 'Rationalities of the Jamaican Modern'. *Small Axe*, no. 14 (September 2003).

Sennett, Richard. *Flesh and Stone: The Body and the City in Western Civilization.* London: W.W. Norton and Co., 1994.

Shilling, Chris. *The Body and Social Theory.* London: Sage, 1993.

Simms, Glenda. 'Winds of change, or Cool Breeze?' *Sunday Gleaner* (June 6, 2004).

Simpson, George E. 'Jamaican Revivalist Cults'. *Social and Economic Studies* 5, no. 4 (December 1956).

Skelton, Tracey. '"I sing dirty reality. I am out there for the ladies". Lady Saw: Women and Jamaican Ragga Music Resisting Patriarchy'. *Phoebe* 7 nos. 1 & 2: (1995): 86–104.

Smith, Adam. *Lectures on Jurisprudence*, eds. R.L. Meek, D.D. Raphael, and P.G. Stein Oxford: Clarendon Press, 1978.

Smith, M.G. *The Plural Society in the British West Indies* [1965]. Reprint, Berkeley and Los Angeles: University of California Press, 1974.

———. *West Indian Family Structure.* Seattle: University of Washington Press, 1962.

Smith, Raymond T. 'Hierarchy and the Dual Marriage System in West Indian Society.' In *Gender and Kinship*, eds. J.F. Collier and S. Yanagisako. Stanford: Stanford University Press, 1987.

Sorenshein, R. *Politics in Black and White: Race and Power in Los Angeles.* Princeton: Princeton University Press, 1993.

Sowell, T. *Three Black Histories in: American Ethnic Groups*, eds. T. Sowell and L.D. Collins. Washington, DC: Urban Institute, 1978.

Sparks, Colin. 'Stuart Hall, Cultural Studies and Marxism'. In *Stuart Hall: Critical Dialogues in Cultural Studies*, eds. David Morley and Kuan-Hsing Chen. London: Routledge, 1996.

Stanley Niaah, Sonjah. 'Kingston's Dancehall: A Story of Space and Celebration'. *Space and Culture* 7, no.1 (2004): 102–118.

———. 'Making Space: Dancehall Performance and its Philosophy of Boundary-lessness'. *African Identities* 2, no. 2 (2004): 117–132.

———. 'A Common Genealogy: Dancehall, Limbo and the Sacred Performance Space'. *Discourses in Dance* 2, no.1 (2004): 9–26.

———. 'Dancin' a Jamaica Middle Name: Musical Hegemony in Stolzoff's *Wake the Town and Tell the People*'. *Proudflesh* no. 3 (2004).

————. 'Making Space: Reading Limbo in Dancehall Performance and Spatiality'. Paper presented at the Ninth Cultural Studies Workshop, Indian Institute of Science, Bangalore, February 2–7, 2004.

Steel, Robert. 'George Kennan at 100'. *New York Review of Books* 51, no.7 (April 29, 2004).

Steinberg, S. *The Ethnic Myth: Race, Class and Ethnicity in America.* Boston: Beacon Press, 1981.

Tafari, Imani. 'Lady Saw ... Dancehall donette'. *Sistren* 16 ½ (1994).

————. 'The habit of violence'. *Universities* and *Left Review* 5 (1958).

Thomas, Deborah A. *Modern Blackness: Nationalism, Globalisation, and the Politics of Culture in Jamaica.* Durham, NC.: Duke University Press, 2004.

Thomas, Helen. *The Body, Dance and Cultural Theory.* London: Palgrave Macmillan, 2003.

Thrift, Nigel. 'The Still Point: Resistance, Expressive Embodiment and Dance'.In *Geographies of Resistance,* eds. S. Pile and M. Keith. London: Routledge, 1997.

Turner, J. *The Structure of Sociological Theory.* Belmont, CA: Wadsworth, 1991.

Walcott, Derek. *What the Twilight Says.* New York: Farrar Strauss and Giroux, 1998.

Wallerstein, I. *The Modern World-System II.* New York: Academic Press, 1980.

————. *The Politics of World Economy.* Cambridge, Mass.: Harvard University Press, 1984.

Welsh Asante, Kariamu. 'Commonalities in African Dance: An Aesthetic Foundation'. In *African Culture: The Rhythms of Unity,* eds. M. Asante and K. Welsh Asante. Westport Connecticut: Greenwood, 1985.

White, Garth. 'The Development of Jamaican Popular Music, Part 2. Urbanization of the Folk: The Merger of Traditional and the Popular in Jamaican Music'. *ACIJ Research Review* no. 1 (1984).

Williams, Francis. 'Fleet Street: Verdict on Terror'. *New Statesman* (October 11, 1958).

Wyman, B. 'Roots: The Origins of Black Politics in the East Bay'. *Express* 9, no. 43. (August 1987).

Yacine, Kateb. 'The Poet as Boxer'. In *Fault Lines: Contemporary African Art and Shifting Landscapes,* eds. Gilane Tawadros and Sarah Campbell. London: inIVA in collaboration with Forum for African Arts and Prince Claus Fund, 2003.

Young-Jin, W. '"Model Minority" Strategy and Asian American Tactics'. *Korea Journal.* (Summer 1994): 57–66.

Discography

Assassin. 'How We Roll'. Personal CD Collection. 2000.

Beenie Man. 'World Dance'. *Strictly the Best* vol. 13. VP Records, 1994.

————. 'Ole Dawg'. *Best Of Beenie Man.* VP Records, 2000.

————. 'Nuff Gal'. *Best of Beenie Man.* VP Records, 2000.

Buju Banton feat. Beres Hammond. 'Pull it up'. *Unchained Spirit.* Anti Inc., 1999.

Captain Barkey. 'Go Go Wine'., *Strictly the Best* vol. 17. VP Records, 1996

Elephant Man. 'Pon di River, Pon di Bank'. *Good 2 Go.* Atlantic Records, 2003.

————.'Fan dem off'. *Good 2 Go.* Atlantic Records, 2003

————. 'Blasé'. *Good 2 Go.* Atlantic Records, 2003.

————. 'Wining Queen'. Studio 2000 single, 2002.

Johnny P. 'Bike Back'. *Punanny.* Greensleeves Records, 2000 [1991].

Merciless. *Ole Gallis* vol. 2 — East Coast. East Coast Records, 1997.

Ninja Man. 'My Weapon. Anything Test Dead'. *Reggae Anthology – Ninjaman.* VP
    Records, 2001.
SuperCat. 'Ghetto Red Hot'. *Don Dada.* Sony, 1992.
Shabba Ranks 'Girls Wine'. *Rough and Ready* vol. 2. 1993.

Contributors

Anthony Bogues is Professor of Africana Studies at Brown University and Visiting Professor at the Centre for Caribbean Thought, University of the West Indies, Mona. He is also a Distinguished Fellow at the Centre for African Studies, University of Cape Town and an Associate Editor of the journal *Small Axe*. His publications include *Caliban's Freedom: The Early Political Thought Of C.L.R. James* (1997) and *Black Heretics, Black Prophets: Radical Political Intellectuals* (2003). His most recent book is *Empire of Liberty: Power and Desire* (forthcoming).

Avtar Brah is Professor of Sociology in the School for Continuing Education, Birkbeck College, University of London. Her books include *Global Futures: Migration, Environment and Globalisation* (edited with Mary Hickman and Martin Mac an Ghail, 1999) and *Hybridity and its Discontents* (edited with Annie Coombes, 2000).

Grant Farred is an Associate Professor in the Literature Programme at Duke University. He is author of *What's My Name? Black Vernacular Intellectuals* (2003) and *Midfielder's Moment: Coloured Literature and Coloured in Contemporary South Africa* (1999). He is editor of *Rethinking C.L.R. James* (1996). His forthcoming books include *Long Distance Love: A Passion for Football* (2006) and *The Phantom Calls: Race and Globalisation* (2006). He is General Editor of the journal *South Atlantic Quarterly*.

Obika Gray is Professor of Political Science at the University of Wisconsin – Eau Claire. He is the author of *Radicalism and Social Change in Jamaica, 1960–1972* (1991) and *Demeaned but Empowered: The Social Power of the Urban Poor in Jamaica* (2004).

Cecilia Green teaches in the Department of Sociology, University of Pittsburgh. She is currently working on questions of transitions in

labour, moral, and disciplinary regimes in Caribbean history, with particular regard to gender. She has published articles in the areas of political economy and social history.

Lawrence Grossberg is the Morris Davis Distinguished Professor of Communication Studies and Cultural Studies, and the Director of the university programme in Cultural Studies, at the University of North Carolina at Chapel Hill. He is the co-editor of the international journal *Cultural Studies*. His books include *Bringing it all Back Home: Essays on Cultural Studies*, and *Dancing in Spite of Myself: Essays on Popular Culture* (1997), *MediaMaking: Mass Media in a Popular Culture* (with Ellen Wartella, D. Charles Whitney and MacGregor Wise, 2005), *New Keywords: A Revised Vocabulary of Culture and Society* (with Tony Bennett and Meaghan Morris, 2005) and *Caught in the Crossfire: Kids, Politics and America's Future* (2005).

Stuart Hall, the subject of this volume, is Professor Emeritus at The Open University, where he served as Professor and Head of Sociology from 1979–97. He was Research Fellow, acting Director and then Director of the Centre for Cultural Studies, University of Birmingham from 1964–79. He holds a Chair at the Institute of the International Visual Arts and the Association of Black Photographers. He has published several books, numerous working papers and journal articles and co-edited many collections.

Percy C. Hintzen is Professor and former Department Chair of African American Studies at the University of California, Berkeley. He is also a former Director of Peace and Conflict Studies at Berkeley and served as President of the Caribbean Studies Association (CSA). His publications include *The Costs of Regime Survival: Racial Mobilisation, Elite Domination and Control of the State in Guyana and Trinidad* (1989), *West Indian in the West: Self-representations in an Immigrant community* (2001) and (with Jean Rahier) *Problematising Blackness: Self Ethnographies by Black immigrants to the United States* (2003) as well as numerous articles in journals and chapters in edited volumes.

Donna P. Hope holds a PhD in Cultural Studies from George Mason University, Virginia and is a part-time lecturer at the University College of the Caribbean and the University of the West Indies, Mona. Her publications include *Inna di Dancehall: Popular Culture and the Politics of Identity in Jamaica* (2006) and scholarly articles on dancehall culture and masculinity in *Interventions: International Journal of Postcolonial Studies and Discourses in Dance.*

Brian Meeks is Professor of Social and Political Change in the Department of Government, University of the West Indies, Mona, and Director of the Centre for Caribbean Thought. His publications include *Caribbean Revolutions and Revolutionary Theory: An Assessment of Cuba, Nicaragua and Grenada* (1993 and 2001), *New Caribbean Thought: A Reader* (ed. with Folke Lindahl, 2000) and the novel *Paint the Town Red* (2003).

Charles W. Mills is Distinguished Professor of Philosophy at the University of Illinois at Chicago. He works in the general area of oppositional political theory, and is the author of three books: *The Racial Contract* (1997), *Blackness Visible: Essays on Philosophy and Race* (1998), and *From Class to Race: Essays in White Marxism and Black Radicalism* (2003).

Rex Nettleford is Vice Chancellor Emeritus at the University of the West Indies, Mona, where he served as Vice Chancellor from 1998–2004. Nettleford has edited the journal *Caribbean Quarterly* since 1967 and has published numerous books, monographs and articles on Caribbean culture, society and politics. He is the founder, Artistic Director and leading Choreographer of the renowned National Dance Theatre Company of Jamaica (NDTC).

Michael Rustin is Professor of Sociology at the University of East London. His books include *For a Pluralist Socialism* (1985), *The Good Society and the Inner World* (1991), *Reason and Unreason: Psychoanalysis, Science and Politics* (2001), and, with Margaret Rustin, *Narratives of Love and Loss: Studies in Modern Children's Fiction* (1987/2001) and *Mirror to Nature: Drama Psychoanalysis and Society* (2002).

Bill Schwarz is Reader in the School of English and Drama at Queen Mary, University of London. Most recently he has edited *West Indian Intellectuals in Britain* and *The Locations of George Lamming.*

Sonjah Stanley Niaah is the inaugural Rhodes Trust Rex Nettleford Fellow in Cultural Studies, 2005 and is Lecturer in Cultural Studies at the University of the West Indies' Institute of Caribbean Studies, Mona She is currently working on three book projects including two edited collections on Jamaican culture — a reader on Dancehall culture (with Bibi Bakare Yusuf, forthcoming), and the other on the production of celebrity. She is an Associate Editor of *Wadabagei: A Journal of the Caribbean and its Diasporas.*

Gilane Tawadros is the founding Director of the Institute of International Visual Arts (inIVA), a contemporary visual arts agency based in London. Responsible for the overall artistic direction of inIVA, she has curated or co-curated numerous exhibitions and has written extensively on contemporary art. Most recently she edited *Changing States: Contemporary Art and Ideas in an Era of Globalisation* (2004) and serves on the boards of the Forum for African Arts and the International Foundation of Manifesta.

Index